Behind the Glass, Volume II

Behind the Glass, Volume II

TOP PRODUCERS TELL HOW THEY CRAFT THE HITS

HOWARD MASSEY

Backbeat
Books

An Imprint of Hal Leonard Corporation

Published in 2009 by Backbeat Books
An Imprint of Hal Leonard Corporation
7777 West Bluemound Road
Milwaukee, WI 53213

Trade Book Division Editorial Offices
33 Plymouth Street, Suite 302, Montclair, NJ 07042

Printed in the United States of America

The Library of Congress has cataloged the first volume as follows:

Massey, Howard.
Behind the glass: top record producers tell how they craft the hits / Howard Massey.
    p. cm
    "[Interviews] originally conducted for a feature series in Musician Magazine called "First Take" (later continued in EQ magazine in the 'From the Desk' series)" —Introd. ISBN 0-87930-614-9 (alk. paper)
    1. Sound recording executives and producers—Interviews. 2. Sound recordings—Production and direction. 3. Popular music—History and criticism. 4. Sound recording industry. I. Title

ML3790.M352 2000
781.64'149—dc 21
00-056052
15   14 13 12 11

ISBN 978-0-87930-955-8

www.backbeatbooks.com

Dedicated to the memory of Gus Dudgeon, Larry Levine, and Norman Smith

Contents

Foreword

by George Massenburg

In an industry that purports to have no rules, it should come as no surprise that the reader of this second volume of *Behind the Glass* will find little consistency between the many interviews contained in these pages, other than the oft-repeated aphorism, "it's all about the song." But the production of iconic records is clearly at least equally about the *record* and about *innovation*.

The other day, I sat with a friend in the business on a flight to California, and we got around to talking about the great recordings—"...the soundtrack of our lives," as Max Langstaff puts it—and...well, try this yourself. Identify a recording or two from 1990 to the present that might be a candidate for being referred to as A Great Recording. C'mon, on the level of a "Yesterday" or a "Stairway to Heaven" or a "Satisfaction," "Fast Car," or "White Christmas." (Or even "Blue Christmas"!) This is not to say that great recordings haven't been made since then. They probably have. We just haven't heard them.

Maybe that's because today there are no "gatekeepers" that recognize great recordings (that is, great tunes, great performances, and/or great innovations) and introduce them to a broader audience. Now, it's many-to-many, with what seems to be at once a hugely democratic opportunity and a denial of the requirement for uniquely individual, idiosyncratic *talent*.

Over the last ten years, give or take a few, we've watched in amazement as the music business has gone through overwhelming upheaval. Horrifically and with an unmistakably steady downwards slide, what once were big labels have simply come apart; today, there's barely any "there" there anymore. At what point it began to veer off course, opinions vary. I say everything started going into the toilet around 1989 to 1991—not coincidentally, the dawn of the age of the leveraged buyout. More specifically, I remember when we started taking direction from accountants rather than the "gatekeepers" we had grown up with.

What happened was that in the late 1980s large music corporations were consolidated, and often bought out, resulting in debt requiring a great deal of cash; cash that labels of the day were hoarding after the huge success of re-releasing their catalogs on CD. Music men—people like Mo Ostin, Lenny Waronker, and Bob Krasnow, among others—were ousted, to be replaced with accountants, themselves responsible only to new managers; managers who simply saw no reason to continue old policy, methodology, and style. Among those axioms brushed aside were the importance of building an artist's long-term career and the expectation that no more than one out of 20 recordings would turn a profit. Labels' bank accounts were stripped of cash to pay off corporate debt, leaving nothing for development, let alone artist support. Projects were directed by numbers alone; gone were the men and women who made decisions from their instincts, quick brains, sincere heart, and guts.

Whatever music recording is—art, process, or science—everything changed: standards, structure, business model, and technology (*especially* technology), and it continues to this day.

And, although it's impossible to know where the record business will next meander in search of, well...*at least* a profit, it is crystal clear that the bell cannot be unrung and that the halcyon early days of recording are gone.

Of course, things aren't all bleak. It's important to note that today far more users are capable of developing recorded music themselves. Pop music production and recording in particular has rarely succeeded when its aspiration was to high art. Talent cannot be so great as to confuse people. As David Foster Wallace has said, "It seems like the big distinction between good art and so-so art lies somewhere in the art's heart's purpose, the agenda of the consciousness behind the text." What's a more abstract art than the making of music, music that touches an audience, heart-to-heart?

So, here are stories from some of the key contributors to the making of modern recorded music. New and old, successful and aspiring, techno-centric and music-centric, egocentric and altruistic, the engineers and producers interviewed in *Behind the Glass, Volume II* present the context of a recording session—the dynamics and interactions, subtle and overwhelming and every shade in between—which combine to yield up a sort of techno-artistic gumbo. They describe various and diverse approaches, plans and preparations, project structures, recording techniques, head-spaces, recording-spaces, and reference points, as well as expectations that have worked in the past. Some of these are ideas we may have marginalized for awhile. But now—*especially* now, as the meltdown continues unabated—it's useful to remind ourselves that real innovation means having to start from the ground up, all assumptions set aside.

Introduction

There is no better way to go forward than by studying the path taken by those who went before you. As someone a lot smarter (and wittier) than me once observed, "There are two kinds of fools: One says, this is old and therefore good. The other says, this is new, and therefore better." As most professionals in the record business will tell you, it's when the tried and true meets the new and bold that real magic happens.

Like the original *Behind the Glass*, this second collection of interviews attempts to answer the question: what makes a hit record? While even the most casual fan understands the contribution of the artist and the songwriter, many people are not aware of the enormous role played by the various technical people involved: recording engineers, assistant engineers, computer operators, and mastering engineers. More often than not there will also be a producer at the center of things—a Svengali-like figure hovering in the background, whose function is a bit more ambiguous. Though it's accurate to liken the role of the record producer to that of the film director, I think team quarterback is a better analogy, since so much of the job involves acting as liaison, trying to find the delicate balance between the creative demands of the artist, the technical demands of the engineering staff, and the commercial demands of the record label. Together this team of people labor to create the recordings we enjoy daily on our stereos and radios, iPods and computers.

So much has happened since the publication of the original *Behind the Glass* nearly a decade ago. The once-mighty music industry has shrunk tremendously in recent years, suffering from the rise of (and lack of timely response to) online distribution and widespread piracy. Those are the events that are primarily responsible for today's drastically reduced recording budgets, which in turn have led to the closings of hundreds of commercial studios and the commensurate rise in the number of records being made in people's bedrooms, basements, and converted garages. Some might argue (and they do, in these pages) that these changes have also led to a decline in the quality of recorded music today.

The universal acceptance of digital recording—mostly in the form of the ubiquitous computer-based Pro Tools system—is another huge change. A decade ago, producers and engineers were debating whether or not the ADAT format (eight CD-quality tracks on a standard S-VHS tape) would take permanent hold (it didn't), and many of them were still mixing to DAT (a smaller, non-standard digital tape format), which has since fallen completely out of favor due to its unreliability and poor error correction. To be sure, some of the interview subjects in this new volume still voice lingering beliefs in the superiority of analog recording, but even the most die-hard of them admit that today's financial limitations, coupled with erratic quality control, makes the use of tape all but impossible most of the time.

You'll find a completely new cast of characters here, but many of the same questions that were posed in the first volume. Again, that's not due to laziness on my part—I genuinely find the different answers and perspectives fascinating, and it's equally illuminating to compare the responses in these pages to those of the folks I interviewed the first time around. While there's a similar focus on aesthetics and the importance of remaining true to one's art, there is also a decidedly noticeable business slant in many of the comments coming from this group, probably in reflection of these changing and difficult times in the industry.

I'm proud to say that there's a little more diversity in this group of interviewees, with more emphasis on contemporary genres. As with the first volume, some come from a musical background, others from an engineering background; and, again, some chose to focus on technical aspects, while others preferred to take a more philosophical approach. There's still a mix of veterans and "young guns," as well as representation from a select group of British producers and engineers, to which I also decided to add a section of interviews with some of Nashville's top studio people. And while you'll once again find a pair of spirited panel discussions, this time the venues are Nashville and London, as opposed to the more predictable music centers of New York and LA.

One thing that hasn't changed is my goal of conducting every interview as if it were simply a casual conversation, as opposed to a series of questions and answers. I've learned the hard way that there is no substitute for engaging on a personal level with your interview subject so that you end up having a true give-and-take with them. It's really no different than the kind of ideal relationship all these producers and engineers try to attain with the artists they work with.

The wisdom imparted by these masters of their craft is at once timely and timeless, perceptive and priceless. As you read these pages, you'll discover that the main recurring theme is a simple one: it is always, always the music that comes first.

Those are truly words to live by.

Howard Massey
Woodstock, New York
November 2008

Nashville Producers Panel

It's All About Relationships

Panelists: Tony Brown, Frank Liddell, Justin Niebank, Steve Fishell

There are, as John Sebastian once observed, some thirteen hundred and fifty-two guitar pickers in Nashville. And while it is equally true that any one of them could play twice as better than I will, I nonetheless find myself one morning in an opulent boardroom at the local BMI headquarters, just off famed Music Row, huddled with four producer/engineers around one tiny corner of a massive conference table discussing the state of the recording industry today.

Music City is like no other city in the world; its residents seem to eat, breathe, and live music 24 hours a day. Country music predominates, of course, but there are a surprising amount of other genres being recorded every day in the still reasonably healthy number of professional facilities in town, supplemented by the rising tide of bedroom-based home studios. Nashville is truly a community, and its unremittingly positive vibe is exactly why I elected to hold my first panel here.

First to arrive is veteran Tony Brown—a legendary figure in Nashville whose career began with a stint in Elvis Presley's backing band—followed shortly thereafter by Justin Niebank (Keith Urban, Marty Stuart, Blues Traveler) and Steve Fishell (Pam Tillis, Radney Foster, The Mavericks). Bringing up the rear ("Man, my alarm clock didn't go off," he explains, red-faced, to the hoots and laughter of the others) is Frank Liddell, a former publisher turned producer who has worked with Lee Ann Womack (to whom he is married); Chris Knight; and, most recently, Miranda Lambert, whose *Crazy Ex-Girlfriend* was voted 2008 Album of the Year by the Academy of Country Music.

As the sun shines brightly through the elegantly draped windows, our panelists exchange opinions, viewpoints, and anecdotes while I become a metaphorical fly on the wall. No doubt the camaraderie that pervades our discussion is largely due to the fact that all four panelists know each other well—Music City is really more like a small town, albeit one populated largely by singers, songwriters, and the aforementioned guitar pickers. Their easy familiarity makes it seem more like we are having a lazy chat in someone's living room than a semi-formal gathering being taped for posterity. And even though the whole event is over in little more than an hour, I have ample time to gauge the diverse personalities of each of the four panelists: Brown, whose quietly commanding presence earns everyone's full attention whenever he speaks, and whose self-deprecating wit keeps things loose; the slightly kinetic Niebank, whose enthusiasm and passion for his craft are both unmistakable and unshakeable; the laid-back Fishell, whose California roots and experience as founder of Nashville's Music Producer's Institute (MPI) provide him with a somewhat more nuanced perspective; and the charmingly "aw-shucks" demeanor of Liddell, which fails to disguise a keen intelligence and analytical mind. It seems as if it ends almost before it begins and I realize that it is the interplay between the panelists as much as their individual insights that has made the event so thoroughly enjoyable for me.

How do you feel the role of the record producer has changed throughout the course of your career?

TB: Well, I can only talk from the perspective of one particular genre: country music—not much western! [*laughs*] I got into this profession after being an A&R person, working for [MCA president] Jimmy Bowen, who liked using in-house producers—he was always a little skeptical of independent producers. Now that I'm an independent producer myself, I'm glad he's not in the business anymore! [*laughs*]

It seems to me that record labels in other genres put a lot more emphasis on producers. In pop music, or in the urban or rock genres, the producer is often a bigger star than the artist. But none of today's producers here in Nashville are viewed that way; in fact, there have only ever been a handful of star, icon country producers—people like Owen Bradley, or Chet Atkins, or Billy Sherrill. I was recently approached by a major label to produce a new female singer, and her manager called me and said, "I've never heard anything you've done—can you send me something you've produced?" That made me realize what a pissant I am! [*laughs*]

But with the record industry in such a decline these days because of their stupidity in dealing with how to deliver our product, there seems to be a lot of extra pressure on producers right now. Budgets have been cut so much that it's really hard to please the label, not only in terms of how well you craft the record and what songs you pick, but how much money you spend. I was at MCA for 24 years, and budget was really never a worry for me. Bowen taught me, "If it takes a quarter of a million dollars to make the record you want to make, by god, spend it. Don't waste it . . . but don't let $20,000 keep you from making magic." Now it's not that way at all. Even major label album budgets are down to $50,000 or less. And on a budget like that, I guarantee you somebody's not getting paid; somebody's getting screwed on every deal.

JN: The logistics of making records has changed dramatically too. The convergence of the shift in the industry and the advent of technology like Pro Tools has changed everything about how people make records. For one thing, it seems as if nobody is planning ahead. I used to get booked months in advance to mix records for major artists. But these days, even if I'm being asked to mix a record for a huge artist, the label always seems to hire me at the last minute . . . and then they want the final mixes in an impossibly short space of time. Not only is everyone making decisions at the last possible minute, no one seems to be ready to commit to a full album, so they do a couple of songs here and a couple of songs there. It used to be that you'd book a block of time to do a whole record from start to finish and have a healthy budget to do it with, but those days are gone. Then you add in the factor of Pro Tools, which in many instances has blown music apart instead of bringing it together—it's a weird time. Record companies aren't making final decisions anymore, and neither are the artists. I have to deal with that all the time.

So how are final decisions being made?

JN: They're dictated purely by the deadline. Mind you, to some degree, that always happened. There are plenty of artists who would tell you, "I didn't really finish the record—the clock finished the record." But Pro Tools has allowed people to put off decisions in a way that we've never seen before, and a lot of times it's a real drag. One of the great things about the way Tony works is that he likes to make decisions on the studio floor. I often wish that people would just use Pro Tools to facilitate that. Instead, it's helped artists and producers put off decisions. And the worst thing for me as a mixer is that I always want people to be passionate about everything on every song they give me. Instead, they tell me things like, "Do whatever you want on the second verse." My

L to R, Steve Fishell, Justin Niebank, Howard Massey, Tony Brown, and Frank Liddell

reaction is, "What?? No, dude, you've got to be way into this. You've got to be crazy passionate about your arrangement so I can get just as passionate about it." But if there's this attitude of, "Oh, I don't know," well, *I* don't want to make that decision. A lot of times it seems that people are afraid to commit, and Pro Tools facilitates that because they don't *have* to commit.

FL: I'd say that the most drastic change that has occurred has been the advent of Pro Tools. I hated it for a long time, to be honest. It wasn't so much the medium that I hated but the fact that people often allowed Pro Tools to take the place of creativity. I agree that the labels seem to be a lot more indecisive now, and they want everything done yesterday. You'll do a mix one day and the next day they're asking for a vocal-up or a bass-down version, and they want it the next morning. But beyond the dealings with the labels, I don't see a whole lot of change in the way records here are made. Tracking for me is the greatest sport in the world, and not a whole lot has changed about tracking sessions. Yes, you can fix things more quickly because you don't have to rewind tape, but the process is similar to when I started making records ten or twelve years ago.

Also, as Tony said, you don't get very much respect from the labels. You're out there trying to create a work of art and they're just treating you like a dog. After a while you start to realize there are a lot of people at the labels that have never even been in a studio—they don't know the names of the major session players and they don't have much idea what goes on. You pour your heart and soul into making a great record, and some of these label people don't know the difference between that and a demo that somebody's done in their house.

SF: I was lucky enough early in my career to be playing sessions for Brian Ahern and Emmy-lou Harris when they were making records in the early eighties, and whatever I know about the studio I learned from them. I moved here in 1988, and worked in mainstream country for a number of years, and, while things have changed quite a bit in terms of budgets and consequently the time that you spend making a record, it seems to me that digital recording has also made a remarkable difference in the way we go about the whole process. I remember George Massenburg once telling me this great quote he heard from George Lucas: "Choice is the enemy of commitment." With Pro Tools, the artist has so many options that it sometimes blurs the process.

Do you feel that the overall quality of records today has suffered as a result of producers having to make compromises due to budgetary limitations?

TB: Actually, I think records are sounding better than ever. Sonically, everything sounds much wider than it did 15 years ago. It used to be that you could only use certain kinds of guitar sounds, for example, but now there's no limit to what you can do as long as you've got the record company behind you and a hit song. There are hit country records today that never would have charted years ago. In many ways, it was Mutt Lange who started that sonic widening of the spectrum by recycling all those Def Leppard licks in the records he made with Shania [Twain]. He actually made more of an impact on how Nashville records sound than anyone I can think of in recent history.

You know, pop artists wait two or three years between records, but here you've got to have that next album ready by the time the third or fourth single has played out on radio, which may be just 15 weeks after the previous album was released. That's the reason why some Nashville labels have such great catalogs; by comparison, I don't think the catalogs of the pop labels are quite as deep. And, trust me, as someone who worked at a label for years, the record companies will try every kind of reformulation they can think of: "Alan Jackson Sings Love Songs"; "Alan Jackson Sings the Songs of the South." [*laughs*] I can't tell you how many times they repackaged the Patsy Cline catalog—it seemed like every year she continued to be the third or fourth best-selling artist, even decades after she'd passed away.

FL: It does seem like artists now have difficulty getting out a record a year.

TB: It's definitely slowing down, and a singer/songwriter like Keith Urban can't turn it around as quickly as a pure singer like George Strait. Mind you, with a George Strait, you can spend a year listening to all kinds of things that you hate, hoping you'll find ten songs that you like. But you can't just write a good song every day. That's one of the reasons why pop artists can't put out an album every year—they're out touring, playing stadiums, and they just don't have the time to write good new material.

JN: I agree with Tony on a certain level, but from a technical point of view it seems to me that some records sound *worse* than ever before. Pro Tools in and of itself is not an evil thing: it's who is sitting in front of it and making the choices that's the issue. The other thing we're dealing with—and it's not just in Nashville, but in the pop and rock world too—is this level wars thing. Everything today is so limited and so compressed that everyone thinks that edgy is what sells. It's hard to tell an artist or someone at the record label that dynamics actually broadcast better. Why do old records sound better on the radio? Because they have dynamics. But you can't tell that to somebody who's been listening to demos all day long where the level is at absolute zero VU digital and full distortion, because they think that's exciting. [*laughs*] They all turn to each other and say, "That thing that's hurting my ears, that's exciting, right?" They've all kind of talked themselves into this; you turn in a record that has soulfulness and dynamics and you're trying to build something that wraps around people, and you say, "Trust me—this will broadcast better," and they look at you like you're crazy. Radio compression loves dynamics, although people don't realize that. But, you give a radio limiter a brick wall of sound—a two by four—and it inverts. That's why some records have this squishy "what- is-that?" sound when you hear them on the radio.

SF: Everything is smashed up to the level of the snare drum or the vocal—whatever is the loudest component of the track—and so it just comes across sounding like a mess.

JN: Thankfully, here in Nashville I personally can still get away with making dynamic records, but when I've been asked to mix stuff for the pop world and I've got a 25-year-old A&R guy saying, "Hey, I put your mix up against someone else's and his is ten times louder than yours," all I can say in response is, "Yeah, it is. But mine's not mastered, while his is, and mine is going to sound better on the radio." Until they hear that, they don't know that. So I agree that some records do sound better these days, but there are also some god-awful records coming out of Nashville that don't sound good on radio. It becomes all cymbals and vocal and you can't pick out any individual instruments.

SF: The trouble with listening to those kinds of records where everything is coming at you like a brick wall is that after five tracks you're exhausted—you just don't want to listen to music anymore.

JN: Which helps answer the question of why people are not enjoying music the way they used to. One reason is that they can't sit through an entire album. You're listening in your car and after four or five tracks you start to think, "You know, quiet is really a lot better." [*laughs*]

SF: Even talk radio is a lot better. [*laughs*]

JN: Again, Pro Tools isn't solely to blame, although it makes it a lot easier to gak things up so that the music being played back makes your speakers fry. But Nashville is unique in that it's so based on publishing and song play and the song demo thing. We have the most amazing system here of studios and songwriters and publishers that do demos that are shockingly good. But at the end of the day, they slam the levels so hard because they feel they've got to compete, and that's what we've got to chase when we go in and record the masters.

FL: That's an interesting point. I've had a lot of songs pitched to me where the demo sounded like a hit, but the song itself wasn't a hit song. You can get fooled because it sounds sort of like a hit, but it really isn't—it's just the excitement of the demo.

JN: I wish publishers would have every writer record two demos: an acoustic-guitar-and-vocal version, and then the full-blown demo, and then let them decide which model to use for the master, because I think people are making the decision to cover a song based on a mix, which may be covering up the fact that the song is just average. It's like layers—we're all just building upon this thing of everything being so aggressive. I'm sick of fucking aggressive! I want soulfulness.

FL: A lot of times everything in the track is loud—people are hitting the drums harder and everyone is playing louder; it's almost as if there's this competition going on amongst the musicians. But go back and listen to a Led Zeppelin record, and [John] Bonham isn't hitting the drums nearly as hard as what some of these modern drummers are doing.

JN: That's true. In the sixties, all the drummers who played on the records that we base our taste on were jazz drummers—they barely hit the drums. And now you go in the studio and people are telling drummers, "Play everything as hard as you possibly can—hit them twice as hard as you ever did before." But in doing that, you kill the tone.

FL: Yeah, it just chokes the life out of the drums.

JN: That's why you get these records where the drums are just dit, dit, dit—they're trying to be loud, but they're not.

FL: It's as though people just get louder or more aggressive and throw in more angst in order to compensate for maybe not being able to be better players.

JN: We're trying to make records that have emotional content, and if the songs are kind of average, it's as if we have to add all this aggression to make them sound emotional. But if the song is devastatingly emotional, you really don't have to do any of that.

FL: I think that the era that brought country music back in the late eighties came at a time when people were stripping down more, and it sounded fresh; it sounded bigger. Tony was a huge part of that. I remember one of the first times I was producing a record and I had this killer track, I just loved it when we walked out of the studio. But then we got to overdubbing and we started piling all these guitars on there. Every guitar was just so cool...but the record just got worse and worse and worse. People think, "If I throw a hundred instruments on here, it will sound huge," but it's often the other way around.

> **"If you layer too much paint on the canvas, it just clouds the whole picture."**
> **— Steve Fishell**

SF: These songs are little stories, and as producer you want to help tell that story; you want to help the artist get to the point where they can get that story across as clearly as possible. If you layer too much paint on the canvas, it just clouds the whole picture. The writers here in Nashville are some of the best writers in the world, so it's a real shame when something gets washed over by bombast. I don't know what's behind this rush to hype things—but I'd love to hear us get back to a quieter time, like when Tony was first making records with Lyle Lovett, or Randy Travis was coming out with his first great records.

JN: It was a time when there was space for vocals.

FL: This town is so interwoven, so a lot of the songs being written back then were dictating the *sound* of the records too. I don't know, maybe a lot of today's hits need all this stuff piled on them.

TB: I think Alison Krauss has the best career in town, because she really just makes records for people to enjoy. She doesn't get played on the radio very much, but she sells platinum records. Dez Dickerson, one of Prince's musicians, once said: "As an artist, if you have a hit, you have an experience, but if you have an audience, you have a career." That's what Alison has: an audience.

Autotuning—automatic pitch correction—is one aspect of Pro Tools that has certainly changed the sound of a lot of today's records. What are your thoughts about its use?

JN: Many people don't realize this, but vocal style is all about pitch versus time: the way an artist moves to each note actually defines who they are as a singer. So when you autotune someone, you're actually taking away all their style.

FL: We're seeing its use on all kinds of instruments now, not just on singers—everybody's getting to the note a lot quicker, and in funny, unnatural ways. But it's those slightly uncomfortable moments when a singer or player is just getting to a note that create a lot of tension and release, and that's starting to become missing from records these days.

SF: I hate autotuning. It should just be a means to an end in an emergency, like when an artist is on the road and you can't get them in to re-sing a note.

JN: Yes, if they've sung something that's emotionally devastating, but they're just slightly out of tune, that's one thing. We used to deal with that kind of stuff in other ways years ago anyway.

SF: I find that autotuned vocals are just uninteresting. I can't hang my heart onto somebody's lyrics or their voice based on the knowledge that they're cheating; I just think if you've got autotuning on from the top of the song, it's unethical. I'd rather listen to Aretha Franklin and whatever flaws might exist in her singing—not that there are many of them. And people should remember that prior to 1995, there were no records that were autotuned, so there's a huge history of great, passionate records that have been made without it.

FL: Some of my favorite old records are the real early George Jones records, and I sometimes wonder what they would sound like if he were autotuned. He hits every note he means to hit, but he never actually hits a *note*. [*laughs*] His pitching is all over the place, but it's brilliant, and it moves you. If they autotuned it, it just wouldn't be what it is.

JN: What concerns me is that I think it's affecting live performance. I can remember the day when you'd go out and hear an artist performing live and they would blow your mind. And if they didn't, they weren't hip. These days, I go out and I see people play live and sometimes I think, hmmm, that's not so impressive. That didn't happen when I was a kid.

FL: Even if you're singing through autotune so that your pitch is perfect, you're still not where Alison Krauss is. I know a lot of people who sell a lot more records than she does, but they'd probably kill for her respect.

JN: Sometimes I see folks singing on TV and I have to change the channel because I can't listen to it. I don't seem to recall that in past years. You can watch reruns of the Johnny Cash show when people used to come out and sing live and you'd be saying, "Oh my god, I can't believe how good this is!"

FL: I guess more people can get away with lack of talent today.

JN: Well, they look good, and they fit a marketing plan. I'm not going to discount that; I understand that this is a business and it's not all about talent, but I do feel that autotuning has had an effect on the quality of singing. Maybe it's just down to pure laziness, because in the old days, if you heard board tapes and you heard yourself singing out of tune, you'd have to go back to your house and work on it and get better. But if nobody says, "You're singing like shit," well, when are you going to get better?

TB: I think the use of autotuning depends on the kind of artist you are given and the kind of song it is. I mean, Steely Dan spent, what, a hundred years per record to make everything perfect. [*laughs*] They didn't use Pro Tools; they just used heaps of time. But a lot of pop music and contemporary country music is built around the perfection of the track, the tightness of the track, and the harmonies being really dialed in. It's unrealistic to compare the country records of today with the records of George Jones or Tammy Wynette. I remember cutting a song with Patty Loveless years ago, and I had a bunch of LA session guys playing on it, including Leland Sklar on bass. Years later, I listened to the track again with Leland and I remarked, "God, I never realized how sloppy that was." Leland said, "That's not sloppy; it's just as good it was the first time you heard it. You're just listening to it differently now—you're analyzing it, as opposed to enjoying it." So I think autotuning is a good thing on certain kinds of country songs. When I first started producing, I worked with a singer who had to sing every song down 60 times; you'd be punching in over and over again. In a sense, you were doing the same thing as autotuning, only you were doing it the hard way. Pop artists like Steely Dan or Toto or Celine Dion, as well as producers like Walter Afanasieff and David Foster—they're all about perfection; I'd put Rascal Flatts and Carrie Underwood in that category, too. Their approach to emotion is the same, and their record labels want hit songs that sound like radio, as opposed to songs that make your heart bleed. It's that perfection that makes their particular records appealing.

How do you deal with the conflict between your own goals of creating a work of art that has emotional content and true value with the goals of a record label, who are demanding commercial success?

FL: I'm the newest producer here, and I admit that I'm easily swayed, but I can't imagine the other three guys here being told what to do by the labels in terms of songs or approach. Do you all get a lot of interference from the labels?

JN: It depends on the label.

SF: When I was making records for Arista years ago, they would encourage me to make sure I had some singles on each album, but also to make what they would call "album tracks" so there was a full body of great songs that made for a great listening experience. It wasn't as important then to have ten singles on every record as your only goal. Artists want to have that sense of freedom, to know that they can express themselves on different levels . . . but, by god, you've got to have some singles too.

JN: Ten or fifteen years ago, you'd finish the record before the label picked the singles. Nowadays it's completely different. You go in and track and the first thing the label does is pick the single and you finish and mix that song first. The rest of the record may not get made for months, which to me is crazy because you've put this many great people in a room together—the musicians, the songwriters, the producer, the engineer—and things are going to happen that the labels have no idea about. Invariably artists are getting shortchanged because there may be a song down the road that may be their biggest hit, but it gets missed because everyone's focusing instead on that first single. That happens a lot.

TB: Jimmy Bowen always felt that the artist should lead the way and have a couple of songs on each album that they believed in as hits. There have been times when I've cut songs that I didn't think were singles on the demo but they ended up turning out like hit records. There are no set rules, except that there's got to be a real good bond when you're making music in a studio, or it does not work. You can have the best players, the best engineers, and even the best songs, but if it isn't coming together, you get nothing. There's a certain intangible magic that has to happen.

> *"My job is to do whatever I can to help the artist make the record they want to make."*
> **— Frank Liddell**

FL: I've always felt that my job is to do whatever I can to help the artist make the record *they* want to make. The greatest A&R people were the ones who had the ability and vision to be able to step back and just let the artist do what they do. When Aretha Franklin was making those great records, I doubt any A&R man was interfering and saying, "I need rough mixes on my desk by Monday morning."

JN: I'm sure there are some young A&R people today who would love to take that approach too, but ultimately they're answerable to the people above them. There are always lines drawn, and I don't blame people for acting the way they do, especially the way the business is right now, with everybody scared and pulling up the drawbridge a little bit. The system just isn't allowing things to happen that way right now.

FL: The artists that have made the bulk of the money in this business had a vision all their own, and they had a strong identity. The Beatles were not created by a label; the Monkees were. The Monkees may have had their relevance, but you can tell that there were a lot more people wanting to have their fingerprints on their identity. But at the end of the day, what instructions do you need to give a Tony Brown when he's making a record? What can you tell him that he already doesn't know?

What do you look for in a new artist? What are the things that will capture your attention and make you want to work with them?

TB: When I was an A&R man, I was always on the lookout for new artists, but now that I'm an independent producer, to be honest with you, I prefer being approached by acts that are already selling a shitload of records. [*laughs*] But I wouldn't turn down the opportunity to work with a new artist who just blew me away, either. I might suggest that they go get a deal first, because to just go in and experiment for free is very time-consuming, and now I can appreciate how hard it is to actually get paid for making records. But I still love hearing about a new songwriter in town, because I'm always looking for songs.

When I was at MCA and I would get pitched a new act, I'd ask them if they could write, and they'd always say, "Yes, I do, and I'm going to write a lot of good songs for you." They thought that's what I wanted to hear, but I actually preferred if they didn't, because the problem with an artist writing all their own songs is that if their songs suck, that's a real tough hurdle to overcome.

I also look for an artist who's willing to come into the studio and *perform*. That's one thing about Pro Tools that's not so good—a lot of artists come in and they think they can get it later. They just kind of hum through the verse during tracking, but what they don't realize is that if they give it their all, it's like a kick in the ass for the band and the tracking session can turn into a lovefest.

Then there are the artists who want to push the envelope, but they don't even know when the envelope has burst; they try to do things that they can't do. Like the Peter Principle, they rise to their level of incompetence. [*laughs*] But good is good, and at the end of the day, you have to trust your instincts. I'd rather fail at doing something good than fail at doing something mediocre. And if I've succeeded at doing something mediocre, I just won't admit it was me! [*laughs*]

> **"I'd rather fail at doing something good than fail at doing something mediocre."**
> **— Tony Brown**

FL: I think that if you do something good, then you *have* succeeded. But if you make a bad record just for the money and it fails, then you're in real trouble because it will end up damaging your reputation.

TB: Speaking of doing things you wish you hadn't done, I remember producing this record when I was at MCA—it was a hit, but it was pretty cheesy. I was sitting at a restaurant a few weeks later and a friend of mine came over and said, "Hey, Tony, did you make that record with so-and-so?" I said, "Yeah, I did." He got a pained look on his face and said, "Oh, man, don't tell me that!" [*laughs*]

But you learn from those kinds of things. If you become an elitist in this business, you won't get a lot of work. You can be idealistic and use that to feed the art you want to make, but you also have to at least be something of a businessman in order to keep your job; otherwise, you might as well be working in a factory somewhere. Trust me, everybody at the label wants to produce records, especially the A&R people. Everything these days is approved by committee, and you just have to deal with that stuff. And you have to realize that on occasion they're right. I've done my share of whining and moaning about remixing or re-cutting tracks, and guess what? Sometimes it was the right thing to do.

But how do you deal with situations where both you and the label feel that the record sounds right, but the artist is dissatisfied?

TB: That's a problem. The artist and the label and the producer *all* have to love it. That's the only way you can go forward.

SF: A lot of times it's down to interpretation. As Tony said, everybody's opinion matters, but one of the most interesting aspects of being a producer is being able to interpret what people say. Someone might say a mix is muffled, or that they hate a guitar part or something, but they might actually mean something completely different. You have to listen to what they're saying with that in mind and interpret what they're reacting to.

JN: That's absolutely true. If someone's is saying, for example, that the vocal just doesn't sound right, it may mean that there's something distracting from the vocal. It could be something totally bizarre, and you've really got to pay attention to what people are saying. Once I figured that out, things started working a lot better for me.

TB: That's one good thing about Pro Tools, especially if you mix in the box—you can turn on a dime and give the A&R people every option that they want. What do you guys think about mixing in the box? It actually sounds pretty good to me sometimes.

JN: Well, everything I do is with the idea that somewhere in the world there's some kid working in his bedroom making a record that sounds better than anything I could ever do, because it has a certain spontaneity and emotion. So if someone comes to me with a great song and an amazing performance, I should be able to make it sound good no matter what format I choose to work in. In the last three months, I've had to mix three records in the box because of budgetary considerations, so it's a reality for me. The thing that I've learned is to do as little as is humanly possible, because when the computer has to work that much harder—because you've piled on loads of plug-ins, for example—the sound seems to get smaller and smaller. But that's the same thing I do when I'm breaking out the tracks to an analog console, anyway; I'm wary of turning knobs. I still believe that balance is what is important. People seem to give up a half hour too soon on some mixes. You have to think balance first, and a good balance inside the box can sound just as good as one created outside the box.

TB: If it sounds good to me and I like it, I don't care how it was done.

JN: Exactly. If it has emotion, it's a good mix.

FL: I used to record and mix to analog, but unfortunately the quality of tape has gotten really bad. The last time I started to make a record in analog, I came in the next day and the kick drum was all but gone. At that point in time I started tracking in Pro Tools and I kept thinking I was still going to mix to tape, but by the time I was done months later, I decided to mix it digitally and it ended up sounding great.

I did a record once on a [Yamaha] 02R [console], with ADATs, and I remember saying to someone, "How in the world can it sound that good?" He said, "It's because a great engineer on an 02R is a hell of a lot better than most people on a Neve." The important thing is who's doing the driving. I'll have some fundamental thoughts and principles whenever I'm working with an engineer, but as long as we're seeing eye to eye on those things I'll defer to him in most technical matters.

SF: The great thing about Pro Tools is that it's democratized the whole process, especially for someone who's starting out in a development situation. Back in the day, if you were working with an artist from the ground up and you didn't have the help of a label, you had to get the funds together just to do demos. But with the tools that we now have, you can do a heck of a lot with relatively little investment and create a home demo that gives a solid impression of who the artist is.

JN: I'm actually excited about the changes in the music business because I think the cream is finally going to rise to the top. It's because everything is happening at once that people are getting a little freaked out, but I think these changes are going to ultimately improve quality.

FL: The record companies used to have the final say, but now there are so many different ways of getting music to people that you can prove them wrong.

What kind of advice can you offer to a young person who wants to forge a career as a record producer?

SF: The month I turned 18, I was lucky enough to go see the Allman Brothers Band with Duane Allman; it was just weeks before he died in a motorcycle accident. They weren't trying to play loud—they were playing dynamically—and that experience impressed on me the incredible power of how well-crafted, well-played music can move a person. I've sometimes wondered, "Was that concert as good as I remembered?" Fortunately, there are a lot of live recordings of them from that era, so it's easy to go back in time and realize that, yes, that really was a great time in music. To this very day, whenever I'm in the studio, I try to capture that vibe and that feel. So I would suggest that young people starting out make sure they never lose that vibe that they started with. Whatever it was that inspired you to get into music, try to hang onto it as tightly as you can and carry it with you throughout. Whatever you do in the studio, keep the fun and the passion in your music and let it run its course; good things will follow.

JN: I've made every mistake possible in my career. The turning point for me—the moment when things started really falling into place—was when I made the conscious decision to quit chasing the brass ring and focus instead on people and relationships. The moment I made that decision, everything changed for

> *"It's not about the producer...or even the artist or the musicians around him or her—it's about creating a circle of art that is bigger than everyone involved."*
> *— Justin Niebank*

me and I started having hit records. It's not about the producer, anyway, or even the artist or the musicians around him or her—it's about creating a circle of art that is bigger than everyone involved. So the best advice I can offer a young person is to take the self out of it and realize that it's all about relationships. Once you come to that realization, everything will amazingly flow a lot better for you.

TB: I would say, in everything you do, do it good, because you never know where it's going to lead. When I started out, I just wanted to be a musician; I wanted to play with big artists and I wanted to play on records. Eventually I got good enough to get to that point, but then, watching producers like Brian Ahern and Rodney Crowell and the way they worked, I realized that I might actually make a better producer than musician. I saw it as a way of being part of the creative side of things without having to actually pick up an instrument and perform or go out on the road.

I also always wanted to be around people who were better than me. My thinking was, if I can keep up with them, then I must be getting better. So try to hang around people who you admire and who you feel have things to offer—experience, talent, insight. As Justin said, it really is all about relationships. I've had opportunities come my way that I never would have believed possible—in fact, everything I've ever wanted to do, I've gotten to do—and it was all due to relationships. I can still remember the first time I met Vince Gill and Lyle Lovett; I can remember where I met them, and who made the connections. It's like a chain, and I kept broadening my circle. I know people who are much more talented than me but they still have that little circle they live in, and so they're not doing anything meaningful with their lives; in fact, they're all pissed off and they have a chip on their shoulder. I just kept widening my circle. Not only is it great fun, there are a lot of interesting people out there, and you can learn from all of them.

FL: First and foremost, you've got to love what you do. It may sound trite, but you need to pour everything you have into what you're doing. I'm in my early forties, and I'm still learning. I have a lot of young people who work for me, and they just want to run things right away. I tell them, "Slow down. If you're learning, you're getting there. You're getting paid right now to go to school, so just make sure you learn something new every day." I actually think of myself as more of an instigator than a producer—I go off and I stir stuff up with a lot of people and then I end up saying, "Oh, no, how am I going to get out of this?" [*laughs*] But the way to succeed is to surround yourself with talent and good people. Just work hard, have a hell of a lot of fun, and always, always keep learning.

Inspiration

Daniel Lanois

Nothing Is Sacred

Daniel Lanois is excited.

"Look at this," he says, proffering a tiny Edirol digital recorder. "This little box, which records on a card, is only about the size and weight of a cigarette package. It runs on batteries, it's got a nice onboard stereo mic and an automatic level control. I could make an entire album with just four of these!"

An entire album? "Sure," he says amiably. "Let's say that during this interview we decide to pick up a couple of instruments, and let's say I have four of these in my coat. I'd put one out in the room to capture the overall sound, one near my guitar amp, one near your amp, and another one in front of whoever is singing, and then I'd press Record on all four of them. I'll end up with four nice stereo recordings of the same event, occurring at different spots in the room. Then when I get back home, all I have to do is transfer the individual recordings to a computer in order to sync them back up. And when you do that, the most incredible thing happens: you get a certain imaging and depth of field that you wouldn't get from static mono microphones, with results that are wild and wonderful."

Lanois calls this concept "the walking multitrack," and it shouldn't surprise anyone if he actually does do an album that way one of these days. In fact, a notion like this is typical of his outside-the-box thought processes. For more than 30 years, the radical approaches he and his sometimes production partner Brian Eno have taken have resulted in some of the most significant and sonically distinctive records ever made: works like U2's *Joshua Tree* and Peter Gabriel's *So*, not to mention Bob Dylan's career-rejuvenating *Time Out of Mind*, which netted the iconic singer-songwriter an Album of the Year Grammy in 1997.

Lanois is also a master guitarist who has forged a significant career of his own as an artist, with six solo albums to his credit, and more on the way. In typical forward-thinking fashion, all are available for download through his website (www.redfloorrecords.com), and not only in the standard low-resolution MP3 format, but also, at no extra cost, as full-resolution CD-quality WAV files. Despite his hectic schedule, Lanois was kind enough to invite us to his beautiful Los Angeles home one sunny winter morning for a long, detailed chat.

You're really sold on these little portable digital recorders, aren't you?

I am, especially since they only cost three or four hundred dollars, so anyone can afford to make records with them. Just keep fresh batteries on hand, keep a notebook so your indexes are accurate, and off you go.

I recently had a nice experience putting one of these inside a grand piano too. I just placed it on a little sponge so it wouldn't rattle around, put the lid down, and we got an amazing sound. These little recorders won't distort, either. They'll compress, but they won't distort.

You know, I initially embraced them because of their ease of setup and flexibility, and because they're unobtrusive—they aren't intimidating to musicians like big microphones on stands can be; they're actually just like having a few snapshot cameras laying around. But then I started really liking the sound of them.

Video cameras have something similar—they'll usually have a little onboard stereo microphone, and you can get interesting results from those too. We filmed one of my live performances awhile ago where we had the front of house [FOH] mix going to a DAT, and then my brother was running the camera, moving around relative to the action on the stage. When we viewed it back, we thought, okay, let's route the good sound—the mix that the audience was hearing—into a pair of good stereo speakers. The camera sound was just coming out of the little TV speaker. But something magical resulted, because the FOH sound was static and the camera sound was constantly changing. Rather than turning up a fader to feature a soloist, the microphone was moving closer to the soloist, so the job was already being done. And when the solo was over, the camera just moved back to the singer. So without having to touch any knobs, the music was actually mixing itself, which got me thinking about a whole new way of working.

Many of your best-known recordings, though, were done to analog tape. Do you still prefer the sound of analog to digital?

Not necessarily. When I listen to my records from the seventies and eighties and compare them with newer recordings, I can hear a difference, but it's not just the tape—it's where we have traveled in our minds and where our expectations have taken us. It's a slow creep, and year by year a little bit of the old way of doing things just disappears. It's an erosion rather than a hardcore change of technique. So I don't really miss the sound of tape, but I miss some of the philosophies that we operated by back in the day. I think that was probably more significant than the sound of tape versus digital.

What philosophies are you referring to?

People were really excited to be in the studio and it was an amazing day to look forward to; there was a hopes-and-dreams aspect to it. Now every day is a day in the recording studio, because every other house seems to have a Pro Tools rig in it. In fact, I hear that some condominiums come with Pro Tools and the Internet, as well as a microwave. [*laughs*] It's just regarded as a contemporary communications system. You get to download your in-house condo demos directly to iTunes! [*laughs*]

It's funny, but there's truth there: there's less mystique to the recording process today. You can almost compare it to when you went out on a date in the 1950s. You'd put on your best suit and your best shoes and your date would put on her best dress and you just knew it was going to be a great night; it was a great night because you didn't get to do it all the time. Then you wind the clock forward to where that kind of Saturday night romance might have disappeared, and therefore people are more sloppily dressed and the night is not as special as it once might have been. I think that's the main difference.

How do you feel about digital plug-ins, particularly the emulations of vintage analog gear?

I've not used plug-ins all that much, but when I have used them I've enjoyed the fact that there were quick and easy effects available. I tend not to compare plug-ins with the original analog equipment anyway; I think that would be unfair. As usually happens, a certain piece of equipment will lead you in a certain direction because of the available trinkets onboard. I think that happens much more than, "I need an LA-2A but I don't have to buy one because I've got a plug-in that emulates it." Whatever your system happens to be, it will promote a certain way of working, and that's the beauty of it, whether it was my old Sony TC630, where I was pinging from one track to the other, or whether it's my "walking multitrack" concept. I've never found myself in a conventional studio doing conventional things but wanting to use plug-ins rather than old equipment. Whether an LA-2A plug-in sounds better or worse than an actual LA-2A is not all that significant to me. If all I had available to me were plug-ins, I'd try to do nice work with whatever I had.

So what you're saying is that it's not down to the tools, it's down to the expertise of the person using the tools.

I think so. I have a friend who's a chef, and he owns one of the great restaurants in Los Angeles. He comes over here and there's hardly anything in my kitchen, but within 20 minutes, there's amazing food coming out, beautifully laid out on plates. He says that's the mark of a resourceful chef: when you can whip something up on the spot with what you've got. Isn't that the fun part of life?

So I wouldn't want to insist on a certain list of equipment and expect every item on that list to be there; if I did, then probably every record I'd make would sound the same as all the other ones.

Has the transition from analog to digital recording caused your choices of microphone and mic placement to change through the years?

Perhaps, but what has never changed for me is my respect for my stations. Let me define the concept for you. "Stations" are positions of sound, and they include instruments and their microphones, as well as whatever integrated technology you use to make that station be effective. A fundamental station, for example, might be a well-chosen acoustic piano, miked with a single ribbon microphone, positioned correctly. Put it in there, close the lid, put a blanket over it, and you will get a beautiful sound. I like mono recordings for piano because it gives me a very focused single point source, but I've also used a C24 [AKG stereo mic], which gives a beautiful sound as well. But if a track is going to be dense, i.e., if the piano is not an up-front main feature but is instead a little melody part panned over to one side, then I'd rather use a mono mic source.

So once I get that station sounding good and the piano is in the sweet spot of the room, the good RCA 77 is in the piano, the blankets are on, we've chosen the right preamp, maybe we've hit a compressor, we've got the right EQ—now my great piano sound lives at the end of one patch cord, and it says "piano" on it. You can be drunk and blind and you walk into my studio and you pick up the plug that says "piano" and bang it into whatever track you want, and you're recording; you don't have to go fishing out of cupboards or have people get flustered trying to figure out why it's not working or anything. That's my reason for having stations, and they are completely independent of the recording medium.

Brian Eno gave me some DX7 sounds some years ago that are beautiful; he personally spent some time designing these sounds, and so I keep my old DX7 as a station as well. I pipe it through a Roland JC120 guitar amplifier, which works well as a keyboard amp, miked with a large diaphragm dynamic microphone; I like the Sennheiser M409, which has been discontinued. It's a real winner; you can put it right up against a speaker and get a great sound without a whole lot of spill from the rest of the room, so it's good for tight-miking. And that's it: my Brian Eno sounds live in that one station. And it never gets interrupted, either: we never steal the amp out of there to do a guitar overdub, for example.

By the way, my main console, my listening console, is never my preamp console; it's only ever in mix mode. I have side consoles and side preamps—mostly API or Neve—that accommodate the microphones, and that's what goes to the recorder. I just find that it makes for a faster way of working. You lay down the track, do a couple of overdubs, and then you're mixing. You turn on your two-track and you've got it, and there's something lovely about the blends of the day. You've seen a track come to life, and the overdubs have been significant relative to the excitement, the ideas in the room.

And on that playback, on that day, there will be a certain unspoken knowledge of that piece of music. The people in the room are operating on instinct, and so your blend is not cerebral, it's doesn't have too much thought going into it other than that you're just serving the room—you're playing it back for the musicians to hear for the purpose of doing overdubs; everything has a practical reason to live on that day. Those are often the great blends, so I keep my main console ready to accommodate the blend of the day. That's my technique, and I've made entire albums out of the blends of the day, like the Willie Nelson record called *Teatro*. We'd lay down a track, I'd do a bass overdub and maybe some percussion, this and that. Then we'd listen back, and while we were listening back, we would mix. Oftentimes those were the lovely, full-bodied musical mixes that worked. It just means that you don't have to go back in a month later to try to recreate the vibe of the day.

You're renowned for treating the drum kit as a single instrument, as opposed to a collection of individual drums. Can you elaborate on some of your mic selections and placements for drums?

I've had excellent results consistently now with a Coles ribbon mic a couple of feet back from the bass drum and a nice old [Neumann] U47 tube mic used as a mono overhead, and then maybe one other mic in the high-hat/snare area, slightly favoring the high-hat, and that can be just a Shure SM57. If the drum kit is sounding good in the room, and you have a good room, it's hard to miss with that combination.

But I also like tight miking; no broad regulation applies to every day. The thing I'm most excited about in the drum department these days is having a few different drums around that I know and love. They're usually hand-picked drums that I've experimented with and found the sweet blend of two specific heads. For instance, I have a 26-inch [Slingerland] Radio King bass drum up in Canada, and it has the original calfskin head on the beater side. We put a little bit of a pillow on the resonator head, and then the bass drum beater was a kind of furry one, and the sound in the end was fantastic—it had a little bit of a marching bass drum sound to it, but not crazy wishy-washy; it just had a lot of body in the sound, a lot of low mids. It turned out to be one of my favorite sounds.

The moral of the story is, if you have a drum that sounds beautiful, keep it nearby. And if you're having trouble with your bass drum sound, don't fiddle with the mic, because a Coles mic two feet in front of a bass drum doesn't lie; it just gives you the business, the actual flat sound. So if the bass drum doesn't work, just swap it for a different drum until you find a more sympathetic marriage with your bass guitar.

It's interesting that you are describing placing the pillow against the resonator head, as opposed to the beater head.

Well, if you have two heads on the bass drum, the resonator head plays a big part in the decay of the sound.

Do you typically cut a hole in the resonator head?

I have a few heads with a small hole cut, and I also sometimes like having the whole front of the bass drum open; you still have a head on it, but you cut a big hole in it, leaving maybe one inch all around. By leaving your lugs intact, you're not messing with the stability of the drum itself. That can be a nice sound; it's more like an RE-20 straight inside the bass drum vibe. That sound turns up a lot on seventies recordings, where the bass drum was more like a pop, with a 200 Hz emphasis, not a lot of decay, and, if you were to look at a frequency graph, it would be operating a little bit above the bass guitar, so its job was not to provide a big, full, furry bottom—it was more of a boomph, like somebody knocking on a door. That's an amazing blend that shows up on a lot of rhythm and blues records of the seventies. Bill Withers records would have that sound, for example.

I hear that in a lot of your productions, too, where the bottom end is coming from the bass and not the bass drum.

It's a funny thing with bass, because it's an education. I grew up in the Toronto area, and we didn't have a lot of examples of great bottom end on records there; that was more of an American thing. Canada was more interested in storytelling and melody; there were just different priorities up there. But then when I went to the southern U.S., I understood why the bass was better down there—it was because the players came up with such great bass parts. I got to work with George Porter Jr. of The Meters when I was working with the Neville Brothers in New Orleans, for example, and suddenly I was exposed to bass lines, and they were very economical and specific and not blurring everything. [*hums a few staccato bass lines to illustrate*] By having those holes and spaces there, you can make the instrument louder, because it's not smearing everything. That was really quite a lesson for me.

What are your thoughts on MP3s having become the primary means of music distribution?

There's a part of me that wishes we were never in the race to the changing of the medium. It's always kind of bothered me every time it's changed: "Oh, we were just starting to do some nice work. Now what are they bringing in?" I liked it when analog got to its peak with those beautiful Studer and MCI multitrack machines. I used MCIs for years; they were really rockers, with great bottom end. Those machines have become doorstops today. It's a great time for making records now, in a way, if you buy up a whole bunch of old equipment.

But the idea of having to completely change the way you work to accommodate a medium just doesn't appeal to me very much. I have a beautiful Nikon 35 mm film camera that I've taken a lot of nice photographs with, including Bob Dylan's *Time Out of Mind* record cover. Not only does it take nice pictures, but when I push the shutter button on it, it takes the picture right away. Digital cameras are not quite as fast; sometimes it takes a split second for the camera to decide whether it's the right moment to take a picture, even though you're pushing the button down.

Yes, there are more options, and it's more convenient, and you can edit right in your camera—you can see an immediate result. But it's not as fast, so it's not as good for capturing the moment.

You know, wherever he goes, people take pictures of Bono, all the time. He usually doesn't mind it, but he's told me that digital cameras have kind of ruined his life because for every picture that gets taken, there's a lot of delay: what used to take a second or two has escalated into some guy standing there fiddling with a camera and he can't get it right and other people have to help. Waiting for that flash has turned his life into a misery. He's actually talked about doing a fun book called "Waiting for the Flash," which would show the minutes of his life that he's wasted waiting for that picture to be taken.

The classic records of the sixties and seventies were, for want of a better word, human: there were mistakes, the tempos would speed up or slow down, or there were lyrical fluffs or notes sung out of pitch. The goal today, however, seems to be perfection, with every vocal autotuned and every mistake edited out. Is that a change you welcome?

Well, I like high-tech records when they're really high-tech, when I can't figure out what's going on. If there's a smart kid out there somewhere—a young Stravinsky or Beethoven—he or she may well be in a bedroom with a computer, doing amazing things. So I'm interested in the works of that person because I'm interested in the genius of that mind. The genetic gift of music never changes, but the time that you're born in, and the tools that you're given, that always moves along. So I never look to high-tech futuristic computer work to replicate a seventies record. In a way, that would be an unfair demand.

> *"I like high-tech records when they're really high-tech, when I can't figure out what's going on."*

When I hear some of today's heavily compressed, multi-mic rock records, I sense the competition, and the competition is dealt with by adding more top and midrange so that things cut, and by adding more compression so that the sounds never disappear and are there all the time. So consequently the presence of that kind of work is demanding on the ear, because it's a very congested sound; it's a hyperactive sound, and you can't deny the excitement of it. But I think a very important ingredient in records is to keep them welcoming to the listener, and if you create a record that does that, you've succeeded artistically. Some modern records that I hear don't have that in them, but I still love the evidence of a brilliant mind having access to a toolbox that includes technology. Obviously some kid working at home isn't going to have drum kits all around the house or people coming over to play them, so they're going to have to do beats with something else, and that limitation might just push them to do something special within what's available in their paintbox. I wish I knew more about those kinds of records, though I do hear them on occasion, and clearly everything has been done with loops and samples, but I still hear it as good work.

The thing about loops and samples is that they are relatively static, and you might say that's going to eventually wear out a listener, but that non-moving part—that component that never has an ebb and flow or emotion in it beyond its two-bar loop emotion—could be regarded as a pillar, almost like a building. It's the Louvre or the Eiffel Tower; there it is, it's up against the sky and it's not going to move. What *is* going to move is the weather, and what you choose to put in the foreground of your picture. So I'm not afraid of static modern technology because it means that I can make my central characters be more animated. Let *them* be the emotion.

I made a record with Dylan in the late eighties called *Oh Mercy*, and funnily enough a lot of that record was made with a drum box—a Roland [TR-]808. It was just Bob and I sitting on two chairs, like two guys on a porch, and we had a large stage wedge right in front of Bob into which we piped the sound of the 808. Sometimes we'd EQ the signal so it would be more of a heartbeat. [*sings section of "Man in a Long Black Coat" to illustrate*] Now you might think, okay, you've got a static 808 there, so what's going to give the emotion? Well, obviously, the lyric, Bob's delivery, and his phrasing. And he happened to hook right into it; he had no problem with it, never gave it a lot of thought, and it was my work technique for the building of that project: a little bit of technology contrasted with a human playing on tape. That meant that we were operating with the luxury of fixed time, which makes it good for repeat echoes, plus you can easily edit between takes. After all, when you've got Bob Dylan in the room, you don't want to say to him, "Do you mind doing it again, because we didn't get the intro right?" If his delivery was brilliant, just use the intro from the earlier version instead, where it was played better.

As a bonus, by getting the vocal and the two main guitars recorded simultaneously, playing to fixed time, you now have a license to go multi-dimensional, to increase your depth of field by overdubbing unlikely ingredients. That's essentially a folk-singing setting, but the vocal will be big and emotional, and will be very well in pitch with the source ingredients of the two guitars. Once you have an emotion and the pitch is great and the vibe is there, you can do anything you want. Bob gets to go home and I can strap on my Les Paul Junior and crank my amp up to 10 with echoes, or I can have Willie Green overdub drums on top of the 808, and then you can start stacking, and you never lose the breadcrumbs of your original vibe.

> **"Once you have an emotion and the pitch is great and the vibe is there, you can do anything you want."**

That's something that's very, very important, and it's the only principle I ever operate by. Whether I'm using an 808 or having an entire band crashing away in a room, no matter what it is, that first stage has to have the emotion and the vibe; the playing and technique, in a way, is less significant than the emotional bedrock. The only question is: what's that bedrock going to be? Some rap people might say, "Here's how we do it: we sample somebody else's record that's got an emotional bedrock, and we build on top of that." That's cool, too. I've done that: I've sampled old blues records for Bob's *Time Out of Mind* record, old Little Walter records, and then we played on top of those old blues record samples. Then we got rid of the old blues record, but at least it provided us with an emotional bedrock springboard for us to work off of.

In previous interviews, you've talked about viewing a complex piece of music as a "network." What exactly did you mean by that?

Here's what I mean by that: if you and I are playing instruments, I start playing a certain way, and then you'll accommodate my way of playing in the way that you play, out of respect for being harmonious and trying to get good results. But if you have a static, fixed ingredient, like a beat that never changes no matter what, then you won't have that kind of ebb and flow. So in the case of a trio, which is a very powerful triangle, like the Jimi Hendrix Experience, none of the three elements are static; in that case, even the drums were playing a melody of sorts—the accents were built to accommodate Jimi's guitar, etcetera. I suppose it's that interplay that we love on those records.

In a trio you can never just play filler; you can't just play a keyboard pad or something like that. I think that as human beings, we provide what is necessary to make a situation work, so the fewer musicians you have, then people rise to that place of responsibility to make that part really be significant and harmonious to the other two [parts].

I feel that way about musical situations that have four parts as well. That exists in a lot of different areas of music. There's no room for laziness in a string quartet, for example. You can't just stray; you have to play the written note because it was planned that way, so you can harmonize with your mates. It's the same thing with choirs, where you have the four divisions of a choir. Or a gospel quartet, or a barbershop quartet.

Funk is built the same way, where there's never evidence of filler or someone just playing along. You'll have that solid beat coming from the bass and the drums, and the guitar accents, and then the vocals: listen to some of James Brown's vocals and they are like trumpet lines. I love the economy of arrangements. We have to remember that there's another Stravinsky out there, another Beethoven, another Mozart, and it will be a young kid somewhere, and that brilliant mind will understand the power of four parts and how to optimize their placement.

When you're working with a solo artist, as opposed to a band, do you prefer the backing track to have the minimum number of musicians, or do you like having a lot of players in the room at the same time?

It depends on the artist. When we were making Peter Gabriel's *So*, we built that record with three people: Peter, [guitarist] David Rhodes, and myself. We used prepared rhythms; Peter had done a lot of work with beat boxes. His songs were not fully written, but his beats were there, and we would be chasing after an idea relative to a beat that Peter was excited about, or a certain kind of chord sequence. As a result, we had a nice starting point. In that kind of scenario, it's not a good idea to have a lot of people around because you get nervous that you're wasting people's time while the song is getting written. But by having just the three of us, we had this "turning up for work" kind of humor: we'd wear these construction-worker hard hats. What was nice about that was that there was not a lot of candy or icing sugar to cover up any weakness in an arrangement or song structure, so we were able to dedicate that time to the building of the songs for Peter, and we could quickly change the course of an approach, because there were only three people in the room—it was less of a large ship, or barge; it was more of a canoe at that point and you could quickly make a turn. Plus it's less of an emotional investment when you have a smaller group of people, because you don't have to communicate an idea to ten different people. The more people you have, the more expensive it gets, and the harder it is to put a twist in an approach.

So that worked out very well for Peter, and once we had our songs finished and our structures there, we overdubbed drums and bass and horns and everything else afterwards. The emotion came from Peter, and we were building on something that was reliably soulful relative to the input of three people.

Now let's wind the clock ahead to Bob Dylan's *Time Out of Mind*. Bob had the songs written beforehand, because he comes from that world: he writes the songs ahead of time, and then he brings them into the studio, more or less complete. We put 11 people in the room with him, and that worked out well because in that case there was no mystery about things; Bob was not about to change the chorus or write a new angle for the song—everything was pretty much carved in stone ahead of time. Maybe we would modify a riff or give it a certain musical identity on the day, but we never went into the bedrock and changed it. When you have the luxury of the song being already written ahead of time, the job at hand is to serve the song and to come up with as cool and as soulful a vibe as you can.

There's also an automatic depth of field that you get by having 11 people playing together in a room. Every microphone is open literally to someone 50 feet away, who's going to sound literally 50 feet away through the vocal mic. As a result, *Time Out of Mind* is dripping with ambience. It paints such a picture that you can really feel the presence of people in the room, and that's an exciting sensation. It's like hearing a great Miles Davis record, where you know that everyone was doing it in the room at the same time.

So that's two ends of the spectrum. It depends on the artist and what you have to work with song-wise. If the songs are written beforehand, you do it one way, and if it's more jam-based, you do it another way.

I'm guessing that you end up using a lot of guide vocals on your records.

Oh, yes. This is something that I learned from Emmylou Harris: she has said that she never bettered a vocal on another day. She might have done a good second or third pass on the same day as the band track, but vibe-wise they would still relate to her backing track vocal. But a week later, two weeks later, a month later—she's never bettered it. That's where it all gets mysterious, because it's all beyond measurement; if it's the same mic and the same vocal chain and the same woman and the same room, then it should be the same . . . but it's not. That's where you get into psychology and spontaneous combustion and freshness and all those aspects.

Psychology is clearly such a big part of record-making, and it seems like you're all about providing a comfortable, safe environment for your artists to be creative in.

Preparation is still my best friend, especially for anything technical. It brings us back to my stations: I respect my stations and I keep them well-lubricated, and I work with people who understand that my stations must be kept well-maintained so that when people walk in we're not dragging cables out of the closet. But the psychology aspect is so important. Part of the process is, I play a waiting game. A lot of times I don't tell people what to do, or ask anything of them; I just put them in a room and I wait for something that I like to happen. Then I'll say, "I really liked what you played there. Could you play it again?" And then we start from there.

Will you have tape rolling constantly during rehearsals?

I'll at least have a two-track running all the time so that if somebody comes up with something while they're fiddling around, we can at least reference it and have a conversation about it. There's a momentum that I tap into that's usually based on the thrill of an idea. It doesn't matter where the idea comes from; what's important is that you chase after it. And if a result comes from the idea, then that usually triggers a second idea, and a third one, and you start capitalizing on the potential of the momentum in the room. There's a power that exists when you have a group of folks in a room. You sort of go down this labyrinth that you might not have expected beforehand.

Making music is a funny thing. You might get up and think, "Oh, I drank too much last night—it's going to be a bad day," and then you go into the studio and you're dragging your ass. But then when someone else in the room sinks a couple of baskets, you think, "Whoa!" and then it puts a little juice in you and off you go: a slow day can become a very productive day. So I've stopped measuring days in anticipation; I measure them when I'm actually in there working, and it's usually all about ideas. The best people I've worked with have been the best ideas people.

You often play on the records you produce. Do you like playing with the band as they're laying down the backing tracks, or do you usually just do overdubs?

I like to be part of the band, especially during the first stage of a record where you've got to juice up the room. It's been different on every record, though; I suppose on Bob Dylan's *Time Out of Mind* I was very much the music director because I'd been living with the material for awhile and so I'd built up a lot of knowledge about it. The musicians that came in were great players, but some of them had not heard the music before, so they needed me to coach them through an arrangement. I'd just keep a communication mic close by and I'd announce a section as it was coming up.

I do my homework, which is having a good understanding of what the song is made of. To that end, I create these elaborate charts, laying out the entire song in these big charcoal drawing books. The way they work is that a song starts on the left and ends on the right, just like the way you write words, and every little turn in the song gets a signpost: a signpost might indicate a four-bar intro, and then the band entry at the fifth bar; then at the ninth bar, melodic signature; then at the twelfth bar, verse vocal comes in. I position the song in the center of the page so that I can draw lines from each particular section, and then add signs that are almost like thought bubbles. Each thought bubble will have a thought relating to that spot in the song—a reminder about a vocal level, or a background vocal, even processing equipment instructions if I come up with a nice delay on the vocal, for example. I keep adding thought bubbles as people keep coming up with ideas. As a result, when you look at the entire chart, you can see what is carved in stone in the arrangement of the song, as well as all the ideas people have come up with.

So the chart holds all the information that I'm going to need to have a nice communication system in the room. After all, you can't be standing in there like an idiot; you can't just be a cheerleader. Perhaps you can get away with that for a minute, but when somebody says, "You know, in the second bar of the third verse there was a little skip in the high-hat," as the producer, you have to be able to say, "I know *exactly* what you mean." Not, "Oh, where's that?" and waste people's time. You have to be able to say, "That happens at 2:42, and it's track such-and-such, and we're going to go in the other room and repair it right now." That way, you can actually do something about a suggestion in the room and not be a dummy. That's one of the reasons I like to play along with the band on the backing track—because I want to have full knowledge of what's going on—and that's why I make my charts: so we can speed the process up and quickly accommodate repairs and suggestions that are made in the room. Cheerleaders not allowed.

So there's a real practical aspect to playing with the musicians, but surely there's got to be a psychological aspect too: you're one of them, not some shadowy figure in the control room looking down on them and passing judgment.

That's very well put. If you're a member of the band, you're pulling the oars along with everyone else; you're not the guy hitting the drum or cracking the whip. After all, you don't want a mutiny on your hands. [*laughs*]

Can you contrast your approach to recording when you're on your own, as opposed to when you work in collaboration with Brian Eno?

Eno and I play very well together, so without speaking a lot of words, we just walk into a room, go to our rigs, and within a matter of minutes there's something happening. We're usually able to come up with a vibe very quickly, and that's the gift of our partnership. Consequently, we play on the records we produce together. Eno will almost always come in with some kind of beat, or a sound that will have a powerful emotion within it, something that might be the perfect complement to a lyric.

So we're a good tag team, but we have a couple of rules that we operate by. One of them, which Brian explained to me very early on, is this: whatever I say, you agree with, and whatever you say, I will agree with. That's because it's better to agree on something and get the ball rolling. That's much more important than suffocating the subject matter with too many opinions;

being in agreement matters more than whether one person's idea is better or not. We made that pact a long, long time ago and we stick by it.

Then we have some fun techniques we apply. For example, we keep an independent station in the control room with an external console—something like a 32-track Mackie—which is receiving the multitrack information all the time. This station will have a set of cans and some processing equipment, so Eno can go and sit there, put on the headphones, and do something to the song that's appearing on the main console without changing the vibe of the room; he's just quietly in the corner doing his thing. The output from his station appears on two faders of the main console, and occasionally he'll stick his hand up, signaling that you should pull up his faders so you can listen to what he's done. That's a nice way of maximizing Eno's talent: just give him a station and let him play with the tracks until he comes up with something he likes.

> *"It's better to agree on something and get the ball rolling . . . than to suffocate the subject matter with too many opinions; being in agreement matters more than whether one person's idea is better or not."*

I have a similar station, with my little loop machines and pedals and sometimes in a quiet way I'll be coming up with something too. I'll put my hand up when I feel I've done enough fiddling and I've hit on an idea, and that in turn might trigger another idea from Eno.

We've taken this concept into mixing as well. The way it works is that one of us—it doesn't matter which—sits at the console and begins mixing a song on our own. But the rule is that you have to lay down a mix onto two-track within fifteen minutes. Then you get out of the chair and the other guy sits down, working from where you left off—he never pulls down all the faders and starts from scratch. Now he gets another fifteen minutes to do another mix, and the one rule here is that nothing is sacred: he can change whatever he wants. Fifteen minutes later another mix is laid down.

We swap back and forth like that for two hours, which gives us eight mixes. The especially good thing about this is that you've only put in two hours of your time, so you're not emotionally invested in what you've done. You've focused instead in curiosity and fun, and maybe you've tried a few crazy things because, hey, it's only a fifteen-minute mix. But at the end you have eight mixes to play for the artist. Together, you sit in a room and listen to all eight of them, and there's invariably going to be something special about two or three of them, and those mixes get to be a kind of character fundamental at that point, a reference as you keep working towards a final mix. You're simply not going to get that if you've got everybody in the room and you're just inching towards a final result over the course of twelve hours.

That's a fascinating approach to mixing. But I'm even more interested in how you're able to stick with the first rule. What do you do if you totally disagree with the other person's suggestion, if you honestly feel it's totally the wrong approach?

You just shut up. You just go with the other person's idea. The thing about ideas is, if you don't chase them up and see them through to their conclusion, you may have frustration living in a corner of the room. And I've never had a disagreement regarding result. Somehow it always works out that everybody agrees on the approach that sounds best.

So you're saying that if it really was a bad idea, everybody will pretty much realize it at the end of the day.

Well, we never call them bad ideas. There are only good ideas that don't work out. And even if they don't work out, that doesn't make for a bad feel, because we gave it a try, anyway.

What advice do you have for someone who wants to be the next Daniel Lanois?

Well, I still adhere to the philosophy that it's good to hang on to tools that have served you well along the way. Just keep them in your box, and you'll always know that a certain tool will give you a certain sound. But I would also say that you need to walk before you can run. Get yourself a portable digital recorder and whenever you hear something that sounds cool, record it. Start with that; it will be as good a recording as any, within its limitations. If I hold one near a drum kit, it will yield a great drum sound if the drum kit sounds great. It might be as great a drum sound than what you'd get if you spent two days dragging mics and cables around; in fact, it might even be a *more* exciting sound, because of the onboard compressor.

Bring the musicians to the recorder, or the recorder to the musicians. Make some recordings and see how you can mold them into sounds that you like. Then go out and buy three more of them and a computer-based system like Pro Tools so you can really go to town!

Of course, you also need to have a belief in yourself. I thank God that I can wake up every day and be excited about an idea or an approach. The naïve spirit is still within me, and within that naïvete is a fearlessness. If you're wide-eyed and innocent, you're not going to know about the bad things that can come your way, and I think that's what fearlessness is. The opposite of that would be, "Hey man, be careful, that's not going to work." Then you get 20 reasons why something's not going to work, and you're operating from a place of needing something to fall back on, taking precautionary measures, walking on eggshells, and those are the fears that could choke a day's work. But if you're wide-eyed and you believe, it's the same as love being blind, really. You and the person you're in love with might have a terrible domestic dispute six months from now, but today it will be the most wonderful kiss you've ever had.

Selected Listening:

Daniel Lanois: *Acadie*, Opal, 1989; *For the Beauty of Wynona*, Warner Brothers, 1993; *Belladonna*, Anti, 2005

U2: *The Joshua Tree*, Island, 1987; *Achtung Baby*, Island, 1991; *All That You Can't Leave Behind*, Interscope, 2000; *No Line on the Horizon*, Interscope, 2009

Peter Gabriel: *So*, Geffen, 1986; *Us*, Geffen, 1992

Bob Dylan: *Oh Mercy*, Columbia, 1989; *Time Out of Mind*, Columbia, 1997

Willie Nelson: *Teatro*, Island, 1998

The Neville Brothers: *Yellow Moon*, A&M, 1989

T-Bone Burnett

A New Dimension in Sound

Talking with T-Bone Burnett is like entering an alternate universe of free-flowing creative ideas. Within minutes it becomes obvious why such a wide variety of artists, in both the musical and visual worlds, are so comfortable working with him. With no apparent effort, he manages to pull off the seemingly impossible feat of being at once cerebral and literate, yet warm and down to earth.

Burnett's story starts with his teenage years in Fort Worth, Texas, where he was exposed to a steady stream of not only the best musicians of the '60s, but the finest visual artists of the era as well—a training ground that would prove invaluable later in his career. After opening a small studio where he recorded local bands and honed his musical chops, Burnett relocated to Los Angeles in the early 1970s, where his skills as a guitarist soon landed him an invitation to join Bob Dylan's 1975 *Rolling Thunder* tour. Once off the road, T-Bone formed the short-lived Alpha Band, which enjoyed some critical acclaim but limited commercial success, before leaving to launch his own solo career. Along the way, he found himself increasingly in demand as a record producer, giving him the opportunity to work with such seminal artists as Roy Orbison, Elvis Costello, Los Lobos, Counting Crows, Gillian Welch, and the Jakob Dylan-led Wallflowers, as well as overseeing the soundtracks for the films *The Big Lebowski*, *Cold Mountain*, and the Johnny Cash biopic *Walk the Line*. Most recently, Burnett helmed jazz singer Cassandra Wilson's *Thunderbird* and the lush Robert Plant/Alison Krauss collaboration, the 2008 Grammy-winner, *Raising Sand*.

But it was his phenomenal success with the bluegrass-laced soundtrack to the 2001 film *O Brother Where Art Thou* (which sold almost nine million copies and netted four Grammy awards) that catapulted T-Bone Burnett into the headlines. Ever since then, he has come to be seen as the guardian and protector of the American musical heritage—something he has a deep and abiding interest in. But there is so much more to the man than that: a decades-long friendship and collaboration with playwright Sam Shepard; a songwriting talent marked by a faculty for droll lyricism unmatched by few since Dylan; and, in conjunction with a hand-picked team of musicians and technicians, a quest to simultaneously preserve and expand the soundscape of contemporary music. Yet for all that, the soft-spoken Burnett retains a humility—not to mention a contagious sense of humor—that belies the profound influence he has had on the worlds of music and film.

Let's get the trivia question out of the way first: where did you get your nickname?

I got it when I was a kid, when I was about five years old, so there's no telling. I just got it around the neighborhood.

You're renowned for your knowledge and grasp of American musical history, yet that's not something that you studied formally.

No, I didn't. It's just come from never stopping listening, I guess. I grew up in an incredible time. The Top 40 radio down in Fort Worth would play Peggy Lee and Little Tommy Tucker and

Hank Williams...and then The Beatles, four songs in a row. So it was really pre-genre, and also there was a group of young artists that all hung together because we were so far out of the mainstream. There was always this interesting flow of people coming through town—people like Andy Warhol and Robert Rauschenberg and Kris Kristofferson—and a lot of different ideas. I had a friend whose dad owned a record store in town. It was one of those record stores that was all about the music and not about sales, so they carried all kinds of crazy records like Wilbur de Paris and His New New Orleans Jazz, stuff like that. Why in the world would a record like that ever end up in Fort Worth, Texas? No telling, but there it was.

Why did you decide to open a studio of your own instead of going to college? Did you always have a desire to work in recording?

I've always been into sound. When I was in high school I was in a couple of bands and we went into a studio to do some recording and I realized that you could just turn a knob and incredible things would happen. The reason I got into music in the first place was that there was an old Gibson guitar leaning against the

wall at a friend's house and I hit the low E string and it did its thing. I thought, "Okay, what is that? I want to know what that is." And that was it. I was gone, right there.

So are you saying your were first attracted to the *sound* of music, or to its emotional content?

I can't differentiate between the two. It's like color and line in painting; it's part of the same thing—the tone is part of the emotion. But whatever it was, it was complex. Even before I first hit that guitar, there were songs that connected with me. To me, there was just this dark, mysterious world that music could evoke, and that's all wrapped up in the tone.

Who have been some of your mentors through the years?

I've had some incredible teachers. The first tour I went on with Bob Dylan had Jacques Levy directing it, so you had an extraordinary artist and a brilliant stage director with a lot of vision. And then I began working with Sam Shepherd, who has all these different ways of looking at things. I never was part of that musician thing where it was just about being able to play hot licks: there was always that visual element to music for me. I remember that when I first heard the Stanley Brothers, I somehow knew what kind of car they were driving in, I could see the road they were driving on, I could see the trees rushing past.

And when I moved to LA, [Warner Bros. executive] Lenny Waronker was certainly a mentor. He showed me how to make records that can penetrate the zeitgeist and simultaneously stand the test of time. He taught me that you should continue working until everything sounds really great, that it's always best to leave no stone unturned and not to be in any hurry to finish. If a mix isn't absolutely right, you do it again, and if it's still not working, then maybe you need to change a couple of parts.

Waronker also pointed out to me that even producers need producers. His point was that we all lose perspective. That's what he was for me: when I was producing records for him, he was my executive producer. I would go in every week and play him what we had done and he would say, "You've missed this," or "This is what's wrong here."

> **"If a mix isn't absolutely right, you do it again, and if it's still not working, then maybe you need to change a couple of parts."**

Do you feel that every artist needs a producer?

I'm sure there are some that don't need another perspective; Dylan is probably one of those people. But, you know, T.S. Eliot had Ezra Pound; we all need editors. Even in terms of lyrics, we need somebody with the kind of eyes that can look and see that you put the same word at the end of one line and at the beginning of the next one.

But you've always produced the records you've released yourself as an artist.

You know, I've always tried to get other people to produce my records, but they were never able to do it, so I've ended up being my own producer.

If you could pick anyone in the world to produce your next record, who would that be?

Well, nobody now, because I feel my team has gotten to a place that only we know about. Also, the yardstick I use as an endpoint is a very personal one. The place where I first heard live music, back in Fort Worth, Texas, was a juke joint called the Skyliner Ballroom, and all the best musicians came to town to play there. It was a big, long ballroom with a huge dance floor on springs, with a bandstand at each end, from back in the old days when they used to do marathon dance contests. There were strippers too. [*laughs*] It's become an exotic, almost mythical place in my memory. I remember hearing Ike and Tina Turner playing there when I was 14 or 15 and how overcome I was by the sound and spectacle of it—the girls, and Tina, and Ike, who in my opinion is one of the unsung geniuses of rock 'n' roll.

A few years ago, I wondered if I could go online and find a recording of them from that night, and I did. As soon as it arrived and I played it I could immediately hear the room, and it hit me that it sounded like all my records! [*laughs*] That's quite a realization, that I've been trying to reproduce the Skyliner Ballroom in everything I've ever done my whole life. It's because that's where I first experienced that sonic excitement . . . and every other kind of excitement too.

It's not just the sound of that room that I'm trying to capture—it's that *feeling* of being there, that freedom, the whole dynamic that I'm trying to reproduce. So I'll work until I get that kind of feeling out of the record.

You've expressed a philosophy of always wanting to be the worst guy in the band. Why is that?

I've had that view since I was kid and first started playing music. If you're the best guy in the band, you have to pull everybody along with you, and that's a lot of work! [*laughs*] But if you're the worst guy, you're learning all the time. If you play tennis, you like to play it with people who are better than you; it makes you a better player. I never had the desire to be the lead guitarist or the hot instrumentalist; I've always just gone for the groove. I really don't look at things from a musician's perspective; my main concern is, how is the story getting told?

There seems to be a pretty distinctive "T-Bone sound" that runs through not only your own records as an artist, but the records you produce.

It's been a long, long process, but it's been accelerating, especially the last ten years, when I started putting a team together that I work with all the time. Everybody on the team is extraordinarily adventurous, and we've developed this notion of sound and music and rock 'n' roll. I wouldn't claim it as a "T-Bone sound," but together I believe we have invented a new dimension in sound.

I used to cast different engineers for different records, according to the engineer's strengths and what I felt they could bring to the record. But finally I decided to work with Mike Piersante exclusively; he was a second engineer at Sunset Sound and I pulled him out of there and we started working together. Together we very consciously started to develop this very complex low-end world of sound. It grew out of an interest in modernist music and their approach to sound and composition. I wasn't as interested in the very notes they were playing as I was in all the overtones that were being created.

How exactly do you go about creating complexity in the low end?

First of all, I think of everything as a drum. An acoustic bass fiddle is just a big drum with strings attached that you attack with your fingers or a bow, but it's still just attack and resonance. A piano is just 88 little drums—in fact, by combining notes, you can make thousands of drums out of it. Even a flute is a resonating chamber that you attack by blowing wind over it. And for me, it's all to do with the tribal storytelling that happens with music, so I don't really care what's hitting the backbeat, whether it's a snare drum or a mandolin . . . as long as it's getting hit in the right place with the right meaning.

So the attack of the instrument is just triggering the tone, and we've been spending all of our time for the last ten years minimizing attack and maximizing tone. All of these other rhythms and beats get set up in the overtone structure, which creates a lot of mystery and a real sense of place. In contrast, the thing that a computer does best, which is to just put all the notes on all the right beats, becomes completely uninteresting.

Do you accomplish that by using of a lot of compressors and limiters to hold down the attacks and emphasize the body of the sound? None of your productions sound especially compressed.

That's because we actually accomplish it in another way: we do it by playing very, very quietly. The more quietly you play, the less attack there is and the more tone there is. If you hit a guitar too hard, it chokes the note off; the volume of sound that's attempting to escape from the box turns in on itself and cancels itself out so that the sound just collapses. The same with a drum: if you hit it too hard and leave the stick there, nothing happens. But if you just tap it softly, you actually get a much fuller sound.

Does that approach require different kinds of miking techniques?

No, it mostly involves the kinds of instruments the musicians use—we have them play very reso-

> *"You can change the feel of a piece of music by changing the equalization of it, by changing how quickly the note arrives in your ear."*

nant instruments. I use a lot of semi-hollowbody guitars, and the drums have mostly calfskin heads and they're all double-headed, so there's a lot of resonance going on. We're not focusing on the slap of the bass drum; we're focusing on the boom of the bass drum. So you look for ways to set up the biggest boom.

That might explain why you lean towards acoustic bass on a lot of your productions.

Right, though I do use both acoustic and electric quite a bit. I love the acoustic bass because it's a less specific boom. Blending it with an electric bass can work well too, and sometimes I even add in a third bass—a six-string bass, perhaps, playing low chords. The whole idea is to get a great density of sound on the bottom end.

I've also long been fascinated by the way you can change the feel of a piece of music by changing the equalization of it, by changing how quickly the note arrives in your ear. By changing the tone, you can emphasize the back end of the note, the low part of the note that arrives later than the first part. If you de-emphasize the high part and emphasize the low part, you can slow a song down tremendously, just by equalization. In a way, it's a psychoacoustic illusion, but more than that it's probably calculus; it's actually a physical thing I'm talking about.

Were you surprised at the commercial success of the soundtrack to *O Brother Where Art Thou*?

No, I actually wasn't. That was one of those rare times in life when there was a very clear path in front of us, and it was also clear that no one was on it. So I did think the soundtrack was going to enjoy success. Perhaps that's because I knew a lot of young people who were getting into that kind of music at the time. People who were more absorbed in labels and genres were surprised by it, but to me it just sounded like a really great rock 'n' roll record, with all these incredible musicians and voices on it. Plus it had a great film to go along with it, so I thought it would do well.

You've been quoted as saying, "I try to use the technology in a way that's either absolutely transparent or absolutely apparent; any of the middle ground is distracting." What exactly do you mean by that?

I'm talking about the fact that if you're looking at a film and the lighting is too obvious, then it distracts you from the story that's being told. Even if you find yourself saying, "that's the most beautiful lighting I've ever seen," it takes you out of the story.

> **"I don't want singers to attract attention to the fact that they're singing. I just want them to say the word."**

So you want to light it so that, even if it *is* the most beautiful lighting ever seen, the audience doesn't notice it. That's what I mean by transparency: being able to use technology in a way that attracts no attention to itself.

I could say the same thing about singers. I don't want singers to attract attention to the fact that they're singing. I just want them to say the word. That word has its own meaning; you don't have to give it meaning, so just say it. If they do some affectation at the end of it, then they obliterate the word and you don't hear it.

On the other hand, technology becomes absolutely apparent when you metaphorically shine the light right in the audience's eyes, when the light follows into the frame. That can be interesting, too; then you're sort of playing with it and at least having fun with it.

Selected Listening:
T-Bone Burnett: *Twenty Twenty*, Columbia, 2006; *Tooth of Crime*, Nonesuch, 2008
Robert Plant and Alison Krauss: *Raising Sand*, Rounder, 2007
Original Soundtrack: *O Brother Where Art Thou*, Mercury, 2000; *Cold Mountain*, Columbia, 2003
The Wallflowers: *Bringing Down the Horse*, Interscope, 1996
Elvis Costello: *Spike*, Warner Bros., 1989
Roy Orbison: *Mystery Girl*, Virgin, 1989

Roots

Larry Levine

The Wall of Sound Deconstructed

He was making hit records long before most of us were born. Together with a legendary producer, he fashioned a distinctive sound that was to dominate the industry for decades and inspire countless musicians and producers (including a young genius by the name of Brian Wilson) to creative excellence in the recording studio.

His name is not nearly as recognizable as Phil Spector's, but Larry Levine was arguably just as responsible for what became known as the Wall of Sound. Born in 1928 in New York, Levine spent most of his life in Los Angeles. Shortly after returning home from service in the Korean War, he began working at his cousin Stan Ross' fledgling Gold Star studio in Hollywood. "Stan couldn't afford to hire anyone, which is how I got the job," Levine recalls with a laugh. "Because I wasn't married at the time, I'd hang around the studio in the evening because there were always some show people there, and they were fun to be around. Then when things started getting busy, they asked me to work there. They really couldn't pay me anything, but I was able to do on-the-job training under the GI Bill, so I earned enough to live on...barely."

By the mid-1950s, Levine was an established engineer at Gold Star, recording many of Eddie Cochran's greatest hits, including "Summertime Blues" and "Twenty Flight Rock." A few years later, Spector began working at the studio, initially with Ross, and then with Levine. The two of them made for an unlikely partnership—Spector was a fast-talking, eccentric producer barely out of his teens, while the soft-spoken Levine was by then a veteran of the Hollywood scene—but they would work together for more than two decades, crafting a unique sonic signature that no one else has been able to duplicate to this very day. Their hits included The Crystals' "He's a Rebel," "Da Doo Ron Ron," and "Then He Kissed Me," as well as Darlene Love's "Chapel of Love" and The Ronettes' "Be My Baby" and "Walking in the Rain." In the mid-1960s, the pair shaped two of the greatest R&B records of all time—the Righteous Brothers' "You've Lost That Lovin' Feeling" and "Unchained Melody"—and in 1966 raised the bar further still with Ike and Tina Turner's legendary album *River Deep, Mountain High*, a release that only garnered limited commercial success but is now considered to be one of the greatest recording masterpieces of all time.

Though he worked extensively with Phil Spector, Levine also engineered numerous outside projects, including multiple albums with Herb Alpert and The Tijuana Brass (their hit "A Taste of Honey" netted Levine a Grammy for Best Engineered Recording in 1965); he also worked closely for a period with Spector disciple Brian Wilson, participating in "Good Vibrations" and the legendary *Pet Sounds* album. As his career wound down in the early 1980s, Levine began the important work of passing the torch on to the next generation of engineers, getting involved in one of the earliest training programs launched, at A&M Studios. "I was fortunate enough to be able to get into the business without any training, so I always felt I should do all I could to open the door for other people," Levine says.

It's a statement that cogently summarizes the generous spirit of Larry Levine, one of the nicest and warmest gentlemen ever to grace a recording studio. Sadly, Larry passed away on his 80th birthday, just a few months after giving this extensive interview in which he deconstructs the Wall of Sound for the next generation of engineers. It seems like such a fitting gift from a man whose legacy will stretch far beyond the hits he helped create.

How important do you feel training is in becoming a good engineer?

Well, I think the term "training" is kind of a misnomer in this industry, because every studio is different and every console is different. To me, being an engineer is 85 percent creative and 15 percent technical. You really don't need any more technical knowledge than that; it's just a matter of knowing what button to push. Once you learn signal flow, it's really a matter of, what do you hear?

It seems to me that you either have this magic ingredient that allows you to be a good engineer, or you don't; I don't think it's something that can be evolved. When I was involved in that apprenticeship program at A&M, I could usually tell within a week whether someone had that certain something. Frankly, though, I've found that those people who have the makings of being good engineers often don't do as good a job in the mundane aspects like setting up a studio as those who don't have that capability; it's almost as if they weren't cut out for the job.

> *"Being an engineer is 85 percent creative and 15 percent technical."*

What do you think that magic ingredient is?

It's when somebody's head is so into sound that they instinctively understand what it's all about from the word go. With the people that didn't have that instinct, you could sense that everything you told them was going over their head. I know it's a pretty broad statement, but you could almost tell who was into sound just by talking to them. Then it came down to who had good ears, and who was tuned into the client. Obviously it's important to be able to understand what the producer and artist has to say; so much of this job is about communication, verbal or otherwise. You can tell who the good communicators are, too, because producers want to work with them over and over again.

The job seems to be as much about psychology as technical ability.

Well, I don't think it's a matter of knowingly trying to get people to bend to your will; it's a matter of merging personalities. Stan Ross, the owner of Gold Star, was a great engineer—one of the best—and he had an ability that I wished I had, which was to make every client feel that what he was doing was really good, and that he was a hundred percent behind them. With me, if I felt that what was happening wasn't good, I couldn't hide it. I regretted not having that ability, and I'm sure it cost me some work with certain clients, but at least I was honest.

So Stan not only had the ear, but people loved him too. He didn't manipulate anyone, though, which is what the word "psychology" implies to me. I don't think that works, anyway—it certainly wouldn't work with someone like Phil! [*laughs*]

If you were as blunt as you say, how is it you were able to work successfully with Phil Spector for so many years despite the fact that he had a reputation as being difficult to get along with?

I think it was just a meeting of the minds—he knew that he could deal with me on his level, and I knew that he could deal with me on his level. Looking back 40 years later, I think of all the times it could have gone the other way, and how fortunate I was to have been with Phil,

even through all the drama. I also think about how tenuous it was that I even ended up with him; if I went astray in a couple of places, that would have been it, insofar as his trusting me.

Did you already have a reputation as a hit engineer before you started working with Phil?

I had made a few hit records, but Stan was the big name at Gold Star, and rightly so. I had worked with a songwriter called Wayne Shanklin, who produced and wrote, and one of the hit records I did with him was a song called "Primrose Lane," with Jerry Walls. He also wrote another hit song that Stan recorded—Toni Fisher, singing "The Big Hurt"—which was the first use of phasing on a record... though it wasn't *intentional* phasing. [*laughs*] Stan had made both mono and stereo mixes—at that point, we only had two-track and mono anyway—and Wayne liked the mono mix, but he felt that Toni's voice wasn't out quite far enough, so the next day he asked me to make a tape copy and to run the two mixes together in order to double the sound of her voice. I explained to him that wouldn't work, because the two tape machines wouldn't stay in sync, but he insisted that I try it anyway. So I did—I lined up the two tapes and started the two machines simultaneously... and it stayed together, pretty much, for the first eight bars, and then one went out of phase with the other. It just happened to be at a point where the strings went up in the air and disappeared and then came back after the null point.

My reaction was, "See, I told you it wouldn't work," but he was falling on the floor, saying, "Wow—can you make that happen in other places?" So I figured out which tape was moving a little bit ahead and I started it slightly later so it would catch up. In the end I made about six edits. It ended up being a big hit record when it was released back in 1959, and people were trying to guess where it was made—a lot of disk jockeys were talking about it on the air, wondering if it was made at an airport with a big jet passing by. So it wasn't something intentional to start with, but, like many innovations, pure luck.

How did you first meet Phil?

The first record I did with him was "He's a Rebel," and the only reason I did that was because Stan [Ross] was on vacation. The truth of the matter is that I was Phil's second choice; he'd already done a bunch of records with Stan by that time, including "To Know Him Is to Love Him," which had been a huge hit. I guess what was instrumental in my becoming Phil's regular engineer was the fact that I was able to mix all the many instruments together into what became the Wall of Sound. In fact, I'm quite sure that had I not put the sound together that he wanted to hear, he would have gone back to Stan.

Phil was actually pretty scary to work with. I wasn't a novice, but I was still generally a bit nervous with anyone I worked with, especially during mixing. I could never understand guys who could eat lunch and do a session—any session—because there was no way I could hold any food down if I were going to record or mix something! Maybe that's because my attitude was, if it's not right, it's all my fault.

So to be with someone like Phil particularly was pretty tough for me. On the second record we made [Bob B. Soxx And The Blue Jeans' "Zip-A-Dee-Doo-Dah"], things were starting to get out of hand and I knew that I wasn't going to be able to successfully record the sounds on tape at the levels he was instructing me to set. It still took me five or six minutes before I could gather the nerve to turn everything off and say, "You know, this is not going to work." That was because I knew he was going to scream at me, and he did—after all, he was a big-shot producer, and I was nothing at the time. [laughs]

I guess there was another turning point in Phil's decision to use me regularly, and that occurred a couple of months later. We were in the studio one night, overdubbing background voices on a song. It was around two o'clock in the morning and we had done the first eight bars and were listening back. Of course, with Phil, I could never just lean back in my chair and listen in a relaxed way—he had me working all the time, constantly mixing what was there. We'd probably heard this track a dozen times when all of a sudden he shouted out, "Okay, this is where they come in!" I was so surprised I instinctively reached for the Record button and pushed it—and, of course, there was no Record Safe mode on the Ampex three-track machines we were using in those days. I immediately realized that I had erased something, and Phil knew it too. We had a little folding card table set up at the front of the control room, and he just crawled right under it, sitting there with his knees pulled up to his chin. [laughs]

Fortunately, I managed to stop the tape almost immediately—just two beats before a chord change that is never repeated anywhere else in the song—so I was able to fix it by editing in a copy of the same section from later in the song. Phil was sure the edit wouldn't work, but it did. He'd never let me edit before, either, because he'd had some bad experiences with cutting tape. Before then, whenever we did a track and something was wrong, even if it was near the very end, he insisted that the musicians play the whole thing all over again rather than allow me to cut tape. But because I had made this repair work, from that point on, we would edit tracks if necessary. So it became a question of trust.

You must have thought your job was on the line at that moment.

No, because I knew it wasn't my fault. It was just a reaction, and the worst that was going to happen was that we'd have to go back and re-record the song. I still felt as bad as you can feel, especially since we had the backing track done and were working on the vocals by that point. But I kind of felt that I could save it—otherwise I never would have even tried to make that edit. I had confidence in my abilities, and I guess I've always been a lucky person too.

Do you have a musical background, or is your approach purely technical?

No, I was mostly just a music fan. I studied violin at college [for one semester], but my family couldn't afford to buy me one.

So you can't read music? I always had the impression that all the musicians in Phil Spector sessions played from scores.

No, the music was written out as a lead sheet only, usually written by [arranger] Jack Nitzsche, and it was only ever viewed as a starting point, not an end point.

Can you deconstruct the Wall of Sound for our readers?

I'll be glad to do that, but I want to begin by saying that I've come to the conclusion that the Wall of Sound only played a small part in Phil's ability to create hits. It was always about the song; without the song, you've got nothing. But the key sonically was that you couldn't really pick out the individual instruments—it was a "wall" that had a texture of its own.

> *"The Wall of Sound only played a small part in Phil Spector's ability to create hits. It was always about the song; without the song, you've got nothing."*

To start with, Phil would always have pretty much the same musicians playing on his sessions—the so-called "Wrecking Crew." He'd begin by having just the guitarists play their parts over and over again; there would be anywhere from three to six guitars, all basically playing the same part. He'd tweak their parts and change things until he felt he had something worthwhile, and then he'd add in two pianos, also doubling the same part. If that didn't work all together, he'd go back to the guitars. I always felt they should be paid double scale, because they worked longer and harder than anyone. [*laughs*] The irony was that Hal Blaine, the drummer, was actually the only one getting double scale, even though he didn't come in until the end.

Once Phil was happy with the parts being played by the guitars and the pianos, the basses would come in next—two or three of them, with at least one acoustic and one electric—followed by the horns and then the percussion. As I said, the drums were always the last thing Phil would add in, and because the studio was so small, their sound would leak into the other microphones, so that's when the real work began, particularly in terms of trying to get some presence on them without losing the sound of the guitars; that's where most of the drum leakage was coming in.

Another big part of the Wall of Sound was the actual air pressure in the room—it was a very small room with a lot of musicians playing all at once, quite loudly, too, so there were all these sound waves bouncing off the walls.

Does that mean that you couldn't create a Wall of Sound in a large room?

I don't know, but I always felt that the sound in any studio was always better when the room was filled with people rather than being half-empty, regardless of whether you could get isolation or not. Also, bear in mind that the echo chambers at Gold Star played a role, although in retrospect it seems to me a little too much credit was given to them as being an integral part of the Wall of Sound. The biggest part of the equation was the room size, and the fact that the musicians were hearing each other play, live, not on headphones—we didn't use them. So it was a true ensemble in every sense of the word. It was just a matter of creating the right blend so that you heard this overall sound and couldn't isolate or identify any one instrument in it.

You know, the one thing we could never get at Gold Star was the Motown drum sound, which Phil loved and listened to all the time. Try as we might, we just couldn't achieve that, even though Hal [Blaine] was one of the best at playing in a controlled way so that the drum sound didn't blare all over the room, yet it was a very strong sound.

Hal was one of those guys who *own* their instruments. It's as if they're not even playing their instruments—they're actually part of their instruments. With musicians of that calibre, all you have to do is put a microphone up anywhere in their vicinity, and they give you everything you need. With some other musicians, you'd have to work hard to try to pull out the sound, and you'd never quite get there.

I only ever used two microphones on Hal: one overhead and one on the kick drum. The kick mic was usually an RCA 77 ribbon, and the overhead mic could be almost anything—it really didn't matter what you used, although I would sometimes put up a Neumann if it wasn't already in use on the percussion instruments.

Were Hal's drums screened off from the rest of the room?

Well, we didn't have any high screens, so he wasn't ever completely screened off. We did eventually build some screens that were waist-high. Again, when you fill a room, you get the damping from all the bodies in there.

Were the piano lids down?

Usually. One of the pianos was an upright, anyway, and Mike Curb would sometimes bring in his electric piano so he could pick up a rental fee. [*laughs*]

Musically, was each part being doubled or tripled exactly?

Generally that's the way the arrangement was written. The guitars and basses were usually doubling each other exactly—but the pianos often didn't play exactly the same notes, though they would play the same rhythms. I once asked Phil why Leon [Russell] was playing lead piano, because I thought that Al DeLory was so creative. He said, "It's because of how big Leon's hands are; he can reach octaves, and that's really important for playing lead piano."

Brian Wilson was a huge fan of Phil Spector's productions, and you worked with Brian as well. Do you think he was successful in emulating the Wall of Sound?

Brian did idolize Phil, and he often used the same musicians Phil did, but I don't think he was exactly trying to recreate the Wall of Sound in his own sessions. I remember him telling me that he had written "Don't Worry Baby" for Phil to produce, but Phil was too busy at the time, so Brian did it himself. Certainly it would have been a natural for Phil and for the Wall of Sound approach.

How would you contrast your experience working with Brian versus working with Phil?

Well, basically Brian was a nicer person. He didn't have any swagger about him at all; he just wanted to make music. He was actually one of the nicest kids you'd ever want to work with.

Brian was also right up near the top in terms of knowing what he wanted, plus he knew how to communicate, he was willing to listen, and he was willing to adapt if something sounded better than what he had envisioned. Phil was similar in some regards. He would listen, although he wasn't necessarily waiting for people to present him with alternate ideas. But if something didn't happen one way, he'd try to get it going another way, and if it worked better the other way, he'd go with that.

You were one of the many engineers in LA who worked on Brian Wilson's masterpiece "Good Vibrations," weren't you?

Yes, I recorded some of it, but I don't remember precisely which part I did. I do remember that he didn't have a clear idea of what the whole thing was going to sound like; I guess he was waiting to piece it all together.

> "[A] big part of the Wall of Sound was the actual air pressure in the room— it was a very small room with a lot of musicians playing all at once, quite loudly, too, so there were all these sound waves bouncing off the walls."

Both you and Phil had high hopes for *River Deep, Mountain High*, which didn't do nearly as well as either of you had wanted or expected.

That's right. I think I was actually a little more disappointed than Phil, because I felt as if I had let him down, or perhaps it was the technology that let him down. With that record, he was trying to go a bit further up that ladder towards perfection. With hindsight, I think the acme was reached with [the Righteous Brothers'] "You've Lost That Lovin' Feeling." We did things there that hadn't been done before, and we just never quite reached that same point with *River Deep, Mountain High*, although it was great working with Tina Turner—she was stupendous.

The real disappointment to me was when it didn't even get a Best Bet bullet in *Billboard*. To take someone with Phil's proven record in making hits and not even give him that was really an insult, and I know it hurt him a lot.

The echo chamber at Gold Star had a very distinctive sound, but wasn't there also something unique about the way the console routed signal to it?

Actually, we had a series of echo chambers at Gold Star. Stan and I had tried building echo chambers of all kinds, and most of them sounded terrible when we were finished. For a while, the best echo chamber we came up with was located in a bathroom, and we'd actually put the singer in there. One day we had a singer come in and do a demo of a song called "Well of Loneliness." [*laughs*] After that, we didn't use that particular echo chamber much any more.

But before we even had any echo chambers, the way we'd create that effect was to just open the door to the hallway at one end of the studio and have the vocalist—the only one who ever got echo, by the way—stand half in, half out, and then we'd put a microphone down at the end of the hallway to pick up the delay.

So, really, our concept of echo was distance—not an enhancement of a voice or an instrument, but just distance from that voice or instrument. To our way of thinking, when you put echo on something, you made it go farther away. Consequently, Dave Gold, the co-owner of the studio, designed our mixing console so that when you raised the echo on a channel, the level was also lowered automatically—it was all one integrated control, which no one else has ever done, to my knowledge. In other words, as you fed more signal to the echo send, you simultaneously sent less level to the output bus. That had a lot to do with why the Gold Star echo sounded as good as it did.

In a way, it's similar to sending echo pre-fader.

No, it's not the same, because in a pre-fade send there's no direct relationship between the amount of signal being sent to the echo and the amount being sent to the output bus. The way we had things set up, it was as if every time you turned up the echo send, the fader was automatically being lowered correspondingly.

Again, it just came from our concept of echo being the opposite of presence, so that as you increased the echo, you decreased the presence, and vice versa. Somehow it worked very nicely for the kinds of records we were making at the time. In essence, we were just playing with depth of field. And I don't know that we would have done the same thing if we had stopped and thought about it; we might have just thought, "Hey, let's just come up with a way of sending signal to the damn echo chamber and not worry about reducing presence at the same time." [*laughs*]

I remember going to another studio with Phil when we were making a record with Ronnie [Spector], and he kept asking the staff engineer there for more echo; every time the poor guy turned it up, Phil kept saying, "No, I want more!" He was getting quite exasperated, and the engineer couldn't satisfy him. That was because he was used to hearing it the way we had things set up at Gold Star—he wanted to not only hear more echo, he wanted to hear less direct signal. In the end, the engineer just turned the echo send all the way up and Phil turned to me and he said, "What the hell is this guy on?" [*laughs*] That's one of the reasons why Phil would have difficulty with certain engineers.

I guess he just had a certain way of working, and very few engineers except you understood what he wanted.

I guess so. I was his sounding board; he'd say, "What do you think?" and I'd usually say, "I love it." And if I didn't say "I love it," that was usually the end of it, because he generally wasn't willing to take a chance on a sound if I didn't give it that seal of approval.

Other engineers who've worked with Phil Spector have said that he was actually very insecure.

Absolutely. Sometimes, though, he'd go the other way where he'd just display more and more bravado, which would turn everybody off. I never had that problem with him, though. I did send him away once, after we did *A Christmas Gift for You*, because it was just too tiring working with him; I didn't want to work that hard any more. Of course, once I got some rest, I missed making hits with him and we started working together again.

You were present at the birth of stereo. How did you feel about things opening up from a single speaker to having a left-right soundstage to work in?

Well, it was a natural transition, though at first what we were doing was not true stereo—instruments were either on one side or the other, with no panning control. But once we got panning controls, it felt very natural. I didn't mix very differently, though, because for a long time after stereo came in there was still no FM radio, so all the radio broadcasts were in mono. So I can't honestly say that stereo opened up a whole new world for me, or anything like that; it was just another advance. The only advance I hated was when we went to quad.

Why was that?

Because it was the tail wagging the dog. It was not an innovation created by creative people—it was an innovation made by manufacturers who wanted to sell equipment. You had to go in and do a new mix, and there was nothing creative about it. Producers didn't want to have anything to do with it, either, because they'd already made their stereo mix and used up all their creative juices doing that.

So it just never felt natural to me. I never wanted to be in the middle of an orchestra—I just wanted to have the orchestra onstage in front of me, but with as much clarity as possible.

What were your thoughts about the advent of multitrack recording?

That was super. We went from two-track to three-track at first, and that was tough because the Ampex machines didn't provide good quality when you were playing back off the record heads. But once we changed over to four-track, the record heads sounded as good as the playback heads, so everything sounded clean even when you were overdubbing, and things got better yet when eight-track came along, and then 16 and 24. I welcomed those additional tracks because they gave me more opportunity to separate things out and change the balance afterwards if necessary.

Multitrack allowed artists to make a recording that didn't have a finished sound to it—they'd simply record things that you'd build on. The problem was that you never knew what the final sound was going to be until you finished mixing the record. So from an engineer's standpoint, mostly it was boring, and boring is frustrating. When we'd do something like a [Burt] Bacharach date, for example, you got to hear the whole thing, all at once, so you knew you were involved in making music.

What about the advent of digital recording?

Well, I have to confess that at first, I didn't like the sound of digital, although I eventually learned how to make it sound more like tape.

What was the secret?

Mostly putting the signal through tube equalizers, which round the sound off nicely—you can actually get pretty good results that way. I was still doing projects with Phil into the '80s, including the Ramones and Leonard Cohen, but we were still going to tape; Gold Star never really got into digital other than automated mixing. It was shortly after digital technology was introduced that I started cutting back, but I never really completely retired until Phil was producing Celine Dion in the mid-'90s. He had asked me to work with him but we just kept mixing and remixing the same songs over and over again. Finally, out of frustration, I said to him, "That's it—I'm retired."

Even then, I never *completely* retired. Just a few years ago, Herb Alpert called me and asked me to mix some previously unreleased tracks for a compilation album [*Lost Treasures*]. We had to do that digitally, of course, but I didn't like the sound of Pro Tools, so we did it in RADAR, which I thought sounded much more like tape.

Do you think someone is born with good ears, or is that something that can be learned?

It's only in contemplation that I've come to realize to my own satisfaction that, yes, I do have a genuine affinity for music. Like any art form, music has different colors and textures, and when I think about it I realize that I had to have been at one with the music in order to create some of the records I made. What I mean by that is that I knew instinctively to not hurry through the mixing process. I'd start by just *listening*, and I might listen to a song all the way through eight or ten or a dozen times before even moving a single fader. I was trying to create a picture in my mind of how the instruments were laid out; I'd envision myself actually in a room with all these instruments, not necessarily the way I would have physically seated the musicians if I'd recorded them in the first place—just a picture. If I could get a picture, it was terrific. That's when I knew the mix was really good.

So it's a matter of being one with the music, and getting the music to what it wants to be, if that makes any sense. One of the reasons I loved working with Phil was that he would leave me alone to mix. If you've got someone looking over your shoulder the whole time you're going through the process, that really can disturb your concentration.

There's a thing called nuance, too, and I really identify that with Herb Alpert. Herb loves to mix, and he thinks things through, and he's obviously got a good ear. When I listen to what he's mixed against what I've mixed, there isn't a great deal of difference in balances, but there is in nuance. That nuance comes when your fingers don't tell your ears what a good job you did—they're divorced from it—so all you're hearing is the music, unadorned. Mind you, it's not easy to get to the point where your hands are not part of the sound you're crafting.

That's what I realized later, in contemplation—that I had those kinds of instincts. That's why I think it's beneficial to spend adequate amounts of time listening before mixing, so you get to the point where you're *with* the music. If you do that, the music will tell you what it wants to be, rather than you forcing it into something that it doesn't want to be. At the end of the day, it's all about serving the music.

Suggested Listening:

Albums:

The Ronettes: ... *Presenting the Fabulous Ronettes*, Philles, 1964
Ike and Tina Turner: *River Deep, Mountain High*, Philles, 1966
The Beach Boys: *Pet Sounds*, Capitol, 1966

Herb Alpert and the Tijuana Brass: *South of the Border*, A&M, 1964; *Whipped Cream & Other Delights*, A&M, 1965; *Going Places*, A&M, 1965; *Christmas Album*, A&M, 1968

Phil Spector: *A Christmas Gift for You*, Philles, 1963 (various reissues since then)

Singles:

Eddie Cochran: "Twenty Flight Rock," 1957; "Summertime Blues," 1958

The Crystals: "He's a Rebel," 1962; "Da Doo Ron Ron," 1963; "Then He Kissed Me," 1963

Bob B. Soxx and the Blue Jeans: "Zip-A-Dee-Doo-Dah," 1962

Darlene Love: "Chapel of Love," 1963

The Ronettes: "Be My Baby," 1963; "Walking in the Rain," 1964

The Righteous Brothers: "You've Lost That Lovin' Feeling," 1964; "Unchained Melody," 1965

Bruce Swedien

A Responsibility to the Music

Spending an afternoon with Bruce Swedien is like having a visit with your favorite uncle. It's easy to imagine this big bear of a man, with his trademark walrus mustache and deep, booming voice, spinning tales around a pot-bellied stove at a local trading post... only his tales involve people like Michael Jackson and Quincy Jones.

Born in Minneapolis in 1934 to parents who were both professional musicians, Swedien decided that he wanted to be a recording engineer when he was just ten years old. As he describes in his 2003 book *Make Mine Music*, "By the time I was 15, I was working in a small basement recording studio. My summer vacations from school were spent recording any willing musical group... everything from polka bands to black gospel singing quartets." He went on to earn an Electrical Engineering degree from the University of Minnesota and in 1954, with the help and support of his parents, purchased his own recording studio—a converted movie theater that is still in business to this very day.

However, it was a casual contact his parents had made some years earlier that was to have the greatest impact on the young Swedien's career. "I was still in high school when my mother and father had to take a business trip to Chicago," he recalls. "They knew I was a big fan of Bill Putnam, who was the owner and chief engineer at Universal Studios there, and so they made a point of visiting the facility. They walked right up to Bill and said, 'Our son thinks you're the greatest.' They told him all about me, and the next thing I knew I got a phone call from him." Though it was to be a few years before Putnam was able to give Swedien a job at Universal, he provided a lasting influence on the young engineer's life, which in turn led to a friendship with another pioneer in the burgeoning recording industry—guitarist (and inventor of multitrack recording) Les Paul. "The main thing I learned from Les," Swedien says, "is that the best recordings rely heavily on intuition."

Once settled in Chicago, Swedien recorded a number of hit records, including Frankie Valli and the Four Seasons' "Big Girls Don't Cry" (for which he received the first of a staggering 13 Grammy nominations), and also began working with some of the biggest jazz artists of the era: Count Basie, Duke Ellington, Sarah Vaughn, Woody Herman, Jack Teagarden. It was at one of those sessions, for singer Dinah Washington, that he first met a young arranger and record company executive named Quincy Jones. When they next reunited in Los Angeles in the mid-1970s, Swedien and Jones embarked on an ambitious series of recordings that were to forever change the history and sound of popular music—particularly the records they would make with ex–Jackson Five lead singer Michael Jackson.

The sonic tapestries that the production/engineering duo wove for Jackson on his mega-hit *Thriller* are the stuff of legend, but no less impressive was their work on his follow-up albums *Bad* and *Dangerous*, or on Jones' landmark records *Back on the Block* and *Q's Juke Joint*. Together, these five albums would win Swedien five Grammys for Best Engineered Recording, and in the process, he and Jones developed a unique technical approach that they named "Accusonics," described in detail in this interview. Other memorable Swedien projects include the temporarily reunited Jacksons' *Victory* album, as well as the soundtracks for *The Wiz, Running Scared, The Color Purple,* and *Nightshift,* plus engineering and mixing work for George Benson, Barbra Streisand, Donna Summer, James Ingram, Ricky Martin, and Jennifer Lopez.

Despite the fact that he has been making hit records for more than half a century now, Swedien is showing no signs of slowing down, other than relocating his studio and home a few years ago to central Florida. "I just recorded Jennifer Lopez here a few months ago," he enthusiastically reports, "and I've been working with a couple of local bands that I think have real potential." The mixes he plays us and the deftness with which he manipulates his beloved Harrison console prove definitively that this is one old master who hasn't lost his touch.

You developed an affinity for recording at a very early age, didn't you?

That's right. For my tenth birthday, my father gave me a disk recording machine, and after I spent just ten minutes with it, I knew what I wanted to do for the rest of my life. It wasn't a conscious choice; it just happened. And I didn't ease into it, either—it happened right away. My mom and dad wanted me to be a classical concert pianist, but after awhile I realized that I simply didn't have the ability to do that, so I had to think of something else if I wanted to stay involved in music. Fortunately, it didn't take long to find the answer.

Why do you think your father gave you such an unusual gift?

I don't know, other than that he had always been interested in recording. I guess he just thought it might be something that would interest me too.

You've seen so many changes in this industry since you started. What are some of your earliest memories as an engineer?

Well, when I started in this business, wire was the main format, though the first studio I worked in recorded directly to disk—there was nothing in-between to affect the sound—and I do remember tape coming in. The first famous client I had was Tommy Dorsey, and eventually I did records for the Dorsey Brothers. I've been very lucky throughout my whole career to be able to work with world-class musicians; even the polka bands I recorded in Minneapolis were really good. One of the best of them, in fact, was Harold Loeffelmacher and the Six Fat Dutchmen—a name that will live in history. [*laughs*] When I moved to Chicago and started working for Bill Putnam at Universal Studios, some of the polka bands followed me there, but my first big assignment was Oscar Peterson, and I did 16 albums with him, which really left a lasting impression. What a great player, and what a sweet man—a prince of a guy.

What lessons did you learn from Bill Putnam?

He didn't really teach me anything about engineering, truth be told, but he did teach me a lot about studio etiquette and how to work with top-level artists and survive. [*laughs*]

Bill welcomed me with open arms when I arrived in Chicago; I think I was not unknown to him when I got there, though, because I'd already worked with Tommy Dorsey and done a few things in Minneapolis, including building my own studio, which to this very day is still a world-class facility. We couldn't afford proper acoustic treatment there, so we glued egg cartons to the walls until we were blue in the face, but what a great-sounding studio—it was unbelievable.

So are you saying that egg cartons are a viable way to go if you're constructing a studio on a budget?

Absolutely! Find out where you can get lots of egg cartons and you're good to go.

But getting back to Bill Putnam, he couldn't give me a job at Universal right away because Studio B still wasn't finished, so he got me a temporary job at RCA Victor instead, where I ended up recording the Chicago Symphony Orchestra under the baton of Dr. Fritz Reiner. Now *there* was a guy who taught me some things! He immediately made me part of his incentive program, which was: one mistake and you're through. [*laughs*] We were experimenting with three-track and four-track half-inch tape at the time, but everything was musically oriented, so he didn't want to know about the technical aspects; all he wanted to know was that the proper balances were there.

Fortunately, I had the advantage of being able to read music and orchestral scores. Ultimately Quincy [Jones] and I ended up doing a lot of movie scores together, and in those kinds of sessions, the engineer absolutely has to be able to read music in order to be successful. In that way, everything came together full circle for me.

Les Paul was another very important influence on you, wasn't he?

Absolutely. "How High the Moon," which he made with Mary Ford, was a record that changed my life because for the first time they issued a performance that could not possibly have existed in reality. Fortunately, I got to know Les because he and Bill Putnam were close friends. His approach to making records was right in line with my own idea that reality shouldn't be an issue. Where does it say that a recording of music has to be real? It doesn't. Sometimes the best approach is to create a fantasy and add in just a little touch of reality, like a patch of blue sky somewhere.

What do you feel are the main qualifications for being a successful engineer?

Well, first and foremost you have to have an innate love of music that surpasses everything else. You can like the equipment and enjoy the equipment, but you can't *love* the equipment. That's not why we're there. We're there because of the music, and nothing else.

There are some engineers who will look down their nose at someone who doesn't focus exclusively on the technical aspects, and I think that's wrong. I will never trade a musical value for a production value. It's all about the music, and you'd better get that ingrained right away.

Yet you went to university to study electrical engineering, so you yourself are actually far more technical than most other recording engineers.

That's true. I can solder my ass off and I understand circuitry... but not like George Massenburg, who is the king of that kind of thing. [*laughs*] He's the one guy who can actually explain *every*thing.

But certainly not every engineer needs to have an EE degree. Personally, I wanted to be able to understand what was going on inside the equipment, but I don't have a burning need to know how to take it apart and put it back together. In a similar way, I want to know what the fuel injectors in my car do, but I don't necessarily want to pull out a wrench and be able to replace them myself.

In terms of recording equipment, you need to be able to understand every parameter and know what every knob is controlling, because you can't properly fulfill your responsibility to the music if you don't have that knowledge. We as engineers have a responsibility to the music, and you have to know at least basic technical principles in order to record music properly.

It's not just engineers, though. There are some musicians who are resistant to formal training because they think it will somehow limit their creativity.

That's pure bullshit. Maybe there are some exceptions, but understanding what the rules are doesn't make you less creative—it makes you *more* creative. In terms of equipment, you can get much more out of gear if you first know how to push the parameters as far as you can . . . but not too far, not to the point where it can degrade the music.

Again, our responsibility as engineers is to present the music in the best possible way, and you can only do that if you know the rules . . . and anybody that tells you differently is a liar.

Do you think that great engineering can take things a step further and actually *enhance* music?

Absolutely. An engineer that knows how to get the most value from the equipment can actually enhance the reproduction of the music to the point where it really is something special.

Most of the time you're the engineer on projects—it seems that you're rarely the producer. Is that by choice?

There are some engineers who prefer not to have the added responsibility of producing, but I never understood that. I was actually co-producer on Michael's last three albums, which was a bit of a change. Even though I'm fascinated by the technical side of things, that's not the real adventure—the adventure is in the music. That's where all the emotion is, and everything I do has to be on an emotional level. So I don't think of it as the producer's chair or the engineer's chair: I'm in *my* chair. You'd have a hard time pinning me down as to exactly what it is I do, because even *I* don't know. [*laughs*]

> "I don't like overanalyzing things . . . I prefer things to be instinctive, because the best recordings are very intuitive."

All I know is that people bring me music and I record it or mix it . . . and sometimes produce it too. But it is true that whenever I produce, I engineer as well, because I love the engineering part of it, as well as the mixing. That's why I built this studio here in my home, which was designed very much to my personal requirements.

I don't like overanalyzing things, anyway; I prefer things to be instinctive, because the best recordings are very intuitive. I think you can always tell intuitive records from the ones that are thought-out or created with one objective in mind. Those records, to me, are not very sincere.

But surely a lot of planning and preparation went into your most famous recordings.

Absolutely, but being instinctive about something does not exclude planning and thinking about the project beforehand. You still have to leave space, as Quincy says, for God to walk through the room. [*laughs*] I'm always up for those creative accidents that nobody's expecting.

Can you tell us more about the "Accusonic" process you developed with Quincy Jones?

Well, for starters, the name is just kind of an in-joke. Michael and Quincy and I were working at Westlake Studios in Hollywood one day and we were sitting out in the lobby, listening to mixes, when Quincy said, "This stuff really sounds great; we should have a name for it." [*laughs*] The basic concept is that most of the sounds get recorded as stereo pairs—but true stereo, not bullshit stereo. Not binaural, either, which is designed to be listened to on head-phones and does not work on speakers, but true stereo, meant to be listened to on speakers.

Binaural is a social impracticability—you can't have a whole lot of people standing around sipping martinis with headphones on. Even the thought of that is kind of weird! [*laughs*]

By "true stereo," I mean stereo where the room acoustics become apparent as part of the image, where the acoustic stamp of the room is preserved. Early reflections play an important role in that, of course.

Mind you, I've never seen a proper definition of stereo; if there is one, I've never seen it. My personal definition would be a recording system that preserves the acoustics of the room in their natural order. Stereo is not about having one thing coming out of the left speaker and something different coming out of the right speaker. That's just two-channel mono; it's not stereo, and it has nothing to do with stereo.

That said, true stereo pairs don't always work as well as mono. There are times when certain elements of the music—particularly in popular music—have to be point sources: important sounds like lead vocal, for example, or solos. That's because single monophonic images, typically derived from a single microphone, can be really dramatic when they're mixed in with all that stereo. Combining multiple mics onto a single track provides a different perspective, but I think one mic generally works best when the idea is to provide a mono point source. I've tried recording lead vocals in stereo, but there's something that happens when you do that which to my ear is very irritating—it's called "wandering," where the image moves a little bit, and it's not very pleasant.

What advice can you give someone who wants to improve the quality of their home recordings?

Try to learn the difference between a good room and a bad room. The best way to train your ear is to go out and listen to good live music in an excellent acoustical setting. That's the only way you're going to know what music *really* can sound like. When I've done master classes, I encourage my students to put away all their records because you don't learn what music sounds like by listening to records—you learn by listening to reality. Then you can take that knowledge and make recordings that have your own imprint but still preserve the reality of the music.

Are you saying that a great recording cannot be made in a bad-sounding room?

No, I'm not saying that. I've actually heard lots of great records that were made in bad-sounding rooms, but the way you get around that is with great mic technique. It takes a lot of time and a lot of listening to get to the point where you can distinguish between a good room and a bad room, but it can be done.

Do you think that critical listening is something you can learn, or do you need to be born with "golden ears"?

It's something you can learn, same as perfect pitch. If you work at it long enough, you can train yourself to listen to a group of different instruments playing together and intellectually isolate any one of them. So in theory, anyone has the potential to be a great engineer, but it takes a funny mind to actually *be* one. [*laughs*] First of all, you've got to be a control freak; you've got to want to know how to manipulate the audio and make it do what you want it to do. You have to be very detail-oriented, and you have to be willing to spend the time it takes to learn your craft and develop the ability to shape sounds skillfully. And, of course, you've got to have good people skills—you've got to be able to get along with people in the studio environment and learn proper etiquette.

I've been lucky in that I've gotten to work with some of the nicest people you'd ever hope to meet. Quincy Jones, for example, is one of the most ethical people I've ever met. Musically, he's a giant, and personally, a pleasure to work with. He didn't even attend the mixing sessions for *Thriller*—that's how much confidence he had in me. Ed Cherney is another person I'm glad to have had the opportunity to work with; I'm so proud of him.

And, of course, there was Bill Putnam; I can't say enough great things about him. Not long after I started working at Universal, I was watching him do a Stan Kenton session when he said, "C'mon kid, you take over; I've got to go to the men's room." The next time I saw him was five years later, after he'd moved to California! [*laughs*] Evidently he thought I was ready.

Your recordings all have a distinctively clean sound, yet they're not cookie-cutter.

More than anything else, I want my recordings to sound a little different. They don't have to necessarily be realistic, either; it's not just about capturing a performance accurately. Originally, the purpose of recording was to recreate a real acoustic event. That got me real excited at first, but then I began to think that it shouldn't necessarily be the goal. Why not record music in such a way as to inject some fantasy into things? That's when it started to get *really* interesting to me. All you have to do is listen to *Thriller* to understand what I'm talking about. It's got a wide range of dynamics in it, and they're all real—there's no bullshit there—but it's also not necessarily a realistic version of how musicians sound in a room.

One of the tricks I used on that album, for example, was to not take the direct signals from the synthesizers, but to play them out into the room over speakers. That adds early reflections and the kind of acoustic support that you can't possibly get from a direct box, or even from a reverberation device. There aren't any of them that really address that issue properly, anyway. Some of those reverb devices have a control on them labeled "early reflection," but it's pure baloney; they're trying to emulate reality, which can't be done.

> *"Every individual microphone has its own distinctive sound . . . and you can't codify that in a piece of software."*

As someone who is an expert in mic technique, do you think it's possible to emulate microphone characteristics digitally?

No, I don't think it's possible at all. For one thing, every individual microphone has its own distinctive sound; I have two [Neumann] U 47s that I use a lot, and they sound quite different from one another. You can't codify that in a piece of software. Some people look to Pro Tools to be an end-all, and it can't be, any more than a tape machine could be. Don't get me wrong—I love Pro Tools, but it is only a tool, and it can't do everything. And, again, it's not about the tool; it's about the skill of the person using the tool.

Obviously, digital recording provides a lot of conveniences and features, but do you prefer the sound of it to analog tape?

Actually, I don't have a preference. I know that a lot of engineers from my generation still sing the praises of tape, but analog tape can mess up really bad, and the wonderful thing about digital recording is its consistency. Its predictability is a thousand percent; I always know what I'm going to get on every playback, whereas every tape playback is a bit of an adventure. That said, Pro Tools really works well when it's coupled with a beautiful old analog desk. My Harrison console is singular in its ability to make music—I used it for all of Michael's big records, and all the Abba records were made on it too.

Do you see sound as colors, like many engineers do?

I think it's a disease with me! [*laughs*] And Quincy has the same thing; in fact, there's a name for it: synaesthesia. As soon as I hear a sound, it's immediately represented in my mind as a color. Lower frequency tones are usually represented in my mind's eye as purple, while higher tones appear as silver or gold—bright colors. It can be a bit distracting at times—sometimes it drives me nuts, in fact—but it can also be a help. It also explains why, for me, mixing is like painting with sonic colors.

Does sound also appear in three dimensions to you?

Well, left-right, of course, and also front-back, which is depth, but not vertically. Depth is associated with wetness; a more reverberant sound will give the illusion of being farther away than a drier sound. Early reflections aren't necessarily just about depth, by the way; they can also be left-right, because the room may respond differently on one side of the stereo panorama than it does on the other, and sometimes I'll look for a room that does exactly that.

Do you ever notch out frequencies in order to get instruments to layer together and better localize?

Never. I think that most people who do that lead themselves into traps, and the result is usually not very natural; not only is it irritating to my ear, but it misrepresents the acoustic space. Each acoustic space has its own personality and is really important to the sound of the recording, so it has to stay intact. That's something that's in the forefront of my mind while I'm doing a recording. If I'm mixing material that I didn't originally record, that can be a problem, but I'll tend to deal with it more by using different reverbs; I won't notch out frequencies with an equalizer.

Do you often print effects?

No, I usually record everything totally dry, and also usually with very little EQ or compression or limiting. That way, I have all options available to me when I mix.

Can you take us through your typical mixing process?

No, I'm afraid that's impossible, because I never do it the same way twice. All I can tell you is that it's driven by the specific music being mixed. There's no set formula; the purpose of the mix is to complement the music, nothing else.

That's why, if I'm given a project to mix that I didn't record, I'll always ask for a demo of it ahead of time. That way, early in the process, I can get in my head what the artist's concept of the music is. Otherwise, it might hit my ear a little differently, and I might take it somewhere where it shouldn't go. Listening to what the artist has to say really helps prevent that and keeps me true to the original concept. But from that point on, there are no set rules, and you really can't approach a mix any other way.

> *"[A mix] is done when the music feels complete, when the song has successfully made its musical statement."*

I firmly believe that what we do as engineers can never win out over the personality of the music itself. In other words, if I think, "Oh, man, wouldn't it be great if there was a better bass drum sound," the song may not want that, so my desires become not only irrelevant, but counterproductive. As I've said before, nobody ever walks around humming a bass drum sound.

How long do you typically spend on a mix?

I mix a song until it's done...and knowing when it's done is part of the reason why people hire me. You can't overthink things too much: Quincy used to call it "paralysis through analysis." [*laughs*] Take it from me: that's not a pretty sight. You need to know instinctively when a mix is done. It's done when the music feels complete, when the song has successfully made its musical statement. It's done when I feel that, no matter who I play this recording for, they will get it.

I know that people have a problem letting go. But there is a point where the music will say, "Get your ass outta here; I don't need you anymore." That often happens after mastering, and it really used to depress me; it was almost like post-partum depression.

Are you equally depressed about today's trends in mastering towards maximum loudness and over-compression?

I guess so. Maybe that's why I'm sometimes not invited to mastering sessions these days! [*laughs*] I love dynamics; they're a really important part of music, and they need to be preserved. The big problem with overusing compression is that it sounds awful; I just don't like what it does to the *sound* of music. It takes a lot of the presence away, and it takes high end away, especially those compressors that are frequency-selective. Even the limiters that radio stations strap on—they may give the illusion of energy, but it isn't real power. A lot of people get led astray by thinking that they have to use compression. It isn't necessarily true; the only thing you *have* to do is serve the music.

Another thing I really hate is when people say to me, "I looked at this piece of music on my computer, and...." You *looked* at it?? What is that about? That's crazy. You're supposed to be *listening* to music with your ears, not *looking* at it with your eyes. People with that mindset don't make good records.

Yet many of today's recordings feature surgical precision, where every beat is perfectly aligned and every note played or sung is perfectly in tune.

It's so foolish, because that has absolutely nothing to do with music; in fact, to some extent, that kind of approach takes the music out of it. When I hear a record like that, I won't listen to it all the way through, and I certainly wouldn't buy it. Any one of Michael's scratch vocals, sung through from start to finish during the tracking sessions, would have been perfectly acceptable for a final mix, mistakes and all. Of course, I'm sure I could have chopped them up and tweaked them to perfection... but then they would have sounded horrible.

Even though I feel as if I've never met the onstage Michael Jackson—he has such a totally different personality when he's performing—there was that same energy in all the vocals he did for us in the studio. In fact, if you listen to the mixes I did for him, you can actually hear him dancing and moving to the music. Many engineers would consider the finger-snapping and things like that superfluous, but I felt they were important in conveying the emotion of the music, so I left them in there. You have to be open to spontaneity and thinking outside the box; a lip-smacking noise is not necessarily something that always has to be edited out or muted.

How do you feel about the fact that most people are now listening to music as low-resolution MP3s over tiny computer speakers or earbuds?

Well, recordings are not sacred. And once an engineer has made his imprint on the music, it's then frozen. After that point, you can put it on a cassette or even an iPod, and it will still have those values as part of the soundscape. Personally, I think iPods are wonderful—I love them! And MP3s really don't bother me at all. A good MP3 can sound surprisingly good. Mind you, a bad MP3 can *really* sound bad! [*laughs*]

I do honestly think that the listening ability of the average person today has improved in that most people can tell the difference between an old recording and a new one. That might be because good recordings are so much more available than they were years ago. All music is subject to the same conditions, and it really doesn't matter what the medium is; a really good recording is going to still sound really good, regardless of the medium. Similarly, a really bad recording is going to sound really bad whether you're listening to it as a low-quality MP3 or on the best 24/96 playback system, and anyone can easily tell the difference. They may perceive it as not being as clear, or not being as full of energy as a really good recording, whereas a really good recording played back as an MP3 can sound gorgeous. It's that old saying: "garbage in, garbage out." Start with a great recording and it's going to end up that way, regardless of the medium and regardless of the monitoring.

I am not a technocrat when it comes to that sort of thing... though you'd have a hard time getting me to mix anything outside of my own room! [*laughs*] Mind you, I always check everything on low-end monitors as well as high-end; I still rely on Auratones, which Michael [Jackson] and I always called the "truth speakers." I've never liked headphones, though, so I think it's pretty foolish to check mixes on those, or on car stereos, for that matter. But if you can get a mix to sound good on Auratones, it's going to sound great anywhere. And that's the mark of a good recording: it will sound good anywhere, without requiring high-volume playbacks over high-end speakers. It *is* a lot harder to get a recording to sound good over a low-quality speaker, but it certainly is possible.

Suggested Listening:
Michael Jackson: *Off the Wall*, Epic, 1979; *Thriller*, Epic, 1982; *Bad*, Epic, 1987; *Dangerous*, Epic, 1991
Quincy Jones: *Back on the Block*, Qwest, 1989; *Q's Juke Joint*, Qwest, 1994
The Jacksons: *Victory*, Epic, 1984
George Benson: *Give Me the Night*, Warner Bros., 1980
Jennifer Lopez: *This Is Me... Then*, Epic, 2002; *Rebirth*, Epic, 2005; *Brave*, Sony, 2007

Sense and Sensibility

Think American popular music in the late 1960s and several names spring to mind: Janis Joplin. Blood, Sweat, and Tears. The Band.

They all have one thing in common: producer John Simon.

The Connecticut native was a child prodigy of sorts, already playing fiddle and piano at the tender age of four and writing songs before he was a teenager. By the time Simon was an undergraduate at Princeton University, he had authored two musicals and was composing scores for full-blown stage productions. Landing an entry-level job at Columbia Records, he began training under legendary label head Goddard Lieberson, learning the industry from the ground up. By 1965 he had been promoted to staff producer, enjoying his first national success just a year later with The Cyrkle's "Red Rubber Ball," a catchy if somewhat lightweight pop tune that dominated the summer airwaves at the dawn of psychedelia. Following his production of Blood, Sweat, and Tears' debut album *Child Is Father to the Man*, Simon struck out on his own as an independent, leading to work with, among others, Joplin, Cass Elliot, Gordon Lightfoot, Leonard Cohen, and Simon and Garfunkel.

In 1968, a chance meeting with several oddly attired musicians in Woodstock, New York led to the most lasting work of Simon's career: production of the first three albums by the group soon known to the world as The Band. The broad musical scope and vision of Robbie Robertson, Levon Helm, Garth Hudson, Rick Danko, and Richard Manuel meshed perfectly with Simon's own jazz-oriented sensibilities, yielding what many still feel are the perfect recorded embodiments of the best of nineteenth- and twentieth-century American music.

Following his success with The Band, Simon launched a solo career as an artist, augmented by production work with Emmylou Harris, Al Kooper, Seals and Crofts, David Sanborn, and Gil Evans, as well as session work as a keyboardist and horn player with Eric Clapton, Dave Mason, Howlin' Wolf, Taj Mahal, John Sebastian, John Martyn, Peter Yarrow, and Garland Jeffreys. He reunited with The Band in 1978 for their live *The Last Waltz* concert and film, serving as producer as well as playing keyboards and providing string and horn arrangements.

Today, Simon continues to remain active in the upstate New York music scene, producing local artists and gigging and recording with the John Simon Trio. We met with him one beautiful summer morning in a Woodstock studio where he was putting finishing touches to a new CD. Lively and highly articulate, it quickly became clear from our conversation that Simon has lost none of his youthful passion and enthusiasm for music.

How did you get your first job in the industry?

I was actually recruited out of college back in 1963—there were interviewers who came to Princeton and after my graduation I was offered a trainee job at Columbia Records, where I was paid a whopping $85 a week. I was 21 years old at the time, and my initial duties included helping Goddard Lieberson record original cast albums—I'd go out on the road with various shows during their pre-Broadway tryouts and get the timings of the songs down, things like that. It was good training in that I got to know every aspect of the record business, from making record jackets to the operations at pressing plants. Goddard was a record man from heaven—he was musically erudite, with a great sense of humor, and he was a fabulous gentleman. He was also as hip as could be—he was a pal of John Hammond's and the two of them had gone down to the Deep South in the 1930s to record spirituals in an effort to preserve the roots of African-American music.

I was also put to work on what Columbia called "special projects," which were coffee-table items—albums accompanied by books. One of the first of the ones I helped on was called *Bad Men*—a collection of songs about outlaws. Thankfully, some of them never saw the light of day, like one called *Doctors, Drugs, and Diseases*. [*laughs*]

One early stereo project I worked on was called *Point of Order*, which was based on a movie about the McCarthy Senate-Army hearings of the fifties. It only had a mono soundtrack, and we had to make a stereo mix out of it, so we put the judge's dialog in the middle and then panned the army lawyers to one side and Joe McCarthy and [lawyer] Roy Cohn on the other side. Then we manufactured a stereo ambience track by getting a bunch of people to walk around the studio coughing and murmuring. Of course, this was long before digital, so we made this huge five-minute tape loop of it that went around the room, using coat racks to give it tension.

Eventually, the top brass decided to fold original cast albums into the Masterworks label, which was Columbia's classical division. I was very ill-suited for that, especially compared to some other guys who had been there for years and knew the repertoire cold. I had been a music major at Princeton, but I had never been heavily into classical music—my love had always been jazz.

Finally, one of the executives there realized that I was in the wrong spot and he moved me over into the pop division. Of course, when I first started, they were only giving me the acts that nobody else wanted because they weren't making much money: acts like Frankie Yankovic, America's Polka King. [*laughs*] Working with him was a real experience because the Chicago studio we used to record him in was outfitted with World War I–vintage equipment: the faders were not even linear—they were rotary, mounted on a vertical deck—and the sound system was equivalent to something you'd get out of a cereal box. I did Frankie's *Fiftieth Birthday Party* album and all of his middle-aged groupies showed up, complete with scary bouffant hairdos. [*laughs*]

Your first hit record was "Red Rubber Ball," by The Cyrkle.

That's right. But I didn't discover them—I was assigned acts. The Cyrkle had been together for awhile before I started working with them—they were a college group from Lehigh [Pennsylvania], so they weren't manufactured. Tom Dawes, the leader of the group, was actually a very talented guy.

Shortly after that, I was assigned Blood, Sweat, and Tears, and that's where I met Al Kooper, who told me that I should be an independent producer. I said, "What's that?" He explained that it would be a better situation for me because I would get royalties. Again, I said, "What's that?" [*laughs*] I was pretty naïve at the time. They were the first artists I worked with as an independent producer.

What were the main lessons you learned during your years at Columbia?

One of the main things was timing. A record, of course, is going to live forever, so of course you want to make sure you capture the best possible version of the song. But to my mind the best possible version can only happen after the artist has already performed the song for ten weeks on the road, because by that time there's no problem with technique and the artist has already explored every possibility. Then all you have to do is get in the recording studio and somehow heighten the event by doing something special.

It's a technique that admittedly doesn't always work with singers because they may get tired of the message they're singing—the song may lose meaning to them, to the point where they're just singing words. That's where the magic of the first take can come in. But it really depends on what you're going for. If you're going for the very best version of a song, then I really believe that the more rehearsal you can do, the better. Of course, in order to retain freshness, you need to leave it for a little while before you come back in and record the song.

PHOTO BY C.C. LOVEHEART

Speaking of timing, the Columbia Records sales department had cautioned us producers that every single had to be under three minutes or it wouldn't get played on radio, and the length of each song was printed in huge letters on the label of each DJ copy. So if that number began with a 2, you were okay. As a result, I put out a few singles with times like 2:74 or 2:93. [*laughs*]

You've seen a lot of changes in the industry, in both technical and commercial terms, since you first started making records more than 40 years ago.

Yes, I have. I was talking about this with a friend just recently, and it occurred to me that, before rock 'n' roll came along, musicians had no special status—they were just like plumbers or anybody else. Then all of a sudden they were gods and had all this fucking *power*. [*laughs*]

I was there when eight-track recording came in, too, and it's always been my contention that the ongoing development of multitrack recording was accelerated by the inadequacies of the musicians of the era. When I started, there were professional musicians who did the backing track and then there were singers who sang over them. Even Simon and Garfunkel never had their own band; they just used great session players, people who could cut it. But then when The Beatles started the whole trend of self-contained bands, we producers had to find ways to cover our asses because the guitar player couldn't play his solo all the way through, so you had to have him do it several times and then piece it together, or overdub with a ton of punch-ins.

And once you started getting 8, 16, 24 tracks to work with, suddenly there was all this *clutter*. There was too much of a temptation to say, "Well, I don't know if I want this or I want that," so people would record multiple versions of everything and decide later. But then, when you put the next overdub on, you don't know what to relate to. Do you relate to the loud guitar part, or the soft one? The intense one or the mellow one? Then there's always someone who wants to mute other parts when they're adding a new part, but then when you try to bring everything up to mix it together, nothing makes any sense any more.

So I essentially became a minimalist. I decided that I wanted to be able to hear everything very clearly and to make sure that everything in a track worked with everything else on there. I always enjoyed the challenge of making decisions on the spot, anyway, to the point where I'd even print effects on tape. Doing that commits you to an attitude. If you put a certain Elvis Presley delay on a vocal, for example, all of a sudden that colors everything, affecting the performance and all subsequent overdubs.

That approach really came to fruition when I was working with The Band, because we worked very carefully, with the luxury of a lot of studio time. In fact, on their second album, we weren't even actually in a studio with an engineer—we were just in someone's house with me in the room with them, operating the mixing console.

Today, of course, artists have unlimited tracks to work with, which I presume you feel makes matters even worse.

Well, I guess that unlimited tracks provide a way for producers to make extra money because they give everyone the temptation to work on songs for months on end, but things really don't have to be that way. Sad to say, the number of tracks matters even less nowadays because it doesn't seem to be about music anymore—it's more about how you look and how you move. Even though George Martin made a huge contribution, The Beatles were the first band that were self-empowered, but that was because they were making so much money for their record label. In their wake came a whole bunch of bands that looked the part but didn't have the talent or the musical chops or the experience, and it was left up to their producers to make a piece of vinyl that might stand the test of time. But, like The Beatles, The Band had been together for years before they made their first record, and that makes a huge difference.

I get demos all the time from new bands, and the problem seems to be that they want to start making records too soon—everyone today seems too anxious to become a rock star. Usually I tell them to go out there and practice; most of these groups are just not ready yet.

From a production standpoint, what are the common mistakes you're hearing in the demos that aspiring artists send you?

Mostly lack of focus. You need to be aware of what it is you're selling. If you're selling a singer's voice, you don't need a guitar solo on the demo; if you're selling the song, you don't need a big, overblown production—a simple piano/vocal or guitar/vocal will generally work much better. If it's excitement you're selling, then don't put any ballads on the demo; if the lyrics are a feature, make sure the listener can hear all the words. In other words, put your best foot forward.

"Most A&R people will only listen to the first minute or so of each song on a demo unless they're completely blown away, so make sure each song opens with a bang, and put the best songs or performances at the beginning."

Also, there's got to be something special about your music—there are just way too many copycats out there. Sure, we all start off as copycats, but at a certain point you have to find your own thing, whether it's a combination of different sources that you've drawn together or something totally new.

Finally, don't make your demo too long. Short and sweet is best. Most A&R people will only listen to the first minute or so of each song on a demo unless they're completely blown away, so make sure each song opens with a bang, and put the best songs or performances at the beginning. We always used to take a lot of care in the way we sequenced albums, and people should do the same with their demos. A good example of that is the very first Band album [*Music from Big Pink*], where we opened with something very atypical—"Tears of Rage." It was a ballad with a very melancholy tone to it, but it grabbed the listener's ear and made you want to hear more. Of course, we led off the second album with "Across the Great Divide," but by that time people knew who they were.

The Band's second album was even more of a success than their first one, something that rarely happens. What's your take on the so-called "sophomore jinx"?

Well, that's always the case with every new artist when they get signed. It happens because they typically have a whole backlog of songs that they know well, all ready to be recorded, but then they go out on the road and they don't have sufficient time to write new songs, so when they return to the studio they run into problems; even if the new songs are good, the other guys in the band don't know them all that well.

That was the case with The Band's second album: the so-called "brown album." Robbie [Robertson] was writing the songs as we were recording them, and we'd work out the arrangements on the spot. One of my most important jobs as producer was to give my opinion, based on my sensibilities, and make suggestions about what I thought could be changed to improve the songs. Again, we'd rehearse each song over and over again and get all the parts worked out, but once we'd gotten it to where everybody

> *"A producer's job is not only about having an objective set of ears, but an objective sensibility too."*

was happy, we'd go to sleep. By returning to it the next day, we were able to add some freshness to the process; we'd usually cut the track by lunchtime, and then we'd be starting on the next song by the middle of the day.

When you're giving your opinions, are they based purely on personal taste, or on what you think the public might like?

I think purely in terms of personal taste, because most of the time I have no idea what the public might like. I suppose if you're thinking in terms of a possible single, where people are going to be moving their feet, then you might go for a take that's got a little more of a groove to it, as opposed to one that's got some more subtlety and musical elegance. A producer's job is not only about having an objective set of ears, but an objective sensibility too.

Still, you've made plenty of hits in your time.

I've been lucky. I was fortunate enough to be able to work with people who saw things the same as me, and I guess their audience had the same sensibilities as me.

What was it that initially drew you to The Band when you first heard them?

I met them through a common friend, [film editor] Howard Alk, while he and I were locked up in a house in Woodstock putting together the music for a movie called "You Are What You Eat." These four guys—Levon [Helm] wasn't with them—came by one night to serenade Howard because it was his birthday, and it was shortly after Halloween, so they were all wearing these funny costumes. We got to chatting, and I really liked them as people. At one point, Howard said, "You know, this is Dylan's band, and I think they have a record in them, so you guys should get together." All Howard had heard was part of their early basement tapes, with Garth [Hudson] singing on it, and it was really wacky, crazy stuff, like the kinds of things I was doing at the time, so he thought we'd be a good fit.

It was just serendipity that we also shared the same musical sensibility. Besides being an excellent musician, Robbie was a very canny guy, and so he invited me up to Woodstock two or three times before he would even let me hear any of their music—I was living in New York City at the time. He kept talking about what they were doing, but he wouldn't let me actually hear it; it was as if he was dangling a carrot on a stick. Then Levon returned from the oilfields of Louisiana, just a day before I came up for another visit, and they finally played me a couple of songs up at the house they were calling Big Pink: "Tears of Rage" and "Lonesome Suzie." They were asking me lots of questions about possible arrangements, so I got a good sense that I could be actively involved, which is what I like—I don't like just being the guy who sits there and says, "Nice take." I'm an arranger, and that's what I really like to do.

You're largely credited with bringing brass to the sound of The Band.

Well, Garth was a horn player too, so it gave us something to do together. I played piano on a couple of their tracks, too, when Richard [Manuel] couldn't quite cut it. I sometimes was able to picture brass in their songs, but I didn't always get it right: later on, a CD version of the album was released that contained an outtake of a version of "Lonesome Suzie" that I had put brass on, and it didn't work at all—it was totally wrong for the song.

Are there any technical details you remember about those first three Band albums that you'd care to share?

Well, I tend to leave the choice of microphone to my engineer, but I do remember using a lot of [Sennheiser] 421s, and a U 87 as a vocal mic.

The Band were somewhat unusual in that Robbie Robertson was the main songwriter, yet he rarely sang lead. Were there ever times when Levon, or Richard, or Rick [Danko] wanted to interpret one of his songs in a way that differed from his vision?

Actually, no, because they would pretty much follow Robbie's leads—he would sing the songs for them during early rehearsals, and they would generally emulate his style. Those guys really were sweethearts to work with, and none of them took a "my way or the highway" approach.

You're not credited on Janis Joplin's seminal album *Cheap Thrills*, though by all accounts you were the producer on that project.

I was, and one of Janis' biographers later made an incorrect assumption that I kept my name off of *Cheap Thrills* because I didn't like either the album or Janis. That's not true. The real story is that my friend Howard Alk—the same film editor friend who introduced me to The Band—was something of a philosopher and at around that time he had convinced me that, in his words, "credit corrupts." His point was that, if you know your name will be on something, you modify its purely artistic values because your reputation is involved. That made sense to my 27-year-old brain—it still does, actually—so I resolved not to take any more production credits. *Cheap Thrills* just happened to be the next project that came up for me, so I decided to try the plan out with that album and left my name off. But I soon realized that, logical as it sounded, doing so wouldn't help my career much, so I went back to taking credit from then on.

How do you balance the aesthetic concerns of the artist with the commercial requirements of the record label?

Well, the producer is always stuck in the middle of that, but my allegiance was always to the artist. I was never a Phil Spector; people didn't want to work with me because I had a certain kind of sound. I always felt I was there to serve the artist, and there were a lot of artists who I turned down working with—even those who had had a lot of hits under their belt—because they just weren't pushing my buttons musically.

How do you deal with the inevitable conflicts that occur in the studio?

Any project manager—which is what a producer is—has to face the fact that co-worker friction is possible, and the chances go up when you factor in youth and the fact that the spotlight of fame blows egos up to I-can-do-no-wrong heights. That's why, as you say, conflicts in the studio are inevitable.

But there are ways of dealing with it. For one thing, you need to realize that there's generally one main songwriter in every group, so it's largely a matter of syncing up the performance curves. When that songwriter comes into the studio with a new song, he's ready to go because he already knows the song inside out, but the other guys in the band don't know it nearly as well, if at all, and the engineer's not ready to go, either. So the job of the producer is to try to facilitate the other members of the band to learn the song as quickly as possible—to get all the kinks out and all the problems solved—and at the same time let the songwriter know that we're not going to be recording the song for hours, so he doesn't start getting frustrated through this learning/teaching process.

The length of that varies, of course, from artist to artist, but you have to time it so you get that magic moment, that magic best take, when everyone knows the song well enough that they're not worried about the technical aspects of playing it, yet they haven't played it so many times that they're bored with it. And that ties in with another piece of advice: don't go too late. There is a maximum amount of time that people can function efficiently in the studio—I'd say six hours, at most. After that, productivity starts going down, and your rate of return in terms of quality goes down. Better to knock off and do it some other time.

A producer also has to be aware of the fact that people—especially creative people—are sensitive. You're going to be spending a lot of time with the artist, so you have to make sure that you get along. You can't just come down on somebody, either. Sure, you have to be able to tell them that their part isn't working, or that they're dragging or speeding up, but you have to do it in the right way. You have to be kind, and you have to be able to see things from their perspective. The artist is under a lot of pressure, after all—they're getting pressure from all sides, plus they have their own self-imposed expectations for themselves. When all is said and done, at the end of the day, it's *their* record.

Mind you, I didn't know that the whole time I was making hits! I once had an artist let the air out of my tires because she was so pissed off at me—and, no, it wasn't Janis Joplin. [*laughs*] In fact, I once got mailed a box of shit! It looked like this candy sampler, but it said "Road Apples" on the cover, and when you opened it up, there were these little bags of horseshit in straw. I was working with a lot of different artists at the time, and the saddest thing was that I didn't even know who it was that I had offended so much that they had sent it to me! [*laughs*]

At that point, I realized, "This is bad karma," and I actually stopped producing records and got out of the business for a while. It was [Dylan manager] Albert Grossman who got me back into making records—I think the first one I did after that hiatus was an album for Gordon Lightfoot.

Which brings me to another point: the producer needs to remember that there's always a manager involved, too, so if there are poor dynamics within a group, it's really not the producer's job to figure it out. In a case like that, it's best to simply say to the manager, "When you've got their personal problems solved, we'll start making the record again." Then, if the record company starts breathing down your neck, you can just say, "Hey, I'm ready when they're ready."

Do you find it easier working with solo artists than groups for those reasons?

Well, most solo artists already know they're prima donnas, which is a good thing. I've found that the best approach is to therefore treat them like prima donnas, but with tongue in cheek. Maybe you need to start calling them "maestro" or "madame"—whatever it takes to make them comfortable and perhaps be able to laugh at themselves a little bit.

Do you think that today's records sound as good as the ones you were making 40 years ago?

Sure, but I'm not a stickler for that. I can quite happily listen to something recorded with just one or two microphones and find it wonderful. So I don't think that records are necessarily any better, or any worse, than they used to be.

I don't even mind listening to something that's badly recorded, if the song is good and that's the only version available. Of course, everybody prefers hearing things with a good balance of instruments, and I've always liked to be able to hear every syllable of the vocal. Early in my career I was always mixing vocals too soft; now I'm careful to keep them at a good level. That's another thing about some of the demos I hear—very often, the voice is mixed so far back that you can't make out the lyrics, or the quality of the singer's voice. I always tend to think that people are embarrassed about the way they sing when they do that, same as I was when I made my solo albums back in the seventies.

Did you find it really difficult to produce yourself on your solo records?

Well, the one time I did have an outside producer work with me, the results were so much better. Even after all these years, I still get nervous in front of a microphone. I'm still able to segment my brain, though; when I make a mistake, part of my brain goes, "Okay, play another chorus and make sure you get that part right so you can splice it in later." But it's much better to have somebody else there—it's so much easier, and you can forget about having to concentrate on those kinds of things. If nothing else, I always try to use an outside engineer when I'm making my own solo records. You need to have someone who's both honest and friendly; those are two good things to be when you're working in this business. [*laughs*]

> *"When a door opens, go through it . . . but if that door closes, don't try to force it back open."*

What advice do you have for young people who want to get into this business?

The main piece of advice I have applies to aspiring artists as well as producers and engineers: broaden your musical perspective. Listen to classical music, listen to world music, listen to jazz, listen to drum and bugle corps, listen to vocal choirs, listen to birdsong; listen to anything and everything outside the one little thing that you're into. The more you listen, the more creative you'll be in the studio, and the more interesting your ideas will be. You need to be focused, but you also need to have an open mind. In other words, when a door opens, go through it . . . but if that door closes, don't try to force it back open.

Suggested Listening:
The Band: *Music from Big Pink*, Capitol, 1968; *The Band*, Capitol, 1969; *Stage Fright*, Capitol, 1970; *The Last Waltz*, Warner Bros., 1978
Janis Joplin/Big Brother and the Holding Company: *Cheap Thrills*, Columbia, 1968
Blood, Sweat, and Tears: *Child Is Father to the Man*, Columbia/Legacy, 1968
The Cyrkle: *Red Rubber Ball (A Collection)*, Columbia, 1966
John Simon: *John Simon's Album*, Warner Bros., 1971; *Baroque Inevitable*, Sony, 2006

Russ Titelman

Sweet Apprenticeship

Russ Titelman's discography reads like a Who's-Who of pretty much all the major recording artists of the past three decades: Eric Clapton. Stevie Winwood. George Harrison. Paul Simon. Brian Wilson. Randy Newman. James Taylor. The Allman Brothers Band. Little Feat. Ry Cooder. Rickie Lee Jones. Chaka Khan. Jimmy Buffett.

What's more, he learned his craft at the feet of the absolute master—Phil Spector, for whom he served as regular guitarist and backing singer on dozens of records and demos alike. Those of you old enough to remember *Shindig* in the '60s might have even spotted Russ, who held down the guitar chair in the house band when he wasn't busy writing songs for the legendary Don Kirshner, working alongside the likes of Carole King and Gerry Goffin. For more than 20 years, Titelman served as A&R man for Warner Brothers records before leaving in 1997 to pursue his interests as an independent producer.

Soft-spoken and measured in his thinking, Titelman took some time out from his busy schedule to chat with us in his New York apartment about the craft of making records, with specific reminiscences about his work with Clapton and Winwood.

How involved are you technically in the records you produce?

Well, I usually let the engineers do what they do. I have great guys who I work with, and I trust them implicitly. We'll discuss things like miking, and if something doesn't sound quite the way I want to hear it, we'll go move mics around. But during recording, I don't get involved in any of the EQing or anything like that. I might suggest something, or we'll just cut it flat and I might fiddle with the monitors to get it sounding the way I like. But in mixing, if I don't hear what I want to hear, I'll go in and roll my sleeves up.

Do you have a sonic vision when you start a record? Do you have a certain sound in your mind and work towards that goal?

That's a very difficult question to answer. For the most part, recordings with live musicians are living things, and you have to listen to what's going on. You can guide it, but the most important thing is the casting—who you have in there playing. In the brave new world of everybody working in his own little room with a computer, that question is a moot point. But if you're talking about recordings with musicians playing together, they have a life of their own and you have to be ready for whatever happens, even though it may take you down a road you didn't expect.

> **"Recordings with live musicians are living things."**

You're talking about flexibility, about being able to not just be married to preconceived ideas but to be open to new ideas as they appear.

Yes, to be ready for the unexpected, and for mistakes. You know, sometimes you make suggestions that don't work; they're terrible. And sometimes you might make a suggestion to a

great musician, who then takes your idea and makes it into something that's so great, you never could have imagined it. That's why the casting is so important.

Though even for people working on computers, there's a certain degree of their personality that goes into the samples they collect and how they put things together.

That's absolutely true. I always feel that it's the person with the creative force behind the thing that dictates where it goes. You can have a perfect machine record, with perfect vocals and everything perfectly in tune, and have it be absolutely soulless—which, for some things, may be just fine.

Speaking of working with machines, I remember when we were doing *Back in the High Life*, which was, at the time, *the* pinnacle of machine and human working together. And I think it was on "Higher Love," where [Steve] Winwood wanted the snare drum to rush in the bridge, so it sounded like a person who was getting more excited. So we programmed it in. All kinds of little things like that happened during the making of that album.

That really doesn't feel like a machine album, even though it is highly synthesized.

I agree; it doesn't sound mechanical at all.

How did you accomplish that?

Well, Steve had worked on demos for a year, so he had loads of drum and keyboard programs. We actually restructured a lot of the songs by editing and fixing them so they worked better, because some of them were pretty linear. Even "Higher Love" just kind of went flat. It was great, but it was flat. So we made the crazy instrumental, and put a little instrumental thing in the middle of the first verse; those things didn't exist beforehand. We also created the breakdown at the end, and then I brought Chaka [Khan] in. So that was a living thing until the very end of the mix—we were constantly doing stuff to it. But in any case, after we re-edited the songs, Steve rewrote the programs. Then I brought in Robby Kilgore and Jimmy Bralower to do the drum machines, so the sound of the drum machines was really fabulous. We did the whole album bit by bit—we'd lay one part down, then the next.

Did you ever throw any of the sounds out into the room or was it all DI?

We did, occasionally, sometimes through an amp. After we laid down the basic keyboard and drum machine parts, Steve sang a little bit. Then we brought in musicians. Somebody might play a rhythm guitar part, and then, when we brought the drummers in, we put a real high-hat on first. Or we'd have them play drum fills to the track that was already there, then we'd sample the sound of the drummer and key it off the machine so when the fills happened it would all sound the same, but we'd also have a real high-hat in there, so the feel was very human. There'd be real high-hat, machine high-hat. Real conga, machine conga. Real tambourine, machine tambourine. So it had a very human feel to it—smoke and mirrors.

You once commented that Eric Clapton will work with machines, but he always wants to jam along with them live.

Yeah; that's what we did on *Journeyman*. If we ever used a machine, the whole band would play, and then we would mix and match. Plus we made comps of the solos, which is a kind of manipulation. Everyone gets up in arms when they think it isn't the actual part that was played live, but I always say it's the difference between going to a play and going to a movie—do they get mad at editors of films just because there's a bunch of performances and they edit them all together so that all of a sudden there's a *Gone With the Wind* or a *Citizen Kane*? [*laughs*] No, people still like the movie.

My theory is that people go to plays because, in the back of their minds, they hope somebody will have a heart attack on stage.

Or make a mistake. The unexpected.

And that's the thrill of live performance, too.

Absolutely. Who's going to hit a real clinker, or maybe you'll witness the most glorious thing that ever happened, and you were there.

But how do you achieve those magic moments in a studio, when there isn't the energy of an audience to build on?

Prayer is one thing. Seriously, you do your best to create an atmosphere where there is that feeling of trust and excitement when everything happens. You try to make it sound as good as it can sound. And *then* you pray.

But the studio is such an artificial environment, such a non-real place.

Yeah, it is, but it's something you kind of get used to, though it definitely is artificial. A lot of people like to record at home these days, do vocals at home, do guitar overdubs at home.

Is that a good thing, or not a good thing?

If it works, it's a good thing. You know, part of the job of being a producer is allowing things to happen. If an artist wants to go and sing at home, or do guitar overdubs at home by himself, you say, "Go, do it." And then you listen to it afterwards and say yay or nay, or, "This part was really great, but why don't we do this?" Because that relationship—the collaboration between artist and producer is extremely delicate, and it's a very special and powerful relationship.

How do you know when a record is done?

It's just instinct, touched against something you know of that artist. If you're producing someone, you need to know their limitations and what they can and cannot do. Also, for me, if it strikes me emotionally, if it's something that speaks to you subconsciously, you can spot it. Even if it's not perfectly in tune, that's stuff you can fix later—you can fix pitch so easily or manipulate the time of something if it isn't exactly right. Or maybe what's wrong with it is what has the charm and makes it great.

What are the common mistakes people are making in the demos they are making in home studios?

I don't know if people are doing anything wrong. What hasn't changed is when you hear a great song. Songwriting styles *have* changed, though; to me, standards of writing have been diminished in a way. People don't use the language as cleverly as they used to. And that tradition

> *"The collaboration between artist and producer is extremely delicate, and it's a very special and powerful relationship."*

of lyric writing, using complicated chord progressions and things like that, were part of what got the message across; the technique itself. It's like the music of poetry in that the way it sounds is part of the message. If you have very clever Cole Porter or Ira Gershwin lyrics, there's something that tickles your brain about how cleverly their rhyme schemes go and what they're saying. So there was that tradition, and then you have our generation that came in the late fifties, early sixties—the Tin Pan Alley group of Carole King and Gerry Goffin, and Bacharach and David, all the greats who wrote in that tradition, but they simplified it. They took the people's music—doo-wop and music off the streets—and made sophisticated versions of what was going on. Plus they were interested in symphonic arrangements to accompany these little tracks. I guess The Beatles were the pinnacle of that tradition. They weren't the first, and they weren't the last, but they may have been the best at it.

Also, because so many people heard them, they exposed us to all kinds of music—particularly George Harrison's bringing Indian music to the attention of the world. What a thing! Indian music—now *that's* exotic; that's intellectual and passionate music that no one would have heard otherwise. Only nuts like me and other crazy people I knew would go to Ravi Shankar or Ali Akhbar Khan concerts before that ever happened.

Now there's the new tradition of the guy sitting in his room, working on a computer, one guy doing it all, but there's still the tradition of bands playing out there, and I think that will become more desirable for people because live music is still the greatest thing in the world. I think the thing that's difficult to overcome is that, because of the technology, it's almost too easy to make something *sound* good, thanks to sampling and all these tricks at your fingertips now. We used to have to create things from scratch, but now people just sample things and make new records out of them. So, yes, you have the ability to make something that sounds professional in your living room, but you don't have the ability to write a great song in your living room. But even a piece of junk can sound good, so it can be deceiving: you might accept something because it sounds great instead of polishing the song to perfection.

> ## "Live music is still the greatest thing in the world."

These days, there are unlimited options and unlimited tracks. Do you see that as a helpful in making better recordings, or harmful?

[*long pause*] Well, I worked on two albums recently that were made very quickly on a small budget. My wonderful production coordinator made me sit down and she said, "Okay, what are you going to do on each track?" I've *never* had to do that before; I've never had to pre-conceive every track. So I had to sit there and go, "Okay, well, this one will be like a Nat Cole Trio song with piano, guitar, and bass, and we'll have two saxophones and a trombone. And this one will have a big band, and the horn section will be this, and we'll have this many strings and the band is going to be this." And then we had to go in like we were conducting a battle. First day, just piano things with vocal. Next day, the trio things and then these people leave and the horns come back in and they overdub on this, and then the small string section comes in the next day—it was incredible. I recorded on analog tape to get that warm sound, and the tracks would then go into Pro Tools so we could manipulate and fix things and do what we had to do. And that's what we did; in five or six weeks, both of those records were done.

That really was an amazing experience, because you had to be on your toes. Everybody had to do his job *right now*; be great *now*. All the decisions about what we were keeping and weren't keeping were made as we went along, because of time and money constraints.

So, for somebody working in a home studio, are you saying it's a good idea to pretend you *don't* have unlimited time?

I recommend it, yeah. It does something to your creative juices, and it does something to your decision-making process. Then again, it depends on the kind of music you're making. I don't know how to make hip-hop records, for example, but some of those records are creative and fantastic and wonderful, though a lot of them are, like anything else, cookie-cutter kind of records—a lot of it sounds the same. And then there are these amazing creative leaps made by people with great imaginations using the equipment in creative ways.

You cut your teeth with Phil Spector. [Engineer] Larry Levine once told me that Phil used to say he could make a hit record with anybody.

Well, I once heard Norman Whitfield say, "I could cut a hit with a chicken." [*laughs*]

Could he?

I think at the time he could have. The mighty Norman Whitfield!

How do you feel about the Spector approach, with the producer being the main creative force in the studio and the artist almost irrelevant?

Well, when you're working with a great artist, the producer and the artist are collaborating on creating something that hopefully will be exceptional and memorable, and will live on and stand the test of time. I doubt that a lot of the stuff on the charts today is going to be listened to 30 or 50 years from now in the way that an Irving Berlin or George Gershwin song is still listened to. A lot of those songs are still being recorded today, even though some were written almost a hundred years ago. To say nothing of Mozart and Beethoven, who were writing 250, 300 years ago. Now *that's* a hit! [*laughs*]

But what happens when you have a great artist doing a not-great song, versus a great song being done by a not-great artist?

Well, there was a record that I listened to recently that I thought was really great, but then I went and heard the singer, who shall remain nameless, and she couldn't sing at all. But her record was fantastic: the sound of her voice was great, and you could hear she had a thing, she had attitude. So I just thought, "Well, this is a really good producer. He made something really terrific out of something that was not so terrific." But the vibe and the writing—the whole thing—was substantial.

As a guitarist, do you find yourself focusing a little bit more on guitar than the other instruments when you're working?

No, I don't focus more on guitar. The sound depends on the guitar player, on what he's giving you. It's difficult to go into the studio with Eric Clapton and get a bad guitar sound. [*laughs*] Even with him, though, we did miking things and other tricks. I remember once during the *From the Cradle* sessions, Eric came rushing into the booth, saying, "Come listen to this on these phones—this is how I want it to sound!" The guitar was monstrously huge in his headphones, so our job was to get that same sound coming out of the speakers.

Was it a matter of taking the effects that were in the foldback mix and putting them into the main mix?

No, it was largely a matter of echo and balance, and it was the same echo—it was just that he could hear more of it. Plus the guitar was really loud, things were out of balance, and that's what he likes, so we did our mixes like that.

The other thing Eric did during the making of that album was to play the old original blues records and he'd say, "I want to capture the spiritual quality of this." If you listen to those records, the guitar and the voice would be way out here in your face, the band would be back here, and the drums would be *way* back, but it would sound tough, the sound is monstrous. If you listen to Beatles records, a lot of their stuff is like that, too. The drums are back, but they're clear, and they have a sound. So it was just a matter of using echo, and taking that basic approach like an old record, like it was recorded on one microphone. The singers got up to the microphone, and then the saxophone player came up, then the harp player. We used old-sounding echo, slap echo. Not a lot of tricks, but a little of everything. We had digital slap, we had real slap. We did that record quickly, too. We got to the end of the last mix in the late afternoon or early evening, and I said, "Okay, let's listen to all this stuff." During that final playback, there were five songs where I said, "We really have to fix these things," so we started all over again—we put them back up and tweaked them. We remixed five songs, and we got out at 7:30, 8 o'clock the next morning—we just went for it.

Similarly, when we were doing Eric's live album [*24 Nights*], I spent a lot of time walking around the venue, listening to the way it sounded in different parts of the hall—going way up high, way in the back, so that when I went to mix the record, I had a sense memory, like an actor, of what it sounded like in there. We had ambience mics, but we also created echo to enhance, to make the drums sound the way they sounded live. I think that we were successful in recreating the sound and the feeling of that hall on that record. That's a beautiful sounding record. Alex Haas is the guy that mixed it, uncredited, to my horrible chagrin. What a job he did!

As a former A&R man, what is it in a demo that catches your ear?

Again, a great song is the main thing. But another question is, is there a creative musical force there? I'm less interested in the sound, because, as we were saying before, anybody can make a good sounding demo these days. But if there's a great arrangement, or a quirky kind of different feel, or an emotional thing that hits you, that's what has always interested me.

Would you rather receive a fleshed-out, arranged demo, or would you rather hear a bare-bones demo, without any frills?

It doesn't really matter to me. If the fleshed-out one is a good version of it, I'll think, "Hey, great—maybe that guy's a good producer, too." But when you listen to something, you listen for the song first, so it could be a simple guitar/voice or piano/voice demo. Then again, if it's a band, you want to hear what the sound is like and what they can do.

How do you handle situations where you and an artist don't see eye to eye on something?

Well, it's a rare occurrence. When you're working with someone, you're usually in tune, most of the time. You're there to facilitate the artist, and to make something great happen—you want them to do their best work, and I also want it to be the best *I've* ever done. That's a matter of having a real atmosphere of give and take, and trust. So if I have an idea, or an artist has an idea, you do it; you say, "Go ahead, we'll see what happens." I suppose that, under certain circumstances, if you really think it's going nowhere, you might try it a little bit, and then say, "Look, I really don't think this is working; why don't we do this instead." Sometimes the roles are reversed, too. I was doing something with James Taylor recently, and I got some stupid idea. We went down the road for about half an hour or an hour, and finally James said, "I don't think we should do this anymore." And he was absolutely right.

But what about those situations where you and the artist prefer different takes?

Under those circumstances you have to have a certain amount of trust in your artist. If you think there's something there, you can make a sound argument but if they still want to go there, then you go there.

So at the end of the day it's the artist's call.

Yeah, I think so; you have to trust in them. When you're working with someone who is a really great artist, they know *something*.

But what if you're working with someone who is not a really great artist?

Then you have to fight for what you think is right. If you're good enough at it, you can convince them. If you believe in something strongly, you make that known, and you make a good case for it. If the artist you're working with has enough trust in you, he'll often go along.

What are the most important skills that a young person has to develop to be a successful producer?

Record production is a craft as well as an art. When I was starting, I learned by doing, but mainly by listening. If you're going to be a movie director, you've got to watch all the great movies so you know what the masters did, and go from there. So my advice is to listen to the great records of the past and see what inspires you. You have to have an open mind and you have to have a good ear. As far as technical stuff goes, you just learn by doing. These days, of course, you can go to schools and learn engineering technique; I don't come from an engineering background, but I know something about it by doing it. But everything that happens gets funneled through your awareness, your experience, so when things happen in the studio, you're able to make judgments about it and lead things a certain way. That comes from your experience and your taste, and from doing what you love. That's what leads you down whatever road you're going, so it's like a creative force, no matter what technology you're using. That's what we're talking about, basically: there's all this new technology, there's all this ability to do things quickly and you practically don't even have to work with musicians anymore! [*laughs*] You can even create things *without* musicians these days—what a scary proposition!

You have to build a base to work from; you have to build some knowledge and gain some experience in order to make an emotional connection and find out what you like. That may be an antiquated concept, but it will allow you to accomplish all you want to accomplish.

Suggested Listening:

Eric Clapton: *Journeyman*, Reprise, 1989; *24 Nights*, Reprise, 1991; *Unplugged*, Reprise, 1992; *From the Cradle*, Reprise, 1994
Steve Winwood: *Back in the High Life*, Island, 1986
James Taylor: *October Road*, Sony, 2002
Randy Newman: *Little Criminals*, Reprise, 1977
Rickie Lee Jones: *Rickie Lee Jones*, Warner Bros., 1979
Keb' Mo': *The Door*, Epic, 2000

Veterans

David Hewitt

A Lifetime of Live Recording

David Hewitt's name may not be quite as well known as some of the other engineers and producers in this book, but his work most certainly is. If you watched the past few years' Academy Awards, or the Stones' 2002 HBO concert, or the star-studded Concert for New York that followed the 9/11 tragedy—or if Neil Young's classic *Rust Never Sleeps* or Jackson Browne's groundbreaking *Running on Empty* grace your album collections—you have heard Hewitt at his finest.

Live recording is, in Hewitt's words, a "guerilla" art, and not for the fainthearted. Despite the rigors of the road, he has managed to not only build one of the most famed mobile facilities the world over (the "Silver Studio"), but to forge a unique career capturing the live sound of some of the most major events ever staged. Following an internship at Philadelphia's fabled Regent Sound (the original Cameo/Parkway studio in the '50s), Hewitt landed a gig at New York's equally famed Record Plant. One day, as he tells the story, he was commandeered by a crew of Plant employees—including a young Jack Douglas, who was later to produce John Lennon, Aerosmith, and Cheap Trick—to help out on a live radio broadcast. From that moment on, he was hooked. "It made my hair stand up," he recalls of that first live gig. "All the things that were going on, everything you had to do in one day just to get to the point where you could bring the faders up and make this thing work—it was one big adrenaline rush!"

Within a relatively short time, Hewitt became chief engineer in the Plant's truck, and eventually branched out on his own, founding Remote Recording Services, where he provides facilities for major-league engineer/producers like Phil Ramone, Bob Clearmountain, Elliot Scheiner, and Ed Cherney, and often mans the truck's Neve VRM console himself. We joined him one clear, cold afternoon for a behind-the-scenes tour as he and his crew prepared to record the New York Metropolitan Opera for a television production of *Live at the Met*.

You got into live recording largely by chance, not by choice.

Pretty much, but I loved it. It was so exciting, so full of the moment—the energy of a live band, and the truthfulness of it. A live show is the culmination of all the musicians' talents at that point in time, and there's no bullshit: no overdubs, no fixing . . .

. . . theoretically, anyway. But a lot can and often does happen in the studio afterwards.

That's very true; what they do afterwards is often antithetical. But from the moment I started doing live recording, I just loved the variety of it—a rock concert one day, a TV show the next, an opera the day after.

Can you compare and contrast the process of doing a live remote recording with that of doing a studio session?

In the studio, you walk in and the session's set up—you sit down, play it down once or twice, and then start recording; then when you're finished, you walk away. And you take a lot of things for granted—that your equipment is set up and that it all works. You're not worried about the power, you're not worried about whether or not the union guys are on break when you want to do something. But doing live recording is like warfare: you're charging in there and dealing with all the house guys and the union guys, the musician's union, things like that.

"Doing live recording is like warfare."

I'm reminded of the old roadie saying about how the show is that little inconvenience between the load-in and the load-out. [*laughs*] It's true, in a way, because the bulk of the work is everything that gets you up to the point where you hit the Record button. And once you do start recording, you're on a tightrope because it is, after all, a live show, so if something does go down, you have to fix it in real time—and you're suffering in real time! If the bass DI goes out, then you don't have a bass for that song, and you've got to explain that to somebody. [*laughs*]

Is that why you need to build a certain amount of redundancy into what you're doing?

Sure. But it's a whole different world these days, in terms of the professionalism of the touring companies. When I started back in the early 1970s, the sound reinforcement companies were just inventing themselves, and, boy, there was a lot of really flaky equipment and bad attitudes and amateur stuff going on. So there were a lot more failures in those days—a lot more buzzes and nasty problems. These days, it's pretty reliable because both the equipment and people are all seasoned—second or third generation.

Do you supply onstage equipment like DI boxes and microphones, or do you just collect the signal that's presented to you by the sound reinforcement company?

It depends on the client and the situation. We are prepared to do the whole thing, if need be. Obviously we're not going to carry a complete orchestra's worth of mic stands in a truck, but if called upon to do that, we have them in storage. But if you're recording the Rolling Stones, who have been touring for 40 years and know exactly what they are doing—with monitors critically tuned and all that—you're not going to be changing too much. They're already using Neumann mics and the most expensive, reliable equipment available, so in a case like that, we're essentially just splitting the mic signals and sending them into our preamps onstage, and from there, out to the truck.

Especially these days, we're using a lot of ambience miking, because everybody wants to be able to remix in surround. That's something that's kind of come full circle in a funny way, because when we used to do a lot of live radio shows—in the days before MTV—the ambience became very important. Oftentimes I had one guy who was doing nothing but hanging audience mics so that we had a real good ambience for the radio shows. We're back to that again, for different purposes.

Do you feel that your job is to accurately capture the sound of the performance in the particular venue, or to try to make the end result sound like an immaculate studio recording plus ambience and applause?

It's almost a two-part equation in my mind: There's a basic ambience to any of these places—whether good or bad—so you have to figure out where to place the mics to get a decent hall sound. Often you're constricted very much by where you can position them, especially these days, where most of these events are videotaped, so you've got camera positions to worry about. You can't hang mics in front of cameras, and of course that's inevitably where you *want* to hang them!

The other part of the equation is the audience reaction. In television, the camera is often looking at the audience, and on a live show they subscribe to "see a dog, hear a dog"; when they cut to the crowd, they want to hear a little bit of ambience come up. But if you bring up the ambience mics too much, the whole sonic picture balloons. So the idea is to avoid doing that to excess. I deal with the problem by thinking in terms of zones. But that, of course, also raises the issue of delays.

For example, the first zone might be down front, across the swath of the stage, so that's one delay that's within a radius of, say, 40 feet from the band or wherever the sound is emanating from. The next zone might be 50 feet out and over the crowd—hopefully miked in stereo. Then, if it's a larger venue, we'll hang another pair of stereo mics further back, and we'll also often try to get mics out into the corner, sometimes pointing in to the back wall. All of these things can be complicated further still if the sound reinforcement includes delay stacks and things like that.

But do you feel it's your job to capture the actual sound of the venue, or to optimize it, to make it sound as pleasing to the ear as possible? After all, not all spaces are created equal.

Oh boy, is that true! Of course, we're going to try to make the space as useful as possible and get the sound as good as possible. But that depends on a whole bunch of variables: Is it a hall you're familiar with? Are you able to experiment and find where the good spots and bad spots are? Is that something you can interest the producers into putting a little extra effort into? Because it does take time, and it often takes another guy, and if it's a union gig, you're all of a sudden spending another grand or two to get this done. You have to work hard to go after these sounds.

> *"The more acoustic the act is, the more important the sound of the venue, because then you can really hear what's going on in the room, as opposed to what the sound reinforcement sounds like in the room."*

The more acoustic the act is, the more important the sound of the venue, because then you can really hear what's going on in the room, as opposed to what the sound reinforcement sounds like in the room. As you progress towards jazz and classical music, it becomes more and more important, until you get down to the purist end of the things. If you've got the Telarc guys in here, for instance, you're going to hear some spectacular ambience miking, where they're moving things inches to improve the sound, and they'll take the time to do it.

I would think your approach would be a little different if you're doing a pure music recording, as opposed to a TV show.

Right. It's more permanent, and not tied to the camera angles, which makes a big difference. And, of course, it's primarily down to the attitudes of the people who hired you to do the job, what they're interested in. We've done some huge productions where we have just flat out been told, "You can't do that; get out of my way."

It depends on the producer, and the act, and who's got the reins of power. If you can lobby for these things in advance, and you've got a sympathetic producer, you can get the help you need. But there are some producers who just don't want to hear it.

Your son [engineer Ryan Hewitt] is starting to follow in your footsteps. Do you recommend live recording as a good career move for a young person trying to break into the industry?

Well, Ryan grew up working in this business. He's played in bands, earned an Electrical Engineering degree and came up through the ranks at studios like Sony in New York and Cello in LA. So he is way beyond following me! [*See the interview with Ryan Hewitt on page 296.*]

As far as breaking into the business, there are very few people who do this exclusively, and most of us who do this kind of work own our own trucks, so we're kind of locked in and tied to our

own facility. So, frankly, I wouldn't recommend it as a full-time endeavor, but I would recommend it as one of the skills that a good all-around engineer should have. You should have an understanding of live music, because a band makes its living on the road. After all, that's where they are most of the time; they're really only in the studio for a very small percentage of their career.

You're saying that seeing a band play live can give the studio engineer a good feel for what the artist is all about.

Exactly. You can't match the excitement of a live performance in the studio. That's not to belittle the efforts of some studio engineers—there are a lot of wonderful things done there. But often what an artist has done in the studio will become refined in the months and years on the road, and you'll find that songs take on a different life on their own, as the musicians work out the most comfortable ways of playing them live.

Do you do the converse? If you know you've got a gig coming up with a well-known artist, will you get their studio albums and listen to them beforehand as part of your preparation?

Yes, given the opportunity, I will always try to listen to what they've done before. But I listen with the expectation that the live performance will not always be the same [as the studio recording]. I'm there to capture what they're doing onstage at that moment, and oftentimes there will be entirely different band members or other major changes.

These days, do you ever get the opportunity to leave the truck and go back into the studio? Do you find you're able to apply the techniques you've learned on the road in the studio?

I do, occasionally. But as a facility owner—like most of the guys in this business—I can't really stray far from the base because my obligations are here; you've always got to get ready for the next gig. So it's very difficult for me to take time away from the truck to go back in the studio. That's one of the reasons why it's hard for somebody to become a specialist in this area; you really need to keep that studio base to keep your career going as an engineer.

What kind of lessons have you learned on the road that people should be applying to better their home recordings?

Consideration of the acoustics is something that you start to learn about as you're doing live recording. That's one of the big ones, in terms of the control rooms in home studios. Mind you, that's come a long, long ways in recent years. There are all sorts of acoustic packages available now right out of the box, with components you can put up and move around. It's a wonderful opportunity for people to be able to experiment with acoustic treatments for very little money.

There are steps that can be taken to control problem areas. In the home environment, you've got control over your time and materials, but you rarely have that opportunity in live recording. I tend to take the "quick fix" approach. Since I'm creating a nearfield monitoring environment, I essentially try to deaden the room and eliminate the obvious slaps and parallel walls and that sort of thing. At home, you can do the same sort of thing with packing blankets. One easy thing to do is put up some mic stands and join them together and hang packing blankets over them and move them around.

> *"Isolation is a good thing, but it's often a tradeoff with . . . creative leakage."*

Kind of like making a portable gobo.

Exactly. Then you can start attaching absorbers and diffusers to the walls and put traps in the corners and build ceiling traps or reflectors. You can go from here to eternity on that subject!

When you're miking instruments onstage, are you concerned with getting as much isolation as possible, or is leakage a big part of the overall sound?

Isolation is a good thing, but it's often a tradeoff with that concept of creative leakage. The place to start is to just listen to what you've got. In live recording, it's guerrilla audio, and so the first thing I'm looking for is, are all the mics there, period. Then you go to the next stage: Is there some kind of problem? Are any mics buzzing? Does the drummer have a couple of huge wedges that are throwing sound into the mics? Are there a couple of slants hanging in the wings? You listen for all of this sound reinforcement stuff that gets at you. And then you try moving things around and see if you can't eliminate some of the more heinous problems.

Sometimes you can get really interesting sounds by putting mics up behind the band, positioned so that they are looking over their heads—or even by placing mics in front of the musicians. You'll have to put them eight or ten feet up, to get above the actual sound of the people moving around. But there's a lot of ambient sound onstage that can be real useful.

Do you ever find that you sometimes don't need to do close-miking in order to capture the true sound?

Well, it depends a lot these days on the level of the sound in the onstage monitors. Fortunately, we're in a position now where a lot of bands use in-ear monitors.

That must make your job a lot easier.

It does. In fact, I remember the first time that I experienced that—it was a number of years ago, with the Steve Miller Band; that was the first performance I ever heard where the whole band used them, and it was absolutely eerie. There was no leakage at all! The vocals were so clean, so dry . . . all of sudden, I was freaking out, trying to bring up some ambience! I even had to put some reverb on the vocal, which I rarely do. I'm always trying to keep things in the acoustic environment that they're recorded in; I don't put a lot of effects on things. So that presented a different set of problems; you may have to go back to ambient miking and things like that.

You have a lot of dynamics processors here in the truck. I can understand them being used a lot in live broadcasts, but do you use them often when printing to tape?

Yes, I do a little bit of compression and limiting to tape. It's largely a question of the sound I'm trying to get; I'll usually compress the bass a little, maybe the kick drum or the snare. You often need it on vocals, too, because otherwise the dynamic range will be too great. But you can't hit the ceiling of digital—I don't do much analog recording anymore, unfortunately. So I will often have a compressor patched in, even if I'm not really using it.

As a veteran who's been around for a long time, do you feel that the home recording revolution has been good for the music business?

Well, it's a mixed bag. Society is going where it's going, regardless, and the music business and the audio business are such small parts of the overall thing. There's no stopping the evolution of computers, or the evolution of the Internet; all these things are intertwined with where home recording is going.

Of course, the whole record business has been changing dramatically. Going back to the start of MTV in the '80s, the fact is that music is not the main entertainment media anymore. Its commercial viability has been diluted over the years; at the same time, the number of people trying to make a living at it has multiplied in a way that's almost inversely proportional! [*laughs*] So you've got a decrease in revenues, and an increase in the amount of competition. In that sense it's made it very difficult for commercial operations like mine. It erodes the whole bottom end of the business: the smaller audio packages that get added into video trucks take away some of the mid-level work. We've always been at the top end of the spectrum, anyway, but now that's all there is. So we have to make more and larger investments, and charge more money, so we get further and further isolated from the medium- and lower-range facilities.

What about aesthetic considerations? Do you feel that the overall quality of recordings being made today has been improved by the rise of the home studio?

Actually, that's a strange dichotomy as well, because it's now possible to make really good recordings in a home studio. But that doesn't mean that people *will* do that—there's a lot of stuff out there that's just terrible, both artistically and technically [*laughs*] . . . and there's a lot more of it!

I think you're always going to find that roughly ten percent of what's done is worth listening to; some people will say two percent.

Do you think that percentage has gone down in recent years?

I don't think so. There's just so much more of it, so you've got to listen to more to find the good stuff. There are peaks and dips, but there's always good music out there . . . and bad music too! But it's great that a kid can start making recordings without having to be born into a situation where you can afford those toys, or have relatives that have them—now anybody can do that. And you don't have to necessarily fight the crowds to get into a studio to get your training; you can get your training at home now.

Does that mean that the level of engineering skills has decreased in recent years?

Well, it depends on what level you're talking about. If you truly want to be a pro, then at some point you've got to step into the professional ranks and get that kind of training. There are kids now who don't know how to mic up a drum kit, and I do see engineers coming in here occasionally with young bands that really haven't got a clue, that don't even know the basic gain structure of the console. I've seen them making some mistakes that you just can't quite believe, but then there are other young engineers that have come in that are just phenomenal—they're fast and they go right after it and they've got great ears and great training. Again, I think it comes back to that percentage thing: there are a lot more people doing recording today, so there's a lot more stuff to wade through before you get to the good ones.

Suggested Listening:
Neil Young: *Rust Never Sleeps*, Reprise, 1979; *Heart of Gold* [DVD], Paramount, 2005
Jackson Browne: *Running on Empty*, Asylum, 1977
Pink Floyd: *The Delicate Sound of Thunder*, Columbia, 1988
Live: *The Concert for New York City*, Sony, 2001
Woodstock '94: *Box Set*, A&M, 1994

The Magic of Capturing Live Performance

New York's famed Clinton Studios is in many ways the kind of facility you'd find only in the Big Apple. Cavernous and steeped in '70s tradition (complete with an array of vintage gear from that era), it somehow comes as no surprise that it was built on the site of a former multi-story parking garage. Yet it has been home to a huge array of classic orchestral, jazz, and pop recordings, not to mention thousands of jingles and many of Broadway's most memorable cast albums.

Studio owner/chief engineer Ed Rak was the prime architect of Clinton—literally as well as figuratively. The industry veteran is renowned for his expertise in pulling together large-scale recordings and live sessions, with an impressive discography that includes work with Frank Sinatra, George Benson, Chaka Khan, Roberta Flack, Patti Austin, Dave Grusin, John McLaughlin, Maureen McGovern, and one of my personal all-time favorites: Mercer Ellington conducting the Duke Ellington Orchestra for the swinging, crystal-clear *Digital Duke*. We joined Rak recently in a noisy midtown beanery for a wide-ranging discussion about maintaining old-school traditions in a changing world, being fashionable versus being technically correct, and the importance of air and live performance in the world of recording.

You began your career as a musician. How did you make the transition to becoming a recording engineer and studio owner?

I was a drummer for ten years before I ever set foot in a professional control room. But even when I was playing in bands, I always was doing two-track recording for references, and I had the three-dollar microphone—you get to learn some really good mic technique recording a rock band with one microphone. And wherever I lived, I always tried to build a little musical world, whether it was in spare space in the basement, or a spare bedroom, or something like that. I would start treating it so the drums would sound a

> **"You get to learn some really good mic technique recording a rock band with one microphone."**

little better in this corner, the bass didn't have to work so hard here, and the horns weren't too loud there, and the vocalist could see you there. Really early on, I considered architecture as a part of acoustics and music, and then finally, ultimately, as an integral part of the performance.

I worked in a lot of bands, including Phoebe Snow's band. In 1975, we were supposed to do a tour opening for Paul Simon, but then Phoebe called the tour off. I had become friendly with Phil Ramone by that point and one night he invited me to come to A&R Studios—he was working on a Paul Simon record at the time. I remember going into the control room and he was there by himself—there was no assistant—and he was having a little Chinese-food party. I didn't really know it was an interview—I didn't really imagine I could fit into anything going on, but he offered me a job! I think it was a Thursday and I said, "Can I get back to you on Monday?" His reaction was, "What?? I just offered you a job! What do you mean you're not jumping at the opportunity to sweep floors?"

Anyway, I went and I called all my friends and asked them what they thought I should do, because I had been out on the road, being a musician, and Phil wanted me to base myself at A&R and be responsible and, I assumed, start at the bottom. For three days I talked with my friends, and I remember sitting out on the wet grass, weeping, looking at the sky and I finally said, "Okay, if I'm going to do this, I'm really going to do this; I'm going to go in and kick some butt." So I started kicking butt in the high-speed tape copy department at A&R! That was fun, learning to cut tape and edit things and run machines. Then a whole series of events occurred where I kept getting kicked upstairs. I moved into the film production room and learned that, and then on to the tape production room where we did a lot of TV production work and a lot of records. It seems like it was a really long time, but it was only seven months altogether before I started assisting. The first movie I worked on was Schwarzenegger's *Pumping Iron*, and then Elton John came in with Kiki Dee, and I was being trained on that session.

How do you think your musical background benefited you in those seminal years?

Well, I always saw rhythm as being the cornerstone of music, the place that everything flowed from. As a drummer, the right hand is connected to this part, and the foot is connected to that part, and all the parts interplay. But with orchestral work, all of a sudden there's no drummer in the band! So who's laying it down? The trumpet player? I had to learn a lot about that, so I started going to Carnegie Hall to listen to classical concerts, just to find their core.

You really took things seriously.

I did take seriously my promise to myself that I was going to go after it for real. So I stayed late; when I wasn't in the tape copy room, I was standing outside the door listening, I was watching the drummer set up, I was hanging out in the control room. I was already 25 by that point, so I was no kid, but that really helped me because I had a real perspective on the kind of music I was interested in, on how it's built.

I don't know if it's my emotional background, but as a drummer I always felt like I was a support man in the band. I was always massaging the bottom end just enough so that the singer or soloist could take off and say what he wanted to say. And if he was angry, then let's get that, let's get him really pissed off! Or if he's interested in a young lady and he wants to blow flowers out of his saxophone, well then, let him do that. So I started understanding that I could massage the players and suggest to them somehow that they're safe to say what they want to say and that there's support there, and if you need somebody to bounce stuff off of, I can be that, too. The application of that is what I feel I do in engineering—it's setting people up in the right environment, with the right flavor, the right air, the right lighting, the right headphone mix.

What was the first session you engineered?

It was in 1976, Steely Dan's *Aja*, doing overdubs. Elliot Scheiner was doing most of the engineering—I just did vocal overdubs and guitar solos—but what a first outing to be responsible for!

So you really only assisted for about a year.

Well, I got to be on that job because Elliot took me under his wing and he was in the studio all the time. I thought I knew what a good snare drum sound was, having sat over one all that time, but I really didn't until I worked with Elliot! He just clarified the benchmark. Actually, the

only problem I had with being an assistant was that you're an extra six feet away from the left speaker. You can hear the mix perfectly, but it's always right-heavy! That's a habit you have to break when you move into the hot seat, when you finally get into that triangle. [*laughs*]

Anyway, Elliot didn't talk about how to do things very much; he didn't say, "You adjust the mic this way." But I got to watch him in action every day. When you're doing commercials, you do three a day; you set the mics up, get a big sound, and then, "Next!" You might see the same string section three or four times in a day; everybody just gets on with it. That's pretty much how it was with mic technique with Elliot: you just put 'em in the right place the first time. You wouldn't even look, you wouldn't even check. Of course, if it sounded inappropriate, up went the new cable and mic.

Have you developed your own mic techniques as an outgrowth of that, or are you still using that basic mic setup as a template?

Well, Elliot and all the engineers I worked with always used the best equipment possible, but they could put up three [SM] 57s and an [Electro-Voice] 666 in a room and make it sound good. They could corral the sound, they could ease it into the right shape and put it into the right place in the mix.

Did they accomplish that by using signal processing?

Yes—that, and with relativity. If you have good balances, you can pretty much cheat anything. I've heard horrible-sounding vocals on hit records—the worst-sounding bullshit ever, but just in the right place. I don't mean to allude necessarily to Led Zeppelin, but their first record was mixed at A&R, with all that tape slap and stuff. I talked to the engineer who was working on it and he told me, "I didn't necessarily know what I was doing; we were just fooling around." But it was horrible, technically horrible! To the extent that I think if the artist actually got the opportunity to hear themselves on those records without being such a participant, they'd say, "How could I have let that happen?" But in the context, it works incredibly well; it was presented well. And now that sound has been memorialized. It's immortal; it is *the* icon for heavy metal, even though it sounds like Robert Plant is singing through his nose, and despite the fact that the bass drum sounds like it's been filled with water.

From an engineering point of view, what are the differences between doing jingle dates and cast albums versus doing pop albums?

I apply my jingle chops to everything. On a jingle session, ten seconds past the downbeat, you have to be ready to record, because a lot of people are in that kind of hurry. So the mics are up, and they've already been rung out and put in the approximately good spots to capture what they're supposed to. Pretty soon you get a chance to hear them, and you can adjust them as you go. But if you have to print, you print, and you can still make it work. Usually you get ten minutes to get sounds up while the producer makes his phone calls. But at ten after, they whip out the chart and say, "Okay, let's do one," no matter where you are. So now I do that on every session.

Another thing is that, even though you're sitting there in this glass box and the musicians are out there setting up their horn or guitar amp, you have to participate as much as you can, especially seeing as how you weren't at their house yesterday when they were having rehearsals, and you weren't with them a year ago when they wrote the song.

> *"Getting a line to their purpose is the most important thing in all cases: understand what it is the artist wants to convey."*

So getting a line to their purpose is the most important thing in all cases: understand what it is the artist wants to convey. Sometimes they don't even know what it is because it's the first time they're hearing it. When you do a film, they may have done a piano demo or a home synth demo, but now you've got a hundred guys out in the studio and it's the first time the director and the composer and conductor are really hearing it. And they're all trying to massage it, so it has to be represented through the speakers in some kind of appropriate fashion so that they can make their last-minute changes.

The beginnings of all my sessions have to be that way. For Broadway shows, I always go to the show beforehand to get a sense of it, because, when I'm actually working on it, I'm not interested in the sense of what they're doing—the end result is ultimately the important thing. At the end, you may go, "Oh, that was cool, the way they got from here to there," but while you're in it you're looking through this slot in the fence and all you see are just the little things: the cat may be walking by but you just see the little tail going by—you don't really notice the whole cat. It doesn't really help me to have the storyline unless I know that I'm going to have to make some major changes in my engineering at some point down the road in order to under-line that change. It's the sensibility of trying to communicate.

Music is, after all, the most natural communicator: your body vibrates with every note that you hear. There are some rooms that just piss me off—I cannot stay there. It's not just that it's tinny, or too loud—it's that the structure of the room causes the bones in my body to vibrate a certain way. Other rooms allow me to express certain things that I can't express elsewhere. My studio, like a lot of professional rooms, seems to be able to do that very thing. You can walk in from an outside environment and find that spot, that zone that lets you say what you want to say through your art. And that's part of the craft that I was practicing back when I was drummer: being supportive of the creative process.

In terms of the approaches to different kinds of sessions, there used to be a standard Broadway show approach, but it's changed now because the union requirements have eased—you don't have to have the same amount of guys, and they're letting in more synthesizers, so you can really go to an ethereal space without too much trouble.

If you've got very limited time to get sounds together during the initial stages of a session, does that mean you need to spend extra time in the mix stage to achieve the optimum results?

You can't really do much else. But all a mix session is for me is taking out all the shit that doesn't sound like what the writer or artist or really meant. It may be as grievous as somebody kicking a microphone stand during a take—you've got to get it out of there.

But aren't you also adjusting the sounds when you're mixing?

Absolutely. But the more I know the sounds, the more I find I'm just removing the things that I interpret as being less important to a less meaningful position in the mix. That doesn't necessarily mean softer, either.

But the fact of the matter is that I can get something usable in my room in the first minute and a half. And the longer you're in this business and the more experience you have, the more difficult the projects are that are being offered to you. For years, there were people shipping me tapes, saying, "Do something with this, doctor." They called me "doctor!" [*laughs*]

Do a lot of those tapes originate in home studios? If so, what kinds of problems do you commonly hear?

I personally don't get that many tapes from home studios. I'll get live concert recordings, the kinds of projects where there are just misinterpretations and inability to get it happening on the spot because they're high-pressure situations.

But in the home recordings I do get, the problems mostly come from things not going together. The recordist may not have more than one mic preamp, or they're recording everything in the same shitty space in their basement or kitchen. Or they may have a good preamp and a good mic, but may not understand basic things like mic polar patterns—leaving a mic on figure-of-eight all the time, stuff like that. Or they do a piano overdub and don't bother tuning it beforehand.

When people come into a professional environment—whether it's in the studio or on a concert stage—they get fired up because they know that at 11 o'clock, their shit has to be together. But when they're home . . . well, it's good that they can get into their own head and their own groove—and I'm not saying that one necessarily needs the reference point of an engineer—but there is something to be said for having guidance. Even just talking technically, you can go down a path by yourself and lead yourself astray. Most people now are used to 44.1 and the crunchy, skinny 16-bit sound. But there are guys who can make you cry with their abilities as engineers and producers—we're talking about the kind of guy where you would say, "Oh my God, I had no idea that 40 voices could sound like that," or "I never heard a guitar that way before." And then there are people who do exactly the opposite, but even for them I think that going into a professional studio makes a big difference. It can serve as a confluence of the energy to get the project off the ground in a way that can't happen at home; being in the studio itself can become an experience, like a performance.

I know that a lot of people work experimentally—they say, "Well, let's try this, let's try that," especially in their homes and in front of their computers. But when you come into a studio there should be a good idea of how it's supposed to be, and the point becomes just how well you can execute it. And that just entices everybody to come single-mindedly to the job at hand, whether it's an orchestral session or a rock 'n' roll song.

So you see the value of the home studio as a testing ground or as a composing environment.

Absolutely as a composing environment. As far as testing, trying things out . . . well, unfortunately, a lot of the things that I hear on the radio seem to represent two opposites of the same question: how much can I sound like Britney Spears, and how little can I sound like Britney Spears? [*laughs*] That whole idea that you've got to conform to certain standards of rhythm tracks and drum sounds.

You were talking earlier about the idea that sometimes technically bad sounds get immortalized as becoming fashionable; they can even become the standard that people aspire to. You cited the first Led Zeppelin album as having become the standard for heavy metal, for example. As an engineer who is being paid by a record company to deliver a finished product, how do you break that mold?

I don't know that I would. I would protect and defend and enforce the worst garbage anybody would want to put out, if that's what they wanted. If I really thought it was terrible, I'd get myself fired! [*laughs*] But my job is to make it be what it's supposed to be, and I may not be the one to decide what that is. In a lot of cases, I do, but the point is to say what the artist is trying to say. I'm surprised sometimes at the mastering engineer that people have chosen after I do a record, because he or she may not seem to match what it was that we've been doing all along. For example, I've worked on records where I did not use a single limiter or compressor, and they bring it to somebody, and the first thing he does is limit it or compress it: "First I'm going to bring it down about 40 dB so there's no dynamic range whatsoever." So did I misinterpret, or did they misinterpret? I have to do some soul-searching at that point, because I'm always trying to do the right thing; I'm always trying to do what the music is saying to me.

> *"Unfortunately, a lot of the things that I hear on the radio seem to represent two opposites of the same question: how much can I sound like Britney Spears, and how little can I sound like Britney Spears?"*

In terms of benchmarks and standards, there are levels of quality set over the last 50 years that should be maintained. What's a good vocal sound? Do I try to determine the best vocal sound by listening to ten current records, trying to use them as a guide? Technically, absolutely I could do that on every record, but what does it mean to hear a skinny little razor voice, or the drummer not knowing how to tune his toms? Maybe they played bad-sounding tom-toms really well! So for me, the standard is to not distract from the meaning of the song. I think the necessity for doing the right thing exceeds even being embarrassed to have your name put on something because you had to screw it up by the measurement of your personal standards.

Given the rise of home recording and the power of what people can do in their own studios, do you think the professional studio is still relevant?

I don't think home recording has hurt my business as much as the state of the economy and those kinds of things, because 90 percent of the work we do is people-oriented. My space is about air and architecture and performance, interplaying with other people so that everybody can hear the final unitized product, and that's what we've always done best. That's what Clinton was designed for—to capture live performance, from five-piece bashing rock 'n' roll to Broadway shows to operas to classical music. Whatever the type of music, it's about being in the same space at the same time, and that's not something that people do at home.

The thing that I am attracted to most—the kind of business that I always was involved in—is the presentation and evolution of a performance to make a point. When you're doing a recording track by track, you're doing overdubs, punch-ins, manipulations, fixes, pitch fixes, time shifting. You may know what you're trying to get to, and you can eventually get there, but you may have to wait a week, or three days, or 19 hours to find out. But the second a live performance starts in a studio, you get to hear the whole thing, and then you can tell more and more what it's supposed to be.

People who haven't been in a studio before often misuse it; they have certain requirements that don't take into account the unitized outcome. They'll isolate people and separate people just so they have more control, but that's not what it's about. My attitude is that you should be able to capture the entire performance with one microphone, and everything after that is for safety. I really want to hear everything in my center orchestral mic! Sure, I'll also put mics on either side of the conductor, and use spot mics so I have some control, but not for isolation.

You can put glue on a recording track by track and then stick it all together to make a house of cards, but when you're recording everything at once in the same air at the same time, you create an oak tree—a solid thing that has depth and dimension and is right there to see and enjoy immediately.

You're talking about a sound being organic, as opposed to manufactured or artificial.

I'm talking about air moving, and the interplay of the same air moving with two different instruments in it. Play a tuba and you've got to have a microphone with a capsule 15 feet long to actually hear what a tuba is doing. But then have a piccolo player sitting in the middle of that waveform, poking little holes in it, and then have a gran casa coming underneath it, pushing it up above, and you get my point.

It's certainly not the same thing if you're playing a sample of a tuba along with a sample of a piccolo. There are experts and artists out there who can get great sounds and create great samples, but it's not the same as playing all those sounds through a speaker system into one air as it is playing back something that was originally recorded in one air environment.

That's because there are interharmonic relationships and resonances, and the magic is to capture that—and that's so old-school! Everybody now reads about it, but doesn't experience it. There are guys who still work every day, seven days a week, doing that same thing incredibly well, and they're going to hang on for some period of time. But at this point in time, I believe it's starting to become a novelty. The new people coming into the record industry—even the new guys in the film business—walk into my room and say, "God, what Martian place did this come from?" It may be a reflection of our times, but I've called my studio a white elephant twice before—once in the disco era, and once when electronics started coming out—and I was wrong both times. I still remember the first time I saw a drum machine sitting on a table—the producer walked over, put his arm around it, and said, "Hey, c'mon, let's go out for a drink!" He really pointed his finger at the change that was coming. But we survived that era, and we'll survive this one too, because there's always a need for expertise and talent.

Suggested Listening:
Original Cast Recording: *Movin' Out*, Sony, 2002
Duke Ellington Orchestra: *Digital Duke*, GRP, 1987
Ornette Coleman: *In All Languages*, Caravan of Dreams, 1987
Michael Feinstein: *Only One Life*, Concord Jazz, 2003
Mingus Big Band 93: *Nostalgia in Times Square*, Dreyfus, 1993

Don Gehman

From a Cougar to a Hootie

*I*n the sometimes fickle, always fashion-conscious music business, it's not easy to sustain a successful career over more than three decades. But Don Gehman has done just that, ranging from his early production work with Stephen Stills to a long collaboration with John Mellencamp (Gehman produced his massive hit "Jack and Diane" back when the artist was still known as "John Cougar") to Brian Setzer's 1985 solo debut *The Knife Feels Like Justice* to three albums with R.E.M., including their superb 1986 offering *Life's Rich Pageant.* In the mid-'90s, Gehman struck gold—or, more correctly, multiplatinum—once again as he steered a band with the unlikely name of Hootie and the Blowfish to stardom, producing their monster debut album *Cracked Rear View*, home to singalong bar faves "Hold My Hand" and "Only Wanna Be With You."

Gehman got into record production via an unusual route—he began as a live sound engineer in the '70s, slogging on the road for Claire Brothers for more than half a decade. It proved to be quite an education, as he manned the FOH board for pretty much every major artist of the era—groups like the Four Seasons; the Supremes; the Four Tops; the Temptations; James Brown; Loggins and Messina; Chicago; Blood, Sweat, and Tears; and Crosby, Stills, Nash, and Young. It was the latter connection that finally got a burned-out Gehman off the road and into the relative comfort of the recording studio, where he found himself named as co-producer on Stills' 1976 solo album *Illegal Stills.* A stint at Miami's Criteria Studios followed, and in 1980 he hooked up with John Mellencamp. The rest, as they say in cheap novels, is history.

Not content to rest on his heels following the Hootie phenomenon, Gehman has continued to work with a wide variety of musicians, bringing his unique heartland sensibilities and ear for sonic perfection to records by Blues Traveler, Better Than Ezra, Bruce Hornsby, Nanci Griffith, and Tracy Chapman. In the late '90s, Gehman assumed a new role: that of label head, hooking up with MCA to launch Refuge Records, where he develops new artists in engineering, production, and executive producer capacities. We met with the soft-spoken yet quietly confident Gehman at Refuge's LA offices to talk about his singular approach towards crafting hits.

How have your production techniques changed since you first got into this business?

Well, I've bought a Pro Tools rig, so I've certainly embraced the new methods that people are using to record, but I'm still using a lot of old equipment to do it. Because I'm not using a tape machine any more, I'm really relying on the microphones, the compressors, and the equalizers as having a lot of color.

You don't miss tape?

Not at all. Using plug-ins, I've found ways to get a lot of the same stuff that I was used to. It's mostly in the way you master, the way that you limit so that you get rid of all those little peaks, but without the hiss. That's the hard thing to do, because with look-ahead limiting, which is what most of these things are, it's not the same sound as something that doesn't know what was coming, which is what tape was: reactive.

You know, this whole analog/digital argument is not as big of a deal as it used to be—I think it still comes down to picking the right microphone for the right job. But I've misrecorded so many things that you can fix in Pro Tools—it's a very, very powerful medium.

Is your approach still to get a bunch of musicians together that can really play, do intensive pre-production and get the arrangements right, and then get most of the magic from the tracking session?

Pretty much, yeah. I don't make very many records that use drum machines and build up from the bottom.

So you're not doing a lot of copying and pasting in Pro Tools?

Oh, yeah, I do. But I wouldn't say that it's for perfection—I'm probably just as sloppy as I ever was! [*laughs*] I'll copy parts from one chorus to the next, and I use what I call the horizontal editing capabilities that you have with Pro Tools, where you're able to time-compress and stretch things to make things fit.

What's your approach towards recording guitars?

I've been using the Amp Farm plug-in a lot. In fact, these days, I sometimes don't use any amps at all. The advantage there is that it's something that's repeatable. You don't necessarily have to record the sound—you can record a DI and effect it differently way later. You need a lot of DSP power to do that, but if you're dealing with multiple guitar tracks, I find Amp Farm is totally satisfactory, to the point where I don't know that using a real amp would really be advantageous.

But when you were using real amps, how did you mic them?

Usually I would record a guitar amp with a [Neumann U] 67 and a [Shure SM]57 right next to each other and then go through a Fairchild [compressor].

Do you use Fairchilds on drums as well?

I've used them on the room tracks—put five or six mics together and compress them real hard with a Fairchild. I also use it on pianos, sometimes guitars, sometimes vocals.

What's your typical vocal chain?

Lately I've been using the Manley Voxbox. It's got everything in there: a de-esser, a compressor, a limiter and an equalizer, and a front end—just plug the mic in. I usually use [Neumann] U 67s, sometime the [Manley] Gold Ref, sometimes the Manley [Reference] cardioid—those are probably my three favorite mics.

Have you ever found that a condenser mic wasn't as effective as a dynamic on vocals?

Yeah, occasionally, with somebody who's got a very odd voice, somebody who doesn't have a full voice. Sometimes there are just too many harmonics and sidebands, and you have to limit it, which dynamic mics do well.

Do you use Pro Tools for comping vocals?

I don't like that—it's not much fun. No, I have the artist sing it until it sounds right, so I'm essentially comping while I'm recording. I might let the vocalist sing the song down two or three times and then pick the best track, or realize that the choruses are best on this track and the verses still need work, but not, "Let's do ten tracks and then go home and I'll put it together syllable by syllable." I know you can do that, but I'm not prepared to invest the time doing that.

PHOTO COURTESY OF DON GEHMAN

Do you typically record guide vocals as you're tracking?

I do, but I don't find that I use many of them.

So the purpose is basically to provide the vibe?

Yeah, to make sure everybody knows where they're at. The process of making a record often means that the way the musicians have been playing it isn't is the way it's going to wind up, so it isn't so much the magic of the moment. There are no rules to this—I've done it so many different ways. Actually, that's the first rule: there are no rules. [*laughs*]

What medium do you mix to?

I mix inside of Pro Tools. I've completely given up all forms of analog mixing.

Is that just for convenience?

For convenience. Being able to recall in five minutes, being able to work on ten mixes a day that are left the way you left them the night before. To be able to get close to something on each song, have perspective. To only work 5-hour days instead of 12-hour days. And the most obvious one, of course, is that I think it sounds better. It's a more powerful medium—you can dig stuff out a lot better, with fewer phase problems.

I also appreciate the fact that you can mix with the mastering chain in place. I master my own records now, too, so what I've done is to build up templates, which are basically a way to lay out the song so that things just kind of fit in with everything already plugged up, with the kind of EQ and compression that I like, and maybe the 'verbs that are associated with drums, and the ones associated with vocals, etcetera. Everything's grouped together and has group limiting. And then I can master it as well with three or four sets of limiters and equalizers and de-essers. So you're always listening to the mix as loud as you can get it on the disk and squeezed up, like you would from a mastering engineer's perspective.

It sounds like, apart from going to Pro Tools instead of tape, you're still taking the same basic approach to making records.

The changes that have happened to me over the past few years are more because of the fact that I own a record label and I sign bands, so I'm seeing a bigger picture as a result. It has maybe made me more impatient with some of the recording process and some of the preciousness that the artist has towards his work.

How so?

Well, the reality of the situation as far as marketing and getting a band on the radio, having success, has become more and more immediate. Our marketplace doesn't allow for second chances or development or, "Let's make three records and see how things go." There's just no time or resources for doing that. But the purpose of making a record is to make something that is artistically and creatively unique to the marketplace, and then also come up with a hit that you can sell it with. Anybody who's not prescribing to that reality is just spinning their wheels.

But making a great record and making a hit record are not necessarily the same, are they?

Oh, yeah. Absolutely, in my mind. Because great records are all hits.

But haven't there been great records that weren't hits?

Well, they're hits now—we don't know records that aren't great. I'm not particularly interested in it, from a pure "Let's make a great record" perspective. I have lots of great records that I've made that I don't find very rewarding looking back on, because they weren't successful.

So commercial success is really the ultimate arbiter.

Very much so. I don't know very many happy musicians who are out of work; everyone who is a musician wants to be able to live off their work. I rest my case right there. So if you don't have some level of commercial success, either with a fan base, live performance, or a recording on the radio, you're not there. Most of the people I know would like to make a living at what they do—that would be the ultimate. And it's the rare musician who can make a living for his whole life off of his work. There are a lot of sad musicians out there, a lot of frustrated musicians out there.

> *"I don't know very many happy musicians who are out of work."*

Is that basically what you look for when you're about to sign a band to your label? A band that's already done the track work, built up the local fan base, and already hit the pavements and proven themselves?

Yeah. We call it "crossing the street." They've already done a lot of work. That shows that, one, they're capable of doing a lot of work, and, two, that they've already got some fans that we can use as a test market, to show that it can be exploded into a larger market.

Do you feel your experience as a live sound engineer gave you a different perspective on record production?

It gave me a sense of immediacy. Because it's a live show, you realize that you have only this moment to get it as right as you can, and make the experience work for everybody. You gain that sense of having to react to what's happening right now. And, of course, the work ethic of living on the road is very hard, so you have to be disciplined.

Many of your records sound bigger than life. Do you think that might be because you were used to working in stadiums?

I don't know. I definitely like big sounds, but I like my records to be rich, even more than big. But I know what you're saying—I definitely like to double things and use slap echoes.

Do you get very involved in the musical, as opposed to the technical, aspects of production?

I don't get involved with songwriting, but I certainly do with the arrangement of a song. I want the song to complete that cathartic thing that I think is so important. When you have a song arranged correctly, it should really feel like it's taking you through something.

Do you still do a lot of your own engineering?

I'm very involved in what kind of mics are used, how we mic things and tune the instruments and the drums, how the EQs are set up. I still do all that, as well as being totally involved in how the mixes are done.

Do you find it hard to wear both hats?

I don't think so; I think it's actually ideal, because there's a lot of lost focus when there are two separate camps. If you're a producer and you don't understand engineering, I don't know how you can make a record, unless you're working with somebody who's just got such a clear vision of what they do. But then the problem is that you might have your own vision of it and if they didn't realize it, you'd be at the mercy of this other person. So for me, I've always found that it's really easy; I don't have to tell anybody—I don't even have to tell the band. I can just go down this road in my mind, and you can manipulate things very much behind the scenes without anybody knowing that anything is going on. It keeps things quieter—there's not as much babbling going on about this and that—and it keeps the stress level down.

Do you pre-visualize or, more accurately, pre-auralize, most records that you make? Are you always working towards a goal that you have in mind?

Definitely. That's the way I work.

Where does that leave room for spontaneity and creative accidents?

That's exactly what it is—I'm usually looking at the accidents. I'm trying to have my focus be in what I'm experiencing, but occasionally things happen that I didn't expect. What made that happen? That's fine, cool, it's done. I accept it.

How do you encourage artists to go down a different road and try different things?

Producers have many means of doing this, from intimidation to stroking, and we use them all, depending on the person and what the moment needs.

But are you trying to move them towards realizing your vision, or are you trying to move them towards going out on a limb and trying new things that you haven't thought of?

Some of both, because I certainly look at it as a collaborative effort. I don't sign bands that don't have any concept of what they want to do; it's too much work. The thing that's fun about making records is this family that you create. You kind of take everyone's talent, and then my job just becomes filling in the absent spots. I let the band take as much of it as possible, because they have to sell it. So you're looking for their strengths, and propping them up with, "Wow, you do that really well! I've never heard anybody do that—you should do that more, do it on all the songs." That kind of process. Pull out all the best things and make them much bigger than they ever thought they were going to be. Then you look at it and say, "It still doesn't groove, we're going to have to put a drum machine in it," or whatever.

You've said in previous interviews that prior to your experience working with R.E.M., you'd been more of a controlled producer, that they kind of freed you up.

They did. They get all the credit. [*laughs*] They get the credit for making me realize that you have to be more Zen about it. And it was a good lesson; it was certainly a turning point for me.

Is that basically the same approach that you take today?

Absolutely. It's the only one that works. You never really know where it's going to go, but I think you have to have a plan, so that you keep things disciplined. You've got to say, "Okay, I've got to make the best of the time that's been allotted." Focus and prioritize.

How do you think the rise of the home studio has impacted on the way the record industry is changing?

Oh, it's changing everything completely. It's made it more of a mixer's market, because you've got a lot of people that are producing records that are poorly recorded but maybe are pretty good songs; they just need someone to straighten them out. I'm seeing a lot of that.

Can a poorly recorded song really be straightened out in a mix?

Definitely. If it's a good song, it doesn't matter.

But if it's a good song, maybe it deserves to be better recorded in the first place.

Well, nobody minded Alanis Morisette. That album [*Jagged Little Pill*] was low-fi, and it was most suited to that. Or take any record by the Rolling Stones. They're very low-fi, but we all think it's warm and accessible. There's a lot to be said for that.

I guess that's the indefinable thing about record production—that's the mojo.

Yep. So I think that the fact that everyone can do that now means that when a great song comes along, it might actually be best suited to be just that way. You still have to do the work to master it right, so it gets loud on the CD and the radio compressors don't mess it up; sometimes that means remixing it.

You've been in this business for more than 30 years. With the benefit of 20/20 hindsight, what was the biggest mistake you've made?

Probably not doing the next R.E.M. record! [*laughs*] There have been other records that I've turned down that certainly would have made me more wealthy had I done them. The R.E.M. record was one—I already had my foot in the door and I had a good working relationship with them but I walked away from it, and I shouldn't have.

On the flip side, what was the best decision you've made?

Starting a little record label was wonderful. It was time to do something different, and start a family.

What kind of advice can you offer to someone who wants to be the next Don Gehman?

"If you really love doing this, just take every opportunity that comes your way and do the best that you can."

If you really love doing this, just take every opportunity that comes your way and do the best that you can. Sooner or later, you'll get everything out of it that you ever wanted. I think there are so many people in this business that are a little impatient, and are hungry for results, as we all are. But just do whatever you can. That means that you'll be prepared when your chance comes along, and you can really take advantage of it. So, basically, stick to it.

Suggested Listening:
John (Cougar) Mellencamp: *American Fool*, Mercury, 1982; *Scarecrow*, Mercury, 1985
Hootie and the Blowfish: *Cracked Rear View*, Atlantic, 1994
R.E.M.: *Life's Rich Pageant*, IRS, 1986
Jason Michael Carroll: *Waitin' in the Country*, Arista Nashville, 2007
Stephen Stills: *Illegal Stills*, Columbia, 1976
Blues Traveler: *Truth Be Told*, Sanctuary, 2003

Jim Scott

Attention to Detail

How many people can claim that they once quit their job and got promoted at the same time?

Jim Scott can.

Scott had been assisting for several years at Los Angeles' famed Record Plant, and had risen to the top of those ranks when he decided to ask for a raise. Not a big raise, mind you—a lousy 25-cent-an-hour raise.

To his astonishment, then-studio owner Chris Stone turned him down flat. "He just said, 'I'm sorry, but that's top of the scale for your position,'" Scott relates. "Chris told me I could stay if I wanted, but he couldn't pay me any more money."

"At that point, I was tired and a little bit insulted too," he remembers. "Beyond the extra quarter an hour, I was looking for a little recognition; I just wanted to feel a little better about all the hard work I'd done. So I said, 'Well, I'm sorry too, but I guess this will have to serve as my notice.' Chris's reply surprised me even more. Without hesitation, he said, "That's great! *Now* you're a recording engineer. And now you can go out there and bring in clients."

The route Scott took to get to that point was anything but conventional. Born in Missouri, he had relocated to Los Angeles as a college student, attending USC and graduating with a degree in geology, of all things. He spent the next six years doing earthquake studies and writing reports for housing tract and shopping center developers, but he never lost the interest in music that had begun during his teenage years, when he played drums and did live sound for local bands.

In 1979 Scott made the fateful decision to abandon his well-paying job and applied for a minimum-wage runner position—the very bottom of the totem pole—at the Record Plant. He was nearly 30 at the time, and it took some doing to convince a skeptical Chris Stone. "He said, "I know guys like you; you're having a little bit of a mid-life crisis and you want to rock 'n' roll, and you're going to work for me for six months and then you're going to want your old life back and you're going to go," Scott recalls.

But he landed the gig, and used his time wisely, racking up thousands of hours both in the studio and on the Plant's mobile truck. After that fateful meeting in which he was simultaneously relieved of his duties as assistant engineer and promoted to the rank of full engineer (albeit freelance), things began exploding for Scott. An opportunity to work on the *Synchronicity* concert film for The Police led to an invitation to record Sting's first solo album, which in turn netted him a Grammy nomination for Best Engineered Record. Several years later, Scott won the coveted award for his work on Tom Petty's *Wildflowers*. His impressive discography also includes work with an astonishingly diverse group of artists: everyone from the Rolling Stones to the Red Hot Chili Peppers to the Foo Fighters, Weezer, Wilco, John Fogerty, Santana, the Dixie Chicks, Tift Merritt, and Johnny Cash. We met up with him at his new facility, PLYRZ Studios—a converted warehouse some 20 miles north of LA, which houses an impressive array of vintage recording gear, drum kits, guitar amplifiers, and Elvis posters.

You've done far more engineering and mixing than production over the years. Is that by choice?

Well, I never really thought of myself as a producer, to be honest. My goal was always to be a recording engineer, and as luck would have it, it took me less than five years to achieve that goal, from the time I first walked in the door at the Record Plant. These days, I produce perhaps one or two records a year.

Looking back on your career, what do you feel was the pivotal moment?

Getting that first job. Even though I wasn't the younger guy they wanted, I had the energy and the time to start over, even at an older age, so it worked out. To be honest, being older than all my contemporaries was a real advantage; it gave me that little touch of authority. But the graduating class from the Record Plant from the years I was there includes a lot of really spectacular and talented recording engineers—people like Dave Bianco and Mike Clink—and a lot of them are still in the business today. You've got to chalk it up to the training we had, because it does make a difference. If you know how to handle a session better than the next guy, you'll keep working. I don't think anybody automatically knows these things; you just need to have all kinds of experiences. That experience is what trains you to pay attention to detail in the work that goes into making a record.

It's not easy, either. You can't forget somebody's sandwich when you bring the food in, and you can't forget where that good guitar solo or good vocal take is—it's really very much the same thing. Somehow in your mind you've got to know where the good stuff is; otherwise it's just a bottomless pit of indecision. That's why, as a studio owner, I make sure there are light bulbs in all the light fixtures, and sharpened pencils in a jar by the producer's desk. It's as detail-oriented as that, because if someone reaches for a pencil and it's broken, it can break the creative flow. I know it sounds silly, but it's not—you just want everyone to be able to focus on making music, with nothing disturbing the flow and no distractions. If you ask for a cup of coffee with sugar, that's what you want to have. You don't want it to arrive cold, or without sugar, or be forgotten altogether, because that's a distraction.

From my very first day as runner, I was constantly being told by the guy who was training me, "This is the way you do something, and if you do it any other way, you're going to get fired." After every sentence, the guy added the words, "you're going to get fired." As in, "If you move somebody's stuff out of the way, you're going to get fired. But if you don't neaten things up, you're going to get fired." You just had to be in the flow, you had to know right from wrong, good from bad, all according to their very strict rules. I've seen that at a lot of studios, and it's a good thing, because it teaches you discipline and attention to detail.

I guess it's just very important for me to be efficient. If you're making a CD for a client to listen to at the end of a session, for example, it's very important to actually listen to it before putting it in the sleeve and handing it to him. I'm not saying you have to listen to every track all the way through, but you certainly have to listen to the first few seconds of every track to make sure they've actually been recorded. If the client gets into his car at the end of the night and pops the CD in and there's nothing on there, he's going to be pissed, and he's not going to feel good about working in that studio: nobody wants to be discover they've been given a blank CD when they're ready to listen to their work on the drive home. That's the kind of detail I'm talking about, and it's really just a matter of developing good habits. When you're driving, you need to get in the habit of checking before you change lanes; similarly, when you're making records, there are lots of blind spots—a lot of places where you can mess up—and the more prepared you are, the better the final product is likely to be.

> **"The more prepared you are, the better the final product is likely to be."**

I also try to constantly be aware of how things are going, for everyone—not just for me. Is everyone having fun, is everyone doing their best work? Where are they in their process? Are they tired, or are they ready to go? Maybe the vocalist doesn't actually wake up until after midnight, and so we're going to get a great vocal in about 15 minutes... or are we done at 12:30? When am I going to get that vocal? Now? Tomorrow morning? Later on? Those are the things you have to pick up on.

So you're saying a big part of the job is being able to read the situation.

Absolutely. And I've had to protect myself a few times, where I've had to tell a client, "You know what, fellows, I can't help you anymore; I'm done." I've gotten to that point, but it takes a long time because I have a lot of patience. It can actually help people sometimes in the decision-making process if you put them up against a wall like that. If there are a hundred choices, well, let's at least narrow it down to 50. Then we'll narrow it down to 25.

There can be such a fine line between expressing your honest opinion and hurting people's feelings, but I've found that more often than not it comes as a relief when I tell musicians, "You know, this really is not working. We're way off the mark; we're a million miles away: let's stop and think about this for a minute." When you actually get to that point, everybody relaxes because they know you're right; they can feel that it's not happening too—they're just waiting for someone to say it. Especially the older, more experienced guys; they're more on top of things and more prepared to go in a different direction when things aren't working. It's the younger guys that sometimes have a problem with that, and I've found that the hardest records to make are the ones I make with the younger, least experienced people. That's because you have to teach them how to make records... as well as make the record. People that have more experience—even though they may be set in their ways, and even though you may have to show them more respect because of their stature—when they have something, they really have something. You just get out of the way and let them do it.

Have you encountered any young artists who have been the exception to that rule?

Yes, I have, but it's a sad story. Several years ago I worked with a young girl named Shelby Starner. She was 16 years old, signed to Warner Bros. She'd made one record when she was just 14 which I wasn't involved with and we were making the follow-up, and even at 16 years old, she was amazing. She was brave, she was powerful, she knew how to sing with headphones on, she sang in pitch, she looked great, the whole nine yards. But unfortunately she died when she was just 19 because she had an eating disorder. Out of all the young artists I've worked with, she was the most spectacular: a great, great artist. Just a kid, but a real pro.

When you were an assistant at the Record Plant, were there certain engineers that took you under their wing?

Yes, there were. After my first year there, I got promoted to their remote recording department, and I did a lot of my training on the trucks. But during the year I was an assistant, there were three big influences: Lee DeCarlo, Andy Johns, and Ron Nevison. In many ways, my setup is a combination of all of their setups. I'd just go and stand in front of the drums and study their

setup, and just the way they put the stands up was beautiful—everything was symmetrical and neat; there was no chaos.

Of course I'd make note of the mics they'd use too—one of the great things about the Record Plant was that they had all these great mics, old tube mics, pretty much anything you would covet, and they had a room full of them. Not too many studios have that kind of inventory, even today.

Lee DeCarlo taught me about handling people in the room. He was great with a story, and he always knew where he was in the music; in his head, he'd always be counting beats and bars and he'd keep a list of things to fix in his head. He never wrote anything down, either—he'd just start rattling things off in the middle of a session, and I'd have to remember them all. I found that it's not all that hard to do—you can remember five things at once if you just concentrate.

Andy was different. He was an Englishman and had a whole other take on things. With Andy, I remember that things would be going along sort of okay, but when it was time to make something happen, it would go from nothing to "This sounds amazing" in like two takes. If he was doing a mix, in 15 minutes it would go from "What is this?" to "Oh my gosh." He'd just jump on a board and be flying around it, moving everything at once with both hands, adjusting outboard gear and mixing all at the same time, and suddenly it would sound amazing. With another engineer, you might have put in ten hours before you got to that point, so the way he got there so quickly was really impressive. We'd all be saying, "What happened? How did he do that?"

Ron was a great guy, and he was probably the most professional and the most organized of all the engineers there. He was a great record-maker, and he really made popular hit records; he put big hits on the radio, and not always with bands that were that easy to work with.

John Boylan was another very talented producer who was always very nice to me. If you were in the hallway and he spotted you, he'd let you come in and see what was going on. He was just awesome; he got great sounds. He said to me once, "Sloppy records are made in sloppy studios" and that stayed with me a long time. The Record Plant studios, of course, were never sloppy because they were cleaned 24 hours a day by a staff of kids with rags and Windex bottles. But I know what he means: when things get chaotic—you don't know where your notes are, your guitars are in disrepair, the light bulbs are burnt out—if you're struggling to keep up, things won't be as good as when you're on top of your game, when you're more prepared.

How did your experiences on the live truck influence your training?

Well, you had to check a lot of stuff because you don't always get a second chance when you're doing live recording. The Record Plant would send out three guys: two drivers, one of whom would be the in-the-truck assistant, and the other one would be the onstage emergency-repair, dive-for-the-microphone guy. In addition, one of the maintenance engineers would fly in to the gig, as well as the client's own engineer. So we always had a lot of people in the truck, and some of them would be great recording engineers with a lot of experience. But the hours were brutal: loading in early in the morning and getting everything set for the day and then doing a sound check in the afternoon, then doing the gig itself and breaking it all down afterwards, then driving to the next city for the next show. It was really hard work—a lot of days it was around the clock, and that got to be my routine. And a lot of those bands back in the eighties had a lot of musicians onstage and a lot of instruments, so you'd regularly run 60 lines or more. Between getting a drum sound and balancing the sound of all the keyboards, it was a lot to keep track of, not to mention the fact that gigs sometimes got broadcast live too. There were no DATs or CDs in those days, either, so you'd be running a two-track machine constantly to capture the monitor mix, and you'd have to make sure the tape didn't run out, so you'd be dashing around changing reels between songs. . . .

You didn't have a second two-track for overlapping?

No, there wasn't room because we had two 24-tracks in the truck for overlapping and lots of outboard racks. We had to treat everything as if it was the master take, and of course the preference was to give the client complete tapes without edits, so you tried to time things correctly—you had to know how long each song in the set was, and to be prepared for the band possibly playing longer versions on the fly. We'd be doing reel changes every ten minutes or so, humping tape, writing labels—there was a lot of bookkeeping to do, not to mention listening and troubleshooting. After a while you got to be able to recognize the sound of different buzzes and hums. You got to know which hum was a bad mic cable, which one was a ground loop in the bass DI, just by doing it night after night. It was a lot of pressure, but it was great fun.

In fact, it was so much fun that when I finally got into the studio, it actually was a bit boring, to be honest. Not only was there a lot less pressure, but you'd spend entire days just getting a drum sound and tuning tom-toms. It all seemed kind of slow to me, just punching in and punching out over and over again. After you do that a million times, you start getting good at punching . . . and you start getting good at making decisions, because we didn't have unlimited tracks. It was especially tough when you were being asked to erase something that you know was the best the guy's ever played it, and you know he's never going to play it that well again. But if he's saying, "Give me one more," you can't say no. You might say, "Wait a minute, dude: we've got to save this somewhere," or, "Let's listen to that before we start punching in on top of it." That old "give me another try" thing is great . . . up until a certain point.

I also found that the studio hours were a different kind of long. The remote truck was one kind of day, and I was super-physically busy working the whole time—we were just running all the time, and it was total adrenaline and excitement. But in the studio it wasn't that way. It was still 4 a.m. before we got to go home, but I wasn't as physically exhausted, just more mentally drained.

What's the coolest recording trick you've learned through the years?

One of the tricks Lee DeCarlo taught me which I still use to this very day is to put the bass and drums through the same compressor. It's something The Beatles engineers used to do, too, way back when. Even if the bass and the drums aren't really playing together all that well, when you put them through the same compressor, they usually will, amazingly, actually glue together: you can feel it and hear it. That's an old, old trick, but I still use it and it still really works.

Your mixes are very recognizable in that they tend to be very dry and in your face. Is that purposeful?

Yes, it is. These days, I like both recording and mixing things really dry. It's become a no-place-to-hide style that I began developing years ago. I just wanted to hear things clearly, and I quickly got tired of big reverbs. We all went through the era of the big reverb; it coincided with the big hair era. Records from the eighties with too much reverb on them haven't aged well to me, no matter how good the playing or the songs are. I like all the components in the mix to be loud and clear and important. When I find an artist that can actually thrive and survive inside of that sound, and they get it, that's a real "a-ha" moment for me.

The fact is that you have to have a great drum sound out in the studio, not just in the control room. To me, everything has to work really dry. It's a lot harder to achieve, but those kinds of records just sound better to me.

Don't get me wrong: I'm not anti-effects. I do use reverbs and I do use slap echo and delay, but my attitude is that, first everything needs to sound really good unadorned. Then you can only make them better, no matter what you do to them after that.

In what order do you bring up the faders when you're doing a mix?

I approach mixing the same way that I approach tracking. On a tracking date you start by quickly going through all the drum channels to make sure all the signal is arriving and that nothing's broken, but the faster you get the drummer and the bass player and the piano player playing all together, the quicker you know what the drum sound really needs to be. Same thing when I mix: I start by working on the drum sound, but inside the overall music. If you go back and listen to the drums in solo, they might not sound all that great, but when you turn on the bass and the piano, it actually makes sense.

So I try to get all faders up as soon as possible, and balance and EQ everything inside the music. And even

> *"The faster you get the drummer and the bass player and the piano player playing all together, the quicker you know what the drum sound really needs to be."*

with all faders up and the whole thing playing, I find I can zero in on a specific sound as if it were soloed anyway. I can listen to the vocal and not hear the words, which is weird, but I can listen purely with the idea of getting the sound in the right place. Then, when you actually do pay attention to the lyrics, that's another kind of experience altogether.

Do you find that you work on individual instruments in any kind of order?

Like a lot of other guys, I tend to start in the engine room, with the bass and the drums. In five seconds I can know if the drum sound is on the good side of the line or the bad sign of the line. And if it's on the bad side of the line, it usually doesn't take all that long to fix it: just grab an equalizer, grab a compressor, do what you need to do and start mixing. Of course if it's completely unfixable, these days you can just substitute a new drum, using samples.

Next, I fill in the gaps around the side with the guitars and piano and percussion instruments and background vocals. It's all about balancing the rhythm section—the bottom of the record—against all the harmonic information on top of the record, and then the vocal goes right in between, really loud. I like *everything* loud, in fact. [*laughs*]

Do you ever pull all the faders down and start from scratch?

All the time. If a mix doesn't come together quickly, the best thing is to start over. It took me a long time to learn how to mix and I used to spend a full day or two on a mix, but those days seem to be disappearing because there isn't the budget anymore to go round and round with it. Usually, once you just get the balance right, people will like the final result.

Do you strap a stereo compressor across the bus when you're mixing?

Yes, I do. Depending on the music, I'll either use Neve 2254s, or an old pair of [UREI] 1176s... sometimes even both. Bear in mind that just because you're using compressors doesn't necessarily mean it's going to sound compressed. If you set the controls carefully, it just kind of glues the sound together so it sounds like a record. Using a compressor across the stereo bus also protects the input of Pro Tools a little bit from distorting because it's not as tough as a tape recorder. Hit the input of Pro Tools too hard and it really sounds bad. It's really not about hitting it hard, anyway; it's about filling it up so you use all the bits, and then you let the mastering engineer do the rest if it needs more level.

> *"If you put a good mic in front of something that already sounds pretty good and just get out of the way, the result will be pretty darn good."*

Do you ever use digital plug-ins?

For the most part, no, I don't use plug-ins. I will use a vocal tuner if it's necessary, and I'll occasionally slip in a sample, but for the most part I think of Pro Tools as just a really smart tape recorder.

What are the things a beginner can do to improve their recording technique?

Well, you can't just spend all your time fixing everything: it doesn't make for good music. So start by hiring the best musicians you can afford and then put the best microphone you've got in front of the best-sounding instrument. Trust me, if you put a good mic in front of something that already sounds pretty good and just get out of the way, the result will be pretty darn good. That approach will work whether you're working with a young band making their first album or an established band making their fifteenth album.

Try to remember too that the harder you have to work to get something above the line of acceptability, the more that means something's wrong. I've been practicing my craft for a long time now, and so I've developed lots of options available to me now that are tried and true. If the sound of a bass isn't happening, I've got three or four options that will fix it. And if we find ourselves going down to option number five, then I know that something is seriously wrong.

What are those three or four options you turn to, to fix a bass that isn't sounding right?

The most likely thing that would be wrong with a bass track would be distortion. If that's the case, you've got to round it out; bass is supposed to be round and sweet in the bottom anyway, as far as I'm concerned. So I'd use a compressor, or an equalizer, or both, to try to eliminate the fizzy, hazy, bad sound and add some low end and roundness to the bottom. Bass is usually the second countermelody, and so it should be strong and clear and sweet. When it comes to bass, dull is actually preferable to distorted and crispy.

If I couldn't achieve that using an equalizer and compressor, then I would re-amp it: I'd route it out of a bus and put the signal into a sweeter amp. Even if the signal itself is distorted, the sound of a new speaker and new air will definitely help. It's a matter of finding the sweet spot of the low end, whatever frequency that is, and accentuating it. Something's got to be at the bottom of the track, but it should always just be one thing, not two: either the bass guitar or the bass drum. One has got to be lower and bigger and louder than the other; they both can't be in the same exact space. So you need to decide which one sounds better and make that one the bottom. It's okay if it's the bass—it doesn't always have to be the bass drum. If it is the bass drum, then fine—just make sure the bass guitar sits above it. If you have to, use an equalizer to notch out certain frequencies, but I find it's mostly about levels and balancing. That's probably the biggest thing I've learned over the years. People tend to spend a lot of time fiddling with equalizers when they should probably instead just try to rebalance things.

Hopefully everything has got some kind of natural balance to it, and the quicker you get there, the better. Then you can start to carve things up and pump it up, fill in the gaps and fill in the frequencies that are deficient in some way. Even if the drum mics were kind of in the wrong place, it still should sound like drums and so it should be okay when balanced correctly...unless there's some horrendous, terrible recording technique being used. If you don't have a clue as to where to place the mics, at least look at a picture of a drum kit in a studio that's miked up to give you an idea where to start.

It comes back to listening to the whole mix at once. If you don't know what the song is, how can you just listen to the bass on its own and start EQing it? You need a lot more information. What are you EQing it in relationship to, and why? What's the groove? What kind of song is it? Country rock? Heavy metal? Is it fast? Is it slow? The idea should be to find the natural sound that fits the song and then fill it up. That's how I do things, anyway.

How would you summarize your overall approach to making records?

Well, most of the bands who gravitate to working with me tend to be rock bands with a sound of their own, so my job is basically to just hold a mirror up to them, only now they have a little makeup on and a new haircut, a new hat...and then hopefully they say, "Wow, that looks pretty good." And if you're working with a great band who are recording great songs, it really is like a day in the park: great music is happening, great sounds are happening, creativity is flowing, everybody's happy, love is in the air. Truthfully, that really is a fun way to spend the day.

Suggested Listening:
Tom Petty: *Wildflowers*, Warner Bros., 1994
John Fogerty: *Revival*, Fantasy, 2007
Sting: *Bring On the Night*, A&M, 1986
Red Hot Chili Peppers: *Californication*, Warner Bros., 1999
Weezer: *Make Believe*, Geffen, 2005

Jimmy Douglass

Hey, Either You Get It or You Don't

"**H**ey, either you get it or you don't."

After more than three decades in the business, producer/engineer/mixer Jimmy Douglass has found a way to condense his entire philosophy of record-making into those eight simple words. "That's kind of become my mantra, especially these days of recalls and changing and tweaking, pulling this up and that back," he says with a laugh. "I mean, either it's a good song or it isn't."

Douglass' no-nonsense approach and rapid-fire speech inflections reflect his New York background, but this is one cat who's been around the block a few times. His career began when he was just a high-school student; a friend of a friend got him in the door of Atlantic's famed in-house studio in midtown Manhattan, where he landed a job ostensibly making tape copies. But Douglass couldn't resist the intriguing sounds coming from the rooms down the hall, where industry legends like Jerry Wexler, Arif Mardin, and Tom Dowd were weaving their magic with artists like Aretha Franklin and the Young Rascals. Dowd in particular took the young Douglass under his wing, encouraging the young bass player's nascent abilities as a record producer.

As one of the perks of the job, Douglass was allowed to bring young artists in and record demos with them during the studio's downtime. Despite having limited success in getting them signed, his sonic abilities soon netted him a promotion to engineer, leading to gigs with many of the top acts of the '70s and '80s, including the Rolling Stones, Foreigner, Roxy Music, Hall and Oates, Bette Midler, Donny Hathaway, and Chaka Khan; Douglass also produced multiple albums for funk pioneers Slave.

In the mid-1990s, Douglass entered into an ongoing collaboration with producer Timbaland, with whom he has recorded and mixed a who's who of today's top R&B artists, including Missy Elliot, Jay-Z, Ludacris, Ginuwine, Jodeci, and, most recently, Justin Timberlake. In between busy sessions, he took time out to chat with us about his unique perspective on the past, present, and future of record-making.

You did a lot of record production early in your career before becoming known primarily as an engineer. More recently, though, you've returned to your production roots.

"I was always the guy that was producing everybody: I just didn't know that's what you called it."

Well, I was always the guy that was producing everybody: I just didn't know that's what you called it. Even when I was just a kid, playing in bands, I was always telling the other musicians what they could do to make things sound better. I used to find these artists that I wanted to work with, and after I had the job at Atlantic Studios, I was allowed to bring them in. When I asked who was going to record them, they said, "Well, you do it." In essence, the bands made me their engineer in order to get free studio time. I really wasn't one—I just had the good fortune to observe great engineers like Tom Dowd at work. Not that he would say, "Here's how you do it, kid." He'd just allow me to stand there and watch.

One of the first acts I brought in sounded just like Crosby, Stills, and Nash. When [Atlantic staff producer] Jerry Wexler heard the tape, his comment was, "They sound like CSN," and I got all excited. But then he pointed out that Atlantic already *had* CSN. [*laughs*] As a young kid, I didn't understand that concept: I thought that if something sounded like the hits I was hearing on the radio, the label would want to sign it.

There was never a producer on those sessions because nobody could afford to hire them, certainly not for a demo. So what would happen is that I would serve as the producer as well as engineer. The fact of the matter is that I really didn't care about sonics. I know a lot of engineers who are really meticulous about what they do, but that's not me. Most of the time, I was just scuffling to get the music down on tape. I didn't know anything about how to work a limiter, for example. When I was recording Aretha [Franklin] or Daryl [Hall], I'd just sit there and watch them, and when I saw that they were getting ready to hit a high note, I'd lower the fader and ride the gain; in effect, I was acting as a live limiter.

It sounds like you take the same basic approach whether you're acting as the mixer or engineer or producer.

Totally. In essence, my production comes from a mixing standpoint. In other words, what I can or cannot make happen is based solely on the parts that have been laid down. If they don't exist, I have to create new parts. Sometimes the best I can get from mixing the existing parts is not good enough because there's simply not enough to work with.

> *"In essence, my production comes from a mixing standpoint: what I can or cannot make happen is based solely on the parts that have been laid down."*

Do you feel that the role of the producer has changed drastically over the last thirty years?

To some degree. In the '70s, I was constantly asking Jerry Wexler to make me a staff producer. His reply was always the same: "Make a hit, and I'll make you a producer." I'd tell him, "Hey, if I could make a hit, I wouldn't need *you*." [*laughs*]

That hasn't changed. People think the record business is different now, but it's the same as it's ever been. But it wasn't an easy world—it was the same world as it is now, but with less technology, and with fewer people looking to break into the field.

Do you feel as if technology has gotten in the way of good music, or is it helping more good music to be realized?

It hasn't exactly gotten in the way, but it's facilitated a lot more mediocrity, because a lot more people that really have nothing to say can now get in there and say it. [*laughs*] It makes it harder to weed out what's really good from what's not good; it's easier to fool people now.

Lately, I've been looking for writers and singers on MySpace, and occasionally I'll find people there who are doing some pretty decent stuff. Just recently I invited someone I'd found there to fly down to my studio to do some writing with me. But when he got here I discovered that he could not even mimic a note I played on the piano, and I suddenly realized, "Holy shit, it's all due to Auto-Tune!" Of course: these days, just because you hear someone singing a part correctly does not mean they actually can sing. You simply can't tell that anymore; everyone's covering up a lack of talent with machinery. There are people who can't play, who don't have a freaking idea, but they quantize their parts, they do it a million times, they throw a dozen plug-ins over it, and then they call themselves producers. I'm not saying they shouldn't call themselves producers— in a sense, they are—but they're not throwing a straight-ahead fastball over the plate, either.

Mind you, there are still some old-school producers around today who operate as if they are the extra member of the band, people who watch what the players are doing and show them how to do it better. They focus in on the parts that they feel are really good, and they develop those ideas. That's exactly the kind of producer Rick Rubin is: he's even less hands-on than me. He just walks around the studio, lets the musicians do their thing, points his finger at one or two major places, and boom! And you know what? It makes a difference. Puffy [Sean "Puffy" Combs] to some extent is still that kind of producer, too. Whatever you want to say about the man, he does know sounds and he does know the marketplace.

On the other hand, you have your hands-on producers who go from soup to nuts. They create and they visualize the whole thing from beginning to end, all by themselves, like Timbaland does. I respect him a lot; to me, he's the man of the decade. But there are plenty of people who are not Timbalands who are trying to produce records that way, and they often fall short.

Is talent all it takes to make great records?

No. When you look at The Beatles and you break it down, sure, they were talented. But remember this: nobody ever told them no, either. And when nobody ever tells you no, whatever you do, you do it from a different place. It's as if you're announcing, "I'm going to step in this little piece of quicksand," but there's nobody to tell you not to do it. So when you go ahead and do it and you walk out the other side, everyone says, "Wow, it's alright to do that!" But for the guy who's in the middle—the guy who's not at the top of his profession—it's a lot tougher, because everyone is all too ready to tell him "That's a really bad idea," and when it doesn't sell, they say, "See, we *told* you it was a bad idea!" The worst thing about that is that the next time you have an idea that's really special, instead of trying it out, you go, "Nah, maybe I shouldn't try that." I've thought about this long and hard, and I've come to realize that many times that's what makes the difference between success and failure.

Are you talking about having the courage of your convictions?

Not really. I'm talking about the luxury of not having people tell you no. There are plenty of people who have the courage of their convictions but don't necessarily have the support or the thinking process that allows them to write a song that's totally unique. If you stop for even one second and look around and think, "Maybe I shouldn't," then you probably won't go out on that limb. "Maybe I shouldn't" is actually the one thing you should *never* say.

Do you have a set approach to how you start a mix?

Not any more. In the analog days, you'd start with the drums and then do the bass. You made them thick and fat and rich, and that was your bed. But with the advent of digital technology, the sounds are no longer necessarily acoustic. They can be anything at all; a lot of records don't even have bass on them any more—they'll just have a keyboard part. So the challenge is to make a traditional record from components that are non-traditional.

The hard thing about mixing now is that there is no standard. The samples can come from anywhere, made from anything. Artists will take a cardboard box or the sound of a window slamming, and that will be your bass drum. It doesn't sound wrong in today's records. So when you get something like that, your role as a mixer is to try to perceive what the artist thinks they perceive.

So your role is to try to decipher and interpret the artist's vision.

When I'm a mixer, yeah. But as a producer, I'm the guy trying to convince the artist to put a sound in there that we can all understand. The production role to me is all about trying to get stuff that we can *all* relate to and make sense out of. Many times artists will find sounds or try ideas that just make no sense to me. They'll say, "Yeah, that's great, it's crazy," and I'll say, "Well, it may be crazy, but I just don't get it. I'm not saying it's wrong, but can't we just do something that we can *all* get?" If

> **"If everyone in the control room can't get a buzz off of it, how can we expect the buying public to get it?"**

everyone in the control room can't get a buzz off of it, how can we expect the buying public to get it? Our only hope is to have everyone involved be a hundred percent behind what we send out; after all, if the ten people in the room don't all like the record, how can we expect ten *million* people to like it?

Another reason why working with many of today's artists is such a problem is that nobody's telling you what they're doing. That's a big issue for me, because it means you're not a part of the process. You can't make the music better or worse, because you don't know what the hell the artist is doing until the time that it's almost done . . . and by then it's too late.

So these days, it's really hard to know what producers are contributing. There are so many singer-songwriters now working out of their home studios, and what they're creating sure sound like records to me. Yes, there are some that don't sound particularly good, but of the few that really come shining through, they're pretty special. It's not such a mystery; it's really not so hard to do. If you've got talent, and you've got a good ear for this stuff, I don't doubt that you can make a good record on your own.

At the end of the day, it all comes down to instinct. Not long ago, I was doing a seminar, and this kid came up to me and he said, "Listen, I've got a Pro Tools rig and I've got it down; I went to a school and I've got the engineering thing down. Now all I need to know is: how do you produce?" [*laughs*] The sad thing is that only a non-producer would even ask a question like that. Sure, I can teach someone the mechanics, but when it comes to actually making a record, that's where you're on your own, dude.

Suggested Listening:
Matisyahu: *Youth*, JDub/EMI, 2006
Duran Duran: *Red Carpet Massacre*, Epic, 2007
DJ Milo: *Wild Bunch: The Original Underground Massive Attack*, Strut, 2002
Slave: *Show Time*, Atlantic, 1981
Creation: *The Creation*, Atco, 1975

Steven Epstein

When Worlds Collide

OK, trivia fans: name this producer. Here are your clues: he was the longest-running staff producer to ever work at Sony (formerly Columbia) Records and has won nine Grammys (out of a staggering 26 nominations).

Admittedly, the name Steven Epstein might not be familiar to those of you who are into rock, pop, rap, hip-hop, or electronica, but he is an icon in the rarified field of classical and jazz recording, as evidenced by the fact that six of his Grammies are for Classical Producer of the Year (1984, 1995, 1997, 1998, 2000, and 2003).

The artists that he has worked with during his career range from almost every internationally renowned symphonic orchestra to such groundbreaking artists as Wynton Marsalis, Yo-Yo Ma, Placido Domingo, Isaac Stern, Midori, and Bobby McFerrin. Shortly after this interview was conducted, he was off to Vienna to record Billy Joel's critically acclaimed album of classical compositions.

The New York–born Epstein vividly recalls wanting to be a classical record producer since his childhood. As a high school student, he demonstrated that commitment by boldly writing to his future boss—Tom Frost, co-music director at CBS Masterworks—and, in recognition of that initiative, he was offered a staff position as a music editor shortly after graduating from college. Today—more than three decades later and now an independent producer—he's still turning out some of the finest recordings you'll ever hear.

In this far-ranging interview, Epstein reveals the unique techniques he's developed and the philosophical approaches he takes to capturing the finest performances of the finest classical and jazz musicians in the world.

What do you see as the essential difference between the role of a classical or jazz producer versus that of a pop producer?

I would say the intent is the same [for both]. That may seem obvious, but the goal of all kinds of producers is to yield the best, most interesting product musically; to get the most out of the artist; and to make the surroundings for the artist comfortable so that he or she can be at their inspired best.

Of course, rock or pop recording is generally different in the sense that a whole album is rarely put together in real time; one section or group of instruments is layered, and then the vocalist does their thing over already recorded material. In classical or in jazz, the idea is to do it all in real time. There are some producers that might not have a problem recording jazz with a significant amount of overdubbing, but my feeling is that, since everyone is spontaneously supposed to play off everyone else and derive their inspiration at that moment—that, after all, is what makes jazz exciting and wonderful—it should all be recorded in real time and without overdubbing.

A classical music producer has to very closely follow the musical score and make sure that all the notes that are being performed are the same as all the notes in the score. In pop, on the other hand, pretty much anything goes. In jazz, it's also a case of pretty much anything goes; you have a lot of latitude in what is correct and what isn't correct—you can get away with what are called "dirty" notes or slight blemishes, whereas in classical music, that's unacceptable. In jazz, those notes impart a color to the sound. As a result, a jazz artist might say, "What do you think of that solo?" and you might have one feeling while the artist might have a different feeling—it can be quite subjective. Then, the next day when each of you listen back to it, your impressions can easily be reversed, unless there's something obviously wrong with it.

One big difference on the technical side is the much wider amount of dynamic range in both jazz and classical recordings than in pop releases. Is your goal more to capture what actually happened in the studio than it is to enhance it?

Yes. In classical, my goal is to capture as naturally as possible the illusion of the reality that takes place in a concert hall. I like to use as few mics as possible; many of my symphonic recordings have been done with only two microphones, even though I like to set up more than two and send them to other tracks just in case we need to call on them during a mix.

> *"In classical [recording], my goal is to capture as naturally as possible the illusion of the reality that takes place in a concert hall."*

Many times I work with a conductor or artist and explain that the approach is to get a two-mic balance, which means that, once we position the microphones accurately, that balance is going to be locked in, without room for manipulation later on. Often the artist is excited by that, though many times during playback, I warn them, "I just want you to be sure that you understand that we can't change anything with regard to the balance later on." That's what I call "natural" recording. But you can also do a natural-sounding classical recording using 20 mics. It depends on the acoustics of the venue that you're in; you basically have to tailor your setup to the acoustics of the hall.

In jazz recording, I aim to get the sense of an ensemble performing in a real room, rather than in a dead studio. That's why I like to go to venues that have some life in them, and I like to have all the musicians in the room at the same time, with the drummer usually semi-enclosed, so there's some drum leakage into the room—but not *too* much. It's necessary to have some control over the drums, because so much of the time the drum leakage will spill into the bass mics, so if you're trying to increase the bass level you're raising the drums also.

> *"Sometimes the headphone mix will dictate what the final performance sounds like."*

I also like to have all the musicians work without headphones because sometimes the headphone mix will dictate what the final performance sounds like. And if the headphone mix isn't exactly the way it should be—whatever that means—the musicians will be rebalancing and playing with different dynamics, based on what they're hearing in their headphones. You get a much more cohesive performance when they can all hear each other in a room without having to use cans.

That said, sometimes we have to use headphones for the drummer and the bass player—depending on how they are physically situated in relation to each other—so they can really lock into their groove.

Presumably, though, you never use a click track.

Only if we do overdubs, and the only overdubbing that I've done in the classical realm is when we've had to lock to visual cues, or when we're approaching making a recording like a pop album, layering tracks together. When we were doing the soundtrack for *Crouching Tiger, Hidden Dragon*, for instance, we actually recorded Yo-Yo Ma, on his own, before we recorded anything else. Normally we would record the orchestral and ensemble material first, and Yo-Yo would overdub to it later. But due to scheduling considerations, we needed to approach these sessions somewhat uniquely. We had him play as he watched the parts of the film he was performing in, with the composer and director both present to provide their input. But all of the orchestral backing and the other Asian folk instruments had to be married to Yo-Yo's performance, so we obviously had to put down a click track for each of the cues prior to the recording.

When you record an orchestra with just two mics, what are your mics of choice?

My favorite microphones—which I've been using almost since their inception—are B&K (Brüel and Kjær) omnidirectionals. When they were first made, I started off with the 4003s, either as two spaced microphones or in a Decca tree–type configuration. Then they came out with the 4009s, which were a matched pair of 4003s, so I used those. I've used them for most any classical ensemble; they have a very open high end and a natural response; not as tight a bass response as, let's say, some of the Schoeps omnis. But, overall they are a more natural-sounding microphone—though I like using Schoeps MK2s and MK2Ss occasionally, too.

What mic do you use on Wynton?

My favorite mic on Wynton is an [AKG] C12VR, which was modified at Sony Studios by our chief engineer. Most of the time when I record Wynton performing jazz, I experiment with different microphones, comparing them against a main mic that I was happy with; that's how you evolve, that's how you hone your art. The great thing about working for Sony/CBS all these years was that I was encouraged to experiment with different techniques and different microphones.

Do you ever compress his signal?

Rarely, unless we run into problems. I try to leave Wynton's sound as flat as possible, though occasionally I might add a little bit of low midrange EQ, at around 700 Hz. Sometimes I compress the bass to keep a fairly linear dynamic, usually using the onboard compressors in an Oxford console; they're very clean.

What's your mic of choice for recording Yo-Yo?

It depends on the type of music we are recording. I've used [Neumann] U 89s on Yo-Yo for some chamber recordings, but, again, my overall philosophy of doing classical recording is to use as few mics as possible. Therefore, if we're making a concerto recording, I like to have the body of the sound of the solo instrument be picked up by the main mics. Not necessarily the complete sound, not necessarily to have the optimum balance, but just to get the body of it. Then I define the solo sound with a spot mic, and on Yo-Yo I've used everything from a [Schoeps] MK4 to a [Neumann] KM 84; usually a small-diaphragm condenser.

One recording I did with him called the *New York Album*—an album of concertos for cello and orchestra by different composers—was a very unusual situation where, with exceptions in just three places, I actually did the entire recording with two B&K microphones, capturing not only the orchestra but Yo-Yo as well. The only way I could do this was to balance the mics during rehearsals—not to record, because the union won't allow you to record rehearsals—but just to listen while moving the microphones to find the optimum position. In a concerto recording, it's almost unheard of—for me, anyway—to use just two mics. But in this particular recording, the acoustics were perfectly suitable, plus David Zinman, the brilliant conductor, had a great sense of balance with the very fine orchestra he was leading—the Baltimore Symphony. So everything was clicking and, as a result, I was able to optimize the dynamic range and achieve a more accurate soundstage with better depth than a multi-mic setup might yield.

When you're recording drums for jazz, is it also a minimal miking, or do you stick a mic on every drum, as is normally done for pop recording?

In the old days, I close-miked every drum; then I wanted to try something different. At one point I was recording a version of *West Side Story* with the original orchestrations, and the drummer was Shelley Mann, the great jazz drummer—it actually turned out to be his last recording. I tried something a little different, and he commented, "You know, it's really refreshing that you're using fewer microphones on the drums." I was pleased, because I was happier with the sound as well.

Again, pop music is a different beast, but for jazz I prefer to minimally mic the drums. I usually use two B&K 4009s as overheads, and I let them basically pick up the entire drum set as an organic unit, allowing the drummer to create his own balance. I supplement the overheads with a bass drum mic and a snare mic, and the snare mic sometimes doubles as a high-hat mic. Occasionally we use a separate mic on the high-hat for greater control.

What mics do you like to use on the snare and kick drums?

On the snare I like to use a B&K 4007, which is also an omni. It's a great snare mic—it's got a high SPL and can take a beating. Sometimes I use an AKG 451; same with the high-hat. On kick drum I like to use a [Neumann] U 47; I used to use [AKG] D112s, but I felt that the 47 has a little more character. I prefer using a tube 47, though in a pinch a FET does the trick, too.

But if the drummer is in a fairly dead booth because I need to get more isolation, I don't like using omnis for overheads, because then you're more apt to pick up the sound of the booth and whatever anomalies or resonances are within it, so you end up losing a bit of punch and brightness in the drums overall. In that case I'll use either two B&K 4011s for overheads—they're cardioids—or two [AKG] 414s in cardioid; they get a little more sizzle, a little more punch out of the drums when they're in that kind of configuration. If we're able to have a more open drum sound, though, I prefer to use the 4009s as overheads.

You say that it is critical in recording classical music to strictly follow the score, which not only has all the notes, but all the dynamic articulation clearly defined. How is a classical artist able to add their own interpretation when they're having to work within such a rigid structure?

Making sure that the notes are correct is *not* actually the most important thing, in the sense of prioritizing. It's a tricky question, but basically, you can't leave a classical recording session with incorrect notes—you can't come out with a recording that either represents the artist having made mistakes, or does not speak truly of the music, of what the composer intended to do.

However, within that framework, the producer must make sure that the artist is free to perform, free to interpret the music without feeling that he or she is constrained by having to play the correct notes. I remember the days of direct-to-disk, when people were saying, "Well, you know, you can't do any editing, so you're getting an actual performance." But, frankly—and my conversations with musicians have borne this out—when you got to the last two minutes of a direct-to-disk recording, the artist would tend to give a very safe performance because they didn't want to make any mistakes and have to start all over again! So, paradoxically, what you can end up with if you don't have the option of editing is a safer performance. Having the option of editing allows the artist to be much more free with the performance. Preferably, though, you do as little editing as possible so that you don't destroy the overall performance.

When I sit down in the studio to record a piece of music, I discuss with the artist how we would like to approach the session and ask for their input and their ideas, what would make them comfortable. I always suggest that we do at least two or three takes of a complete movement, so we get a full performance and a full overview of the piece; then let's see where we stand. If we have to, we'll touch up or fix places, and just lay in what we need to lay in—though we may do larger pieces than just the part to be fixed so we get the complete context of the passage. Generally speaking, if the artist has a clear conception of how he or she wants to play a piece of music, then it usually doesn't matter how much editing is done, because the performances are all of the same character and style. That way, you'll undoubtedly have a seamless performance even if you have to resort to a lot of editing.

Chamber music, by necessity, usually requires a lot of editing, because you only have one instrument to a part, as opposed to in an orchestra, where you may have 40 string players, a massed group of instruments, so that, if somebody's playing a little out of tune, it's hardly going to be obvious at all. But in a string quartet, for instance, every note is critical—every pitch, every nuance becomes magnified a hundredfold. Because of this magnifying glass effect, you are usually compelled to do more editing.

So in a classical recording, there are no overdubs; if there's a problem, you edit in a piece from another performance. But in a jazz recording, if someone is playing a great solo but hits a clunker, will you punch in that one note?

It's been done. But in jazz, it's rare that there's ever a wrong note! [*laughs*] Sometimes an artist feels that a phrase within a solo has been poorly executed and asks to just punch in, but that can't be done if the musician was in a room together with the other players and not in an iso booth—obviously, there's going to be leakage on the other mics; as minimal as it may be, you're going to hear a ghost of the original solo. So, unless it's something that the artist wants to punch in where no one else was playing, I would generally just record another take of the passage (or the complete piece) and look for a suitable edit point.

I also shouldn't say that we *never* do overdubbing in classical. For instance, I've recorded operas, and sometimes, because of scheduling problems, a singer might not be able to perform with the orchestra at the time of the session. So it is conceivable that, because of the realities of an artist's touring schedule, we might have to do an overdub like that. But it would be extremely rare to overdub in a concerto; you're right, fixing problems is a matter of editing different takes together.

What advice can you give the reader who wants to get into this field?

The most important thing in becoming a classical or jazz producer is that you have a strong musical background. When I started, there weren't colleges offering specialized programs in recording, so I went to Hofstra [University, in Long Island, New York], studied violin, and majored in music education. Now, of course, there are some wonderful colleges that have programs in recording.

> *"You can always learn the technical aspects as you go along, but you should have a fundamental knowledge and understanding of music so your ears can always be focused."*

You can always learn the technical aspects as you go along, but you should have a fundamental knowledge and understanding of music so your ears can always be focused. As a kid I frequently listened to Columbia/Masterworks records, analyzing them, imagining what I might do differently. I also had a scrapbook in which I collected pictures from magazines of microphone setups. I know producers who have sort of fallen into the position, but, frankly, I have greater respect for those who have shown that it is part of their life's blood.

Suggested Listening:

Wynton Marsalis: *Hot House Flowers*, Columbia, 1984; *The Majesty of the Blues*, Columbia, 1988
Billy Joel: *Fantasies & Delusions*, Sony, 2001
Yo-Yo Ma: *Premieres*, Sony, 1997; *Appalachian Journey* (with Edgar Meyer and Mark O'Connor), Sony, 2000; *Obrigado Brazil*, Sony Classical, 2003
Original Soundtrack: *Crouching Tiger, Hidden Dragon*, Sony, 2000
Joshua Bell: *West Side Story Suite*, Sony, 2001

Kevin Killen

Trust Your Instincts, Decide on a Course of Action, and Follow Through on It

Sometimes a little humility—combined with tenacity—can go a long way. Consider the career of engineer/producer Kevin Killen, who was willing to start at the bottom rung of the ladder not once, not twice, but three times before he finally broke through to the pinnacle of his profession, manning the board for the likes of U2, Peter Gabriel, Elvis Costello, Jewel, Lindsey Buckingham, Tori Amos, Kate Bush, and Paula Cole.

Rewind the tape to 1979, when a young Killen began working as an assistant engineer at a small demo studio in his hometown of Dublin, Ireland. After six months of doing jingles and low-budget sessions for local artists, he worked his way up to engineer, and then moved on to the more prestigious Windmill Lane studios—despite the fact that he had to return to assisting.

There he met an up-and-coming Irish band called U2, working with producer Steve Lillywhite on their *War* album before engineering their 1984 release *The Unforgettable Fire* (with producer Brian Eno). Later that same year he made the fateful—and gutsy—decision to relocate to New York, even though he knew hardly anyone in the Big Apple and had to essentially start from scratch, working as an assistant engineer once again.

It wasn't long before Killen's perseverance and self-confidence began paying dividends big time, garnering him production duties with the '80s techno-pop band Mr. Mister and the first of a long series of engineering and co-production gigs with Elvis Costello. We met up with Killen at New York's famed Avatar studios. Articulate and thoughtful, Killen shared his philosophical approach towards making lasting records, focusing on both aesthetic and technical considerations.

How do you see the rise of the home studio as having had an impact on your career?

The way the industry has been going the past couple of years, I've been forced to be creative in stretching a budget and finding ways to make a $100,000 record sound like a $500,000 record. Like a lot of people now, I'll go in and track at a recognized studio for two or three weeks, and then for the vast majority of overdubs I'll go to somebody's house or a low-budget room with Pro Tools LE and a couple of reasonable-sounding microphones and mic pres—I've got a couple of friends who literally have little studios in their bedrooms. Then I'll go back into a big room to mix.

If you're on a limited budget, do you think it's more important to have a good mic, or a good mic preamp?

In the home studio, it seems to me that the most critical thing is the chain from the microphone into the recording media, followed by the monitoring system.

A good mic pre. It will make a not-so-good sounding microphone sparkle a little bit more while a bad mic pre will diminish its response. Fortunately, there are many good mic pres out

PHOTO BY KRISTINE LARSEN

there that are affordable for the home recordist on a budget.

Do you tend to favor the straight-wire approach in a mic pre, or do you look for one that imparts a little character or color to the signal?

It depends upon the project. For home recordings, a mic pre that has less coloration is probably the one that I would advise using, if you're trying to accurately represent what you're hearing. But if you're trying to take a sound and morph it into something else, then the chain of processing doesn't really matter because you're going to seriously alter the sound anyway. If you want to get an accurate representation, then you need to spend the time listening to the musician and moving the microphone around.

What if the microphone itself isn't that great—perhaps because you've spent most of your budget on the mic preamp? Wouldn't you then want to use a preamp that enhances the sound of that not-so-great mic, as opposed to one that delivers the sound in an uncolored way?

No, I still think the straight-wire approach is the way to go. That brings to mind a project I did with producer Pat Leonard in Los Angeles; the artist was a classically trained pianist. We had a nine-foot Bosendorfer [piano] and a seven-foot Yamaha with the MIDI module. We miked the Bosendorfer with a pair of B&Ks, but the Yamaha was miked up with a pair of [Shure SM] 57s, running through a pair of Neve mic pres. We were looking for the distinction between a very elegant piano sound and one that would really suit a pop recording, with a lot of elements surrounding the piano, so we didn't want it to be all that broad-sounding. So I do think the mic pre is the critical element, along with the placement of the mics and the touch of the player, and of course the quality of the instrument itself. It's a combination of events that really articulate the sound.

Was the Yamaha piano miked in a standard stereo configuration?

Yes, just standard stereo, one 57 picking up the treble strings and the other picking up the bass strings, about a foot and a half apart. No real trickery involved; again, I took the time to listen to what it sounded like in the room. Interestingly, on Elvis Costello's *North*, I used an [AKG] C24 on the piano, just right down the middle of the soundboard, but I spotted a couple of [Neumann] KM 86s on the outside to see if I could add a little width to it. On some songs they really helped, and on some songs they didn't. So you pick and choose, depending on what kind of sonic landscape you're trying to create.

You cut your teeth recording a lot of jingles. A lot of recording engineers say that they found the experience of doing jingles invaluable because it taught them to work quickly.

In a two- or three-hour jingle session, you may cut three or four different spots; plus you overdub them with voiceovers and additional information, mix down, edit, and copy, and they're out the door with a whole neat package. In comparison, making a record seems like a long drawn-out process that takes weeks or months, but as an engineer you still need to be able to work fast when the artist is ready to record. If you broke down how much time during those weeks the creative juices are actually flowing in terms of performances, it's really a very small amount of time. But you're waiting for time to happen, and you're trying to do everything you can to manipulate the environment so that when the artist feels they are ready, they can just fold into it and you're recording. All the rest is just setting up for that moment.

It's probably easier with home recording, because you're in a very comfortable environment. Even for a lot of seasoned musicians, just the notion that they're in a studio environment gives them red-light fever: "Okay, we're putting it under the microscope." Musicians often comment, "It was much easier in rehearsal," and they're right, it *is* easier because you're not thinking about it.

I was just reading the other day about [famed jazz producer] Rudy Van Gelder's first studio in Hackensack New Jersey, which was in his father's house—the original home studio. He's quoted as saying that the reason a lot of the seminal Blue Note recordings were so great was because people just felt so comfortable in that studio—he even had home furniture there. The musicians would think, "We're not recording," but here were all of these classic recordings being created.

If a classic recording that stands the test of time can actually come out of a home studio, what is the role of the professional studio?

To provide the technical backup and a level of excellence that's hard to match in a home studio. In most top-line studios, the sound is just so superior, and if you have a problem there's somebody there to fix it immediately. You're not questioning the wiring or the tape alignment, and usually the room you're listening in is a more critical environment when you're trying to make final decisions, especially during mixdown.

> *"Anytime I've spent weeks or months doing a home recording, I've always felt an enormous benefit as soon as I've come into a professional room to mix."*

Any time I've spent weeks or months doing a home recording, I've always felt an enormous benefit as soon as I've come into a professional room to mix. It's not that I've been dissatisfied with what I've recorded; I just feel that the sound I visualize in my head can be more readily achieved in a professional studio when I get to the mixdown stage.

It seems that one of the popular myths of home recording today is that because the technology allows so many ways to manipulate or "fix" a signal, that it's less important to start with a quality recording.

It *is* a myth. Why spend the time to fix something that's basically subpar? Why not just get it right? If you think about a record as an emotional context in which a performance resides, then you should be willing to accept certain imperfections as long as it tells a story when it comes out of the speaker. All of these elements combine to make the listener feel removed, or engaged. Personally, I'd much rather have somebody be engaged and accept the warts. If you try to fix it and you find that it's better technically but not better emotionally, I'd sooner go with the more emotional performance.

I find that this kind of philosophy is common in engineers who come from having to record a lot of real musicians over a long period of time, and in different genres of music. Many of the young engineers who are coming up are technologically savvy and are into the manipulation of sound, and they do amazing work—it's really fascinating to see what they do with audio—but I couldn't even remotely try and replicate it. Even though some of it's not my aesthetic, I can certainly listen to it and go, "That sure as hell is cool." But it's also unreal, and there's no way they can recreate it live onstage. Of course, nobody says you should have to be able to do that—it is a different medium, after all.

If the performance is great, that's the thing that's going to come across, time and time again. As far as the notion of constantly correcting something, there's a consequence to every correction. It might sound perfect—whatever your version of "perfect" means to you—but you're going to remove a tangible ingredient. The question with new technology is, how much do you leave and how much do you correct? It depends on the artist. If you're working with someone who has gotten away with masking their inabilities and you're using technology to correct their imperfections, then it makes the job more difficult. Ideally, you want to go in, set the microphone, get a sound, hit Record, and get a wonderful reading of what they're trying to do. Of course, we all know that's not necessarily the case—and you can only hide behind the technology for so long. Maybe that's part of the reason why some new artists have an initial success with their first album release, but then when they go on the road, they can't even come close to replicating those performances. People see through that. Personally I feel cheated when an artist cannot deliver a credible performance onstage. As the saying goes: "In time. In tune. With feeling." Is that too much to ask?

"There's a consequence to every correction."

When you produce records, you engineer as well, which seems like quite a tall order.

It is a tall order, because it's always good to have another set of ears in the room. It's easy to convince yourself that something is working when you know instinctively it's not—you just want to move the process along. And then, in the cold, harsh light of day you come back and say, "What was I thinking??" Whereas if you had another set of trusted ears around, you might say, "Okay, we need to try something else here."

When you're starting a project, do you have an end goal that you're working towards sonically?

It depends. If the artist has an identifiable sound that they just wish to expand upon, then I have an idea of what I think it can sound like at the end, so I'll try and move towards that. But I'm also willing to go with the flow, because the best-laid plans don't necessarily materialize, so you've got to be flexible. Sometimes it takes you a couple of songs to really identify the strength of the collective group of people in the room. All of a sudden you go, "Okay, this is what these people really do exceptionally well," and then you hone the sound towards that.

I still try to make it different enough from song to song so it doesn't sound like I just repeated the same trick, but also sounding familiar enough that it feels cohesive from top to bottom. I'll try different drums, different drum kits; maybe instead of using a full-size drum kit, I'll use a smaller-sized kit. Things like starting out with one sound in the verses and expanding on it in the choruses, or vice versa.

And so much of it is dependent on the lyrics. If it's a lyrically intensive song, then I think so much of it is about space and not about the constant musical backing.

So you're saying you actually shape the music to fit the lyrical content.

Oh, yeah. I love the musical backdrop, but I usually start my mix by pushing up the vocal fader so I'm building from that perspective. At some point I'll turn the voice off for a couple of minutes and listen to the musical balance, but I'm always thinking in terms of telling a story. The voice is the thing that's leading the story; the other elements are supporting components.

What criteria do you use to determine whether you want to work with a new artist?

Good songs, the ability to perform, and a strong personality. I'm looking for somebody who's got a vision and a passion. I don't want it to be so considered-sounding that they think, "I can be a musician and an artist because I'm smart and I'm technically able to do these things and my level of musicianship is high enough." I want people who are really *passionate* about music, because that's what ultimately comes across. There are some artists out there who are really good, who may be very competent musicians, but they don't have the desire to be incredibly successful.

Some producers try to avoid working with strong-willed artists, preferring instead to work with people who are willing to be shaped and molded.

Ultimately the artists who are most successful are the ones who are most driven. That doesn't mean you have to butt heads with them; they can be incredibly affable people, even if that desire burns within them. I distinctly remember working with U2 and thinking that the whole band was so driven, but it didn't seem overt. They just wanted to be the best band in the world. They didn't have to step over a lot of people to achieve it, either—they just let their music do it for them.

I was fortunate enough to do the first Paula Cole record and she had that same passion. She had the drive to want to succeed—same with most of the artists I've been fortunate to work with. Some have been more successful than others, but they all had that passion.

Often, an artist has a successful debut album working with an established producer and then they decide they can take over the production themselves on the second album and fall short.

Well, producing a record is not just about making the musical decisions. There are so many other things, from choosing the right musicians to choosing the right studio. Then there are all the intangibles, like figuring out how to work the budget. You need to understand how all the decisions you're making on a day-to-day basis affect the bottom line, and how that's going to impact on how you finish the record. Knowing how to coax the best performances out of people, having the ability to step back, keeping the overall vision. Some artists have that vision themselves, of course—Prince is a great example—but it's a tough job.

Coming from where I sit, I think the best records are made in the collaborative process. Most artists will tell you that their record turned out sonically different and probably much better than they ever imagined because of that interaction of the collective in the room. Sometimes it happens by accident, sometimes it happens by design, but who cares as long as the net result is a compelling piece of music?

Perhaps it's that lack of collaborative process that is the biggest negative about home recording.

Unfortunately, the same is true for musicians as it is for engineers—in a home studio they not only don't get to work with one another, they don't get to work with other people that might be floating around in a professional studio complex. People that you admire are suddenly in the room next to you and you think, "Wouldn't it be cool if I had so-and-so come in and play on a track?" Those kinds of accidents can be wonderful things.

People doing all their own recording and mixing at home tend to work in isolation. They even try to do their own mastering—you give someone a [Waves] L1 and they think they're a mastering engineer! I would never even remotely think I was a mastering engineer; I don't know anything about mastering, other than that I have a good sense of who the great mastering engineers are. I learn every time I go into a mastering suite—watching the incredible clarity they get out of a recording just by making a tiny adjustment. It's amazing, but they spend years training to do that, so why not take advantage of all that accumulated experience?

You're known for not putting decisions off, for not giving yourself tons of options to deal with at the end of a project.

Absolutely. It's a very simple philosophy: trust your instincts, decide on a course of action, and follow through on it. If that means printing a particular effect, don't be afraid to make that decision. You always have the option of saving the session in various different ways—one with a printed effect on a particular instrument, and another with just the raw data, so that if you decide at a later point that there's something wrong, you can rebalance.

> *"There's nothing wrong with making a commitment to the sound; that's what we're supposed to be doing, after all."*

But there is something special that happens when you make a decision. For those of us who had to work on 16-track or 24-track analog, when you only had a certain number of tracks, you didn't use 16 tracks on drums or even 8 tracks—you used 4 or 6 tracks. So you committed to that sound early on, and that became the basis and foundation from which all your other judgements were made. By the time you got to mix, you felt that the record was already pretty much done—you just pushed the faders up. It wasn't that you were trying to achieve the sound [in the mix]—you'd already established the sound beforehand. So at that point you were just trying to correct some minor imperfections that you perceived. There's nothing wrong with making a commitment to the sound; that's what we're supposed to be doing, after all. Why put it off until later? You might lose the sound—you might be monitoring through a particular delay or reverb but when you come back the next day it doesn't sound the same anymore, and that affects how you view the performance. Just print it. If you don't like it at a later point, just erase it. But if you at least print it, there will be no question as to what it was. That's definitely still my philosophy.

But if you print every effect you try, you'll end up with lots and lots of tracks, hence lots of decisions to make at mix time.

I don't necessarily print the effects separately, though. Let's say I'm recording a guitar and the musician has some effects of his or her own and I add some more effects to make a nice stereo spread. I would then print it as a single stereo track, rather than doing individual tracks for each effect. If I feel—and if the musician agrees—that's a great sound and that's what we want to hear every time we come into the control room, then I'm going to commit to it.

I find a lot of artists are reticent about doing that: "Oh, let's make the decision later on." No, I say let's make the decision *now*, so that your future decisions are based upon something that you're actually going to use, as opposed to something you think you *may* want to use. You make those decisions and then the mix doesn't take five days to do; the basic mix should be done in about five or six hours. With the overall tone and shape of the recording already set, you can take the luxury of time to step back and get into the details.

What advice can you give the young reader who wants to be the next Kevin Killen?

Well, corny as it sounds, I would just say follow your dreams, wherever they take you. My dream was to take what I learned in Dublin and to see if it would work on a bigger stage. I was heartened by the fact that it seemed to, and I take incredible comfort from the knowledge that I've worked on some great records, but it was pure luck. Yes, I had the aptitude and I had the talent, but it was also being in the right place at the right time.

So it's about not giving up, and like so many things in this business, it's also about your personality. There are a lot of people out there who are incredibly gifted, but their personalities don't necessarily lend themselves to being embraced by a lot of people. You just have to keep remembering that the person that you met today who you think is of no consequence could be somebody of consequence tomorrow. That doesn't mean you have to brown-nose them all the time; it just means you have to treat them as you want to be treated. Ultimately, if you're good enough, you'll get there.

The final piece of advice is to respect your hearing. Be safety conscious when you go to shows and monitor at reasonable levels. Remember that your mix has to sound good at *any* level. Do not be afraid to protect your most valuable commodity.

Suggested Listening:
Peter Gabriel: *So*, Geffen, 1986
U2: *War*, Island, 1983; *The Unforgettable Fire*, Island, 1984; *Rattle and Hum*, Island, 1988
Elvis Costello: *Spike*, Warner Bros., 1989; *The Juliet Letters*, Warner Bros., 1993; *Kojak Variety*, Warner Bros., 1995; *North*, Deutsche Grammophon, 2003
Shakira: *Oral Fixation, Volume One*, 2005; *Oral Fixation, Volume Two*, Epic, 2005
Shawn Colvin: *Steady On*, 1989
Paula Cole: *Harbinger*, Imago, 1994

Tchad Blake

Breaking the Mold

I t's true that Tchad Blake began his career in a conventional enough fashion, working as a runner at the famed Wally Heider facility in Los Angeles in the early 1980s before shifting base to a funky eight-track studio called Mad Dog, where he began engineering and eventually hooked up with longtime collaborator, producer Mitchell Froom. But in the years since, Blake has marched to the beat of a distinctly different drummer, working with artists as diverse as Peter Gabriel, Sheryl Crow, Bonnie Raitt, Elvis Costello, Tom Waits, Pearl Jam, Fishbone, The Bangles, Los Lobos, Cibo Matto, Spinal Tap, Crowded House, Neil Finn, Richard Thompson, Ron Sexsmith, and Soul Coughing.

I met up with Blake at LA's Sunset Sound Factory one rainy morning shortly before he relocated to England (where he's currently based at Peter Gabriel's Real World Studios). As the raindrops pelted down on the roof over our heads, we chatted at length about his unusual techniques and approach towards making records.

When you're starting a new project, what's your thought process? When do the gears start spinning? Is it the first day the artist turns up at the studio or do you go into preproduction with them?

It really depends on the artist, but I'm not big on preproduction. If it's really needed, I'll do it, but most of the things I gravitate towards for myself are things that I think need spontaneity.

I usually don't think about a new project very much until I'm in the studio, on the first day of recording. I like to have something new to use on the date; it doesn't have to be anything big. It can be something simple: a new guitar pedal or a new filter box or something. I'll bring it to the studio and somehow it gets used—often, the first day. That's about the extent of my preproduction: buy something new. [*laughs*] It seems to work well for me.

I usually don't take stuff home with me, either. When I leave the studio, I pretty much leave the studio. It doesn't mean that I don't take a CD sometimes and listen, but I don't go home and think about the songs.

When the band first comes in, do you have them set up and then go out and listen before you put mics up? Or do you have a generic mic setup that you begin with?

I have a template setup of mics I like to use. Certain things, like drum overheads, never change. I always use the [Neumann] Binaural Head for my overheads.

I usually start with a [Shure] D-112 on the kick, and a [Shure SM] 57 on the snare. I'll put a [Neumann] KM 84 or a 57 on the hat, and [Sennheiser] 421s on the toms. I rarely mic top and bottom—it's either one or the other, depending on the drummer. Sometimes the Binaural Head picks up enough of the top, so then I just put a mic on the bottom.

Then I always have a floater mic, which is usually a [Sennheiser] 441, and I can do a number of things with that. Sometimes I use mechanical filters—I'll put the mic in a pipe for resonance or a filter effect. I can then gate it off of anything later if I want it to open up the snare or the kick, or whatever. Sometimes I just run that floater mic through a really distortable, crushable, cheap compressor. I usually like to have that on tape, just a mono track; I love the sound of it, mixed in a little bit.

What do you mean by "mechanical filters"?

Anything that alters the sound that's getting to the mic. Something like a pipe or a didgeridoo, metal pipes, metal plates that I would put the metal pipes up to, trash cans, tin cans. Anything you can find that you can put a mic in or on top of, I consider a mechanical filter.

Where will that be generally positioned?

The way I've used it the most is where the sound is getting collected; maybe just laying on top of the kick drum, maybe pointing at the knees of the drummer, or at the snare. Who knows what it's going to pick up? It just depends on where it is.

Sometimes I'll lay pipes around the drummer, on the floor. Sometimes I'll put a guitar amp in the room with the drummer, with a microphone on the kit but just running through the amp so it's in the room. Maybe there's a tremolo on the amp, or a chorus, or a flange or something so you almost can't tell what it is. Mix that in with the drums and it yields a different sound.

> **"A little distortion goes a long way."**

What's your generic bass guitar setup?

I've got a couple of different DIs—a custom one made by the guy that built the Distressor, and I also use the Little Labs DI. I'll bring the DI signal into the console and send it to a SansAmp, then bring that up on another channel. I usually take the DI direct out to tape—99 percent of the time I use 24-track, 15 IPS, Dolby SR—and I'll print the SansAmp on another track. Depending on the music, it might be compressed by a [dbx] 160x or an Anthony DeMaria Labs tube compressor or maybe a Distressor.

The SansAmp just blows my mind; I actually have one for the bass, one for the kick, and one for the snare.

So bass amps are not in your vocabulary.

Well, they are—I've got some. But more times than not, I'll put the SansAmp track up and the sound is so much better than an amp would be; it's got really good growl to it. It's funny—a little distortion goes a long way.

Do you compress just the DI signal on the way to tape, or both?

Usually both.

Do you find that you often have to put one of the two signals out of phase?

I'd say half the time, depending on the setting on the SansAmp.

> **"I'm not that fussy; I like to do things fast. The thing I am fussy about is carving a space for each instrument."**

Let's get to guitars. You're a guitar player, so you're probably very fussy about guitar sounds.

I'm not that fussy; I like to do things fast. The thing I *am* fussy about is carving a space for each instrument; I don't like things that occupy too much of the same range. I'll do radical EQ to get instruments out of one range and into another. To my ear, that creates a depth.

So you're talking about doing lots of filtering?

Yeah. The guitar can sound big and full, but if it's getting in the way of the bass I'll just whack off 50 Hz; it'll still sound chunky and big, but it won't get in the way of the bass.

PHOTO COURTESY OF TCHAD BLAKE

It's interesting that you create near-far with EQ. Most engineers create near-far with reverbs and delays.

Well, it's just how you hear things. Low frequencies drop off pretty quick in proportion to the distance, so if you roll some low end off, it can sound further away. I do use delays a little bit, but mainly it's EQ. I don't know how conscious I am of it; I just twiddle knobs until it sounds right to me. I tend to pull out a lot around 180 [Hz].

How do you generally record electric guitars?

I like small guitar amps for recording; I like the distortion, I just prefer the sound. To get the low end, I mic real close—an eighth to a quarter of an inch from the grill cloth—so the proximity effect alters the sound. If I want a woofy sound with not a whole lot of edge, I'll go farther over to the edge of the speaker. If I don't want a lot of low end—if I want more top and mid—I'll go closer to the center. I like using 57s on guitar amps; I also like KM 84s, and ribbons—I use Coles often.

Surely you can't put the ribbons an eighth of an inch away!

No, no. Actually, on the small amps they'll be maybe four inches away. I can't do that with a big amp, though. [*laughs*]

What's your miking technique on acoustic guitars?

I have a Countryman Isomax mic that I tape to the inside of the soundhole; I love that thing. It's not a pretty, wispy acoustic sound; it makes the guitar sound more like an archtop. It's midrangy; you can hear the clothing on the back of the guitar, all of those little extras. I have this old '48 Martin, it's an 00-18, a really little one. There's all this noise you hear on the guitar, but I just love the sound of it.

With all the inventive keyboard sounds you come up with, I assume it's rare that you simply take a DI into the board.

It's not that rare; it depends on the keyboard. Mitchell has some pretty weird keyboards that you don't have to do anything to, except maybe there's crackling or some other noise you want to get rid of.

But they're not typically amped?

A lot of SansAmp. Analog delays to distort, Octavias, fuzz boxes, a bunch of different Leslies. We like the POD, and, yes, sometimes amping.

You're renowned for using almost anything as a vocal mic, from a Telefunken to a square plastic Lafayette open-reel tape recorder mic.

[*laughs*] Yeah, that's true. I'm not one of those people who gets a vocalist in and then puts up ten mics to have him sing down. Not because I'm lazy, but normally whenever the vocalist wants to sing, he wants to sing. I'd rather get the performance and worry about the sound later. There have only been two vocalists I couldn't use a Telefunken 251 on: Elvis Costello just wouldn't work on it, and neither would Maria McKee—their voices were too edgy. But for everything else, I always start with the 251. Of course, if you want a weird sound, anything goes.

Do the vocals get compressed on the way in?

Yeah, they'll get a minor amount, depending, again, on what I'm going for. If it's something where we just want a nice vocal sound and I don't want to hear the compression or use it as an effect, then I'll just use a small amount of tape compression. Vocalists usually like that; they like to hear that pumping sound. The vocal normally will get recompressed during mixing, depending on how it needs to sit on top of the track.

Will you ever strap a compressor or limiter across the headphone mix during tracking or overdubbing?

It doesn't usually happen. I think I've only been asked to do that a few times through the years. A vocalist might want a special EQ on their vocal, but not often. I've worked with a lot of vocalists who don't want *any* effect, nothing.

How do you typically begin a mix? Do you have a certain template that you start with?

During mixing—even in tracking—I've always got a stereo compressor, usually an Al Smart, on the mix bus. I usually leave the vocal in all the time—from the start—and just kind of work my way around stuff, going back and forth on things, EQing, compressing. I never go through and just work on one channel and then bring up another channel and then another channel. I think that's the most important thing—always mix with everything in. You can solo stuff up and create incredible individual sounds, but when you put it all together it just falls apart. Or the opposite can happen: you can solo the kick drum and it'll be just awful. But then listen to it with the bass and it can be fantastic.

Is the reason for monitoring through a stereo bus compressor to give a "finished record" kind of feel?

Yeah; I want to know what it's going to sound like with that on it. It changes your depth of field, and it also changes the stereo width. Everything starts to tighten a little bit and I want to hear that, so I can be panning and deciding where I want to put the toms, for example. I know that I'm going to use it when I mix, so I might as well have it on all the time.

How long do you typically spend on a mix?

On average, I'd say five to eight hours. Again, it depends on the artist and the material: with somebody like Richard Thompson, we did a double album and mixed it in seven days. With Neil Finn it was probably two songs a day. Sheryl Crow, that would have been a song a day. When I'm mixing I usually don't work more than eight hours at a stretch.

As you're mixing, do you tend to assign discrete effects to each track or do you have two or three generic effects that you use for everything?

It's all mixed together. I might only have three main effects that I end up sending a lot of different stuff to, but then they might go by different routes. On one instrument it might be direct to that effect; on another I might have a short delay before that same effect, which gives you a whole different sound. I also like to record effects with instruments. If there needs to be a delay on the guitar, I'll record the delay on the guitar.

On a separate track?

No, on the same track.

It seems that you don't use long reverbs very much. On most of your records, whatever reverb is there tends to be very short and clean.

I'll go to great lengths not to use reverb. I like reverb, but I think I started doing that just to be contrary. Eighties records had lots of reverbs, but whenever I put up reverbs I could never fit anything else in; it just always seemed to get messy. I used to try to do it but it sounded horrible and it was really frustrating. I think I probably stopped doing it because I wasn't any good at it. I had to find another way.

And you actually developed a style out of it.

Yeah! [*laughs*]

It seems that you've built yourself a career on breaking the "rules." Is that the way you see it, too? Was that a conscious decision?

Not really, but in creative things I *do* like to be contrary. If there's somebody doing something, I just don't want to do the same thing. It can be really good and I can love it, but I just won't want to do it; I've got to find something else.

Having a sense of abandon; that's the only way I can think of to describe it. In the studio, you have to be open for things to just happen. You have to be willing to turn something up too far, or have that high-hat way too loud, or have the kick drum sound

> **"In the studio, you have to be open for things to just happen."**

sloppy and funny, put all the drums on one side if you want. This is all stuff that's been done before; I'm not doing anything new. But my tastes were developed on the early '70s records that I love so much. I've gone back and listened to some of them recently and I can really hear where some of my influences came from.

Well, you're certainly not formula, which is to your credit.

Yeah, but there's an art to making something really artistic and at the same time making it popular. That's a whole other art, which I'm still trying to learn.

How does your approach differ when you're producing, versus just engineering?

When I'm producing, there are a lot more responsibilities, and I usually have to get more involved with preproduction. But the approach in the studio is not that different. I'm an engineer; I'm not like Mitchell and a lot of other producers who are composers in their own right. He comes in with that, first and foremost; he can rearrange the blocks. I can really only do that after the fact. Usually when I hear something, I like the quirks and I don't want to fix it: my attitude is, let's just record it, let's get it down. But a lot of time during mixing or overdubbing, I'll hear that we need to do something extra or that something's not quite right, that it doesn't hold up over time—and that's when you do something. My arranging comes in mixing, in using the mute buttons, dropping stuff out, or maybe flying something in—creating a new part out of the things that are there.

Do you always engineer when you produce?

So far I have, yeah, but it's hard. For me to produce it needs to be a special kind of artist. Soul Coughing was perfect, and Lisa Germano was another record that I loved doing. These are people that really had a strong sense of what they required on their record and looked to me to be a sounding board. They didn't need someone to come in and go, "Right, we need to rearrange these songs, we need to do this, we need to do that." They just needed the frosting on top. I'm an engineer who produces when the artist has a real strong sense of themselves and knows what they want out of a record.

Suggested Listening:
Soul Coughing: *El Oso*, Warner Bros., 1998
Lisa Germano: *Slide*, 4AD, 1998
Sheryl Crow: *The Globe Sessions*, A&M, 1998
Bonnie Raitt: *Souls Alike*, Capitol, 2005
Phish: *Undermind*, Elektra, 2004
Pearl Jam: *Binaural*, Epic, 2000

Joe Chiccarelli

Adaptability

Joe Chiccarelli is a chameleon.

Not literally, of course. But unlike many producers whose sonic stamp is immediately recognizable (a Roy Thomas Baker or a John Shanks, for example), you'd be hard-pressed to identify a Joe Chiccarelli "sound." It's hard to believe that the same individual who produced the rough-and-ready White Stripes' *Icky Thump* was also responsible for the ephemeral, moody ambience of the Shins' *Wincing the Night Away* or the smooth, slick jazz tones of Kurt Elling's *Night Moves*. But not only was it the same guy, it was a body of work that netted him a 2008 Grammy nomination for Producer of the Year.

Chat with the soft-spoken, self-effacing Chiccarelli for just a few minutes and it becomes apparent why artists in so many different genres gravitate to him. "Honestly, I don't think I'm confident enough in my abilities to have a sound and a strong direction," he admits disarmingly. "It's more important to me to study the song and the artist and figure out what's strong about them and then help the record be the best it can be."

Originally from Boston, Chiccarelli relocated to Los Angeles in the late 1970s after playing in a series of failed rock bands. Always interested in the technical aspects of music-making, he landed a job as an assistant engineer at Cherokee studios, but his big break didn't come until the day that Frank Zappa's regular engineer was held up in London with visa difficulties. As low man on the totem pole, the 20-year-old Chiccarelli was given the assignment to work with the notoriously difficult and demanding artist. Seven albums later, he had a career.

Since then, Chiccarelli has worked with an astonishingly diversified group of artists, including Tori Amos, Oingo Boingo, Black Watch, American Music Club, and My Morning Jacket. And every album he works on, it seems, sounds totally different from every *other* album he's ever worked on.

"When people ask me, 'What's your approach to producing records?'" Chiccarelli says laughingly, "my answer is, 'Well, what day is this?' But on a creative level I think I would be dead if I just made the same record over and over again. The personal challenge for me is to try to make something that's unique to that artist." Clearly, he's succeeding.

What do you think it was that Frank Zappa saw in you that made him want to continue to work with you?

I think it was because I was very much an open book. At the time, my only experience was in making good, clean contemporary pop records, while Frank's whole thing was to try the most outrageous things possible in order to make the music interesting and dynamic and over the top. It was a new place for me, but I was very willing to go there. Perhaps he just viewed me as someone who hadn't done a lot of records and so wouldn't be as set in his ways or closed to new ideas.

Frank was all about breaking rules and challenging the norm. I learned pretty quickly during my first few days with him that you just didn't say no. [*laughs*] He really had a great sense of the big picture. Before I even had a chance to make a statement or try to do things my way, I realized that this was a guy who could see five steps down the line, so I had to learn to trust him and know that in the end it would be okay.

A lot of producers and engineers I've talked to have stressed how important it is to be ready when your big break comes. Looking back with hindsight, what preparations had you made to be ready for that moment?

To be honest, I didn't know where the Frank thing would lead. I was fortunate in that I fell in with an artist who was a workaholic and went from one album to the next. But I didn't know at the time that this was going to be a break; I thought it would be a very transitory thing, that I

" [Learn] not just engineering and music, but also learn about art, poetry, literature, psychology."

would work with Frank for however many weeks and then go back to Cherokee and resume my assisting gig.

In terms of preparation, I'm not so sure that I did anything specific, but the one thing I tell people who want to become an engineer or producer is, "learn everything." Not just engineering and music, but also learn about art, poetry, literature, psychology. The job really involves a lot of things, and it changes from project to project.

As someone who appreciates good sound, do you ever find it frustrating to work with an artist like Jack White, someone who's into rough edges? Do you ever find yourself thinking, "if only we could work on this mix a little more we could get it sounding so much better?"

Yes, and there are many times where I will say something just like that: "Give me another half hour and let me fix this and fix that." But the thing that makes rough mixes good is that you just kind of go for it, as opposed to laboring over it and making sure that every corner is polished and every little detail is in place. That's why they often find their way onto records, and that's one of the things I respect about Jack: he's so much about spontaneity and honesty—the *reality* of something—that he doesn't want to spend a lot of time on sounds, on mixes, on anything. Jack is a big fan of old-school recording; he's the kind of guy who thinks that nothing's sounded good since 1972. [*laughs*] But if you go back and listen to a lot of the music from the '60s and '70s, the thing that it's got more than anything else is a feel and an emotion. So I actually think Jack is correct in that things sometimes just get polished to death.

With the White Stripes, my basic role is to capture the performance and protect the energy and the magic that Jack and Meg have. And they're a pretty powerful combination, I have to tell you. I've recorded Jack now with three or four different drummers, but there's a chemistry between him and Meg that's unique. They're so respectful with one another, and they work hard, and they push each other. Whatever people say about her abilities, it's immaterial, because there's something that she does that lets him do something very special.

Do you prefer to record digitally, or to tape?

It really depends on the project. When I feel confident that the band has got it down in terms of performances and things will probably be just a matter of a few takes, then I'll do it in analog. With the White Stripes, we recorded to 16-track analog, which was Jack's preference. But if it's a situation where there's still some uncertainty as to arrangements and structures, then I would choose the digital approach. Having the Shins project done in Pro Tools was a godsend, because I was able to say to [singer/songwriter] James [Mercer] something like, "You know, it would be wonderful if the chorus happened again at the end," or "Let's put a whole new section in the middle with different textures, and let me show you real quickly how it could go." Working digitally gave him lots of options. For example, there's a track on the album called "Sea Legs" where the chorus only happens twice in the song, and that was slated for release as a single. But for radio, sometimes that doesn't really work. So we tried doing the song with a more traditional pop structure, where there are three choruses and it ends on the chorus, and it worked, but we all felt that it was a little too normal-sounding. So we opted to go off on this crazy, quirky, almost Latin jam thing because it sounded really exciting when the song took a big left turn, and that's the version we used for the

> **"I view mixing as a process of balancing and refining, not reinventing."**

album. But when it came time to prepare the track for a single release, we went back and used the file that had a shortened jam section and a third chorus at the end.

Both analog and digital work fine, and they each have their strengths and weaknesses, and their own distinctive tonality. To me, it's like having another microphone or compressor to choose from. But even when I record digitally, my goal is still to get the sounds the way I want them on the way in. I've always taken that approach, and everyone I ever learned from back when I was just starting out took that approach. In those days, you were limited track-wise, so my attitude was, every time you put up the faders to do a rough mix, that was your record, or at least it was 90 percent the way you wanted it. I viewed mixing as a process of balancing and refining, not reinventing, and that's still my attitude.

What do you think it is that makes a song great?

In any kind of pop song, you want to be able to tune in and tune out at the same time. In other words, you want it to engulf you and captivate you every second of the way, but you also want it to take over your body in the sense that you don't want to have to work too hard; you want to be able to turn off and just kind of sing along. I think great songs work that way, in that you can view them from afar or be really inside them, just like a great painting or a great movie.

What do you think is the most important quality in a successful producer?

I think the more you are a fan of the music and are moved by it, the better the job you will do with it. And if you are really in love with the music, you will protect the artist's integrity at all costs, and that's all-important. Of course, you do need to know a little of the technical side of making records as well as the musical side of it, but mostly you need to be well-rounded as a person. I'm always inspired by people that create works that are long-lasting, in any art form. I think that what we do can sometimes be a very ephemeral thing, and I'm always awestruck by the Bob Ezrins and the George Martins in this business—people who have made records that will indeed last for a long, long time. But I often try to gain my inspiration from art forms other than pop music—painting, or filmmaking, or novels, or great architecture: something that's been around a hundred years, created by some guy who really broke all the rules. If I go to a museum on a Sunday and I get motivated by some new young painter or sculptor, that's more fuel for me to go into my medium and try to do the best that I can do.

> *"The more you are a fan of the music and are moved by it, the better job you will do with it."*

Suggested Listening:
Frank Zappa: *Joe's Garage*, Zappa, 1979
My Morning Jacket: *Evil Urges*, ATO, 2008
The White Stripes: *Icky Thump*, Warner Bros., 2007
The Shins: *Wincing the Night Away*, Sub Pop, 2007
Kurt Elling: *Night Moves*, Concord, 2007
American Music Club: *San Francisco*, Reprise, 1994

Carla Olson

Falling in Like

There are laughs, and there are big laughs. And then there are *Texas*-sized laughs. Carla Olson's got one of those—a honking great guffaw that makes you want to bust out in a big ol' grin yourself.

Little surprise that she was born and raised just outside of Austin. Forming a self-described obsession with the Rolling Stones when she was a teenager, Olson made the fateful decision to take up guitar and eventually teamed up with future Go-Gos bassist Kathy Valentine, first in a punk band called the Violators and then relocating to Los Angeles in the early '80s, where they formed the Textones.

Following Valentine's departure, Olson began two important long-term collaborations, both with ex-guitarists of famous bands: Gene Clark, formerly of the Byrds, and Mick Taylor, formerly of the Rolling Stones. Shortly after the release of their second album, the Textones disbanded and Olson struck out on her own. It was, as she freely admits, a difficult time for her. Then one evening she happened to catch a musical performance by actress Mare Winningham.

"Her lyrics and her voice and her sense of humor just grabbed me by the heartstrings," Olson remembers. "I could really feel what she wanted to do, but nobody was interested in making a record with her. We ended up going into a studio in Oakland and made a self-financed album. It was a learning experience for me, but after that, I guess I just fell—well, not in love; let's say in like—with producing. Performing live is still my first love, but now what I like doing second best is producing."

Since then, Olson has produced records for an eclectic group of established and indie artists, including Phil Upchurch, Barry Goldberg, Jake Andrews, Joe Louis Walker, Dona Oxford, and Davis Gaines. In between a busy schedule of sessions in LA and London, she's even found time to write songs for R&B legend Percy Sledge. Is there anything this Texas firebrand *can't* do? Picture that big Texas guffaw as your answer to that question.

Were you always interested in becoming a record producer?

Well, I've always been much more of a performer—I was a ham when I was five years old, singing and playing piano for anyone who would listen. I was never a techie, but as a teenager I remember listening to 45 RPM singles—Yardbirds, Jimi Hendrix, Jeff Beck, Cream—and playing them at 33 RPM so I could figure out the guitar licks being played. Even when I got to the point where I was a professional musician playing on sessions, I was never really all that interested in what was going on, other than wanting to make sure that everything was being recorded correctly. If I heard something that didn't sound like me, I was pretty vocal about it, though. Luckily the people I was working with had a good sense of humor.

In the Textones, [guitarist] George Callins and I were pretty much in charge, so if things weren't happening, we didn't hesitate to let the engineer know. [*laughs*] He and I had been partners for years, so we knew what kind of sound we were trying to go for, and between the two of us, we made sure that what was going down on tape was what we wanted. Our producer would be looking after the big picture, while we focused on the minutiae; we were the ones going, "Nah, that guitar sucks," or "The snare's not bright enough."

I learned a lot from those studio experiences, so when my career got the point where nobody was really knocking down my door to play a gig, it seemed natural to move in that direction. Looking back, I guess I was starting to feel a bit lost before I got into production because I didn't have an outlet for all the cumulative knowledge I'd gained through the years.

Now that you're sitting in the producer's chair, do you find you're able to focus on the big picture while continuing to look after the minutiae?

Yes, because that's really the producer's job—a lot of time, the artist is seeing the minutiae, same as I used to do. That's not to say that you're letting them make all the decisions, but with certain artists you simply have to defer to their judgment or you're not going to get the project done. In fact, a lot of times, their independence is the very reason you want to work with them. But very often, headstrong artists see their weaknesses as something they don't want to reveal, whereas the producer may see it as a vulnerability, which can be very appealing.

The idea is to utilize those things to the best outcome. For example, I never wanted to sing softly or in falsetto; it was like pulling teeth to get me to sing anything softly. Then, on a Gene Clark album I did in the mid-1980s, I was forced to sing that way because he sings so softly, and it taught me something about my weakness, because a lot of people were saying, "Wow, I never heard you sing like that—that's really cool." [*laughs*] Here I was thinking that it was something I never wanted to do again, but that's actually something that people like to see in a singer they think of as a belter. Take Linda Ronstadt, for example. She rarely sings anything soft, but when she does, it really stands out.

So what you're saying is that an artist's perception of a weakness in themselves might actually be an asset, and that only a third party like a producer would be objective enough to realize that.

Exactly. Take, for instance, the Honeydrippers album. It probably broke Robert Plant's heart that he had to sing in a regular voice because he's so used to getting up there and grabbing his crotch and wailing. [*laughs*] But that's actually one of the best Robert Plant voices I've ever heard. I do find that a lot of artists are resistant to trying new things, but sometimes if you can get them to just try it and then magnify it for them a little bit, they can see things a little more clearly. You certainly don't want to make the recording process unpleasant for them, because it very often already is for a lot of artists. Mare [Winningham] had worked with somebody before me who just broke her chops constantly. She was so happy working with me instead, she ended up paying me double! I called her up and said, "Mare, this isn't right," but she said, "No, you deserve it." She was just really pleased with what we ended up with, and I was too. Sure, there were definitely some things we could have done better, but you can't think that way. You can't go back once the work is finished, because you'll always have regrets. It's not fair to the artist, and it's not fair to you.

> *"A lot of artists are resistant to trying new things, but sometimes if can get them to just try it and then magnify it for them a little bit, they can see things a little more clearly."*

It does seem that the hardest thing for most artists is letting go.

True, but I'm a great believer in spontaneity—I love the first takes, and so I'm always rolling tape. In fact, some of the best takes I've ever gotten were when we had the attitude of, "Come on, let's just get some sounds together."

You said, "rolling tape." Does that mean you still record in analog?

I do, whenever I can. I love tape; it really is luscious to my ears, especially the sound of two-inch 16-track. For me, analog is like painting on an empty canvas, while digital is like typing on a typewriter. I think it's to do with the jagged edges of digital sound versus the rounded edges of analog sound. When I'm sitting in a movie theater, I've got to cover my ears now…and it ain't just because I'm old—I have no problem listening to music loud when it cries out for it. But digital recordings just bother me. I know I have to adjust to it, and I'm sure that eventually I'll find a happy medium, but if I've got the budget and the time, I'll still use tape.

> *"Analog is like painting on an empty canvas, while digital is like typing on a typewriter."*

Another thing about tape is that it imposes track limitations, which I think is a good thing. By knowing your limitations, and working with them, you can actually turn them to your advantage—just look at The Beatles for proof of that. Think about your favorite restaurants: are they the ones that have menus with 300 different dishes offered? [*laughs*] It's only the all-night greasy spoons that have those kinds of menus.

Is making the artist as comfortable as possible always the best approach to take?

Well, you don't ever win by intimidating the artist; you might get what you want, but you're not going to get what *they* want. I remember being so demoralized by one of the engineers on my first solo record when I was doing vocals; he was just pushing me and pushing me and pushing me, and I didn't like it, so I wouldn't want any artist to work like that. Yes, I was happy with the final results, but I don't have fond memories of that particular session; I can remember feeling less than myself, and it was a terrible feeling.

> *"You don't ever win by intimidating the artist; you might get what you want, but you're not going to get what they want."*

Even when you go into the studio with an artist you don't know, you can usually suss out pretty quickly whether they want to be guided by you, or whether they're counting on you to get the best out of them and onto tape. Most of the time you've chosen to work with an artist because you think they have something very special to offer, so why wouldn't you want to nurture them and do all you can to make them feel comfortable?

Yet there are some producers—and some film directors, too—who insist that the only way to coax the best performance from an artist is to get them on edge.

Well, musicians are on the edge already. Hello? [*laughs*] And actors certainly are on the edge too, because they're all dying to work. At least we musicians can sit down and practice our instrument; they've got to wait for someone to hire them so they can go someplace and act. So artists are on the edge all the time. You may not see it, but that's the reason they are who they are: they've got the muse inside them that's pushing all the time. So I don't think anybody has to push an artist to get the best out of them. And as producer, it's not your job to push them, anyway; to the contrary, the best thing you can do is to ingratiate yourself with them, because then they're comfortable and at ease. If they're out there in the studio trying to get their headphones right and you're sitting behind the glass, you've got to be the one to reach out and be as

Carla Olson with Mick Taylor

helpful as possible. Say to them, "Tell me what you need in order to be more comfortable; tell me what I can do to help." That's the way you get the best out of an artist.

So much of the job seems to be psychology.

It sure is. The funny thing is that I never wanted that kind of job—I never wanted to be a personal manager, for example, which is all about being a wet nurse and banker and attaché. But you really have to be careful with artists even though they often need that helping hand. Sometimes it's a matter of just being a little bug in the ear—a little tsetse fly—to help make them realize that they're going in a wrong direction.

Do you tend to spend a lot of time in preproduction to try to get to know the artist, or do you prefer to just go into the studio and start recording?

Well, very often there's no time for pre-production, especially if the album is being sandwiched in the middle of a tour. All you can do then is to try to talk things through a little bit. With guitar players, I usually break the ice by talking about guitars, amps, and pickups—they all love talking about pickups, for some reason. [*laughs*] Pre-production is always wonderful if you can get it, but a lot of times it's just not possible. Many times, the only pre-production I do is just learning the artist's previous work. I always try to listen to their most recent work, and it can also be really helpful to listen to their early work, too, so you can see where they've moved from. And because you've bothered to listen, they know you respect them, and that's really important.

Do you prefer to work with new artists and help shape their sound, or veteran artists who already know what they want?

Well, even if you're working with a new artist, you still have to listen to them if they have strong opinions, because if you don't, you're in danger of them losing confidence in you. You need to defer to them just enough, but it's also fine to be opinionated, as long as you shade what you're saying in a way that's not overt. You also need to accept that there are some people who simply don't take to criticism—even constructive criticism—at all. Sure, the reason the artist hired you is because they think you can do good things for them, but if you can sense in them a feeling of, "I know where I'm going, and I'm very confident in my abilities," you've got to defer to it, especially if the player is very good. I very seldom get in the studio with someone who's totally directionless, and it doesn't appeal to me to do that anyway. I'd love to produce young bands, but that may not be my strong point; I'm not one of those people that wants to put my stamp on the recording. To me, my imprint is the way the drums and bass sound.

Not the guitar? I'm surprised.

Well, the thing is that guitar sounds vary so much, depending on the player. Every guitarist has their own sound, but the one constant in rock 'n' roll—though not blues, and certainly not jazz—is the bass and drum sound. I can always tell my bass and drum sounds . . . though I have to admit that very often if I'm listening to an obscure Stones track, I can get fooled into thinking it's something I produced! [*laughs*]

So you're saying your goal is to get every rhythm section to sound like Charlie Watts and Bill Wyman?

[*laughs*] No, but I can always hear the sympathy that the snare has. I don't want a dead snare—I want it to have some character, and certainly I want the bass to blow some air. I don't like the sound of bass direct—I want to hear some movement—and I love for the drums and bass to work together, but every once in awhile somebody's got to take off a little bit. I love working with rhythm sections, and I love having the ability to tinker with that a little bit. You usually get the best results when they've worked together before, but sometimes you get beautiful results with people who have never worked together, too.

Keith Richards has commented that in most bands, the rhythm section is the bass and drums, but in the Stones it's the rhythm guitar and drums.

Well, I was the rhythm guitarist in the Textones, and I always played with the snare—it's what guided me, and so I'm sure that's true from Keith's perspective. Plus he's the greatest rhythm guitarist who ever lived. Mick Taylor is a great lead player, but, god bless him, he's not a rhythm player.

Mick Taylor had a tough time getting his career together after leaving the Stones, didn't he?

There were just too many choices for him. People like Mick need the right venue, and sometimes they don't choose the right venue for their work. Look at his background: first, he was in the John Mayall Band, where he was told what to do. Then he got into the Stones, where he was told what to do. But after he got out of the Stones, there was nobody there to tell him what to do . . . so he didn't know what to do! [*laughs*]

Did *you* tell him what to do on the albums you did together?

Absolutely. He depended on me. And that's why I was there—because I wanted to be a venue for him; I wanted to be the podium for him. I love his playing, so I would work with him in a second, any moment, just to be able to hear another Mick Taylor solo that's never been heard before. Who wouldn't? I know a lot of people who would love to have heard the end of Mick Taylor's solo in "Sway." Jagger had them fade it, but that was one of the reasons I had Mick record it again on the *Live at the Roxy* album—I wanted to hear what he was going to play! Those are the moments that you live for as a producer.

The thing about Mick is that he's just looking for you to give him the go-ahead. In the [Stones] song "Can You Hear Me Knocking," when they come to a stop, right before the solo section, you hear this voice shout out, "Play!" A second later, there's Mick. [*laughs*] They're telling him to play, and boy, did he play. Mind you, he's not looking for you to tell him *what* to play—he's looking for you to tell him *where* to play. I never, ever told him what to play; we started the tape, we rolled the song, and we got what we got.

And all our studio stuff was live, too, with the exception of the occasional keyboard overdub. I love recording live—for rock 'n' roll, there's just no other way to do it; blues and jazz too. I think the more instruments you have out in the studio and the more bleed you get, the better the results.

Did you have a similar kind of experience working with Gene Clark?

No, because in terms of the studio recordings I did with Gene it was a more controlled situation, with lots of acoustic guitars. In that case, I was looking for the music to be the underpinning to the vocal; I wanted it to be subtle, and not the clarion call, so everything was done a lot more methodically. We definitely had to work within the confines of knowing that sensitive microphones pick up [*whispers*] everything.

Subtlety was something I learned from doing live gigs with Gene, because he's such a soft singer and so nuanced. My voice is so loud, I had to back off at least three feet from the microphone in order to do backing vocals with him. That was actually kind of enjoyable, because when I was in a rock 'n' roll band, I got so used to being right on top of a 57; it was a pleasure to be able to actually hear myself.

Why do you think there are so few women producers or engineers?

I have a pretty good theory about that, and I hope it's not too jaded. I think that when women first get into the business, most of them are singers or songwriters; they often don't have a technical background, so they don't gravitate to engineering or record production, at least not initially. And by the time they reach the age where they decide they're not going to perform any more, they've often got families to take care of . . . and men to take care of, too, unfortunately. [*laughs*] I personally was never discriminated against in the studio; nobody ever treated me badly or disrespected me. I mean, sure, sometimes I get funny looks—"There's a chick behind the console!"—but nothing more than that.

You know, when you're in your twenties, you want to be an artist, because that's your moment, that's your angst, that's your time to get the ya-yas out. When you're in your thirties, you start feeling like your moment is slipping by, and you take the mentality of, "I've got to do whatever I can to keep in the game—I've got to look good and go to the gym." But then all too soon you're in your forties . . . and nobody wants you anymore. It's a bit like acting—that's why you see actresses turn to producing and directing, because nobody is giving them acting roles any more.

I also feel that a women's point of view is totally different from a man's point of view in terms of recording, and also in terms of what we hear. I'm not saying it's better or worse; I'm saying it's different.

Are you saying there's a genetic reason that causes women to hear things differently from men?

I don't know, but I do find it to be true, and male engineers tell me that all the time, too. It's not that we hear things totally differently; it's a lot more subtle than that, like the way things sit in a mix. A lot of times the way I mix a vocal is different from the way a male engineer might do it—they'll actually say to me, "Wow, I wouldn't have thought of doing it that way." I don't know—maybe it is a physical thing. Or maybe it's just a vulnerability thing. Women are already paying 75 percent equity in the world, at least in America; we make 75 cents for every dollar a man earns. So as a woman in the world of business, you are already constantly being pushed down. That may be why we have a bit more edge, and a bit more drive, to try to prove ourselves. That's the only explanation I can offer.

I do find it strange that some female producers haven't gotten the recognition they're due in the industry—take, for example, Sylvia Robinson, who was a producer, a record company executive, a musician, and a writer. People like her often get treated as a sidebar or a footnote, but they don't get focused on. Though, to be fair, I do have to say that I've never come across any male musicians—or producers, or engineers—that ever did anything to make me feel any less equal to them.

What advice would you give someone who wants to be the next Carla Olson?

Do what I didn't do: go to school. Learn everything you need to know technically, so that when you walk in the room, nobody can one-up you. And always fly by the seat of your pants at least once in awhile; try something new, something different, instead of constantly relying on what you already know. Finally, go with your heart. If your heart tells you to do something, it's the right thing to do.

Selected Listening:
Carla Olson: *Within an Ace*, Watermelon, 1993; *Reap the Whirlwind*, Watermelon, 1994; *The Ring of Truth*, Evangeline, 2001; *Dark Horses*, Blues Boulevard/Music Avenue, 2008
Gene Clark and Carla Olson: *So Rebellious a Lover*, Razor & Tie, 1987; *In Concert*, Collector's Choice Music, 2007
Mare Winningham: *Lonesomers*, Razor & Tie, 1998
Phil Upchurch: *Tell the Truth!*, Evidence, 2001
Jake Andrews: *Jake Andrews*, Emusic, 2002
Mick Taylor and Carla Olson: *Too Hot for Snakes Plus*, Collector's Choice Music, 2008

Eric Schilling

Miami Heat

When you think about major hubs for music, three cities spring to mind: LA, New York, and Nashville. But the immense success of Latin artists like Gloria Estefan, Enrique Iglesias, Ricky Martin, and Mark Anthony has also put Miami distinctly on the map, and eight-time Grammy winner Eric Schilling is one of the shining stars in the South Beach scene.

With over a hundred albums to his credit—including more than a dozen with the esteemed Ms. Estefan—Schilling is a veteran with that rare combination of experience and a willingness to embrace new technologies. His career began when he was a mere teenager, working in radio broadcast, doing live shows from jazz and folk clubs in his native California. He eventually landed at Sausalito's famed The Plant, paying his dues as an assistant engineer. Several years later, he was offered a job in south Florida in a new facility being opened by legendary producer Bill Szymczyk. The long apprenticeship finally paid off when Schilling was asked to engineer an album for Dion and the Belmonts in 1978. Since that time, he has worked alongside top producers Phil Ramone, Quincy Jones, Peter Asher, and Humberto Gatica, recording major artists such as Elton John, Shakira, Natalie Cole, Janet Jackson, and Natalie Imbruglia, as well as mixing sound for the Latin Grammys and MTV Unplugged. In 2006, while on his way to mix a live gig for Gloria Estefan, he was involved in a serious car accident, which put him in a coma for two months; happily, he made a full recovery and is now back in the studio.

But for all his personal travails and professional success, Schilling remains disarmingly down to earth, and most definitely in touch with the common home recordist—the kind of guy you'd definitely like to have in your corner when it comes time to put your own music on the line.

Do many of your projects begin life in home studios?

Much of what I deal with now starts off in the home environment; I actually view it as one continuous process. I tell people, "I don't care if you record at home, but learn the craft so that you have a respect for what you're doing." It's not that I'm worried that you're going to take my job—it's just, try and do it well. The gear is important, but it's actually the third thing down the list. Number one is that you have some skill, and number two is that you be in an environment where you can hear what you're doing. The gear comes third.

How can a home recordist tell that a room isn't allowing them to hear accurately?

If you do a mix and go out and play it in your car stereo and it's wacky, it means you have a room problem. Mixing if you can't hear is like trying to paint if you can't see.

Most people think that treating a room simply means going to a music store and buying foam. But if it's essentially a square room, it doesn't matter if you have some foam in the corner and a few pieces on the wall—you still won't be able to hear bass to save your life.

I know one producer who has a studio in his house, and he built bookshelves all across the front of the room. It's a terrific idea because they make for a natural room diffuser; it has mass, and each book has a different depth and size. The concept is brilliant in its simplicity. There are a number of techniques like that which are really simple. Bill Putnam's original United Western room had room treatment that was all off-the-shelf materials from a lumberyard, built into modules. It's a very basic design: pegboard over fiberglass in little boxes against the wall, a linoleum tile floor. You've got to put how it works above how it looks: I've been in plenty of rooms that I think look great but don't sound very good. You need to put thought into your home recording environment, even if it's as straight-ahead as, don't put the speakers up against the wall in the corner, where the bass is going to build up. Try and refract the room by putting in a couch, and hang some tapestry so that the walls aren't just hard surfaces that the sound bounces off of.

Use your ears! Play your favorite CDs and start tweaking while you're listening to them. I have a little room that a friend and I built in an office complex. We don't rent it out; it's just for us to go in and work out ideas. I had my friend do a computer plot to determine where the speakers should be placed. We tried it and there was something funny—the bottom just wasn't working for us. Another friend came down, walked around the room, clapped his hands, made some noises, and said, "Why don't you try them over here?" Night and day! He just used his ears to sort out where he heard stuff, in terms of how his voice sounded in the room wherever he stood. It was not very difficult to do.

What are the most common mistakes you hear in home recordings?

Well, the major one is not turning the air conditioning off in the house. If somebody's recording an acoustic guitar and is close to a vent, you just get this constant low-end noise.

That's a problem that's probably unique to Miami.

[*laughs*] That's true. I never thought about that—you wouldn't have that problem in a lot of places, but in Miami everybody always has air conditioning on all the time.

I guess a more universal problem is placement of microphones. It's hard for me to say because I'm not there when they do it, but what I hear tells me that people get a microphone and just kind of point it. My hunch is that what happens is, they look in a magazine, they see a microphone, there's somebody who's saying it's great, and they think, "Well, if I get this and just point it over here, it will sound fine." If they were to spend a little time critically listening while they move it around, it would probably improve their recordings a lot.

And the whole Pro Tools thing leads to another set of problems. When I mix a file that comes in from a home studio, I often need to spend hours cleaning it up first. Because tracks may not be labeled, I can't tell what to use. It's like having an assistant's chops; you just need to go through and take notes as to what's recorded on what tracks and clean out everything that you don't want included in the mix. Actually, this is the worst of all the problems I find with home recordings, and all my friends that mix have the same complaint. In fairness to people who record at home, they're not the only ones that do this. I've gotten material from really well-known rooms with the same problem.

Again, if you're going to do this craft, just try to do it well.

You're probably best known for your work with Gloria Estefan. How did you hook up with her?

In 1982, I had done a project for the guy who was producing Gloria, and he remembered me and called me when it was time to do her album *Eyes of Innocence*. Back then, she was not very well known; she'd had a couple of songs that did well in the Latin area, but there wasn't the kind of mainstream tie-in with Latin music that there is now. She and I got on really well; it was one of those albums where we cut all the tracks in the first week, then she did her vocals and I mixed three songs a day, finishing the whole thing in two weeks. A couple of months afterwards, the producer called and said, "We're looking for some new guys to do our charts and arrange for us." I brought them some tapes of this friend of mine who was one of the first guys to do drum machine programming, and they really liked them. I brought him in on the next project, and the album made a little noise—she had one hit off of it. She liked the team, so we just kind of kept on for many years.

Which brings up an important point: you never know where your next break is going to come from. You could do a tiny gig somewhere that doesn't seem important at the time, but it can lead to big things. So you need to always be prepared.

There's a very consistent vocal sound on all of Gloria's albums. What's the vocal chain you use for her?

For the older albums it was a [Neumann] M 49 into a Hardy preamp and an LA-2A. It's just a really simple chain. I actually bought the Hardy so I could ride the gain. When she would sing loud, I would back the gain down a little bit.

You actually did that while you were recording?

Yes. If you know the singer and the material, it's fine. If you only set the gain correctly for the quiet passages and you don't ride it, then it's going to get buried when she wails. It's just a way to keep the vocal from being too compressed.

And every LA-2A is different, you know; they're like playing guitars. At Criteria, where I was recording her for a long time, they had three of them, and there was only one that I liked; I think it has to do with the photocell element in it.

But then in 1989, as Gloria matured, I started changing to a [Neumann] TLM 170 microphone because her voice changed a little bit, and the M 49 became a little strident in the midrange. It's funny, because some folks hate the TLM 170. It's not commonly used on vocals, but I like it; I think it's really neutral.

I used that for about five years and then switched to a Sony 800G because her voice kept changing. I would change mics as her voice changed.

How exactly did her voice change over the years?

When she was younger, she had a much rounder vocal sound. As she matured, it became a little brighter. I wouldn't say it had an edge to it, but it had more overtones than it used to have.

People's voices do change, although maybe not every vocalist goes through the kind of changes Gloria did. I know that she works out, and she's in great health, so it isn't any of that; it just happened naturally as she matured. If you think about it, it makes perfect sense, because everything else about you changes as you get older.

But I try not to always use the same mics, anyway. I like to try new things, and every once in awhile I find something that I hadn't liked before that I suddenly like. If you're doing drums and are always putting a [Shure SM] 57 on the snare, sometimes you just say, "Can't we try something else?" So occasionally I try something else and it works.

What have you tried that works better than a 57 on snare?

Well, this is a little bit oddball, but on a jazz album many years ago, I used a Beyer M101, which is an omni mic. It was an album that had a lot of brush and sidestick work, and it was fantastic, because it got a more natural sound out of the drum. I'm not even sure why I tried it, but I put a 57 up and the sidestick just sounded real small. Every so often I'll use Audio-Technica mics on drums. I have a pretty good group of mics from them and on jazz sessions I've been very pleased with them; I don't know if I would try them on a rock session.

I know that a lot of people put 57s up against the grill to record guitar amps, but I'm a big fan of the [Sennheiser] 421 for that application. I just don't think that you should always use the same mics in every situation; you should experiment. With Dion, for instance, I used to use a Beyer M88—an old dynamic mic—on his vocals, and I got tremendous results. I'd try my M49 and all these other things, and they just never worked on him. I think you have to think outside the box a little bit when it comes to microphones.

You know, I get a lot of work because I actually know how to record things, which I find very odd; it seems to be becoming a lost art. But for me, any time I get a gig where I know the players are great and I get to record a bunch of them at the same time, I know I'm in my element. I really, really like to do that kind of recording.

> *"From the very first moment the first note of music goes down to hard disk or tape, every person in the chain is crucial, and needs to be just as good as the next person."*

People in our field tend to think that the only really important guy is the one who's doing the mix, and I completely disagree. I think that from the very first moment the first note of music goes down to hard disk or tape, every person in the chain is crucial, and needs to be just as good as the next person. Maybe it's a monetary thing, where people think, "Well, I'll get somebody young for the tracking who's maybe not done a lot of stuff yet, so he's cheap, and I'll save my money for the end so I can pay a high-priced person to do the mix." But the mixer can only do so much with the material he receives. The people who record the tracks—their role is as important as the mixer's role. So people who record at home need to understand that what they do is really important, that it really makes a difference. Even if it goes to Bob Clearmountain or Tom Lord-Alge or Mick Guzauski to mix, believe me, they're going to be really pleased if you did a good job.

It's been rare, but there have actually been one or two times I've said to people, "I can't mix these tracks; you're going to have to go back and fix them."

What was so bad about the tracks?

Well, somebody would record in Pro Tools and gate or EQ everything on the way in. My attitude is, if you don't understand the piece of gear, don't use it. Or just use it for monitoring; learn it on the monitoring side.

Do you prefer working in analog or digital?

It depends on what I'm doing. For acoustic stuff, I still prefer tape. But I'll often start a project on tape and then transfer it to Pro Tools afterwards, because people want to move things around and tune them and edit them, and you just have to deal with it. If the transfer's done well, it'll work out.

I use Pro Tools, but it kind of scares me a bit sometimes, especially when I have 40 people in a room, because if the drives give you any problem, or if you hit the Record button and the little hand icon comes on, then all the players are sitting there, all being paid scale, with the clock running!

Do you find that using digital workstations ever actually saves you time in a session?

No, it doesn't save time; it just gives you more choices. I've never seen a piece of gear using new technology that I felt saved time. The analogy is, if you're writing and you sit and type at a typewriter, your brain functions in a different way, because it's such a pain in the ass to go back and change anything. I think you tend to form your thoughts in a different way than if you're using a word processor, where you can futz with the words and you have a lot more choices. It's no faster writing on a word processor than on a typewriter, it's just a different process. Maybe sometimes it even takes more time because you futz with it more.

> *"Your brain thinks in two ways. One is a mental thought process, where you think about every detail, and the other is a gut reaction process."*

I really believe that your brain thinks in two ways. One is a mental thought process, where you think about every detail, and the other is a gut reaction process. So if you're recording and you've got an effect that you think is so right that it's part of the sound, then print it. If it's really a part of what you think the sound should be, just do it.

But isn't it also good advice to print a dry track at the same time, just in case you change your mind later?

Only in the case of reverb. But it really depends on whether you know what you're doing. If you have a good ear and know how to print the effect and make it right, then, yeah, print it; if you're unsure, then no. But if you put a flanger on the guitar and you like it and you feel it's part of the sound, then it should be on tape.

Mixed in with the guitar or on a separate track?

Mixed in with the guitar. I want to be able to pull up one fader and hear the overall guitar sound. Same thing with strings, or horns, for that matter. I don't have a need to place every spot mic on its own track. If you feel that the balance of the strings or horns should be a certain way, then you should go ahead and give me that balance. But if you don't have that kind of ear, I wouldn't encourage people to start off that way.

You need to not be afraid to make decisions . . . and don't put things off. Often when you're working on an album that's all in Pro Tools, people will say at the end of the night, "We'll take care of that when we come back tomorrow." But they often don't go back to take care of it; they get into something else and you end up with all this stuff that's not corrected.

The producer might be there for 12 hours, but I'll stay two hours afterwards to clean up stuff so that when he comes in the next day we can move on. You just can't afford to put anything off. It makes for a long day, but as Gloria once said to me—one night I was really tired and I was bitching about working late—and she said, "I didn't pick your job; *you* picked your job." [*laughs*] That was great; she was completely right. I just went, "You know what? You're right; I'm just being an asshole." You look at what you choose to do, and you just accept it.

While we're talking about home recording, there's another topic I'd like to touch on, and that's the lack of community. People working in home studios don't have a chance to sit by the coffee machine and talk with other people about what they're doing. Even a lot of players are getting into that. They'll say, "You send me a track and I'll do the drums, then I'll send it on to the bass player and he'll add the bass." I think that affects the production quality of some of the albums that are out now; you just don't get the emotional response the same way. Plus, with nobody to feed off, it can be hard to know when to stop. Same thing when I mix; the hardest thing is to know when I've done as good as I can do.

What yardstick do you use to know when to stop mixing?

It's through experience; I just know from years of doing it. I will say that I have more fun with it now than I used to. When I started, it was much harder for me, because I was always trying to create an exactly perfect mix; I didn't know when to stop. I began doing better work when I learned to relax and trust my instincts.

Do you prefer mixing tracks that you didn't record, or tracks that you've been working on since their inception?

There's no doubt that it's sometimes more fun to mix stuff that I've never heard before, because I have no predisposed concept. Yes, it is harder for me to mix stuff that I've recorded from the beginning, but on the other hand I know exactly what I have on tape or on hard disk.

In the old days, I would really work to do roughs that were great; I would put a lot into them, so I would be a little bit spent when it came time to mix. Now I don't worry about the roughs so much. I save an emotional part of myself for when it's time to do the final mix. That's the key: saving an emotional reaction. After all, if you're in a band, you don't want to blow out your whole performance at rehearsal—you save it for the show. Mixing is much the same way.

At the end of the day, just how important are engineering skills to the success of a project?

Well, when I'm asked about allocating budget, I tell people, "Spend the money on the players; don't worry about the studio or having fancy equipment. If you spend the money on the players, everything else will pretty much take care of itself." I can work in a cheaper room if the guys playing are great. My philosophy has always been: it starts behind the microphone, not behind the console. So if you're having a problem sound-wise, you've got to look at the source. If you record a drum and it sounds like shit, then maybe the drum itself sounds like shit! Or maybe the drummer needs to improve his playing. It's like taking a grand piano and having five different guys play it—you'll end up with five different sounds.

> *"My philosophy has always been: it starts behind the microphone, not behind the console."*

Suggested Listening:
Gloria Estefan: *Into the Light*, Epic, 1991; *Turn the Beat Around* [single], Sony, 1994
Miami Sound Machine: *Primitive Love*, Epic, 1985
Ricky Martin: *Sound Loaded*, Columbia, 2000
Julio Iglesias: *Quelque Chose de France*, Columbia, 2007
Jon Secada: *Secada*, Capitol, 1997
Dion: *Inside Job*, Stingray, 1980

Matt Serletic

Comfort and Challenge

Matt Serletic is the real deal—a thinking man's producer, with an approach to record-making that's truly unique. An accomplished keyboardist, songwriter, and arranger/orchestrator (not to mention record company executive), Serletic is also sharply focused, insightful, and—well, there's no other way to say it—*deep*.

First bursting on the scene in the mid-'90s with powerful debut records by Collective Soul and Matchbox Twenty, Serletic captivated the music industry (not to mention the listening public) with his unrelenting in-your-face production of Carlos Santana's 1999 megahit "Smooth" (off the multi-Grammy-winning *Supernatural* album). That success led to a five-year stint as CEO of Virgin Records, a post he left in 2005. Serletic has also produced a wide range of both established and up-and-coming artists, including Courtney Love, Stacie Orrico, Angie Aparo, and Taylor Hicks, while continuing to work with Matchbox Twenty and their charismatic lead singer, Rob Thomas.

We met Matt Serletic in [the sadly now defunct] East Iris studios one rainy Nashville day as he was putting the finishing touches on a new album. In this wide-ranging interview, he shares his passionate views and philosophies of life, covering everything from his early days as a hopeful adolescent to his groundbreaking work of recent vintage.

How did you get started in record production?

I started as a musician; I learned to play some musical instruments before I could walk, so that was always the basis for me. Even at an early age, I loved combining that with making tapes. I had a little cassette recorder and I'd go out into the yard and record crickets chirping and layer that over my piano playing for the soundtrack of a film project I'd be doing in class, or whatever. Tape as a way to change things was an early fascination for me. From there, it was really just a matter of pursuing it wholeheartedly that led me into learning how to make records at a fairly early age. I was playing studio sessions when I was about 12 years old, playing keyboards and doing little TV car commercials, doing whatever local work there was in Atlanta at the time for somebody that was amazingly cheaper than anybody else—I had no idea what to charge. [*laughs*] "Twenty-five bucks? I'm there!"

I really became intrigued by the recording studio as an environment to make more lasting musical statements than you can possibly make in concert. I was fortunate enough to meet Ed Roland from Collective Soul, and from about age 14 or so, I began playing in his band. Every summer, we'd get spec time in a studio from midnight until eight in the morning, so we would spend every night making recordings, trying to get a record deal. Later, I received scholarships to go to the University of Miami and be a fulltime music student. I was fortunate to be in an environment where the only option to make a living as a musician was to start playing merengue and salsa; there's such a large Latin population down there that there's a lot of those bands, and they look to the University of Miami for some of the better horn players. So I would go and play trombone in these bands. Man, you would get your musical and sight-reading chops together real quick! You'd literally be in the middle of a chicken coop or something, rehearsing in these strange places, junkyards, whatever, and these guys would write this music backwards, forwards, with lines drawn in Spanish and you really had to learn how to be quick-witted.

Were you doing arrangements for these bands?

Well, at first I was just playing, and it was enough to try to survive that—it was very challenging musically, especially when you're unfamiliar with the styles. Then I began doing some arrangements and we started going into the studio to make records, and since I was the only one who knew how to do things in the studio, by default I became the producer. A couple of those records were local hits, and that got me thinking, "Wow, I can do this as a living." That's where I really got a hunger—between Collective Soul and making those early merengue records, I knew what I wanted to do. Producing is the only job that combines all the aspects that I love about music: composing, arranging, and performing. As a producer, you constantly shift between making judgments or suggestions and actually doing those things, and it never gets stale. I love the fact that I get to dance between all of these disciplines.

How do you think the role of today's record producer has changed?

I view making records as a modern orchestration in the sense that the new orchestras of the modern age are bands and electronic instruments. I'm always thinking in terms of scoring, in terms of it being an underpinning, a framework, something that is supporting the melody here and countering the melody there. It's about creating a tapestry of sound, and that's why it's great to work with engineers that have such a knowledge base, because they're really able to hone that picture in. It's like trying to sit down and say, "Okay, the third violin in the back row is playing this note; now place it in the context of the whole orchestra." It's tricky. Some of the records we've been making have had 200 tracks, so it really takes somebody with great skill to have that kind of perspective.

Surely a big part of it is in the arrangement, though. It's not just about knowing how to carve out frequency areas in order to fit all the instruments in.

I agree. It's about working to consistently frame the melody in suitable ways. It's not enough to say, "We've got 200 tracks," as if you won a race or something. It's about what those 200 tracks are doing; if it can be said in ten tracks, it should be said. But if there's a certain power and majesty that comes with that larger, grander landscape, then go for it.

> *"You've got to know how to leave space for that vocal line while always maintaining a respect for the basic melody of the song."*

The arrangement *is* important. You've got to know how to leave space for that vocal line while always maintaining a respect for the basic melody of the song. To me, making records is just about making great songs. It comes down to songwriting; record-making is just an outgrowth of that process. Only a great song can make a great record; one has to exist before the other one can.

Though it *is* possible to make a bad record out of a good song —it's been done many times.

Absolutely. [*laughs*] Hopefully, I haven't done it, but I agree—you can get in the way of a song very easily. The record is really an arrangement. If it's destroying or conflicting with the melody, it can be real trouble.

You come from the George Martin school of record production in the sense that your strengths are primarily in arranging and orchestration, as opposed to in the technical arena.

Song, to me, is great melody. There always should be a dialog between the melody and the sonic underpinning, like the reverse tape kind of stuff that The Beatles did: "Listen to the melody, now listen to this." It's a dynamic interplay between those two elements. There's always melody, even in atonal music. Even in drum loops, you hear a shifting pitch. How to create appropriate sound collages with pitch is what's great about making music.

I don't think music is meant to be totally organized, anyway. It's important to have framework, but if all of a sudden a new addition grows out of it, that's what's so great about the creative process: you cannot define it. Even if you try to keep it within bounds, it works itself in other directions.

So you're saying it's important to be open to new ideas in the studio, to not have preconceptions.

I always feel like, when I'm sitting behind a board and working with an artist, I'm in a constant state of reacting, in a very neutral stance. You have to have a stillness and a receptiveness to allow whatever floating stuff is going on—both the input you're getting from the speakers and what's going on in your brain and creative soul. You throw one idea out and something comes back, and it might be something totally different than what you meant, but—wow!—it could be great. You just wait for those sparks and you have to always be receptive to them. Probably one of the most frustrating yet ultimately enjoyable things about what I do is that you never have the answer—at least not until after it's happened: "Oh, *that's* the answer!" Because as soon as you start saying, "I know what to do," you're committing to a predetermined path. Yes, you have a knowledge base that is ever-expanding, but you're really trying to create that initial moment, always trying to make every record different.

How do you counterbalance that creative spirit against the demands of deadlines and budget?

You know, the funny thing is, in some ways, the music business, fortunately, is less demanding on timelines than some other businesses. Even "we have to have this tomorrow" turns into "if you give it to us a day later, it's not the end of the world." Nobody's going to die if the music doesn't happen tomorrow, so there's a built-in flexibility. Yes, there are always constraints—budgetary, whatever—so you just have to react faster. I always find that at the end of a record, when it's really time to get it done, your mind allows itself to work that fast; it'll keep up with you. Sometimes those ideas are better because they're not mulled over so much.

You seem to be fearless in terms of blending traditional orchestral instruments with modern rock instruments, much as George Martin was. There don't seem to be any boundaries or limits.

I hope not. And mixing urban rhythms and world concepts and traditional reggae; all that stuff. There's a sophistication of rhythm that I seek out. It's really just thought processing and allowing those things to clash. I always found myself caught between the schooled, trained musician and the reactionary who is just all about the vibe of things without even knowing what note it is. Sometimes I find myself knowing what note it is but I refuse to *know* what note it is. It's a clash of two things in me that I welcome and enjoy. Sometimes it drives everyone crazy, but I think it ultimately helps the records I make.

You know, the great thing about making records is also the saddest thing: when you perform, you're immediately getting a reaction from the audience. When you make a record, it just goes out there, and you never really get that visceral, immediate reaction. But it also lasts for so long; it's a document for all time, and, to me, that's ultimately a better statement. So I believe in keeping

some sense of honesty about the performance in that you still have one single point to identify, and that's the lead vocal. That person is singing to you, and it's not my job to get in the way of that with 15 backing parts and 27 guitar parts. To me, a record should be a constant dialogue between a vocal and something else. It might be that right here the bass comes up or in another spot the toms drive up and then all of a sudden there's a glorious organ in the chorus, but it's always about having a dialog.

Are you an analog guy or a digital guy?

I use both. I love the sound of Neve preamps and I'm specific enough that we keep 25 road cases full of gear with us. I've done a lot of A/B listening and tried to define what my ears hear as appropriate. I usually use a vintage front end—great pres and great mics and all that—but I do love the creativity that comes with digital workstations, so we record to Pro Tools. For a lot of the records that I make that are a little bit dense—100 tracks or whatever it may be—that digital presence helps define [the sound]. There are some drawbacks to it, as far as warmth and stuff, but putting a digital source through a couple of great old analog compressors and a Pultec EQ all of sudden gives it what you might have gotten from tape compression, so I think there are workarounds for getting the analog feel in the digital domain. I love the creativity that that system brings, being able to try ideas instantly. You used to say, "Let's put another amp on this," and 30 minutes later it sounded like hell. Now it's just two seconds . . . and it sounds like hell! [*laughs*] It's a lot quicker; you're able to flow ideas faster and see if they work and discard them if they don't.

I'll then come out of Pro Tools into a great analog console, like an SSL 9000. I've done some experimentation with this and I believe the ability to mix in Pro Tools is getting better and better all the time, but there's really something to going through that SSL. Maybe it's as simple as the high voltages physically coming into contact with the audio on every channel that gives the sound a vivacity I don't near coming out of two channels of a converter.

Do you do a lot of preproduction work? Do you rehearse things thoroughly or do you just provide a framework and wait for great things to happen in the studio?

It goes back to the song; the song has to be right. You don't want to be sitting in the studio realizing that, wow, this song isn't really that good! [*laughs*] So whatever it takes to get that song ready, and, if you're working with a band, them being able to effectively perform it. As soon as that's done, that's when I stop. And that defines the timeline; it might be a week, it might be two days, it might literally be a month and a half.

For example, with the [first] Matchbox record, it took us awhile to get the songs together. The process probably took over two months, because we were also working to get the band feeling like a band. We were pounding out 14-hour rehearsal days, plus six hours a day songwriting on top of that. It was really insane, but that's an example of taking the time and waiting for the songs to come. We were completely under budget constraints, so we had rented a total dive. In those circumstances, I think that's much preferable to saying, "Let's just get in the studio now." That's because you can make a bad record pretty easily, and going in before you feel you have a song is one way to make a bad record. But as soon as you *do* have a song, you need to get in there right away, because that creative excitement isn't going to necessarily last forever.

When you've completed the preproduction process and you've got the songs where you want them, do you then have a sound in your head? Do you work towards a sonic goal during the recording process?

For me, it's really about hearing a world, and I hear that constantly; in fact, sometimes it drives me nuts! It might suddenly shift as time goes on, so you can never set it in concrete until you're making the record itself, but it is there as a goal I work towards. It's an ethereal, kind of electric buzzing in my ears that defines where the record should be, and it's different for each artist. I always hear that, and, for me, making a record is about more clearly defining that initial impression, without being predisposed to it.

Let's talk a little about your work with Carlos Santana on "Smooth." It's perhaps the only track on *Supernatural* that could have appeared on any classic Santana album; it's got a modern sound and attitude, but it could easily have been on *Abraxas*. What did you bring to the party that allowed that to happen?

That was a combination of enthusiasm, passion, and honesty. I really respect Carlos as a musician and a spiritual person. He is somebody that embodies a lifetime of music and what all of us associated with music and the arts can hope to accomplish in our lifetimes, yet still being connected to your muse, always totally passionate and committed to the music you make.

What was especially fun for me about that project was that some of the first productions I ever did were of merengue and salsa acts. I'd be the only gringo in the middle of these 4 a.m. sessions that were so alive—all these guys had day jobs and yet would show up at midnight. They were really amazing working-class musicians, and that passion and energy has always stayed with me, in terms of what music is and what it should be and how sometimes it really is the lifeblood of a people. Carlos is connected in a way to that, coming from his background, and from working with jazz greats such as Miles Davis. It was really exciting to work with him and to hear his interpretation and my interpretation and Rob's interpretation of that energy. That's really what that track was about, and it was a lot of fun to do.

I think the record was a success largely because Carlos was open to receiving other people's energy, and the producer ultimately is the traffic cop, the energizer of a session. It's really about taking the temperature of the room and the musicians around you at any moment and pushing that over the top. That's really what happened on all those tracks on *Supernatural*—the different barometers, the different apparatus for gauging Carlos' energy and the energy around the band—each producer made the difference to what direction each track went in. The energy coming from Carlos was the same, but the interpretation of it through the traffic cop, if you will, was different for each track.

I sincerely believe that the glorious part of the human soul is the creative aspect of what we do. That creative energy is inherent in every person, everywhere, and, hopefully, that's what the best part of our lives is celebrating. As we sit here now, you're thinking about things; you're proactively going beyond this conversation and pulling ideas back and forth, as I am. That energy changes, shifts suddenly at any point between two people, and certainly if another person comes into the equation; if somebody else were to sit down here now and talk to us, the whole dynamic would shift. I think there are people that are given the ability to help energize that process and to really stir it up and change it; to challenge it like you're challenging me to answer these questions. People who take on that role would be great producers, because they're gauging at all points: the low ebb of creativity, the high point, how to massage those two intervals, how to change the thoughts in the room, really. That, to me, is what doing it right is about: dancing that dance of gauging the energy that's around you, and effectively getting it on tape in a way that's new and fresh and exciting.

Even though Carlos was this legendary guitar player for whom I had such admiration, when he walked in the room, he needed to know that I, along with all the musicians in the room, was honest and passionate about the music we were about to make. As soon as we got that energy going—and it started with the rehearsals we did even before Rob [Thomas] came in that night—that set a tone for how that record was going to come out. And then it was furthered by getting all those people together and feeling that nervous energy, between Rob being a little awe-struck by Carlos, and Carlos possibly being a little nervous about working with a new team. But that energy was set up; when these guys came in, they could already feel it.

Was that the first time Rob and Carlos had met?

Yes. And we capitalized on that; it was really about pushing the envelope, driving everybody. I would be saying, "Come on—more!" Sometimes you have to verbalize the intangible energy in the room. It wasn't some magical psychological trick; it was really just being a lightning rod for what was already there—getting out of the way when it was necessary, and pushing when the energy was ebbing. We did the solos the next day, but it was still about retaining that energy and creating the right headspace for Carlos to walk in and play.

You can hear in his solo that he's totally inspired.

That also comes from sitting around talking about it with him. He's a very spiritual person, and I think when somebody starts talking to you about what they truly, passionately believe and have discovered over years and years of searching, you have to be respectful of that and show them that you have some notion of what that means to them. Certainly it doesn't mean similar things to me that it does to him, but he needed to sort of get that information reflected back to him—to know that he was connected. That emotional dialogue between us was all spiritually based, and he defined that, not me—that's his personality. So therefore I shifted my language and my comments into that realm so as to be more effective.

> *"I can summarize in two words what I think a producer should do: comfort and challenge. Make the artist comfortable, but challenge him."*

I remember an old childhood story where sorcerers create an illusion of having danced between the raindrops. I always loved that ideology of not letting problems affect you, allowing yourself to drift freely to the good things in life, to live a passionate existence. So I can summarize in two words what I think a producer should do: comfort and challenge. Make the artist comfortable, but challenge him. Not in the antagonistic sense; you create a comfortable environment so that they know that the challenge is coming for the greater good of the project, not for some ego boost.

But let's go to the other side of the coin: How do you deal with situations where you and the artist just don't see eye to eye; for instance, if you feel that a song is not ready to be recorded?

I simply don't record things that I don't feel passionate about. I view it as looking for the key to the door: if I don't get the key to the door, I can't get into the song, I can't get into how I'm going to help make this record. Eventually, you should be able to find the key, after repeated listenings or changing things. And if there's no key, you just don't record it. I've fortunately never been in a situation where a record label has said, "You *have* to record this."

But how can you get an average song—one that's okay but not particularly exciting—over the hump?

You rework the song, and I build my relationships with most of the artists I work with on a song level, so we can go there and it's not an infringement of their artistic sensibility. So you try new things on a song level; maybe that improves it, maybe it doesn't. If you then get to a point where it's still not working for you, you have to really gauge the artist's intent and their attachment to the song. If it's coming from a certain place that you can understand and respect, maybe *that's* the key. Maybe you can try to hear it like they're hearing it and then change it to really represent what they're hearing. A lot of times creative people hear things in this magical world that's perfect, and it's really amazing to them. So instead of discarding something because I just don't get it, I try to somehow understand what it is they're hearing. None of this is stuff is individual vision; it's very much collective vision, so I think you have to respect that aspect. If somebody is passionate about something, then maybe they're right. If nobody is passionate about it, you probably shouldn't record it. That's a defining issue for me.

Some artists view the producer's role simply as a facilitator—they rely on him or her to realize their vision for a record—while others give the producer the freedom to impose his own vision on the record. Presumably, you've dealt with both kinds of artists. Are you able to work both ways?

Yes, but you pick your battles. When you're given that trust, the sky is the limit, but you still want to respect the vision of the artist in the sense that you understand it. You're not necessarily going to include whatever instrument of the moment you might be favoring just because you feel like it; it really has to be in the context of the artist. Because you're putting forward a picture of the artist, and, as producer, you're secondary to that.

But if you're dealing with a person that has very definitive ideas, it's really a one-by-one thing. You weed through them; you try all the ideas. It's really a single creative incident at a time.

What do you do if you see an artist traveling down a road that you instinctively feel is all wrong for them?

You discuss it. You owe them the service of pointing them in a better direction, and the more strongly you feel about it, the more vocal you have to be. And artists definitely head in weird directions at times, but producers can do that, too! The thing can turn back on yourself very easily. As a songwriter, I have to be careful not to be a producer while I'm creating. In those role reversals, you really have to know the boundaries in which you're playing; that goes for steering an artist in the right direction, too.

If you have to, at some point you just say no. You have to be a firm, decisive leader at the appropriate times, and if you couch it in the right creative, vibey way, those times come very infrequently. My style is confrontation at the very last; working together comes first. The budget plays an important role, too: for certain artists, you can afford to try everything out; for others, you have to say, "Nope, this is how it has to be—this is a single that's going on a soundtrack that's going out next week, and this is how we're doing it." [*laughs*] You have to be very authoritarian in those circumstances, but that's what I love about starting in the other place first: because there's a mutual respect between you and the artist, they allow you to be an authoritarian without getting too flustered about it. Or, if they get flustered, they go away and come back. It's not like it's the end of the world and you're never going to see each other again.

Of course, the artist has much more at stake than the producer; they have to go out and tour behind the record they're making, while the producer goes on to another project.

Absolutely, and you have to respect that. So it goes back to, when one of the guys in the band is very passionate about something, you owe it to them to look into it. You've got to step back and let it happen until you catch on. You've got to allow other ideas to filter in.

What's the craziest recording trick you've tried that actually made it onto a record?

[*long pause*] God, there's so many. Two that come to mind are recording drums on a roof on a watershed and getting this weird, bizarre sound. Or doing guitar sounds that literally require nine people to create: "Okay, you're going to hit the Echoplex now, and you're going to turn on the delay now, and you're going to do the Morse code on the guitar while the guitar player actually holds the note." I love involving people in strange circumstances and flipping the rules, because there are so many implied rules in the studio: "This is the way you mic a drum kit; this is where you stand when you sing your vocals." A lot of those are totally time-tested and honored, mind you, so you can use them when you're not looking for anything sonically different or weird.

Some of the funnest things are when you get a roomful of people who have no idea what the recording session is about, and all of a sudden somebody's playing guiro and somebody's hand-clapping and somebody's screaming and you get that crowd response. We've done a few things like that, where the energy of the room is so fun. Half the time it sounds like hell when you're done, but you hear the excitement; the "good time was had by all" vibe translates on the tape.

I really look for signature. That's a big word for me: looking for the signature lick, the signature sound, the signature performance—something that really helps define artistically the song, the artist, the guitar player.

Are you averse to using autotuning if you've got a great performance but it's not quite in tune?

I go back and forth. When I work with a vocalist, I don't listen with an "Oh, we can fix that" mentality; I go for it. And sometimes out of tune is not the end of the world, if it's sung with passion and conviction. So screw it, you know? It helps define the genre of what you're working on, in a way. If it's a big rock record, not every note needs to be in tune. [*laughs*] You know, as new tools become incorporated, the sound becomes somewhat homogenized, and all the best producers have always chosen elements outside of the standard of the day to do something different. Whether it's something as simple as, "Don't pitch your vocals," or using cannon drums when everybody else is using tight snares, we are collectively responsible for shifting the medium.

"A great record should be like you're pulling a string towards you constantly, and you never let up: there's a constant tension that maintains your interest."

What is your definition of a great record?

A great record should be like you're pulling a string towards you constantly, and you never let up: there's a constant tension that maintains your interest. That can be the vocal dipping into the way a guitar line leads into the pre-chorus; there's always this constantly connected thread. Especially when I'm doing a final mix, I'm always looking for that point where the string breaks. Then I say, "Okay, we've got to fix that." If I'm not believing it past this point, I've lost it, it's not right.

It should also contain something of lasting intrigue. You go back to it and you're still fascinated by it, by what the artist is saying or how it sounds. On some level, it just intrigues you. [Don

Henley's] "Boys of Summer," for example, is a great record to me. When I was a kid I loved it, and I still go back to it and listen now and it's still intriguing, from the vibe of the record to the vocal performance to the cool guitar licks that Mike Campbell played. Or you can take any U2 song—say, "Sunday Bloody Sunday"—and behind it stood an album that unrolled itself as engaging. That song sat in that album in a way that encouraged you to roll on into the rest of the album, to really become involved. Same with *The Bends* by Radiohead—an amazing rock album. Or *Let It Be* by The Beatles, and, of course, *Sgt. Pepper*—any record producer has to recognize the brilliance of *Sgt. Pepper*.

It's interesting that you would single out *Let It Be* since most people view that as the *least* great of all The Beatles' albums, mainly because it was made in such dire circumstances.

Yeah, but to me that's still intriguing—the fact that it was chronicling the dire circumstances of a great bunch of creative people.

But they hated each other by the time that record was being made.

Yeah, and you can *hear* that. Same thing with the Eagles' *Hotel California*. It comes down to those albums that raise the hackles on the back of your neck. I can't define it, but I just respond to certain albums that way. I also get that feeling when we're getting it right in the studio; that's the same gauge I use.

Is it your goal to make records that are lasting, even if they don't necessarily enjoy commercial success?

Well, I really believe that making great records equals commercial success, in the sense that, if you're recording great songs and putting exciting or intriguing performances down on tape or disk, it will engage the listener. After all, that's the fundamental principle of what the recording industry is built upon: engaging the listener, who's also the consumer, enough that they're going to go out and buy it. That's a very simplistic, maybe optimistic model, but I believe if more people take that view, it's going to be a better musical world. If we can go back to making great albums, as opposed to a hit song and a collection of other songs to package on the album to trick the listener into buying it, it's going to be better for music. Sure, in this fast-paced world, you have to have the big, blazing billboard that says, "Hey, check it out, check it out!" But if there's something really behind the hit, people are going to gravitate to that artist for a long time to come. As record-makers, I think it's our responsibility to make that happen consistently.

Suggested Listening:
Matchbox Twenty: *Yourself or Someone Like You*, Atlantic, 1997; *Mad Season*, Atlantic, 2000; *Exile on Mainstream*, Atlantic, 2007
Rob Thomas: *Something to Be*, Melisma/Atlantic, 2005
Carlos Santana: *Supernatural* (produced the track "Smooth"), Arista, 1999
Collective Soul: *Hints, Allegations, and Things Left Unsaid*, Atlantic, 1993
Taylor Hicks: *Taylor Hicks*, Arista, 2006
Courtney Love: *America's Sweetheart*, Virgin, 2004

Part Four

Across the Pond

English Master

Gus Dudgeon

Decca Records in the late 1960s was an exciting place to be. Okay, so maybe A&R man Dick Rowe had committed the colossal blunder of turning down The Beatles, but the label still had a huge roster of hit acts, including the Rolling Stones, the Animals, the Zombies, the Small Faces, John Mayall, Marianne Faithful, and Tom Jones. The young engineer who manned the board in Decca's in-house studio for many of those artists was Gus Dudgeon, who later went on to fame and fortune producing a string of hit albums for a then-up-and-coming singer/songwriter by the name of Elton John, including John's 1973 double album tour de force *Goodbye Yellow Brick Road*.

Dudgeon's lush orchestral style was also the perfect complement to what may have been the first "concept" pop song—David Bowie's "Space Oddity." No wonder that when regular Bowie producer Tony Visconti turned the song down as being "second-rate Simon and Garfunkel," Dudgeon was brought in to realize Bowie's vision on tape, resulting in yet another smash hit. Following a parting of the ways with Elton John in the late '70s, Dudgeon continued an active career, crafting hits for XTC, Lindisfarne, Chris Rea, Stephen Bishop, and John Miles. Not bad for someone who once described himself as a non-musician with limited technical skills!

Tragically, about a year after doing this interview, Dudgeon and his wife Sheila died in an automobile accident. He was not only one of the most creative, but also one of the nicest guys in the business.

The piano sound on the Elton John records you produced was very distinctive. How did you go about crafting that?

It's very simple, really. You stand and you listen to somebody playing a piano and you go, "Right, that's how a piano sounds to my ears. Now how do I get that natural piano sound to appear on tape?" I was always scurrying around trying to find out a way of doing it, and the first thing I realized with a piano was, if you mic it too closely, you get an incredible amount of harmonics and a very unbalanced sound. So I was always looking to get the piano lid open, but of course it's very rare that you are in a situation where you can have that kind of separation, because if you've got a drummer thrashing away in the corner, he's going to be picking up all over the piano. Therefore, I developed this bizarre upside-down piano technique for quite a number of Elton's records, from *Honky Chateau* onwards: I had these boxes built that were basically upside-down, empty piano frames, which sat on top of the piano, thereby screening it off. And the microphones went through a hole in the side.

So this was a piano frame that was the same size as the top of the lid?

Try to imagine a piano frame with nothing in it other than a certain amount of padding, and a light so that the man who is going to tune it didn't have to take the thing off to tune it—the front would come off on some magnets and he could reach in—and you'd also have a little stand so he could put the lyrics up. Up until that point, all I was doing was recording pianos in the normal way, trying to get maximum separation.

Did Elton use the same make and model of piano through the years?

Oh, no, no. There were no Yamaha pianos when I first started, and I think that's what he uses most of the time nowadays. Plus he's using an awful lot of piano samples as well.

In the recording studio as well as live?

Nowadays, yes.

Your work on "Space Oddity" was groundbreaking. Did the production ideas originate with you or with Bowie?

The demo was pretty sparse, actually. Bowie played a stylophone, did a few harmonies, and did the countdown before the rocket takes off; there might be a bass on it too. I did a lot of planning on that record. I invented a bizarre wall chart, where I figured out a weird way of using different colored pencils to represent instruments so I could write a line like a graph. Then, if I was talking to [arranger] Paul Buckmaster, I could say, "Look I've come up with this line for cellos and it goes like this," and I'd look at this wall chart and sing it to him. He'd say, "Hang on a minute, let me scribble that down," and then he'd ask, "Well, what about if it went to this note here?" Basically we were chucking ideas backwards and forwards, singing them to each other.

Was the string arrangement conceived beforehand or did you build on Bowie's basic track?

All I can remember is that it happened very quickly—I think we did the whole thing in a day. I'd worked out to the absolute nth degree exactly how I wanted that record to sound and discussed it with Paul, and then Paul went off and wrote the charts. I recorded the backing track during the daytime and then I think he must have come in in the evening, or maybe the following day, to do the orchestration, and then we mixed it. It was all done and dusted in no time.

Did you love the song instantly?

Oh, yeah. Don't forget, I'd already worked with Bowie as an engineer. I did all his early stuff, including his whole first album. I liked him as a bloke, and I loved the fact that, as far as he was concerned, rules were there to be broken. He used to come in with all these bizarre lineups. He was always doing something different; he was an interesting guy to work with.

> *"I loved the fact that, as far as [Bowie] was concerned, rules were there to be broken."*

Did Elton have the same kind of sense of artistic freedom, or was he a little bit more formula in terms of, this is the "Elton John sound"?

Oh, no, Elton was up for whatever. If I said to him, "This song would be great with an orchestra," he'd just go, "Fine." The most amazing thing about Elton was that, as soon as he'd finish doing what he had to do, he was off. He was either going to go and listen to some records or watch a football game or play some tennis or something. He never hung around for any overdubs, be they strings, backing vocals, whatever.

What about the mixing sessions? Was he there?

No, he never came to a mix. He'd come right at the end and listen to it. It wasn't that he wasn't interested—don't get the wrong impression. It was just that, for some reason, he trusted us, right from the word go. He obviously thought, "Well, these blokes know what they're doing; let them get on with it."

Where do you stand on the analog-versus-digital issue?

I got into digital the minute it happened; it was a blessing. When I was working at Decca, analog tape was such a dodgy medium that we used to listen on line out for any dropouts. I can remember situations where we'd be doing a take with a 20-piece orchestra and suddenly there would be a dropout or something weird would happen or a piece of dirt would go over the heads or something, and you'd have to stop them and do another take. It was a very unstable medium. And I always hated hiss. So when Dolbys came in, my attitude was, "Yes! Thank you very much, that gets rid of that problem," or as much as you can get rid of. Then when digital came along I thought, "Yes, please; this is what I've always wanted."

However, having said that, I totally understand why people have a love of analog sound and I must admit that quite frequently nowadays, after I've recorded a whole album, I will dump the whole thing onto analog before mixing it. I will always run a half-inch analog tape when I mix, and I almost always use the analog tape for mastering. But I'm not that fussy about it at the end of the day. People get very anal about this whole business. To me, you are either recording a hit song or you aren't; you've either got something that's worth recording or you haven't. I'm very fussy about what I record.

A lot of music today is being constructed after the fact, in postproduction with editing. Are you big on editing?

Sure, I use Pro Tools; who wouldn't? But I don't use it as the main tool. I use it when I have to because I'm in a situation where it's the only way around a problem. If a bunch of backing vocalists come in and they're going to sing four choruses, in an ideal world, I'll still have them sing all four choruses, rather than record one and move it around. Because then the choruses are different; the balance doesn't stay the same, the blend doesn't stay the same. I think if you just bank on the fact that you are going to get it right once and then fly it in everywhere, you're not really pushing the boundaries musically. I just like to go for the maximum sound from the minimum number of instruments.

> **"I just like to go for the maximum sound from the minimum number of instruments."**

How do you accomplish that? Is it in the arrangement?

Yes, a lot of it is the arrangement. The key can also affect things enormously. If you transpose up a tone, the bass may not sound as good, so I'll perhaps persuade the bass player to use a different bass, or change the EQ completely to make up the missing frequencies. Or maybe ask him if he's got a five-string bass so he can fill in the bottom end that's gone missing because he's gone up higher on the instrument. There's usually a way around it.

Is the vocal range of the singer the primary determinant of which key you pick?

I know an awful lot of vocalists who've decided they are doing it in the key that they think is right, and they are really pushing themselves to the very edge. If they can't get the bloody notes, you spend ages trying to drop in over and over—it's just hell. So I try to make a point of not going through that kind of agony, and say to them, "Look, what are you trying to prove? Do you honestly think that the people listening to the song could care less what key it's in? Most people don't even know what a key is." At the end of the day, you've really got to take a lot of regard for the range of the song. You have to put it in a key that's correct for your voice, so that when you are singing the highest and the lowest note, both are well within your range. Of course you get caught out sometimes because you get a song that's got a large range. Then you have to say, "Well, it's obviously going to be a strain to hit those top notes, but at least the bottom notes are going to be OK," or vice versa. You just have to steer for the safest key and cross your fingers.

Do you do a lot of signal processing during recording?

When I'm constructing a track, I don't bank on doing things later. I try to have a really good mix with a really good sound as near as dammit to the finished sound on everything. That way, when you get to the mixing stage, you don't have to process tons of stuff to get it to sound good. I'm not one of those people who sits and listens to ten different high-hat patterns and sounds and then says "Right, well we'll use this one for the moment and then possibly change it later, and keep another eight different ones up our sleeve." I like to commit and say, "This is the sound I want."

I also can't believe how many people listen to things in solo. Engineers do that all the time; they say, "What do you think of this bass drum sound?" My answer, invariably, is, "Let's hear it with everything else." That's the only time you can tell how it sounds—when it's in with whatever else it's got to work with. Because of that, I always try to set up really good monitor mixes so that people can get off on them.

What order do you usually bring faders up?

I always start with the bass and drums. Until the bass and drums sound dynamite from beginning to end, there is no point in putting anything else in, anyway, because you're only going to wonder what's going on when you start to put your 15th track in. You'll think, "Hmm…the snare doesn't sound very good anymore, though it sounded great before I put this other stuff in." It's because you probably haven't taken the snare sounds or individual sounds as far as you could have done, and I think the bass and drums are crucial; they have to work as a unit.

Are there any specific steps you take to meld the two together?

I think the biggest mistake a lot of people make is, because they don't decide on what sound they want at the time of recording, they wait till it's too late. And, because they wait till too late, they may not be able to make up the missing frequencies. If you've got a really good bass and drum sound on tape, you look forward to hearing it. You can sit down, push up the faders with no EQ, no echo, no nothing at all—just as it is, flat, and it should immediately sound very good because you've already done the work. However, you can make a decision on an EQ at an early point in the recording which turns out to be incorrect because of the other instruments that have been added subsequently and have filled the same frequency slots.

To me, a mix is like a cake—it's a question of layers. There's no point in having cherry and strawberry next to each other

> *"To me, a mix is like a cake—it's a question of layers."*

because they will become "cherryberry"—or "strawcherry." What you need is another layer of pastry in between the strawberries and the cherries so you can appreciate them as individual flavors. And, obviously, it's easier to make a three-layer cake work better than a 20-layer cake; a 20-layer cake is going to take you a bit longer to get it right.

Paul Buckmaster and I used to have these discussions. I used to say to him, "There's no point in booking a cello section if we're really looking for a lot of bottom end, because you're not going to get it," so I'd add arco [bowed] basses. He'd object, saying, "You'll never hear them," but I would say, "Yes, you will—if you write a good part that's placed harmonically where it should be in the sound spectrum, I can assure you I'll make damn sure you'll hear them." But I'll do it subtly, do it to the point that it's audible but doesn't blow the drums out of the water.

There's always a slot; when you're doing a mix there are slots that appear where you can crank something just enough to help it through so it still makes its point but isn't blowing your head off and hasn't gotten lost. It's all about trying to find that subtle point.

Once you've got the rhythm section sorted out, what comes in next?

If there's a piano involved, the piano would definitely be next, because it fills an enormous spectrum of sound; it's the most expressive instrument that's ever been created. And then the guitars are going to have to fit around the piano. That can be tricky, because if they're playing in a similar area in the harmonic structure, it can be hard to get them to come through without buggering the piano up, or vice versa. Sometimes I've recorded a piano in stereo and actually only used it in mono on the final mix because it's occupying an area that the guitars are in. If I've got the guitars spread and the piano spread as well, sometimes they're fighting each other, so the simplest thing is to make the piano less panned and all of a sudden the guitars are there. But if I'm having trouble with a mix, be it computer-wise or hand-cranked, probably I'm using too much EQ. That's a pretty golden rule.

What I would do in that case is either take the EQ off altogether and start again, or if you solo it and you think, "I really like this sound, I want to get *this* sound through," what you do is ease the EQ back bit by bit and turn the level up. Basically, if you use too much EQ, you're trying to force something through a slot that's too small. Maybe you've got a sound you really like, but let's face it, when you solo things, you could have the most fabulous sound in the world, but are you ever going to get that sound to work with the track? Very often it won't, so you compromise. You say, "Okay, maybe I'm pushing it too hard, I'm EQing it too much. What I should be doing instead is backing the EQ off and turning the volume of it up."

Presumably, then, the vocal is the last thing that you fit into the bed of instrumental sounds.

Yes, the lead vocal, and then the backing vocals.

What kind of tricks have you come up with for getting a lead vocal to sit correctly in a dense backing track?

Well, that can be tough. The classic case is that you've got this rocking track and it sounds brilliant and everything is roaring away, and you put the vocal in and all of a sudden the snare seems to have just completely lost it big time. That means that you're going to have to be very cautious about where your vocal level is and then make an adjustment to the snare level. It may be that it actually always was a little on the quiet side, because they both tend to be panned dead center, as a rule.

I wouldn't pan things to different places unless I felt it was absolutely necessary. I have panned vocals to the side for the effect of it, and I've actually panned vocals across a mix sometimes, if it works within a certain kind of piece of material. Maybe you need to compress the vocal or limit it harder; maybe you need to use a different kind of echo than the one you've chosen or a different sort of reverb, or maybe you should dry the thing up completely and take all the effects off and have a listen to that.

I find the quickest way to decide whether something is actually loud enough or not is to run the mix and just turn the signal on and off. If you turn it on and you can hear it, but it's not smack, bang in your eye, it's probably roughly where it should be. If you're running a track where you've got an acoustic guitar and there's all sorts of electrics, you know damn well that you're not going to hear every piece of that acoustic guitar part, and you're not going to hear everything the electrics are doing, either—there has to be some compromise. And if it sounds like you've got both sets of guitars too loud, the thing to do is just to turn one set off and see what you're left with. Probably if you turn the electrics off you'll suddenly think those acoustics are ridiculously loud, or vice versa; turn the acoustics off and the electrics are blasting. Actually what it means is, they're all too loud! The best thing to do is to take the bloody fader out and start again. Creep it up until you think that's probably where it should be and then try switching it on and off.

Suggested Listening:

Elton John: *Elton John*, Rocket, 1970; *Madman Across the Water*, Rocket, 1971; *Honky Chateau*, MCA, 1972; *Goodbye Yellow Brick Road*, Rocket, 1973; *Caribou*, MCA, 1974; *Captain Fantastic and the Brown Dirt Cowboy*, Rocket, 1975

David Bowie: *Space Oddity*, Virgin, 1972

Original Soundtrack: *Tommy*, Polygram, 1975

Richard Lush

The Beauty of the Apprenticeship System

"I remember thinking how amazing it was that they had trusted a session of this importance to two 20-year old kids, alone in the control room."

That's how Richard Lush describes a moment of epiphany during the orchestral overdub to The Beatles' "A Day in the Life," the towering climax of sound that closes the group's monumental *Sgt. Pepper's Lonely Hearts Club Band*. And he was indeed alone in the control room for that session, along with legendary engineer Geoff Emerick, despite their youth and relative inexperience. In fact, Lush would serve as Emerick's assistant for most of the *Pepper* album, as well as a good chunk of *Magical Mystery Tour* and *The White Album*, including the live satellite broadcast of John Lennon's anthemic "All You Need Is Love."

Lush began work at Abbey Road—then simply called "EMI Studios"—back in 1965, a result of innocently sending a handwritten letter while still at school. "I played a little bit of guitar," he explains, "and like a lot of young guitarists back then, Hank Marvin of the Shadows was my hero. One of their albums had liner notes that included a transcript of a conversation at a session between their producer and various members of the band. I began thinking that that might be a quite interesting job, so I looked up EMI's address and wrote them a letter saying that I played guitar and was interested in music, and did they have any jobs for a youngster just leaving school?"

To his surprise, he was called in for an interview and three months later, was offered a job as assistant engineer, or "button-pusher," as they were commonly known. After doing a handful of Beatles sessions with the newly promoted Emerick, Lush became his full-time assistant for the next year and a half, before leaving, like Emerick, in the wake of tensions during *White Album* sessions.

Unlike Emerick (who was asked back to engineer *Abbey Road*), Lush would never work with The Beatles as a group again, but he did stay on at EMI until 1973, when he emigrated to Australia in search of new vistas. Before leaving, though, Lush engineered solo albums for both John Lennon and Paul McCartney, as well as new Apple signing Badfinger...and he also eventually got to record his heroes, Hank Marvin and the Shadows. Once established in Australia, he began working with many of the country's top artists, including Sherbet (co-producing their number one single "Summer of Love" and their triple-platinum album *Howzat*) and Olivia Newton-John. In recent years, Lush has branched out into film music, including orchestral work for *Moulin Rouge*. "As you progress in life," he observes, "you tend to get shoehorned into specific genres, and these days I'm doing mostly jazz and classical sessions. One of the reasons, I think, is that there aren't all that many engineers around today who actually know how to record live instruments!"

Despite his daunting resume, Richard Lush is one of the most down-to-earth blokes you could ever hope to meet. With his easy laugh and self-effacing humor, the hour and a half conversation we had via transcontinental phone flew by in what seemed like minutes. It's easy to see why such disparate personalities as Lennon and McCartney warmed to him, and why he continues to be in such demand to this day as one of Australia's top-call engineers.

Your first opportunity to work with The Beatles came on a handful of *Revolver* sessions. Do you have any memories of those early experiences with them?

Well, Norman Smith was still their engineer when I started at EMI, and I actually assisted him on one *Rubber Soul* session, but that was just a sequencing date at the very end of the project, and none of the band were present. What I remember most about the handful of sessions I did on *Revolver* (assisting Geoff Emerick, who was their new engineer) was that they were always wanting to do things differently, and they were always looking for fresh ideas. On their first two or three albums, they had gone into the studio and performed like anyone else; recording back then was really all about capturing a performance successfully, and then going home. But by the time I got to work with The Beatles, they'd done all that and they'd moved on to a new phase—they were pushing the barrier, whereas other bands of the day were still going in, just recording the song and then perhaps changing a few sounds here and there afterwards. Geoff was into doing things differently, too, so it was a good match.

Was Geoff Emerick your main influence during your days as an assistant engineer?

I would say so, yes. It was all perfect timing—Geoff starting at that period, just when they wanted to do everything differently, and of course I was pretty new too. As Geoff accurately says in his book [*Here, There, and Everywhere: My Life Recording the Music of The Beatles*, Gotham Books, 2006, co-authored by yours truly], Abbey Road was a really square place in those days, probably because so much classical music was still being done there. Having these guys in white lab coats walking around the corridors was all part and parcel of being very British—doing everything properly and correctly. In many ways, he and I were the resident rebels.

What would you say were the most important lessons you learned from him?

Patience, probably; that, and pushing the boundaries. I learned the latter from Phil Spector, too. He was a bit of a wild man; whatever amount of reverb you put on something, it was never enough. He always wanted chamber reverb *and* tape slapback *and* plate. The Beatles, and Geoff, and Phil Spector, always pushed you to go that extra step, which in retrospect I think is a very good thing. It's something that hasn't happened to me for a while now. I guess as you get older, people have less of a tendency to question you.

Like Geoff, you walked out midway through the recording of the *White Album*. What were your reasons for quitting?

Well, it was a combination of things. Geoff was really peeved with the way things were going and we weren't getting any thanks for all our hard work, plus they were getting pretty fed up with Abbey Road—they'd been to a couple of other studios where the engineers probably smoked joints with them, so they felt those places were far more hip—and they were going through a lot of internal aggravation. Not only were they starting to annoy us, the long hours were starting to get to us—sitting there forever waiting for them to turn up, never knowing if we were even going to get a break to eat dinner, that kind of thing. Finally Geoff said, "Bugger it; this is it." The original idea was for us both to leave together—we thought that would really teach them a lesson. [*laughs*] But I ended up sticking it out for another couple of weeks longer, and then I left too.

PHOTO COURTESY OF RICHARD LUSH

Were you invited to come back for the *Abbey Road* sessions, as he was?

No, but I'm not actually sure what happened there. I was working with other people while those sessions were running, and I was engineering by then, so I wasn't needed anyway—they already had Geoff and Phil McDonald handling that end of things. I do have a strong memory of George Harrison sitting in a room with a Moog at some point, working on some sounds. That was actually all I saw of those sessions—I never actually went into the studio to hear anything they were playing.

You're one of the few people who worked on solo albums for both John Lennon and Paul McCartney after the demise of The Beatles. Can you compare and contrast their approach to making records?

The basic difference between the two was that one worked quickly while the other took his time. Even when he was with The Beatles, John was very quick at doing things. He didn't have a lot of patience: he'd go in and sing every song in just a couple of takes. He'd always say he wanted his voice to sound different, too. For one thing, he always wanted tape echo on his voice, and if you didn't have that effect going in his headphones, he'd get quite annoyed. Paul was the opposite: he'd usually spend a lot of time refining things, though sometimes he would do a vocal quickly, too. He was certainly more detail-oriented and thought things through a bit more; John was all about capturing the event, and then moving on.

On his solo albums, many of John's keeper vocals were actually sung live with the band during backing track sessions. Paul did that only rarely—"Live and Let Die" being the main exception; it was sung with both the band and a live orchestra playing together, which gives you a lot more excitement. But most of the time he would lay down a rough guide vocal and then spend a lot of time crafting the final vocal afterwards.

As is well-documented, some Beatles tracks took a very long time to do because Paul would be working out his bass part, again taking it to the extreme, not just playing roots or four to the bar, but trying to work out a countermelody that would complement the song. John, on the other hand, was as fast playing rhythm guitar or piano as he was singing his vocals. I don't think there were any overdubs on the *Plastic Ono Band* solo album other than vocals—all of John's playing was done live during the tracking sessions; it was basically just bass, drums, and piano, with John laying down a guide vocal. That was it—there was no dropping in parts. In fact, there are still a couple of bass mistakes on the album; it was just not a big deal. It simply didn't upset John if there was something inaccurate; getting the feel right was much more important to him.

What other memorable sessions do you remember doing at Abbey Road before you emigrated to Australia?

Badfinger's *No Dice* album, which was produced by Geoff, was one, and it was really fun. They were a great band to work with, and I remember us recording their original version of "Without You," which Harry Nilsson later had a huge hit with.

Paul's "My Love" [from *Red Rose Speedway*] was another session I really enjoyed, although it was a lot of pressure at the time. I remember that Paul had a really bad cold that day, but the orchestra had already been booked to come in, and so he wouldn't cancel the session because he'd have to pay for them anyway. So consequently we got the band sound in the afternoon, with Paul playing the electric piano while singing, and we spent three hours in the evening recording the orchestra, doing multiple takes. I remember him asking my advice frequently as to which takes were best. At that point, I already knew that I would be leaving for Australia in a month or so, so it was a very nice way to end my period at Abbey Road.

Why did you decide to emigrate to Australia?

My decision was based on a number of factors. I'd been at Abbey Road for eight years at that point, and a lot of my friends and colleagues—people like Geoff and Phil—had left by then; plus another ex-colleague, Martin Benge, was already living in Australia, and he was telling me how great it was over there. I guess I just thought I was ready for a change, so when a job opportunity came up at EMI in Sydney, I jumped at it, even though the job was only for a two-year period. I remember when the notice was first posted on the staff bulletin board, people were taking the piss, saying who would go all that way?

At the end of the day, it was actually my mother who talked me into it; she encouraged me to give it a try, pointing out that the weather would be a lot better than in England, for a start. [*laughs*] She was absolutely right, but at the end of the two years, when the job was over, I had to go back to the rain anyway, though I only stayed in London for just three months before returning to Australia. I've been here ever since, and I'm glad I made the move—I've married a lovely woman and raised a great family here, even though it's very hard to survive in Australia just making records; one has to have a lot of strings to one's bow to make ends meet. That's where my Abbey Road training really came in handy: when you've recorded all different kinds of music and taken part in all different kinds of sessions, you know what to do in pretty much any circumstance.

You did some sessions in recent years with legendary arranger Lalo Schifrin. What were those like?

That was quite an interesting experience. Very often, as engineers well know, things go wrong and you have to go to a Plan B, and this was a case in point. Lalo had two pieces of music to record—a 20-minute viola concerto, and a three-piece jazz band with himself on piano, played live with a symphony orchestra. He'd never been to Australia before, and he was planning on recording in a room in Adelaide that's basically a film soundstage, not a proper recording studio. Warning bells went off in my head, so I flew down there to have an advance look, and it was clearly unsuitable for the orchestral recording, both acoustically and in terms of equipment—all they had was a film console. In the end, we did the viola concerto in a large theater in Adelaide, but we recorded the orchestra and band live in performance at the Sydney Opera House. Lalo is such a great arranger, and he was so much fun to work with, plus I got to put a mic in front of Christian McBride, who's arguably the best jazz bass player in the world.

What mic did you use?

Well, I'd sent an email to [engineer] Al Schmitt ahead of time, because he'd recorded Christian before, and his reply was, "Any mic on that guy will sound great." [*laughs*] That turned out to be absolutely true, because he gets such a fabulous sound from his fingers. I ended up using a FET [Neumann] U 47, and when he saw that, he said "Cool, man," so I knew I'd made a good choice. I didn't use any kind of external preamp, either—just the built-in channel preamp on the Euphonix console we were using—though I put it through my beloved dbx 160. I love those compressors! I put them on all sorts of things—French horns, flutes, violins, basses—and it just makes everything sound nicer; it sorts all the levels out without making things sound squashed.

While Christian was here, I attended one of his clinics, too, and that proved to be really instructional. It was held in this little club in Sydney, and he was playing bass with a trio, and after a while, he said, "Hey, I've played enough—now it's your turn." All these other musicians got up and started playing, using the same bass through the same amp... and none of them got the volume or sound quality that he'd gotten out of that rig. It's not that any of the other people were bad players, but it's proof positive that it all starts in the fingers. I can't say I was surprised, but it was very cool to witness that.

The same was true of Paul [McCartney]—his unique sound came from his fingers just as much as from his bass or his amp. You can put his Hofner or his Rickenbacker in anyone else's hands and it won't sound exactly like him. Mind you, if you use the same kind of Altec compressors we did, you'll get a similar kind of sound, but it's not exactly the same. It's a combination of the player and the equipment he uses.

At Abbey Road, you only ever worked with top-level artists and producers, as opposed to someone starting out working in a demo studio who might only get to work with new artists. Do you think that that kind of experience spoils you to some extent? Does it make you less well-equipped to successfully record an artist that doesn't have that level of talent and ability?

Perhaps, but that doesn't change the fact that if you've got a great pianist playing on a dodgy piano, you'll end up with a far better sound than if you've got a bad pianist playing on a good piano. We all strive to make the best records we can all the time, but it doesn't always work out that way. You've got to make a lot of compromises along the way, and these days there are tools that allow you to compensate for lack of ability to some degree. Whether you agree with the use of things like autotuning or not, those tools do exist and you need to be aware of what they can do. A great singer may be able to go out and sing a song perfectly in one take, and, while those moments are fantastic, the reality is that a lot of the time you have to chip away and do it line by line, bit by bit, to actually attain a great performance. In its own way, that's kind of satisfying too. But the fact is that auto-tuning a bad performance will never make it great.

> *"A good engineer can get a pretty good sound no matter where they record."*

Regardless of where you train, I feel that a good engineer can get a pretty good sound no matter where they record. Obviously, it's a lot easier to make a great recording in a great studio with great mics, but it can also be done in non-professional environments with lower quality equipment... if you know what you're doing.

So are you saying that good ears are more important than good equipment?

Yes. If you can't discern between a good sound and a bad sound, or if you can't hear when something is wrong with a sound, it doesn't matter where you're working or what equipment you're using. The best engineers—people like Geoff Emerick—place all the priority on getting it to sound right in the studio. That's something I remember from my earliest days at Abbey Road: the engineer would go out into the studio and stand behind the conductor, listening to how the orchestra actually sounded. It's true that, these days, the engineer often doesn't have the time to do that, which is unfortunate, because if you do stand out in the studio and listen to an orchestra, or a guitar amp, or whatever, you can tell whether it sounds good or bad even before you set foot in the control room. If a guitar sounds shitty coming out of the amp being used, you need to try another amp before you go and start wrestling with different mic placements or EQ settings. Similarly, if a snare drum sounds really rattley and horrible out in the studio, change it over. Don't spend hours messing around with plug-ins trying to make it sound right! As Geoff often says, if it's wrong in the studio, it's never going to sound right in the control room, so don't bother even going in there until it *is* right. If you don't have good ears, the problem is that you may not be able to tell the difference.

As an example, I remember doing a vocal once with a singer in a studio that wasn't all that great, and I was sure that his mic was distorting, though it only happened every time we got to this one particular phrase. I tried all the usual procedures—I routed it into another channel and patched it through a different limiter, but there was no change. Finally, I thought, this is crazy, so I went out into the studio and asked him to sing it for me so I could hear it live. Sure enough, it was his voice! It just got this certain kind of raspiness when he sung this one phrase, and through the control room speakers, it sounded like audio distortion. But if I hadn't gone out there and just listened to him in the room, I would have been chasing my tail forever, trying different mics and this and that. That's the most important thing: listen to the music in the studio. That's also the only way to decide how to record an instrument you've never encountered before: go out into the studio and walk around the bloke so you can figure out where the sweet spot is; it won't necessarily be directly in front of the instrument, which is what you might think. It could actually be in a completely different part of the room, but unless you go out there and get the guy to play for you, you'll never discover that. Even just listening to someone speaking in the studio can tell you a lot about what areas in the room are too live and need extra screening, or which areas are too dead.

You were a fairly early adopter of digital recording technology, weren't you?

I suppose so, but I'm still not completely sold on digital. The first digital recorder we had in Australia was a Mitsubishi, and I first used it to record a Pavarotti operatic piece for a TV commercial. I was really looking forward to hearing the playback, because I'd heard good things about the sound of digital from various people who'd recorded pop music with the Mitsubishi. But when I heard it back, I got the shock of my life; suddenly the width and depth of this orchestra had shrunk in front of my ears. Fortunately, those machines didn't last very long.

Even with all the improvements in technology since then, I'm not convinced that digital is necessarily the way to go when you're recording acoustic instruments. It kind of gives you just the one plane: you don't get the depth that you get from analog. But if you're primarily recording electronic instruments like synthesizers and samplers, there's no real difference between the two, other than that the bottom end will be a bit nicer on an analog machine.

Not long ago I recorded some string overdubs onto a Leo Sayer album and we decided to bring in some tape machines, and it sounded fantastic. I hadn't used analog machines for awhile, and I'd forgotten how warm and lovely they sounded. It's hard to get tape these days in Australia, so most of the time I record digitally, but analog would be my choice for most acoustic recording. At a minimum, I prefer to mix to tape even if I've recorded digitally; it just kind of fixes any funnies that might be there. I don't know whether it's tape saturation or what, but quite often it sorts out all the levels for you—all the little level problems that you thought were there in the original recording resolve themselves. Stuff just happens when you put audio on tape, and it makes everything sound good.

You reunited with Geoff Emerick not long ago for a BBC project, rerecording *Sgt. Pepper* with contemporary bands, in analog and with all the original equipment. What were your most memorable experiences from those sessions?

Well, the Kaiser Chiefs were the first band in, and I remember the drummer being utterly blown away when he heard the first tape playback—all he could say was, "Wow, I've never heard my drums sound like that!" Part of it was Geoff getting the drum sound, of course, but part of it was laying it down on one-inch, four-track tape.

What with all the dropping in, there was a lot of pressure on me—I hadn't been a tape operator for 25 years or so, and I hadn't done it for nearly 30 years with Geoff in particular—so it was quite nerve-wracking, but after a while it all came back to me. The thing I'm proudest of with those sessions is that I never actually wiped anything! [*laughs*] So I guess the old brain is still ticking away. Geoff was a bit nervous too, truth be told, because he was working on a desk that he hadn't used for a long time. Fortunately, we had a lot of the Abbey Road technicians there to help us. At one point, the BBC people who were filming us asked me to turn off the four-track machine because the fan was too loud and so I started walking around the back of the machine looking for the mains switch . . . until one of the maintenance guys reminded me that it's actually on the front of the machine! [*laughs*] Mind you, I don't remember ever having to switch the machines off at Abbey Road—the maintenance staff would have been the ones to turn things on and off.

Another bizarre moment came when we were recording "She's Leaving Home" with the Magic Numbers. The two girls in the group were singing the melody—they were even singing the same note—but somehow they couldn't sing in time with one another. Geoff and I were totally shocked that a professional recording artist couldn't do that, but they explained that normally they rely on the Pro Tools operator to move their parts around. I remember thinking, god, that is so wrong! [*laughs*]

Then there were the Stereophonics, who came in thinking they were going to play the title track, but Bryan Adams had already done it, so they had to do the *Pepper* reprise instead. But they learned it on the spot and they did a really good job of it. The last overdub consisted of maracas, some backing vocals, and a double-track of the guitar solo, all done live and all recorded on one track, just like we used to do with The Beatles in the old days. It's good discipline doing things that way; it's like a high-wire artist having enough confidence in himself that he can do his whole routine without a safety net. In this case, there was no net, either—there was no mentality of, "Oh, we can fix it later."

The great thing about the whole project is that most of the bands arrived extremely nervous but they left on an up note. As we pushed them through their assigned songs, they eventually realized that they actually had to play every part right all the way through and get a really good feel and vibe at the same time, rather than rely on us to edit together a bunch of average takes, and so they began to relax into it. Pulling it off in the end made them feel really good about themselves and gave them a huge boost of confidence.

Even when you're recording digitally, with virtually unlimited tracks, do you still tend to impose limitations on yourself?

Well, I still think the way I did way back when, which is that there's no point in keeping a bad take. A lot of my assistants will ask me after every take, good or bad, if I want to keep it, and my usual reply is, "Well, the singer's still alive, isn't he?" [*laughs*] If he's given me a bad take, I want to do another one; there's no point in keeping one that isn't good enough. People today seem to have this mentality that everything needs to be kept, but when you adopt that approach you end up with 55 really bad takes and one that might be alright if you patch it up. No, it's much better to just keep doing it until it's right. Sure, you may need to drop in one or two bits, but the end result is that you get a great performance instead of a bunch of mediocre ones knitted together.

> **"There's no point in keeping a bad take."**

Also, as Geoff has frequently pointed out, there's the importance of overdubbing to parts that you know are going to actually end up on the final recording; that way, you're always building towards a cohesive whole, with the sound of the backing track actually influencing the sound of each overdub.

What kind of advice can you give a young reader who wants to forge a career as an engineer or producer?

The best thing you can do for yourself is practice. The great thing about today's technology is that anyone can set up a recording studio in their home, so you can fiddle around all the time, refining your skills. It's important to do a lot of live recording of real acoustic instruments, so that your ears get trained to know what things are supposed to sound like. The great thing about my start at Abbey Road is that I experienced all sorts of music—everything from orchestras to bagpipe bands to pop bands. That was the most incredible training anyone could have. It's a shame that young engineers today don't get that kind of experience; there's simply not that diversity of music being done these days in any one studio.

I really treasure the grounding I received at Abbey Road—not just the technical aspects, but having the opportunity to meet important people and to learn how to talk with them, which can be quite daunting. You don't think of it at the time, but later on you realize it was a very important part of your training, especially when you start to meet assistants who always seem to say the wrong thing at the wrong time—someone who might be the most brilliant Pro Tools operator in the world, but doesn't seem to understand what's going on in the artist's head. Those were important lessons we all learned at Abbey Road, and I don't know where today's young engineers are going to get that knowledge and insight.

Another piece of advice I can offer is that you seek out people who've done the kinds of things you want to do, and ask them lots of questions. At Abbey Road, we all learned from those who went before us: Geoff learned from Norman Smith and Malcolm Addey and Peter Bown, and then Phil McDonald and the other assistants and I learned from Geoff in turn. We took a little bit from each of them and molded it into our own individual styles. The beauty of the apprenticeship system is that everything evolves as it gets handed down to the next lot of people. That's

> **"The beauty of the apprenticeship system is that everything evolves as it gets handed down to the next lot of people."**

actually the best way to learn—to start as an assistant engineer and stand behind us old geezers so you can watch how we do what we do, then turn it into your own style.

You know, the great thing about getting older is that you amass a lot of experience. I've encountered every kind of problem there is by now. In fact, not long ago, I had a singer storm out of a studio and go home, and his people were apologizing to me. I told them not to worry, that it's nothing I haven't seen before. After all, I've had John Lennon walk out on me! [*laughs*]

Selected Listening:
John Lennon: *John Lennon/Plastic Ono Band*, Apple, 1970 (with Phil McDonald)
Badfinger: *No Dice*, Apple, 1970 (with John Kurlander)
Paul McCartney: *Red Rose Speedway*, Apple, 1973
Sherbet: *Howzat*, Epic, 1977
Original soundtrack: *Moulin Rouge*, Interscope, 2001
Lalo Schifrin: *Kaleidoscope: Jazz Meets the Symphony #6*, Aleph, 2005

John Kurlander

Lord of the Strings

In many ways, John Kurlander's career at Abbey Road begins where Richard Lush's left off. Growing up in St. John's Wood, about one block from the famed London facility, Kurlander would pass the studio every day on his way to and from school, a journey that might account, at least in part, for the lifelong career path he would ultimately follow. One day in 1964, he and several classmates not only made a field trip to the studio but were actually invited to help add some sound effects to a Shakespearean play being recorded there. "That was the day I realized this was really what I wanted to do," Kurlander recalls.

Upon his graduation in 1967, Kurlander duly applied to EMI for a job, and to his surprise was immediately granted an interview—something he now credits to his English teacher, who, as he was later to learn, was good friends with the assistant studio manager. "Although I didn't realize at the time that I knew somebody on the inside," he says with a laugh, "it turned out that I did."

Following a brief stint in the tape library, Kurlander soon joined the ranks of the studio's coterie of button-pushers, and in early 1969 began working with The Beatles on a series of sessions which would ultimately yield their final album, *Abbey Road*. Interestingly, he has a clear recollection of bumping into Lush in the corridor shortly beforehand. "I asked him why he wasn't doing these sessions," he remembers, "because he was quite famous among the staff for having worked on *Sgt. Pepper*. But after he filled me in on all the downsides to working with the group—the long hours, the lack of appreciation, the general pettiness and bickering, I have to admit I began thinking, 'Why me?'"

Despite his trepidation, the sessions ran smoothly, and Kurlander and two fellow assistants—Alan Parsons and John Leckie, both of whom were also destined to have successful recording careers in the years ahead [*and both of whom are interviewed in the original* Behind The Glass]—soon found themselves increasingly taking on the role of balance engineer, even without benefit of a formal promotion. "I got the point where I was receiving so many engineering assignments, I just began thinking of myself as an engineer. That's when I went to management and said, 'Look, I haven't assisted on any sessions for three months now, so how about giving me the raise in pay that goes with being a balance engineer?'" Kurlander would remain at Abbey Road for a staggering 29 years, and in 1985 worked his way to the top rung of the ladder when he was named chief balance engineer. In the mid-1990s, he began a long collaboration with film composer Howard Shore—one that continues to the present day—and began developing a reputation as a specialist in recording orchestras. In 1996 Kurlander moved to Los Angeles, where his career took off like a shot, earning him three Grammys and the accolades of both the audio and film industries for his work on blockbusters like the *Lord of the Rings* trilogy, *Tomb Raider*, *Blade II*, *Panic Room*, and *Aviator*.

The soft-spoken engineer's thoughtful demeanor and infectious laugh permeate this interview, which we conducted shortly after he'd returned from an extended stay in London and

Paris, where he'd somehow combined a family holiday with the recording of yet another orchestral film soundtrack. Seems that you can take the workaholic out of the studio, but you can't get the studio out of his blood!

What were some of your more memorable early sessions as an assistant engineer at Abbey Road?

My first memorable moment came even before I started assisting. I had delivered some tapes from the library to the studio down the hall, and the producer there, who was known for his vulgarity, turned to the engineer and said, "Who's the new c—t?" I was only 16 years old at the time and I remember thinking, "Okay, so this is the way it's going to be." In fact, I was wrong, because I didn't experience anything quite as offensive as that at any time in the next 40 years. [*laughs*] But it was quite an indoctrination nonetheless.

As an assistant, I worked a lot with [engineer] Malcolm Addey, and he was a strong influence on me. Our mixing consoles at that time weren't very complicated—they had 16 inputs at most—and of course this was long before the days of computers, so Malcolm had come up with his own version of instant recall on the board. Most other engineers would start a session in the normal way, by bringing up the faders for each individual instrument, one at a time, getting a sound for each. It was almost a set routine, in terms of the order in which they'd bring up the instruments: first bass, then bass drum, then snare drum, then kit overheads, then guitar, then piano. But Malcolm had actually come up with preset level and EQ settings for each instrument, based on his long experience, and so when a session started and the producer would ask him, "How long do you need to get a sound?" he'd literally say, "I'm ready; let's start recording." He still does that to this very day, which really makes clients very happy in these times of limited budgets.

You could make an argument that the standard way of doing things—crafting sounds for each instrument one at a time while listening to them—was more creative, but what Malcolm was doing was more expeditious. He knew that they didn't need him to reinvent the wheel for the kind of material they were doing—they just needed to sound good, so he used his knowledge from previous sessions. It was very impressive watching him, especially for a newcomer like me.

Did that mean that there was a sameness to his recordings?

Well, there was a sameness to the type of sessions they were. He was doing mostly middle-of-the-road projects—what we might call "easy listening" today, so they weren't necessarily creative in the way that band sessions might be. I tend to think of it more as well-planned engineering, and I have to admit I've done it myself quite a few times, especially when I'm working under severe time constraints. If nothing else, that kind of approach provides you with a good starting point.

In any event, it's very rare that the first take is artistically acceptable, so you know that in all likelihood, they'll do it again. Most of the time, you can use the first take as your fine-tuning run-through . . . whilst giving the impression that you're totally ready. [*laughs*]

Did you ever have an opportunity to work with [first Beatles engineer] Norman Smith?

I did, but it was on sessions that he was producing, because he'd already been promoted by the time I started at EMI. I assisted on some of his Hurricane Smith sessions, for example.

Was he very specific about how he wanted the sounds on the sessions where he was the artist?

I didn't get the feeling that there were two engineers in the room, if that's what you're asking. He was primarily a songwriter, and he was concentrating on that. I can't remember who was actually doing the engineering, but I didn't get the feeling that Norman was second-guessing anybody or being overly controlling. To me, he was just somebody who used to be a staff engineer at EMI who had recorded The Beatles and was now a producer and artist.

What were The Beatles like as people?

I have a memory of playing multiple versions of "Hey Jude" for them in the control room of Studio Two at one point in late 1968, but that was just a playback session and I didn't really have any interaction with them other than changing tape reels when they wanted to hear different takes. The initial *Abbey Road* sessions in early 1969 were also just listening sessions, because the album was really a compilation of some newly written tracks with some leftover tracks from earlier on. So the first few experiences I had with The Beatles just consisted of me playing tapes for them; there was no recording going on. Everyone was just sitting around listening and making notes as to what might be usable or not.

It was some time later that I was clearing up Studio Two with [technical engineer] Dave Harries, when he casually remarked that George Martin and Geoff Emerick had requested that I assist on the forthcoming Beatles album. I have to admit I entered the project with a fair amount of trepidation, especially after talking with Richard Lush. It's not that I was reluctant to work with them, but that first session was still quite nerve-wracking in that I realized that it was something over and above any other sessions I'd done before. The entire procedure was different, both in terms of the security of the tapes and in terms of the whole booking arrangement—they weren't working the usual three-hour time blocks, for a start.

As has been well-documented, there was always a much friendlier atmosphere when we were working with individual Beatles; things really only became tense when all four of them were together, and on the *Abbey Road* sessions, that only happened infrequently. So generally it was a really good experience.

John was, of course, well-known at Abbey Road as the Beatle with the shortest temper, but if you got him on his own he could be the sweetest person in the world; he certainly wasn't always angry. I think Paul probably went the most out of his way to get to know everyone at the studio on a personal level, whereas I don't think Ringo, for example, took much interest in who was running the tape machine. It's really difficult for me to be objective about them because I had the opportunity to work with Paul post-Beatles, but not any of the others.

Abbey Road was co-engineered by Geoff Emerick and Phil McDonald. Can you contrast their differences in engineering style and approach?

Well, I got the feeling that Geoff was Phil's mentor, and that it was actually more Geoff's project. When Phil was engineering, it felt to me like he was substituting for Geoff, but not vice versa, and it also seemed as if Phil was doing things as he thought Geoff wanted them to be done, rather than doing it his own way. In subsequent years, whenever I've worked on projects being done by multiple engineers, I've noticed that they tend to change everything around and put their own mark on things, but that wasn't the case with *Abbey Road*. Phil is a very casual and laid-back guy, anyway, and, again, he didn't want to reinvent the wheel, so I definitely got the feeling that he engineered those sessions with everything subject to Geoff's approval.

You also have to remember that one of the rules at Abbey Road was that you didn't do things completely differently if you were filling in for another engineer on their project. Yes, there might be slight variations in the approaches different engineers might take, but you're still talking about a team of people who are all employed on staff at the same studio, and, excluding Geoff's new association with Apple, there were no outside engineers—people trained at Olympic or Trident, for instance—ever involved in sessions at that time. Everyone had come out of the same training, so any differences that occurred would have been more those of personal taste.

Would you say that kind of homogeneous training—where every engineer and assistant is expected to follow the same set of standardized rules—is a more valid approach than a more freewheeling one where individual creativity is encouraged?

It definitely is, at least as far as providing a starting point. There was a set way of doing things, and everyone received the same training; we weren't taught to do different things by a series of different teachers. I guess the closest thing we have today is the German Tonmeister course, or the British version at Guildford College, and you can always tell the people that come out of those programs, because they've clearly got a common training. But then once they start working professionally, they can move on tangentially from there. Every once in awhile, you'll still get a Geoff Emerick to come along, someone who will start breaking all the rules and doing his own thing.

The other unique aspect of the Abbey Road training was the sheer breadth of different artists and producers that assistants got to work with, in both the classical and popular genres.

Absolutely. At that time, the same way they had classical and pop EQ modules on the board, they also had classical and pop engineers; very few crossed over. Stuart Eltham was an exception; I worked with him quite a lot. He started as a pop engineer, doing lots of sessions with George Martin, but he ended up doing all kinds of things, including classical.

But if you were an assistant, you worked all kinds of sessions. The studio manager might come up to you and ask you if you wanted to do a session on a Friday night—they couldn't force you to work overtime. You'd try to get out of it by asking what it was in advance, but he would never tell you. [*laughs*] But it could be anything from the London Philharmonic Orchestra to The Beatles. If it was a one-off Beatles session because someone couldn't cover it, you knew it would involve long hours, but it was also likely to be quite interesting.

I understand you used to keep detailed diaries in those days, but that somehow you managed to lose the 1969 diary.

And you had to remind me of that, right? [*laughs*] It's true. I have all the other diaries for all the other years, so I must have put it someplace safe because it was such a special year for me . . . and now, of course, I can't remember where that safe place was. [*laughs*]

In any event, it's not as if I was keeping a record of conversations I had with The Beatles or anything like that—all I wrote in my diaries was where I was every day, and what the hours were. The detailed notes that I kept of the sessions themselves were all stored with the studio's job files, so not having that diary really isn't that big of a deal.

Meticulous note-keeping does seem to be a really important part of being a good assistant engineer.

That's absolutely true, even though the job description has changed dramatically since I was an assistant. Record-keeping now is not so much about getting a yellow pad and writing everything down as it is file management. If you're dealing with thousands of computer files, you can get lost easily unless you stay on top of their chronological history, so record-keeping is still really important.

Do you prefer doing orchestral dates to other kinds of sessions?

Working at Abbey Road provided me with an opportunity to do a bit of everything, but even back in the 1960s I enjoyed doing classical sessions. Because I'd assisted with Malcolm Addey and Peter Bown, I ended up doing a lot of engineering for producer Norman Newell; I actually worked with him until he retired in the 1990s. He really mentored me and got me a lot of engineering jobs, and it was he, along with Stuart Eltham, who taught me about recording orchestras.

In the mid-'70s, after The Beatles had broken up, there seemed to be a bit of a dearth of good pop music sessions that were coming into Abbey Road, with the exception of *Dark Side of the Moon*, which Pink Floyd recorded with Alan Parsons. That might have partly been because EMI artists were starting to record in outside studios. It just seemed that there was more interesting stuff going on orchestrally at the time, so I kind of morphed into that. Stuart and Norman were very good teachers, and I really got into all aspects of orchestral recording. In some ways, it presents a bit more of a challenge than just recording pop bands.

Do you remember the first orchestral session you ever engineered?

I do. Stuart Eltham was due to record an orchestra up in Liverpool, but he had booked a holiday months beforehand and so was forced to take it instead—EMI management were quite adamant about things like that; they even forced me to miss out on some Beatles sessions because I had a holiday booked! Anyway, Stuart cleared things with the producer and arranged for me to do this session instead. He gave me very specific instructions; I remember him telling me, "Look, just do it exactly like this; don't try to be clever and don't use your first session as an opportunity to experiment." So I went up there with our mobile recording unit and I followed his instructions religiously. To my great relief, it ended up sounding exactly the way it would have if Stuart himself had recorded it, as he himself told me later on.

Eventually you became Abbey Road's chief balance engineer. What did the job entail?

It wasn't really a managerial position—it was more like being the head boy at school, or, in American terms, class president. My job was to act as liaison and represent the staff engineers and their needs to management—things like participating in interviews for new assistant engineers and making recommendations about equipment purchases. It was a really big deal when we got our first SSL desk in the mid-1970s, followed shortly thereafter by one that was jointly manufactured by EMI and Neve. In the 1960s, 90 percent of the equipment we were using had been home-built, but by the 1970s, Abbey Road's management had finally realized that gear off the shelf was unstoppable, and that if every other studio in London had a particular piece of gear, we needed to have that same piece too in order to remain competitive.

Why did you decide to leave Abbey Road in 1996 and make the move to Los Angeles?

I was approaching my 30th year there, and so I was starting to reflect on my future. I began thinking then that either I'd stick it out and do my 40 years at Abbey Road and then retire, or maybe I would leave and do something completely different. For the past 15 years, we had begun doing digital recordings of all the classical repertoire because everyone wanted everything released on CD; we had huge budgets, too, which enabled us to do some really great work. But by the mid-1990s that was starting to come to an end: sales were dropping off and many big orchestral contracts were not being renewed. In 1993 I'd done my first movie—*M Butterfly*, with Howard Shore, who hired me even though I didn't have any film experience—and I enjoyed it thoroughly. Movies just seemed like a new thing, something that I hadn't done before, and LA seemed like the logical place to be for that. Truth be told, a lot of us had thought about moving to the States for a long time, and some of us, like Geoff and Alan Parsons, had actually done it, so I decided to take the plunge.

Was the transition to LA a difficult one?

Well, it was an impossibly hard decision to make, and one that I went backwards and forwards on a few times. I found it really painful and difficult to leave England and Abbey Road, and I discovered rather quickly that my resume, as impressive as it was, actually tended to work against me, because a lot of people dismissed it as a work of fiction. There were times when I was actually told that I would not be considered for a job because the people doing the hiring felt that my resume could not possibly be true! [*laughs*] I actually tried dumbing it down at one point to make it seem a little more believable, but then I thought, no, that's crazy—why should I do that?

I also discovered that many film people are not all that interested in your past. It doesn't matter if you give them tons of references and invite them to phone those people up; they won't do that. But if they can phone a friend of theirs who worked with you last week and the session went well, that's more important than anything you may have on your resume.

You're a great believer in digital recording. Why do you prefer it to analog?

Abbey Road went digital in 1979 or 1980—we were very early adopters, and I've been a fan of it right from the beginning. In the late seventies, EMI actually built a prototype digital desk because they knew that it was the coming thing. It was only 16-bit, but it worked and it sounded fairly good. We installed it in a little editing room that was close to Studio One, and we would parallel the mics and route them to both the digital and analog desks, then listen and compare the results.

Unfortunately, after we'd done some comparative listening, we all felt that the digital recordings didn't sound anywhere near as good as the analog ones—in fact, we thought they sounded terrible. But then the boffin who built the digital desk—he was a big, tall, imposing fellow by the name of Reg Willard—came to one of our meetings and I'll never forget what he said: "There's nothing wrong with this desk—it's just that you chaps don't have the experience to know how to use it. You're bringing analog experience and analog techniques—even your mic selection is based on that. But you have to forget all that. You have to think digital."

Everybody thought he was crazy, but he was so big and imposing, you couldn't really argue with him. [*laughs*] And those words have haunted me ever since, because he was absolutely right. You cannot just take the approach of, this is the mic I would use for an analog recording, and this is where I'd place it, and then I'd put the signal through this compressor and this equalizer. You need to start with a totally clean plate and ask yourself what would be best for a *digital* recording. That's when it begins to work. So in orchestral terms, I actually left analog behind in 1980. And, of course, I'm getting much better results now as the technology has improved.

One of the techniques that I employ is to never listen to the input signal, no matter how bad or good the digital recording system is. From the moment you put the first microphone up, if you only ever listen to it through the complete chain, through all the converters, you'll be guided in your decisions much more accu-

> *"From the moment you put the first microphone up, if you only ever listen to it through the complete chain, through all the converters, you'll be guided in your decisions much more accurately."*

rately. You may discover that the mic isn't such a good choice in that particular situation, or that it should be positioned slightly different, or processed slightly differently. The problems come if you start off with an analog mindset.

I remember being hired to do an orchestral session some years ago and I was told I had to record it on an ADAT. I'd never actually heard of an ADAT at that point, so I asked what it was and I was told, "It's really bad-sounding." [*laughs*] I just did my thing of not listening to the input signal at all; instead, I listened to every mic through the ADAT and based every decision on how things sounded through that chain, and you know what? It turned out pretty good.

With that approach, the focus shifts from trying to capture the original sound as accurately as possible to instead trying to craft as good a sound as possible through the analog-to-digital and digital-to-analog converters.

Exactly. As I see it, the whole thing is about bottlenecks, whether that bottleneck is 44.1k or 16-bit—they're all bottlenecks. So if you actually engineer through the bottleneck, you're going to come out with a much better result. After all, no one other than the people in the studio know what the input signal actually sounded like, so it becomes irrelevant, really—it's there only for the duration of the session, and it's heard only by the people in the studio. What carries through is what people hear at the end of the bottleneck.

> *"The whole thing is about bottlenecks. So if you actually engineer through the bottleneck, you're going to come out with a much better result."*

And it's all because Reg Willard had the guts— and the physical size—to stand up to a roomful of EMI engineers and say "You don't know how to use digital." [*laughs*] So yes, digital is definitely my preference for orchestral work. I'm not saying that every digital recording is better than every analog recording. Certainly there are great analog recordings, but there are ways of making excellent digital recordings too.

My thinking about analog tape is that it's an enhancement. When you're recording to tape, you do a lot of listening of line in versus line out, and people often find themselves thinking, "Wow, that tape's really saved me—it's made things sound even better than what I actually put into it." So it's kind of like a crutch. It smooths out transients and so it glues things together, but it's not necessarily an accurate representation at all of what you're recording on it. I'd rather work directly to digital and exclusively monitor the output signal. These days, I really only use analog for effects, like tape slap; I don't view it as a major recording medium anymore.

I know there are still some vinyl aficionados left, too, but it's worth pointing out that vinyl records are remarkably inconsistent from beginning to end. That's due to one of its physical aspects: the fact that the length of a groove is much longer on the outside of the disk than it is on the inside of the disk. So what happens when you play a vinyl disk is that the sonic quality is much higher at the beginning of a side, but as the needle travels towards the center, you start to lose high end and it eventually goes into distortion. Any mastering engineer will concede this, and the way they got around the problem in the 1960s was to make the records shorter so that the needle never got too close to the center. So when people say, "I still love my vinyl because it sounds so much better," my reply is, "Is it the beginning of the record that sounds better? Or the end of the record?" Because they're two different sounds.

What's the basic difference between a classical music session and an orchestral film scoring session?

When recording classical material, the mic setup is pretty much formulated—there are accepted ways of doing things. You can choose different techniques for specific venues—the Blumlein Pair, for example, or the Decca Tree—but you usually take a set approach. Film scores, on the other hand, cut across all genres of music, so there are no hard and fast rules about miking up an orchestra for a film.

> **"There are no hard and fast rules about miking up an orchestra for a film."**

Another thing is that, in classical recording, the majority of composers are deceased, so it's really all about how the conductor wants to interpret that music. But with film scoring, you've got the composer sitting at the desk right next to you, able to collaborate and make changes, so it tends to be a lot more creative at the moment of recording.

The vibe on the two types of sessions is often completely different, too. Classical sessions tend to be very intense. Usually, the producer and the engineer are alone in the control room, both wearing very expensive headphones, listening attentively to every little nuance, every chair creak, every squeak that might occur. In contrast, there are usually lots of guests and visitors attending big film sessions, all hanging out in the control rooms with their laptops and their cell phones.

Actually, I have an interesting story that demonstrates what can happen when you take that to the extreme. Back in the mid-'90s, the Twentieth Century Fox soundstage was closed for several years while it underwent a complete redesign. When it reopened in 1997, they decided to have a celebratory opening party at the inaugural recording session, and I was very honored to be asked to do the engineering. Their control room is huge, and that night it was packed with 60 or 70 guests, with the whole back wall laid out with food and drink. Meanwhile, in the studio there was a 100-piece orchestra, booked to play several different versions of the fanfare that opens all the Fox movies and TV shows. The noise level in the control room was so high, I could barely hear what was going on, but I carried on anyway. I remember thinking after each take, "Well, I have no idea how that turned out, but if nothing else it's great entertainment for the party."

But the next morning, when I came back in to listen to it, I was quite surprised at how good the recordings were . . . and even more surprised to learn that they had decided to actually use those versions on every new Fox film and television production.

Does that story prove that monitors are over-rated?

No, but it does illustrate that the reverential silence that accompanies most classical sessions may be unnecessary. [*laughs*]

Is the mic technique you choose dictated more by the room than the material or the players?

It's mostly dictated by the genre of music, and by what the composer and director are looking for, but the room plays an important role too. Without sounding pretentious, at this point in my career, I've worked in most major rooms in most major cities, so I already know a lot about their acoustic characteristics, but when I know that I'm going into a studio I haven't worked in before, I do an incredible amount of homework beforehand. I spend a lot of time with the floor plans, trying to glean as much information from them as I can, and of course I always try to get into the room a few days before the session, just so I can have a look around. For the most part, I focus on the physical construction of the facility; I'll actually knock on the walls to see how solid they are, and stamp on the floor to see how much give there is and consequently how much resonance there will be. I know, for example, that if I jump up and down on the floor and there's a little bit of give, the bass response will be a lot more generous than if it feels like a thick concrete slab.

Do you always have to deal with the acoustics of a room as it exists, or will you ever apply pop techniques like putting up screens to reduce the reverberant character of a room?

Well, when you're dealing with a room that has 30-foot high ceilings—and a lot of the large rooms are even higher than that—an eight-foot screen really doesn't do very much. An eight-foot screen is a great tool in a room that's 8' 1'', but if the ceiling is 30 feet high, the sound will just go straight up to the ceiling and down the other side of the screen. So I tend to try to work things out by careful positioning and angling of mics. Following the Malcolm Addey lessons, a lot of preparation goes into every session, and that really pays off nowadays with budgets being so tight; you pretty much need to be able to start recording the minute the session begins.

Given that EMI and Decca were archrivals, were EMI engineers ever trained in or allowed to use the Decca Tree for recording classical music?

In the fifties and sixties, there was a very strong directive at EMI to use the Blumlein Pair—a pair of crossed figure-of-eight microphones—exclusively. But in the 1970s, the rules were relaxed a little bit, and so some of the EMI engineers started using the Decca Tree. So, yes, we were allowed to use it, but we weren't especially encouraged to do so.

Something that seems to have gotten lost in the history books is the fact that the Decca Tree is a system that only works well in resonant and reverberant rooms, as opposed to deader spaces; it definitely doesn't work everywhere. At Decca, the producers and recording engineers were actually on equal status in terms of rank, unlike EMI, where the producer was the boss, and the person who hired the engineer. So the Decca engineers could and would actually refuse to work in rooms where they knew the Tree wouldn't work well, and the Decca producers had to accept that. In contrast, the EMI producers would simply say, "We're going to record such-and-such on this date in this place," and if their engineer wasn't too keen on that venue, it was just too bad; they had to be flexible and adapt their mic technique to the room.

Which technique worked best in Studio One?

You could do anything there; that's how good a room it was. Studio One was actually rebuilt shortly after I started work at EMI, in the early 1970s, under Ken Townshend's direction, and ever since then it's been open to all kinds of techniques, Decca Tree or crossed pair. I'm not sure that it was quite so friendly to the Decca Tree before the redesign.

There's usually a lot of editing that occurs in classical sessions. Is that the case with film scoring sessions too?

They have become that way, yes. When I first broke into film scoring in the early 1990s and everything was still being recorded onto multitrack tape—analog or digital—editing was very time-consuming, and so producers would tend to identify one take that was mostly good and maybe insert one edit piece. But now that everything is recorded in Pro Tools, the amount of editing on film score sessions is approaching that of classical sessions.

What's the nature of the collaborative process between the engineer and the film composer?

It's different with every composer. In contrast to a classical session, where you're really dealing mainly with the conductor, here you're working with someone who's only just finished writing the music and in some cases is still changing it on the stand. The composition and the recording become one and the same, so the sound takes on a great deal of importance.

It's also worth pointing out that, while classical composers can write whatever they want, film composers are ultimately answerable to the director, who is always present at scoring sessions. Directors usually talk solely in terms of dramatic impact, and because their requests tend to be musically nonspecific, the engineer can act as an important intermediary, though you have to be careful to make your suggestions in a very tactful way.

How long is a typical film scoring session for a full-length feature film?

Each session is three hours long; a typical film might run three to five days, two sessions a day, for a total of six to ten sessions. Each of the *Lord of the Rings* film scores, however, took three months to record, which put it in a musical and budgetary category of its own. Those sessions were great for me, not only because of my long-standing relationship with [composer] Howard Shore, but also because of my relationship with [director] Peter Jackson. Oftentimes Howard would be out on the studio floor conducting the orchestra while I was alone in the control room with Peter, so I was able to feel his vibe over and above what he was actually saying on the talkback.

Is it true that you show up at your sessions with a steel ruler in an ice bucket?

[*laughs*] That's a rumor that started at one of the *Lord of the Rings* sessions. It's true that I always bring a ruler with me for continuity purposes—it allows me to accurately reset mic distances in the studio in case bits need to be rerecorded weeks or months later, something I learned from Malcolm Addey. The ruler that I use happens to be made of steel, and it has an angle checker on it, kind of like a protractor; it's this little needle thing which looks like a compass. What happened was that one day this little needle had gotten sticky and wasn't working properly. I was just about to throw the ruler away, but just outside the control room there was a drinks table set up. I thought, well, maybe if I stick it in the ice bucket for awhile, it might contract the little bit of the needle that had stuck and get it working again. One of the assistants was walking by at the time and he asked why I was doing such a bizarre thing. I don't know what got into me, but instead of telling him the true story, I said, tongue in cheek, "Because the ice contracts the ruler to a certain size in order to make it more constantly accurate." I was really just taking the mickey out of myself, but to my astonishment, he actually believed me and ever since then has proceeded to spread this scurrilous rumor all over the LA studio scene. [*laughs*] So, no, I don't actually turn up at sessions with my ruler in an ice bucket . . . but the more people believe it, the more I'm inclined to do it!

Selected Listening:

Badfinger: *No Dice*, Apple, 1970 (with Richard Lush)

Ormandy, Philadelphia Orchestra: *Four Legends from the Kalevala (Sibelius)*, EMI Classics, 1979

Toto: *Toto IV*, CBS, 1982

Haitink, Royal Opera House: *Peter Grimes (Britten)*, EMI Classics, 1994

Paul McCartney, London Symphony Orchestra: *Standing Stone*, EMI Classics, 1997

Original soundtracks: *M. Butterfly*, Varese Sarabande, 1993; *Ed Wood*, Hollywood, 1994; *Mimic*, Varese Sarabande, 1997; *The Lord of the Rings: The Fellowship of the Ring*, Warner Bros., 2001; *Blade II*, New Line, 2002; *Ice Age*, Varese Sarabande, 2002; *The Lord of the Rings: The Two Towers*, Reprise, 2002; *The Lord of the Rings: The Return of the King*, Reprise, 2003; *3:10 to Yuma*, Lionsgate, 2007

Hugh Padgham

Rejigging the Model

Ah, the eighties. Every record sounded like it was made in a stadium, every singer working their uppermost range until it seemed as if their vocal cords were about to leap out of their throat, every hit wrapped in a glossy package of shimmering guitar leads and silky bass. And, of course, every snare drum was passing through a gated reverb.

Hugh Padgham is largely responsible for many of those sounds—particularly the latter—but he's also responsible for crafting many of the greatest records of the era, The Police's "Every Breath You Take," Genesis' "Tonight's the Night," and Phil Collins' "In the Air Tonight" among them. His ultra-clean signature sound raised the bar for every engineer and producer of the era and had a major impact on the shift from the dead, close-miked records of the seventies to the open, ambient sounds of the nineties and beyond. Padgham's unique abilities and versatility are probably best reflected in the fact that he's won four Grammys in four different categories: Album of the Year (Collins' 1985 *No Jacket Required*), Record of the Year (Collins' 1990 "Another Day in Paradise"), Best Engineered Album of the Year (Sting's 1993 *Ten Summoner's Tales*), and the 1985 Producer of the Year award.

Padgham's career started at London's Advision Studios, where he served as tea-boy (the British equivalent to a runner), but it wasn't until he moved to Landsdowne Studios in the mid-1970s that he received formal training, quickly rising through the ranks from assistant engineer to chief engineer. In 1978, he took a job at Richard Branson's Townhouse studio (which sadly closed its doors only recently), which gave him an opportunity to engineer for various Virgin artists, including XTC, Peter Gabriel, and Phil Collins. It was also at the Townhouse that Padgham first met a young bass player by the name of Gordon Sumner...soon to be known to the world as Sting. A couple of years later, just as Sting's band The Police were poised to reach the heights of international fame, Padgham was brought onboard to co-produce their massive hit album *Ghost in the Machine*.

We met up at his West London studio, Sofa Sound, one bright summer afternoon, where the affable Mr. Padgham, looking more like a ruffled professor than a superstar pop producer, shared his unique perspective on the evolution of record-making through the past two decades.

Are you fully sold on digital recording these days, or do you still use tape?

I'm not anti-digital per se, because you've always got to stay as current with things as you can. But people who grew up with analog gear can hear the difference, and there's no doubt in my mind that analog sounds better: it's kinder to your ears, and not as harsh. Having said that, there's also no question that digital now sounds better than ever before. These days I'm running all my sessions at 96k, 24-bit, and that's a big improvement over 44.1 or 48. Of course, the original RADAR, which was 44.1, 16-bit, sounded a lot better than other machines, so I think a lot of it is down to the converters.

One thing I really miss about analog recording is tape compression, though. By using it carefully, you can actually get some 10 dB of extra level before a well-recorded transient signal like a snare drum clips. That's one reason that digital sounds so harsh—because you're not getting any of that nice rounding off of the transients. So these days, I tend to do my initial tracking onto 24-track tape and then copy that into Pro Tools. That way, at the very least, my drums, bass, and guitars hit tape. If I have the time and budget, I will continue doing things onto analog, either by premixing and bouncing tracks, or by running a second machine in sync. However, I still never go over 48 tracks; I set that as my limit. It just gets really difficult to manage more tracks than that, especially if you're mixing on an analog console. Don't forget, we used to quite successfully make records on a single 24-track machine.

How do you know when a recording is complete, when it's time to stop adding overdubs and start mixing it?

It's really just instinct. For me it always comes down to one simple question: "Does it sound any good?" Sometimes you run into situations when you suddenly think, "I'm not so sure this sounds good anymore." That's when you realize that the

> **"It often takes a lot of effort to have less rather than more."**

last thing you added didn't need to be there. "Less is more" sounds like a cliché, but it often is true, and it often takes a lot of effort to have less rather than more. I actually spend more time pruning stuff down than adding things. Doing so can often require a musician to learn or evolve an altogether different part to be played, so that what was two tracks is now one track. Every song is different, of course, but I'm always looking for ways to simplify and reduce.

I have one criteria that is probably my bottom line: is it embarrassing or not? If somebody is singing and it's really out of tune, that to me would sound really embarrassing if you put it out on a record. A guitar part could be equally embarrassing—the kind of thing you'd play when you were in your first band in school, when you were 13 or 14 and playing a lot of crap. Something that goes back to the days when the guitar player was focusing so hard on getting the chord shape or string bend right that he couldn't put any feeling into it. Those moments are tough for me, because I find myself thinking, "Oh my god, what am I going to tell them?"

What *do* you tell them?

Well, I hope they'll come to that conclusion themselves when they hear it played back. Still, I always subscribe to the idea that it's not my record, it's the artist's record; I'm making it *for* them. So all I can do is ask the artist, "Are you really happy with that? Or are you going to be embarrassed when you hear that in five years' time?"

What happens if the artist is happy with a part he's played but you feel strongly that it's embarrassing?

I occasionally had that problem with Sting, who sometimes couldn't be bothered, or thought what he'd done was good enough. Usually I'd just fix it when he wasn't looking. Of course, now in Pro Tools you can do things that were unimaginable years ago. I made a record not long ago with a singer who, frankly, was not on the ball—he'd often come in hung over or whatever. We had the usual problem of time and budget, plus he was physically incapable of improving things sometimes. But somehow, by doing a lot of fiddling around and editing, I was able to make him sound really good. The problem was, he thought that was all him! He thought he'd done a great job, when in reality what he'd done was quite embarrassing.

But if there's a conflict with the artist, it's like a conflict in any job or any aspect of life: you talk it through and either you come to a compromise or one person wins and gets their way.

People usually get over it, though. If I have a really strong feeling about something that the artist disagrees with, I'll say, "Look, it's your record, not mine; if you really want it to be like that, that's fine . . . as long as it's not embarrassing." [*laughs*]

How do you feel the role of the producer has changed since you started making records?

The main role used to be quality control, but one of the worrying things about making records nowadays is that the concept of things sounding good rarely comes into it. It used to be that you would run down to the record store to buy a particular new album because you knew it was going to be a work of art sonically; you'd race home and put it on the best stereo you could find and it was an amazing experience listening to it. Sadly, nowadays, kids grow up listening to everything on earbuds. My daughter, who's a teenager, once plugged her iPod into some little computer speakers I have and she said, "Dad, that sounds amazing!" They were just tiny satellite speakers with a small subwoofer, but she was amazed . . . and the reason, I think, is that she had never heard bass before!

It's almost a complete reverse evolution, really. If you look at video quality, things have evolved forward, from VHS to DVD to high-def. But in the world of audio, it seems that things have gotten worse and worse: we've gone from vinyl to CD—and the early CDs sounded way worse than vinyl—and now we've gone to MP3s, which sound even worse than the earliest CDs. Personally, I think the era of the disc is well and truly gone. Hopefully our file sizes will get bigger—meaning better quality audio—and so too will storage capacity. I really hope that, as memory becomes cheaper and more prevalent, we'll be able to restore the quality of audio. Soon there will be massive flash drives with high bus speeds, and hopefully then we'll be able to at least store good quality uncompressed audio. People won't notice files that are ten times the size of MP3s if you actually have ten times the space to store them in. Or perhaps there will be new forms of compression invented that will preserve full-quality audio. Or maybe we'll all just be wired into a central server. The problem with that is, what happens when you lose service? There will be caching schemes, I'm sure, and hopefully they will improve all the time as well. What lies ahead is exciting, and you can't stay rooted in the past.

Another contributing factor to any perceived decline in quality is that budgets are shrinking, so people aren't given adequate amounts of time to hone their sounds in a professional environment.

That's true, and, as a producer, I find that very frustrating. These days, the budgets are so small that the only way you can make an album is to do it as quickly as you possibly can; otherwise somebody ends up not being paid. As a result, there's very little room for experimentation, so it's very bad from an artistic point of view. And they're cutting the budgets all the time—every day, there seems to be less and less available and more and more corners being cut. Yet somehow you don't ever hear about record company executives taking a cut in salary.

Still, I honestly don't think it's been economics that have been the sole downfall of record labels. The problem is that, generally speaking, they have gotten themselves into an irreparable situation, and so they've become very adept at signing music that most people don't want to listen to. That's because most of today's A&R people don't come from a proper musical background. They're much more into trends rather than something being good. If something is on the front page of the newspapers, they want to sign it, and then all the other labels want to sign the same thing. In fact, very often, labels sign artists just to stop other labels from getting them, not because they really believe in them. My daughter likes a lot of current music because she's young, but she often asks me, "Why is it only old stuff that gets covered, or sampled?"

PHOTO COURTESY OF HUGH PADGHAM

What do you think is the solution?

It's a question of rejigging the model. The major labels still have huge overheads—huge offices in New York and LA, and big staffs to run. But if you run a tighter ship and share the ownership of the product with the artist, if you don't con them into thinking you're going to be selling millions of records when you know you're not, and if you keep the costs down, then the artist can make the same amount of money selling far fewer records. That's a model that a lot of people are starting to look into now.

Even in the old days, when a lot of records were being sold by people like Sting or Phil Collins, it was only because they were selling eight or nine million records that nobody was complaining. The people associated with them were making good money—nowhere near the huge amounts of money the record labels were making, but good money—so you put up with it, just as you put up with the fact that you weren't going to get paid anything from certain foreign territories because of bootlegging. You were just educated by the record labels into assuming this was normal. But eventually, hopefully, those kinds of things will be policed properly, so that everyone gets paid what they're owed.

In the old days, artists had to have a record deal because they needed that advance to afford to pay for expensive studio time and they needed the label to do marketing and promotion. Today, people have the ability to do those things for themselves, and it has made a huge difference. Ironically, in some ways it's made it harder for an artist to gain recognition, because how do you get your stuff heard?

How important do you think formal training is in succeeding as a producer or engineer?

Well, I'm all for creativity, and it's true that sometimes not knowing too much is great and having too much knowledge can be a hindrance, but if you want a flute to sound like a flute it

Across the Pond **177**

may not be a bad idea to know where to place a mic, and history has deemed that there are certain ways of doing things that yield the best sounds.

For example, trumpets recorded in the digital domain can be unbelievably hard and nasty-sounding unless you understand the physics of it, and that will teach you to perhaps use a ribbon mic instead of a condenser mic and maybe smooth it off with a tube preamp. But I was taught fairly formally—you'd have to turn up at ten o'clock in the morning and you were expected to wind up cables properly. Landsdowne was actually quite a stuffy place and at the time I couldn't wait to get out of there, but looking back on it later I realized that it was a very good grounding. But I was always trying to break the rules, and that's how I came upon the Phil Collins drum sound, among other things.

Ah, yes, the Phil Collins drum sound—one of the better-known creative accidents in recording lore. *[Ed note: An accident that is recounted in detail in engineer Mick Glossop's interview in* Behind the Glass *Volume One]*

Well, that was one of the wonderful things about the SSL desk. Before then, if you wanted to put a compressor into the sidechain or insert points, or any piece of outboard gear, you had to first pick up a patch cord, think about where you were going to plug it in, and then physically plug it in; it was a very methodical process. With the SSL, you suddenly had a console that presented all these options—compressors and noise gates—on each channel, right in front of you. Having the ability to press a button and compress or gate a signal—literally without having to do anything else—made you experiment a bit more. And once we'd heard the sound of Phil's drums through this mighty compressor on the reverse talkback mic, we all went, "Wow!" Then I had to persuade the maintenance engineer to wire its output to a point on the patch bay because there was no way of accessing the reverse talkback mic. Once I was able to plug that mic into a channel, I started mucking around with a noise gate for some reason, and there was the sound.

"Fifty percent of making a record is the microphones and equipment, and the other fifty percent is the vibe in the room."

Were you flattered or irritated when everyone in the world began copying that sound and appropriating it for themselves?

I was so busy in those days, I barely noticed, to tell you the truth. But I suppose I was flattered, really.

In some ways, it became the sound of the eighties.

Perhaps, but George Massenburg was getting even more live drum sounds on the records he was making with Little Feat at the time—a group I loved then and still love to this day. Perhaps it wasn't quite as crunchy a sound, but it was easily as live. You know, if you stand next to someone playing drums, it's very loud, so I was just trying to find a way of making them sound loud even if the volume was turned down. In so many records of the seventies, the drums sounded like somebody tapping on a bloody cardboard box—dull and flat and non-ringing. There were still loads of dead rooms around in those days, rooms that were trapped to death. When I first got to the Townhouse, it was like that, and it took a bit of doing to persuade the powers there to let me have a live area in the studio where we could put in our own acoustic treatment, which was basically big stones dug out of the garden at the Manor Studios in Oxford.

Do you believe in always trying to make an artist as comfortable as possible, or do you try to keep them on edge?

Well, I know that different producers take different approaches: no two people will crack a nut in the same way. But I've always felt that 50 percent of making a record is the microphones and equipment, and the other 50 percent is the vibe in the room, which the producer is largely responsible for. There's the old cliché, for example, of winding the singer up just before he sings so that you get a better performance out of him.

Does that ever work?

A lot of people have done it and have gotten good results. More often, though, I tend to take the opposite approach—I'll do whatever I can to make a nervous singer feel comfortable. For example, here in my studio I've got table lamps all over the place so it feels more like home and is less intimidating. If you march someone out into the center of the main orchestral room at Abbey Road and just order them to sing their heart out, it's probably quite a difficult thing to do. So evaluating the situation is extremely important, as is pre-reading the situation—knowing when it might be the right time to do this, that, or the other. It's a balancing act the whole time; you're constantly reading the artist to try to determine if they react best to being wound up a bit or being coddled.

Do you spend a lot of time in preproduction socializing with artists, getting to know them as people?

I've always tried to do as little pre-production as possible, because I find that whatever you think you've achieved in pre-production often tends to be not what you thought it was—you won't know if the drummer can or cannot really play until you get him into the studio, for example. Even though the economics nowadays dictate that you be as prepared as possible, pre-production doesn't always work out to be the best way to accomplish that.

Unfortunately, lack of time or budget sometimes prevents you from doing a lot of experimenting, and that's a problem when working with new artists in particular. It's nice when you have a longstanding professional relationship with an artist and you know what vocal chain sounds best on them for a ballad, for example. The last thing you want is for them to have sung their best while you were busy fiddling with a compressor and so the level was moving up and down.

Presumably since you own an SSL console, you don't like to mix in the box.

No, I don't. I admire anybody who can do it, though. [*laughs*] I know that some people who grew up in the era of the analog console are doing it, and they say they love it, but I can't get my head around it. I also don't believe that it sounds as good. You at least need a summing mixer, to my way of thinking, but a lot of people still don't use even those, even though a lot of them are reasonably priced now. I still like pushing three or four faders in each hand at once, and you can't do that kind of thing with a mouse. There are, of course, control surfaces with faders, but even with those you're still pushing all the audio through this little digital pipe.

Having said all that, I think the resettability of Pro Tools is really great—the fact that you can have a mix completely set up, spend five minutes on it, put it to bed, and then get something else up. That whole aspect of digital recording is terrific, and it's a real bonus in live sound too, being able to completely reset delays and things on a per-song basis.

Using an SSL, I can't really jump around from mix to mix as much as I'd like, because, even if you work fast, it takes a minimum of half an hour to reset a song. In some ways, that's good because you tend to get a mix up and then work on it until it's done. There's that old joke about, why does a dog lick its balls? The answer being, because it can. The same goes for Pro Tools. There are times when you ask yourself, why am I mixing this song for the 20th time? I think a lot of us can fall into the trap of not seeing the forest for the trees. So in some ways I regret not being able to get mixes up instantly, but in another way it makes you work harder because you think, okay, this is the time when the song is going to be mixed. Look at the days before automation, when everybody in the control room was hanging on to a fader—that was a performance itself.

Do you think Pro Tools can help an artist achieve the optimum performance?

Well, I've done a lot of live recordings over the years, and nine times out of ten the singer would want to come in and redo a few things, maybe for technical reasons or perhaps because something was sung a bit out of tune. You can get away with a lot at a live gig but a record is forever, so you'd have to get people back in to fix things. Nowadays with Pro Tools you can fix everything afterwards without having to get anyone back in the studio. I think that's a creative use of software— using it to make repairs, as opposed to making someone patently untalented sound acceptable. Hopefully I'll never find myself in the studio with someone patently untalented!

> *"You can get away with a lot at a live gig, but a record is forever.*

Mind you, I've had artists come in and sing and then they say to me, "Alright, I've done my part; now you do your thing." They know that you can do a lot of polishing, and so in some ways artists are starting to get a little lazy. When an artist sings a chorus and says to me, "Alright, there you go, now you can go paste that in," I'll say to them, "Sorry, mate—you've got to sing it again, all the way through" because I simply don't want to work that way. Similarly, if they want a double-tracked sound, I'll make them actually sing the double-track instead of constructing it in Pro Tools.

Most producers seem to come either from a purely technical background as an engineer or a musical one, as a musician. Which set of skills do you think is more important?

These days, I think that having that musical background is much more important, because if you can be involved in writing songs with your artist, that will work out for you much better financially. The old historical model simply isn't any good these days unless you don't mind being poor; the numbers just don't stack up any more.

What kind of advice can you give to someone who wants to be the next Hugh Padgham?

Always do your own thing; don't try copying other people. But my most pragmatic advice would be to develop your songwriting skills. Get in there at the get-go and sell yourself as a writer/producer, because earning your income on the old model, which was points [percentages] of record sales is not a good way to go, due to the drastically reduced sales these days. Even having 100 percent of nothing is still nothing! [*laughs*]

In my day, you started off as a tea boy or a runner, and there was a clear path to becoming an engineer/producer, which was good because you wouldn't want to go into an apprenticeship and wonder if you'd ever get to the endpoint or not, through no fault of your own. But now there is no clear path, because studios stopped having house engineers years ago. So where do you go from being an assistant? It's hard unless you latch onto somebody who happens to like you and is working a lot and takes you under his wing. Just as there are many more genres of music today than there were years ago, there are many more ways of forging a career making records; certainly the path I took doesn't exist anymore. Somehow, though, water finds its way and things have a way of working out if you're really determined.

Another thing I should add is that you should only get into this business because it's something you love doing, not for the money. I heard a story recently about a new American shoe company: after you work for them for a few months, they offer you a thousand dollars to leave. It's a really good idea, because if people take the offer, they know right away that they've got an employee who didn't care about the job.

It's hard to imagine studio owners paying anyone a thousand dollars for doing nothing, though.

That's true—the poor old studio owners are dropping like flies. Mind you, some studios deserved to close down because they'd charge you for breathing. [*laughs*] It's really only those that own their own properties that have any chance of staying in business these days. But in the recording industry, like in all industries, change happens, and you have to adapt, and those who adapt better are the ones who survive. There's a lesson in that for all of us.

Suggested Listening:

The Police: *Ghost in the Machine*, A&M, 1981; *Synchronicity*, A&M, 1983

Genesis: *Abacab*, Atlantic, 1981; *Genesis*, Atlantic, 1983; *Invisible Touch*, Atlantic, 1986

Phil Collins: *Face Value*, Virgin, 1981; *Hello, I Must Be Going!*, Atlantic, 1982; *No Jacket Required*, Atlantic, 1985; *But Seriously*, Atlantic, 1989

Sting: *Nothing Like the Sun*, A&M, 1987; *Ten Summoner's Tales*, A&M, 1993; *Mercury Falling*, A&M, 1996

Peter Gabriel: *Peter Gabriel*, Geffen, 1980

XTC: *Black Sea*, Geffen, 1980; *English Settlement*, Geffen, 1982

Trevor Horn

The Wizard of Sarm

In some circles, he's revered; in others, maligned. Say what you like about producer Trevor Horn; there are few people in the industry who feel neutral about him.

It's nothing personal, mind you. To the contrary, Horn is one of the nicest guys in the business. And it's entirely possible that those who harbor negative feelings towards him do so out of nothing deeper than simple jealousy. But there are still those who stubbornly accuse him of putting too great a signature stamp on his productions (as in, "every record he makes, regardless of the artist, is really a Trevor Horn record"), the same way some criticized Phil Spector half a century ago—particularly ironic, since, as you'll read in this interview, Horn is no great fan of Spector's.

Horn is rather unique among his peers in that he enjoyed a highly successful career as a musician before moving to the other side of the glass. As half of the eighties pop duo the Buggles (he was the one with the nerdy glasses), he co-wrote, co-produced, and sang lead on their smash hit "Video Killed the Radio Star," perhaps best known today as the first video ever played on MTV. He and co-Buggle Geoff Downes were then briefly integrated into prog-rock kings Yes (an experience he later described as "awful") before he made the decision to end his touring days and focus full-time on record production.

After starting his own record label and purchasing London's Sarm Studios in 1983, Horn hand-picked a custom production team and then proceeded to issue a series of sample- and loop-based albums with them under the name The Art of Noise—decades before sample- and loop-based records were the norm. Since then, he's gone on to work with an eclectic collection of artists, meticulously crafting lush soundscapes for the likes of Frankie Goes To Hollywood, Grace Jones, Barry Manilow, Paul McCartney, Cher, Rod Stewart, and Tina Turner, as well as several albums with British soul vocalist Seal, one of which netted him a Grammy award in 1995. As if that weren't sufficient proof of Horn's impressive work ethic, he also collaborated with ex-bandmate Hans Zimmer on the soundtrack for the 1992 movie *Toys* and even wrote the official song for the 2004 Olympics!

So was Yes's 1983 album *90125* a smash hit because of the group's musical and songwriting chops, or because of Horn's production flourishes? Was Frankie Goes To Hollywood really Trevor Goes to East London? Would Seal have attained international success with anyone else at the helm? You can be the judge, but based on this insightful conversation with the genial, soft-spoken Horn, it's hard to believe he's really the Svengali some have made him out to be.

Did you always want to be a record producer?

No, it had never been my intention to become a record producer. I started out as a bass player, but I was always absolutely fascinated by the recording process. When I first came to London, I played on a lot of sessions, and after each take I was always the one who wanted to go into the control room and have a listen.

Then, with a friend, I decided to build a recording studio. Because we didn't have much money, we had to do it all ourselves, and it was a real education for me—I had to learn about soundproofing and a lot of technical things. The studio was in Leicester, though, so I didn't stick around very long after we finished it; instead, I returned to London. I suppose that, like a lot of young people, I didn't really know what I wanted; I just knew that I wanted to be in the music business rather than the normal world.

"Video Killed the Radio Star" took three months to record. That was a really long time to make a single track, even by the standards of the eighties.

Part of the reason it took so long to make is that, even though it may sound programmed, everything on there was actually played by live musicians. Our only concession to programming was playing to a click track.

Another reason is that we had made a great demo of the song, which had gotten us the record deal, but we didn't want to sign a contract with the person who had put the money up to make the demo, so we had to make it again from scratch. But when we started it again, we became a bit cavalier, and we ended up having to scrap everything we'd done because we'd wandered a bit too far away from the good ideas in the demo. It's a very easy mistake to make; there's a great temptation to change

> *"You always need to keep every bit of magic that's on the demo before you try to create additional magic."*

everything, but you've got to be very careful to keep everything that was good about the demo exactly the same. That experience taught me a really hard lesson that has stood me in good stead ever since, which is: you always need to keep every bit of magic that's on the demo before you try to create additional magic.

So, yes, it did take us three months to record. In the end, we got a bit crazy with the whole thing—we didn't know which way was up.

I imagine it's tough to see things objectively when you're producing yourself.

It's part of the problem with producing *anybody*, actually. [*laughs*] In some ways producing yourself is easier in that you don't have to worry about anyone's opinions except your own. Artists can occasionally freak out—especially if things are going on for a long while—and try to get you to do things that aren't right for the record. The thing is, if you spend all your time in the recording studio, like I do, you know so much more about it than someone who just comes in for a couple of months. Making a record can be quite hard: there are so many pitfalls, so many places where you can go wrong, that artists sometimes fall into the first hole that comes along.

In addition, everyone is so much more relaxed when they're recording a demo because they think that few people are ever going to hear it.

That's true, and to retain that freshness when you're making the record, you have to keep listening to the demo the same way you have to keep checking the rear-view mirror while you're driving a car.

These days, of course, most demos that people make are usable, so if you can't recreate that same feeling a second time, you can just import the original demo itself and build on it to create a master. Back when I started making records, demos were usually done on an inferior medium like a TEAC four-track, or half-inch eight-track tape, so you had no choice: you had to do everything again in order to get an acceptable sound. Nowadays, with everyone using computers, that's not an issue, so that's what I generally do: I work on top of the actual demo.

How do you think the role of the producer has changed since you first got into the business?

Well, for one thing, there are loads of songwriters calling themselves record producers today; there seem to be a lot fewer people around like me who are prepared to work on other people's material. Many of today's producers insist on co-writing the song with the artist; they won't just take your song and make it into a record.

Also, now that you don't have to play in real time, there are lots of people masquerading as musicians who are barely literate musically. That's fair enough, but the problem is that it does tend to make for a certain kind of harmonic mediocrity in many of today's records.

I guess another thing that's changed is that you don't hear as many out-of-tune singers! [*laughs*] Of course, there are some people who spent an entire career constantly singing out of tune, and there can actually be something quite appealing about that. Nowadays, every singer seems to be impossibly perfectly in tune. There's something a bit irksome about that.

So I take it you're not a big fan of autotuning?

No, it's perfectly fine. It's a brilliant piece of software, and we all have to use it, because everybody's using it. It is true that it can move you up a division. But if you're fourth division in the first place, it's only going to move you to third division.

Your records are beautifully crafted, yet many of them have also enjoyed tremendous commercial success. When you go into the studio, is your goal to make a great record or a hit record?

Well, making a great record can't be your goal all the time, because sometimes you're working with a piece of material that will never make a great record. In that case, the best you can do is to try to make a good record that entertains people.

I'd actually only describe a few of the records that I've made as great records. One of them would be the Yes track "Owner of a Lonely Heart," but a lot of what made that really good was that I had severe doubts about the song, so I thought I had to do loads of stuff to distract the listener. As it turned out, the song was rewritten in the end, so it didn't need all the crazy bits on there, but we kept them anyway.

Yet musically, it's far and away the simplest song Yes ever recorded.

Without a doubt. And it also had a good feel to it. They were a band that actually usually had a good feel, but it can be hard for the general public to appreciate a good feel when the music is in 9/8. [*laughs*]

Do you feel there is a distinctive "Trevor Horn sound"?

I don't feel all my records have a similar sound, though I seem to be identified with some of the records I made in the eighties. I guess that's because I was one of the first people to make records that sound like modern records today. I suppose my early records were somewhat identifiable in that they had rhythm sections that were perfectly in time, but that was because I was using equipment that really was only available to a few people at the time. I had an ethic of Kraftwerk meets Glen Campbell—the idea of putting a commercial record on top of an electronic backing track. At the beginning of the eighties, that was a really new idea. But as the decade progressed, everyone was able to do that; you didn't need to buy a hugely expensive Fairlight anymore—you could get much the same result with an inexpensive Akai sampler.

I don't know that Seal really sounds like Frankie Goes To Hollywood, but there are certain things that all the records I've made have in common. One is that I'm pretty manic about them being entertaining to the very last note; I don't give up on a track two-thirds of the way through. I like the records I make to build and I like them to have interesting arrangements that don't go exactly where you'd expect them to go all the time. If I have any kind of recognizable sound, maybe that's the reason.

As producer, I have to keep the big picture in mind at all times, but the big picture is often severely affected by the minutiae; there really are times when you have to roll up your sleeves and truly sort something out. So there's lots of hard work that goes into all the records I make because I'm always trying to get things that little bit better. To that end, I always make sure to use really, really good musicians. It's generally the same cast of people that keep popping up on my records, because I haven't found many players that have that little extra something.

Not only do you tend to use the same musicians on your records, you tend to use the same team in the control room, like Phil Spector did. Was Spector a big influence on you?

Actually, no. I think Phil Spector made some good records in the early days, but it seems to me that his great contribution was making musicians do things they didn't necessarily want to do and would not normally do in live performance. Those early "Wall of Sound" records were the first records where the musicians played in a way that they wouldn't play onstage. He deserves credit for that, and overall he was a reasonably effective producer, if a bit heavy-handed at times. But I always preferred George Martin's style of production.

Having said that, I have to say that I hated *Let It Be ... Naked*. Why the hell they took the orchestra off "Long and Winding Road" is a mystery to me. "Long and Winding Road" is a great big cheesy ballad, and it's not going to be any less of a cheesy ballad without the orchestra on there. Even though I'm not a big fan of Spector, I had a little more respect for him after hearing that. But I think once you took Phil Spector away from being the producer of a concept record—records like "River Deep, Mountain High" or "You've Lost That Lovin' Feeling"—he wasn't nearly as effective; once you put him in charge of The Beatles, or John Lennon, I wasn't very impressed.

And if you think of the entire Beatles catalog, there are exactly two cheesy string arrangements: one of them is "Long and Winding Road," and the other one is "She's Leaving Home"... and neither of them was done by George Martin. [*laughs*] George just had a way of arranging strings so that they didn't sound MOR or cheap. His work was understated, and he also made some great records post-Beatles. But then, of course, he never made "Leader of the Pack" or any of those kinds of records.

You were one of the earliest adopters of digital recording. What made you gravitate to it even when it was still in its infancy?

Primarily because of its consistency. If you record a band through a proper analog desk onto analog tape—16-track, 30 IPS, preferably—you'll get a really good sound. But if you record at 15 IPS with Dolby, you'll get a different kind of sound. Good or bad, the problem is that they don't stay like that for very long, because the more you run analog tape past the heads, the more the sound degenerates. If you listen to the *Beatles Anthology*, you can hear that the final masters sound quite small compared to the original backing tracks, which were big and open-sounding. That's because those rough mixes were probably run off at the time of recording; by the time you get to the final master, it's been down a couple of generations, and the tape has run over the heads a thousand times.

There were ways of getting around that, mind you. The last album that I made completely analog would have been Yes' *90125*, and we did all the backing tracks on two-inch 16-track and then copied them and put all the original tapes in a cupboard for ten months; we didn't get them out again until it came time to mix the record.

So when digital came along, it was like manna from heaven for me. It was wonderful, because it meant you could do all kinds of things without losing quality. And I felt that the quality of even the very earliest digital machines was fine—it just took people a long time to get used to the sound. Engineers recording on tape used to print things really bright—the drums, particularly—so that, as the oxide wore off, there would still be enough top end there. That's where a lot of people screwed up in the early days of digital—they'd EQ the hell out of everything on the way in, and then you couldn't undo it.

We never had the same kind of problem with digital, thanks to Steve Lipson, who's a very good engineer. [*See the interview with Steve Lipson on page 189.*] He learned early on to record things flat and to then make any necessary EQ adjustments afterwards, during mixing. I remember going to a Sony event in the early days of digital, when we were one of the few people using it. There were a bunch of old guys there moaning about the sound of digital, and I'll never forget Steve saying to them, "But that's not the point. The point is, the sound never *changes*." With analog, it changes all the time.

It's funny, I was working with a band recently and they were asking me what I thought about analog recording. They were making the argument that everyone used to record that way. I said, "Well, my grandmother used to have an outside toilet on her house." [*laughs*] While there may be certain advantages to having an outside toilet, nobody actually builds a house with one these days. That's how I look at analog.

Do you think that the sound quality of records today has been negatively impacted by the fact that most people are listening to music over earbuds or tiny low-fidelity computer speakers?

How can you even talk about hi-fi in an era when people think that iPods sound good? An iPod is like a cassette. If you play an MP3 over proper speakers, turned up loud, you can hear how shredded the music is and how awful the sonics are.

Sadly, these days it almost doesn't matter, because a fair percentage of records are being made solely from pre-prepared ingredients. It's like a cook in a kitchen who doesn't buy actual meat; instead, he buys cans of processed meat and a can opener. For many people these days, a studio isn't a gourmet kitchen—it's just a sophisticated can opener and a pan for heating things up. And if you're just heating things up—if you're just using prerecorded drum sounds and sequencing the whole thing in Logic—you don't need a great big set of monitors so you can hear the what the drums really sound like and look at the sound through a microscope. Because those drums are prerecorded, when it's all put together, it's going to sound fine...but it's a completely different approach to the way records used to be made, when you'd create all the ingredients fresh, from scratch.

If some records today have poor quality sound, I think it's mostly because they're being made in crappy rooms. I'm really lucky in that I get to work in rooms where huge amounts of money have been spent on acoustic treatment so I can hear what I'm doing and be confident that what I'm creating in that room will sound right on any system—it's like having a nice, clear canvas to paint on. But most people work in their bedroom, or their living room, and they're listening on a set of nearfield monitors, and while those monitors will tell them a bit about what they're hearing, they won't tell them much about what the sound is *really* like. So you can have all kinds of anomalies creep in there—strange frequencies that agitate the compressors or the limiters on the radio, for example. People try to fix it all in the mastering now, but it's not always possible.

> **"It's the noise that ultimately interests people, not the quality of the noise."**

But at the end of the day, all these things—analog versus digital, or the difference between a Neve desk and an SSL desk—are trivial compared to the difference between this guy's bass drum and that guy's bass drum. It's the noise that ultimately interests people, not the quality of the noise.

How do you feel the democratization of recording—the fact that anyone today can make a record in their bedroom—has affected the music business in general?

Music is just like any other area of endeavor. If you were to take a hundred people and give them each a large sum of money and tell them to use that money to go start a business, probably half of them would be broke in a year. Maybe three or four of them would be running a multi-national conglomerate, and I suppose the rest would be muddling along in the middle.

In much the same way, if you give everyone an electric guitar, an amplifier, and a drum machine, you'll get the same results. It doesn't matter what you give people; some people will use it to create crap, and some people will create something worthwhile. It's always been like that. If you think of how many rock groups have been formed since the fifties, you can still only count the number of meaningful bands—the ones that have truly made an impact—on your fingers and toes. Yet they've all had access to the same thing, so, clearly, having access to equipment made no difference.

Obviously, because so many people now have the capacity to make records in their bedrooms, we may be getting a lot more mediocrity...but it is fairly well-recorded mediocrity. In fact, it's a rarity to hear something truly bad these days! [*laughs*] What with autotuning and the ability to line up everything in time, it's pretty difficult to create something that's crap. I suppose that's one of the problems with technology: everything today is so perfect, you tend to hear a lot of perfect mediocrity.

> **"Mediocrity is the enemy of the record producer."**

The thing is, mediocrity is the enemy of the record producer. It isn't being crap that's your enemy, because you wouldn't have gotten to that position in the first place if you didn't know what you were doing. The battle lies in fighting mediocrity, and mediocrity creeps in all the time. Of course, sometimes you really need to know how to use mediocrity to its best advantage; for instance, if you're scoring a film. In some respects that's what film music is all about, because the directors don't want the audience focusing on the music.

What advice would you give someone who wants to be the next Trevor Horn?

First and foremost, don't do anything for the money; certainly, don't make any decisions based on money until you're very successful—up to that point, be prepared to do anything for nothing. And don't get married early on; you can't start having children at the age of 22 and expect to make it in the music business.

But if you work really hard and you keep going, one day you'll get your chance. One day the planets will go into a certain alignment, and suddenly it's your day. It took me about five years to get to that day, and I've seen it happen over and over again, often enough that I'm convinced it happens to everybody. The thing is, you've got to make sure that, when your day comes, you have enough experience and enough ability and knowledge to be able to seize the opportunity and do something really good with it.

And if you see somebody get that opportunity ahead of you, don't be envious, because blowing a big opportunity early on in your career can be the worst thing that can happen to you. All the people you see fall by the wayside are the people who weren't ready when their time came. Whoever you are, you need to have your own thing, and you need to make sure that you do it better than anybody else can do: nobody else can do your shit like you can do it. You just have to make sure that your shit is as good as it can possibly be!

Finally, never be intimidated by people who are loads better than you; there's room for everybody in this business. I never understood that thing musicians have where they get discouraged by seeing someone better than them. I know loads of bass players who would go see Stanley Clarke or whoever and then come back saying, "Oh, man, I give up." I used to go and see those guys too, but all it would do was make me want to play some more, even though I knew I'd never be as good as any of them. So don't ever be envious of anybody, and if you do see someone who is suffering from envy or insecurity, help them; in helping them, you'll actually learn more than you could possibly imagine.

Suggested Listening:
The Buggles: *The Age of Plastic*, Island, 1980; *Adventures in Modern Recording*, EMI, 1982
Yes: *90125*, Atco, 1983
Frankie Goes To Hollywood: *Welcome to the Pleasuredome*, ZTT/Island, 1984; *Liverpool*, ZTT/Island, 1986
The Art of Noise: *(Who's Afraid Of?) The Art of Noise!*, ZTT/Island, 1984; *The Seduction of Claude DeBussy*, ZTT/Universal, 1999
Seal: *Seal*, Sire, 1994; *Human Being*, Warner Bros., 1998; *Seal IV*, Warner Bros., 2003

Stephen Lipson

From Frankie to Annie and Beyond

Being an interviewer is a funny kind of job. Sometimes it feels as if you're playing a game of ping-pong, firing questions at your interview subject, who is returning each volley with an answer until one of you declares the game over. Other times—the best-case scenario—you feel as if you're instead involved in a true dialog, chatting informally with someone who is as interested in what you are asking them as they are in their own responses.

That was unquestionably the case with this interview you're about to read. Stephen Lipson is one of England's top producer/engineers, with a lineage that traces back nearly three decades, including a long apprenticeship with ace Trevor Horn (with whom he co-produced Paul McCartney and Frankie Goes To Hollywood, among others) and sole production of Annie Lennox's first two solo albums, *Diva and Medusa*. He's since worked with a diverse range of world-class artists, including Cher, Whitney Houston, Simple Minds, Natalie Imbruglia, and the Pet Shop Boys, as well as doing soundtrack work for *Bridget Jones' Diary* and an *American Idol* collection. Despite his fame as a producer, he continues to do session work as a guitarist and is an enthusiastic member of a not-so-tongue-in-cheek band appropriately enough named The Producers, along with Horn and veteran producer (and ex-10CC member) Lol Creme.

Thoughtful and unassuming, with an unmistakable dry British wit, Lipson chatted with us at length one bright sunny morning in his upstairs room at London's Sarm Studios, located at the former Basing Street site of Island Studios.

You started as a musician. Did you always want to end up as a record producer? Was that a goal you were always consciously working towards?

No, and it's actually quite interesting how I got into it. I started playing guitar at the age of nine, but I eschewed lessons, so I never really knew how to play properly. I put together a kind of "bedroom band" with a couple of friends, and when the first drum machine came out, I got one of those, and I got a Revox two-track tape recorder and an Allen & Heath mixer with four inputs, plus a TEAC tape recorder that we used for echo. So all three of us would plug into this little rig, and everything went to one track and then we bounced to another track and added more overdubs.

Eventually we were offered a record deal, to our amazement. It was a really good deal, too, but we were really cocky kids and so we said, "No, it's not good enough." Needless to say, we didn't get *any* deal. [*laughs*]

At the time—this would have been the mid-1970s—I was taking a load of drugs, including LSD, and one day I had a bad trip and started behaving like I was Jimi Hendrix. The next day, I thought, "This is not good. Under no circumstances must I become an artist, because I'll turn into an asshole." I was doing a lot of sessions at that point for a friend who had a jingle company, and I said to him, "You know, I'd love to learn how to engineer." My reasoning was that if I knew

how to engineer, I could make my guitar sound better. He had actually just bought a building, and so he invited me to go into partnership with him and build a studio there. It took me all of about a nanosecond to say yes. Mind you, I didn't know anything about studios, but I was given 20,000 pounds to spend and a year to build a studio with that money.

So I built a 16-track studio from the ground up, finding the contractors, figuring out the acoustics, learning how to wire it and what gear to get. We bought this bizarre 16-track machine from a place that had just gone out of business and when you started it playing back, the pinch rollers would lift the tape straight up in the air an inch or so... and if you were lucky, it settled down just enough so that it landed on the reel. Other times it went over and out, and I had to stop it rather quickly! [*laughs*] I didn't know any better; I just thought that's the way things were.

Eventually we open our doors and the first session arrives—it's a jingle—and I have never, ever engineered anything in my life. So I set the musicians up in whatever way I figured they should be, and I get some sounds together even though I was clueless beyond belief, put the 16-track into Record, ran over to the console—there was no remote autolocator, of course—and had to immediately run back because I saw the tape about to head for the floor!

Despite the rocky start, within six months the studio was flying, and by that time the penny had dropped; I realized that all the knowledge in the world wasn't going to make my guitar sound any better, that it didn't come from that side of the glass—it was all in my fingers. So I'd finally ended up in this position, and it was a flawed concept from the start: I'd become an engineer and it wasn't the answer to my question.

One day a group came in called Sniff 'n' the Tears, and I ended up getting a co-production credit because the producer read science fiction books all day long while I did all the work. There was this amazing moment on a song called "Driver's Seat," which became a minor hit.

The way the band had recorded the song, all the parts played all the way through—there were lots of riffs and things. But when it came to mixing, I suddenly discovered the Mute button. I said to the band, "I've got an idea here," and after the song started with all these riffs and things playing, as soon as the vocal came in, I hit these Mute buttons and cut the guitars. Everyone went, "What's happened?" I said, "That's good, isn't it?" and they all agreed. It was a major moment for me.

After that, the band asked me to produce their next album, which was going to be done in France, so I left the studio to make the album, which ended up dying a death. That was another big lesson I learned: producing a record is not just about you, it's about involving every-one...even if only to make sure that everyone is equally as guilty as you if it stiffs! [*laughs*]

I ended up as a reluctant freelance engineer, working with loads of artists, including Gerry Rafferty, who I learned quite a lot from. An old friend of mine was producing Gerry, and so he brought me with him down to AIR Studios in Montserrat to engineer. One day Gerry's band was rehearsing a 12-bar in the key of G and the guitarist was playing chords at the bottom, on the third fret, and the piano player was playing a Wurly, down in the same area. I couldn't get it to sound right, so I suggested to the guitarist that he play inversions higher up on the neck, up on the tenth fret, in the A position, out of the range of the Wurly, so I could get some separation. He said, "That's a really good idea," and Gerry overhead him saying that. He asked, "What's a good idea?" and the guitarist said, "Oh, Stephen's just suggested I play a higher inversion to get out of the range of the piano." Gerry turned to me with a dour face and said, "You just stick to the engineering." It was one of those pivotal moments when I realized that I'd crossed a line. Of course, not every artist is like that; many of them are happy to receive suggestions, especially if they help improve the record.

There is actually a prequel to that story: A few years earlier, our studio had gotten a major booking from Stiff Records. They wanted to record some big new artist they had just signed and they were bringing in a bunch of top session players to help out, but the label head, Dave Robinson, didn't think I was quite experienced enough to handle it, so he sent in another engineer to work with me, a fellow named Phil Brown. Phil opened my eyes to engineering like nobody had ever done before. He sort of did nothing, but it sounded great, and it all just seemed to happen by osmosis. I remember him telling the keyboard player one day that he was playing in the wrong inversion, saying, "There's nothing I can do for you in the control room; it's got to happen out there in the studio," and that really registered with me.

Anyway, while I was bouncing around as a freelancer, the person who was managing me at the time got a phone call one day asking me to do some engineering for Trevor Horn. My first thought was to say no—I loved his records but somehow I just didn't want to get involved in the kinds of poppy things he was creating. Plus I wanted to be a producer, and I couldn't see how engineering for Trevor Horn was going to help me achieve that. But I was talked into it, and I agreed to do a couple of days as a trial. At the time, Trevor was working with Frankie Goes To Hollywood, and something had happened, so he needed a new team. I was brought in as the engineer, and I was so not into being there, I decided to just ignore him and do whatever I wanted. But it turned out that was exactly what he was looking for—he wanted someone to come in and just do it. So two days turned into six years! [*laughs*]

Within the first week, of course, I'd told Trevor that I played a bit of guitar. He completely ignored my comment at the time, but one night he went home for dinner while I stayed behind and continued working on the track—the band weren't there, so I was on my own—and I came up with a guitar part. When he got back from dinner and heard it, he said, "What's that guitar part? I love it!" We ended up making a lot of records together, and then I started producing artists for his label.

These days, you're pretty much an all-digital guy, aren't you?

These days, it's all about convenience; you simply want the gear to not get in the way. This console [Digidesign Icon] is stunning; that one item has really made record-making a joy. Some people have called it a "big mouse." What a stupid remark! If that's a big mouse, then a car is just a lump of metal. With it, the process all becomes natural; I simply can't relate using a mouse to the whole flow of the music.

Regarding plug-ins, I'm not so sure. I can't decide if it's good or bad to see the EQ curve, for example. I find myself putting EQ on something to the point where it sounds good, and then I look at the curve and I start thinking, "Hmmm, that's a bit much." Which is interesting, and probably not such a good thing.

The big issue these days, of course, is tuning, because if you don't do it, your records sound strange: people's ears have become used to hearing voices perfectly in tune. Still, I'm pretty sparing with it, because often the sound of the voice straining is exactly what you want.

Do you ever use digital compression?

I use compressors on pretty much everything on the way in because it allows you to hear things a bit better. I wouldn't dream of recording a vocal without a compressor, for example. Digital compressors are fine for mixdown, but when recording vocals in particular, you need to gently harness a wide dynamic range. I find that's best accomplished with something like an 1176, which gives a gorgeous tone as it starts compressing.

Do you experiment a lot with different compressors or mics or preamps?

Well, if someone's coming in to sing, I think it's inappropriate to say, "Let's try these ten microphones." That's because the very first time they sing might be the best take, or at least most of the best take. That's why having a go-to vocal chain is absolutely essential. I'm lucky: I've got a really incredible microphone that works for everybody, and I've got an incredible mic preamp.

What are they?

The mic is a Wagner, made by this guy Gunter Wagner, who rebuilds [Neumann U] 47s. I have an original, vintage U 47, and it's fine except it's unreliable—it sometime hisses and gets noisy and crackly. I made loads of inquiries, eventually discovered Gunter, spoke with him, and he said, "I'll build you a mic." I've A/B'd it against my 47 and it sounds the same, yet better in every way; I can't speak highly enough about it.

The preamp I now use is a Mercury M76. At my old studio, we had a rack of original Telefunken V76s, but it was the same deal: we kept having to change them out because they went down. So I again made inquiries to find out if anyone made a modern version, and located a company called Mercury Audio. Their M76 is a new version of the V76, and it's unbelievable. The combination of it with my Wagner mic is phenomenal: singers put their headphones on to say, "I'm ready," and then they immediately go, "Wow!" just hearing their voices for the first time through that chain.

I've never heard anyone describe a single microphone or preamp as perfect for everybody.

I know; I completely agree. But these are. And what's really good about this chain is that there's no sibilance to speak of. It somehow calms the sibilance down and it's got beautiful low end; it just represents the voice in the most glorious way.

Having said that, I still feel that we can get a little too precious about these things. What we're talking about here is that final two percent, and I think there are more important things to focus on. The real problem is that to look for that final two percent can cost you 40 percent in other departments.

I guess you have to wonder anyway how much of that final two percent makes it through the conversion process to a highly compressed, lossy MP3, which is the final product most people will hear.

Sure, and then you have to factor in mastering, where everything gets compressed to hell. In my opinion, it's time spent in the wrong area.

I had a big learning curve when I was asked to get involved in the first *American Idol* album, which consisted of songs that they'd done throughout the season. There were ten or twelve singers doing two songs each, and we didn't have long to do it, so I had a friend here in London prepare some backing tracks, and I had another person recording the backing vocals in a studio in LA, and I concentrated on the lead vocals, again with not much time to do it: I had perhaps two hours to do two songs with each singer. I learned really quickly that the best way to accomplish this was to begin by just sitting and chatting, just as you and I are doing right now, for an hour and a half, just talking about anything. And then I'd say, "Whoops, we've only got half an hour left! Quick, let's go sing something!" [*laughs*] Bang! Got the vocals. It worked every time.

The opposite to that approach would be having a singer audition lots of different microphones. It's drawing attention to the wrong things, and all it will accomplish is to make the singer tense, which is totally counterproductive.

So much of production seems to be about getting the artist into their comfort zone.

Absolutely. I'll sometimes spend half a day talking with an artist before even attempting a single take. I find you have to get them relaxed and not thinking about what they have to do in order to get the best performance out of them.

And yet there are some producers that rely on intimidation instead.

Yes, but we'll never know if they could have gotten better results by taking a different approach. They got what they got, and that's all we hear. Do we know whether it could have been better or worse if they'd been gentle with the artist instead of intimidating? It's anybody's guess.

At the end of the day, records are about the vocal. And there's always that point where it's, "Okay, now we're going to do the vocal." I know all too well that when I'm playing

> *"At the end of the day, records are about the vocal."*

guitar—and I often play on the records I make—I play differently when it's in Record than when I'm just figuring out parts. Am I different than anyone else? I don't think so. So to remove that whole level of pressure surely must be a good thing.

Trevor Horn has a reputation for being a real perfectionist who wears out engineers. Is that accurate?

No, it's not quite like that. He doesn't ever get into too much detail on any one thing.

So he's not always searching for that extra two percent you talked about earlier?

Well, he is, but in a different way. He'll put a drummer on a track and then he'll have a second drummer play on the same song, not because he's trying to overproduce but because he's not sure if he got the best drum part the first time around. It's a bigger picture kind of thing; it's not about working on the kick drum sound for three days in a row. Neither of us is interested in things like that; we both agreed on that within two minutes of working together.

Having said all that, of course there are times when that happens anyway. On the [Frankie Goes To Hollywood] song "Two Tribes," we spent three months on the bass part. But that was because the whole song hinged on the bass. I'll never forget [producer/engineers] Clive Langer and Alan Winstanley coming into the studio next door to mix an album while we were recording that. They finished the mix, went away, recorded *another* album, came back to mix that one... and we were still working on the bass part! [*laughs*]

All the Frankie records took a long time to make, didn't they?

Yes, they did, but again the time was spent on the bigger picture, like, "let's remake the song," as opposed to "let's concentrate on the bass drum sound." When we were doing "Welcome to the Pleasuredome," we were using a Sony digital multitrack machine, and I suggested we get another one in, even though it was going to cost a fortune. But I had an idea: by doing an offset between the two machines I was able to double up the length of the track. We ended up doing that four times—quadrupling the length of the original track, which had never been done before. It allowed us to build this thing up into some kind of mad symphonic piece.

You actually played bass on a Paul McCartney track, which is a claim probably no one else can make. How did that happen?

It just kind of worked out that way. Trevor had been asked to work on a couple of tracks on Paul's *Flowers in the Dirt* album, and he invited me to co-produce, which was very generous of him. On the drive down to Paul's home studio we had decided that we would work very quickly and spend no more than a day or two per song. Obviously, the guy's got the talent, and assuming he's got the songs, we felt it would be better to do things that way rather than drag it out over a period of months.

I had a Yamaha RX5 drum box with me, and I'd pre-programmed a bunch of rhythms in it— I guess I was writing beats long before anyone else—and Trevor had commented about one of them in particular, saying, "Oh, we could do something with that," not knowing what. But when we got to Paul's place and Trevor heard him play the song "Rough Ride," he thought he'd found the perfect home for it. We played Macca the rhythm, and he said, "Yeah, alright, we'll use that."

My rig consisted of a PC, this Yamaha box, and a whole bunch of rack-mounted synths, and I had it set up at the console, so I was playing while I was engineering. Just fiddling around, I came up with this extraordinary bass sound—I think it came from a Yamaha TX802 and a Roland MKS-70—and when Macca heard it, he said, "I like that; you play that and I'll play guitar." So off we went, with Trevor and I playing keyboards and Paul playing guitar. I remember thinking, "This is really weird, because the only thing that's actually changing in this song is the bass line, and I'm playing it... even though that's Paul McCartney standing right there."

Weren't you assuming that you were just playing a guide and that he was going to redo the bass later on?

The thought didn't occur to me, quite honestly—the music was just unfolding. I was just freaking out that it was the bass that was making the chorus happening; it wasn't what anyone else was playing, it was what I was doing. So in effect I was creating the arrangement. It did me in a bit. I kept thinking, "I shouldn't be doing this; *he* should be doing this."

We had an issue with the middle eight, too: I thought it was crap, and at one point I said so. All of McCartney's people were in the room with us, and they looked at me like, "Do you know who you're talking to??" Paul himself was looking at me a bit funny, saying, "Oh yeah?" There was this pregnant pause where I thought to myself, "Okay, Stephen, you've gone too far." But then he said, "Well, if you think it's crap, what do you think we should do instead?" I said, "I haven't got a clue; that's your department. My job is to tell you what I think."

Then, to my tremendous relief, he simply said, "Right! I'll go rewrite it then." And he went upstairs and came down a short while later with a new middle eight.

It sounds like you impressed him with your honesty, and by refusing to be intimidated by him.

I guess so. And the bass part I played ended up on the record too! [*laughs*]

I haven't worked with Paul that much, but one thing I loved about him was that everything came from instinct; things happened really quickly. He's just so talented as a musician. I kept thinking, "What a great person to have in a band; he can do anything really well." In fact, he's *exactly* what you want in a band. I think we did four tracks on that album, and it was a great experience. I did the bass on another track as well, though that was different because it had been sequenced beforehand.

I've also worked with Ringo, on one of his solo albums, and, you know, he's a *really* good drummer. If you listen to "A Day in the Life," the fill he plays in the second bar of the second verse is just amazing; it just sums up how brilliant he was. Not just the fill itself, but where he plays it: another drummer would have played it coming into the verse, not at the second bar. And his timing is rock solid, and his feel, and his sound—he has the whole thing down.

I have a good Ringo story, too, which I think illustrates the importance of getting the artist relaxed. On this one track I engineered for him, Paul was producing. At the time, I had one of those old Elvis Presley–type Shure microphones sitting around for show: it was an old chrome thing, and it looked cool but it was rubbish. When it came time for Ringo to do the vocals, he said to McCartney, "I like the look of that microphone. Can I sing into that one?" And Macca said, "Sure, of course you can."

I was appalled because I knew how poor the mic was, so when Macca walked back into the control room, I asked him, "Why are you letting him sing through such a bad microphone?" and he said, "Because he'll sing better." That was a big lesson.

Did you sneak a U 47 a few feet away and use that instead?

No, I just used the Shure, and it ended up sounding fine because he sang great; he was really comfortable with it. Unfortunately, I don't think the track was ever released

Do you think someone can be trained to develop critical listening skills—what some call "golden ears"—or is that something you're either born with or not?

I think you can learn to disassemble what it is you're hearing, but I don't think you can learn taste. And, really, a big part of making records is subjective, just having good taste. How can you learn that? *Can* you learn that?

I don't know; you're the one being interviewed! [*laughs*]

I just don't see how you can.

On the other hand, I suppose there are producers who claim that they somehow know the tastes of the listening public and can give people what they want.

Yes, but you're talking about the machine approach to making records.

I guess so. You're talking about what's good versus what's not good; I'm talking about what a hit supposedly sounds like.

They're two different things. It's true that I'm always thinking about the singles that might come off an album, but every record I've done has been about my personal taste, as in, "I like that" versus "I don't like that." For example, when I'm analyzing a vocal take, I'm always thinking in terms of, "It doesn't sound heartfelt enough at this point" or "It doesn't sound bland enough at that point." The ingredients that go into making a record are purely a taste thing for me. I can't imagine thinking, "It doesn't sound enough like a hit."

On the other hand, I suppose you might apply that criteria to a rhythm: "Is it a hit rhythm?" could be a question you might ask. Perhaps more, "Is it a *hip* rhythm?"

What are the criteria you use for picking the single off an album?

I'm not sure; in fact, I don't know how good I am at that. Trevor [Horn] is very good at it—he's much better at finding the single than I am. I may be underestimating myself, but there are always other people involved, and you get a feel from the way they react too. A good example might be Annie Lennox's first album [*Diva*]. There were two specific songs on the album we were considering for the single: "Why," and "Walking on Broken Glass." Her manager felt strongly that "Why" would be the first single. I didn't question his decision, because he expressed it with such quiet confidence. So it was the first single and I worked on it as if it was the first single, but I didn't pick it. "Walking on Broken Glass" to me was the obvious only other choice, because if you looked at the album as a whole, there really wasn't anything else suitable, and of course it turned out to be a massive hit for her.

There are other times when a song starts coming through the speakers and it just instantly sounds like a single. That happened with the Geri Halliwell track, "It's Raining Men," which somebody suggested I have her cover for a Bridget Jones movie soundtrack. It took me about one second to recognize that I could make it into a hit, and it turned out to be a huge record for her around the world. It was just a no-brainer; I knew instantly how to make it a hit.

What was it that made you instantly realize that? Was it completely visceral?

Well, I already knew that the song was strong, because it had already been a hit, but I somehow knew right away how to give it the energy it needed for her version. Not that I knew exactly what components were going to go into it, but I knew it would be very up-tempo and that the rhythms would be exciting and outrageous. I immediately heard big orchestra stabs and tymps in my head; the record almost constructed itself. There have been a few records that have happened that way, but it's not easy picking a hit, not at all. Nor is it easy writing a hit; I've written a lot of music, but I've never written a hit. I often co-write with my artists, but only to fill in the gaps, to help make the song better; I'm no good at writing hits. Sadly, the cheese often wins, and I'm distinctly anti-cheese.

Are you more interested in making a great record or a hit record?

They're kind of one and the same, in a way. If you make a great record, you want it to be a hit. It won't necessarily be one, because there are so many balls that have to go in the pocket. But if something isn't successful—and I'm not in any way talking financially—but if loads of people don't hear it, it's a shame. Unfortunately, that happens all the time—there are a lot of great records made that are never released, or which are released and go to obscurity. So when I'm choosing an artist to work with, it's sad to say that more often than not, my priorities are: Do they have good management? Is the A&R guy solidly behind the project, or is he about to leave? Is the record going to just get lost because nobody knows what they're doing? It's only after I'm satisfied with the answers to those questions that I turn my attention to the artist and the song.

Do you consider yourself very detail-oriented?

I can be, if the situation warrants. To me, it's like zooming in on Google Earth. Sometimes you need to be able to see the big picture and other times you need to take a really close look at things, like when you're comping vocals. Those are situations where you really can't let any mistakes go, and it can really pay off. And I firmly believe that the artist never should be in the room with me while I'm comping, because a singer's perspective on their performance is extraordinary; they're concerned about different things than I am. I'm not concerned about getting the ultimate performance; I'm concerned with how the song is delivered.

Singers tend to microanalyze. They'll be thinking, "I didn't hit that note correctly," whereas that may not matter to me if I like the way they ached up to the note, if there's a feeling that isn't present on any of the other takes. I simply don't want to have that discussion with them while I'm in the middle of comping; I just want to pick at it and move on, and then play the final result to them and get their input. I don't want them to hear all their bad bits, either—they don't need to hear that.

> *"I'm not concerned about getting the ultimate performance; I'm concerned with how the song is delivered."*

Do you feel the same way about mixing? Do you not want the artist in the room with you while you're mixing?

I can't see the point. To me, it's far more useful to have the artist hear something complete, or near-complete, than for them to hear the whole process of me getting to that point. If they're in the room with me throughout, they're going to be discussing things with me that are completely irrelevant, like the EQ on a particular instrument. If I'm adjusting the EQ on something, I have a reason for doing so—I'm trying to get it to sit with the other instruments. I don't need to discuss that with the artist while I'm doing it.

Of course, if they don't like what I finally play for them, I'll take their opinion into account big time, but they don't need to be here for the process. And all the smart artists know that. More often than not, the artists I work with accept the mixes I present them with. To me, the mix is a bit of an overblown concept, anyway. Generally it always strikes me as quite obvious as what it should be.

> *"To me, the mix is a bit of an overblown concept. . . . Generally it always strikes me as quite obvious as what it should be."*

You play in a band of producers called, fittingly enough, The Producers.

Yes, and we're making an album at the moment which is remarkably good.

Who's producing it?

No one, really. [*laughs*] But I've ended up mixing most of it, just because. It's a very cooperative band—everyone does what they want, instinctively. Generally we're all in agreement about what we like or don't like; it's all pretty black and white and it's worked out quite well because everyone in the band has pretty good taste. We've got huge plans for world domination. Plus it gives me a good excuse for buying lots of gear. Seriously, it keeps me grounded, and it keeps me playing.

Just recently I was mixing this one song for the band, and it came to the final chorus, and whatever I tried pushing didn't seem to do the job. Eventually I pulled out a high-strung guitar—it's called Nashville tuning, the top six strings of a 12-string—and I put a capo on it and played this part. It took all of two minutes; I just swung a microphone around in the control room, put the headphones on and did it, and wow! It just did the business. It was the perfect example of "push something or play something." Somehow it absolutely turned the last chorus into this sort of glistening version of the first two choruses.

Do you find that fame sometimes changes the artists you work with?

Sometimes, and it always amazes me. I mean, nothing's really changed except that they've had a hit. Of course, they now have people all around them constantly telling them how great they are, but it still astounds me how myopic some artists can become, how quickly convinced they become that their world is *the* world. It's a funny thing, that.

It also seems to be fairly common that an artist starts to believe that they don't need an outside producer after they've had a hit or two.

That happens a lot, and it's happened to me personally. I could give you examples that you wouldn't believe... but I won't. [*laughs*]

Perhaps the problem is that a good producer makes it look too easy.

Perhaps. And sometimes the artist just isn't willing to put in as much effort after they've had a hit, particularly in terms of the songwriting. Sometimes they're only looking for sycophants, people who won't give them honest feedback or the grief that they need to push them forward.

Do you have any major regrets in your career? Is there anything you wish you had done differently?

[*long pause*] No, I've loved every bit of it, and I still can't wait to get to work each morning. It really doesn't feel like work, either.

I'll tell you what pisses me off, though: it's when people say, "Oh, you're so lucky, being able to do what you want to do." That really sticks in my throat; it annoys me because I spent years literally earning nothing, literally sweating, literally not having enough money for food. There was nothing easy about my path here. But I decided at an early age not to get on any money treadmill that was going to prevent me from following this route. So I didn't buy property, not for years, because I didn't want a mortgage hanging over me. I thought, "If I have a mortgage, I'm going to be under pressure to earn money, and if I have to earn money, that means I'm not going to get to do what I want to do." So this journey was all completely conscious. That's why, when people say I'm "lucky," I think, what are you talking about? Everyone can get to do what they want to do if they're willing to make enough sacrifices. But it's so much harder to follow your own path if you're on that money treadmill.

So you're saying that commitment is the key.

I suppose so. Just do it. I always tell my kids, "Do what you want to do, and if you do it well, the chances are that the money will follow." When I was younger I wrote songs with a friend who was always talking about money and contracts, and he never got anywhere in the business. I've done so many projects for nothing, I can't begin to tell you. But often they pay off in the end.

Are your children following in your footsteps?

One of them, unfortunately, has chosen the music business. He's a manager, and he's quite brilliant at it. That's a really tough road, but he has good taste and good skills, so if anyone can succeed at it, he can.

What kind of advice do you have for someone who wants to be the next Stephen Lipson?

The first thing is, keep your day job. Do whatever it is you want to do musically, but don't lose your day job until you can afford to. That's how I got the money to buy the gear to be in my first "bedroom band."

The next thing is, figure it out. I know I'm sounding a bit vague, but if you can't figure it out for yourself, you're not going to get anywhere. On occasion a son or daughter of a friend of mine will ask to come down to the studio and watch me work and they ask a whole bunch of questions: "How do I do this? How do I do that?" and I can't help thinking, "I can give you the answers to these questions, but then you'll just get stuck on the next hurdle because you don't have the wherewithal to answer this much for yourself." So figure it out. At the end of the day you've pretty much got to work it out for yourself—it's not like going to work in a bank. This is a weird business, and it's getting weirder by the minute.

Are you talking about figuring it out in the technical sense?

In every sense.

But there were mentors in your career—people like Phil Brown and Trevor Horn—who gave you additional information and guidance.

Yeah, but that brings to mind the old adage, "The harder I worked, the luckier I seemed to get." They didn't just *give* me the information—I *gleaned* the knowledge. I ended up in a position where the knowledge was available to me.

I'm not saying that you shouldn't ask questions. I'll always talk to anyone who has questions, every time. But, really, the only way forward is under your own steam.

So you're saying that if you're not self-motivated, you're not going to get very far in this business.

Exactly. The people who approach engineering thinking, "Oh, that seems like a good job; you get to meet famous musicians and it doesn't seem like especially hard work"—those are the people that get nowhere. You need to be completely motivated. There's just no way to be guided through everything that's entailed.

It's quite funny how the stars seem to align sometimes, you know. Things just seem to happen in this cosmic way. You're in a certain place, you meet someone, and then something happens as a result, which leads to other things happening. But it's not just about recognizing opportunity and taking advantage of it when it comes your way; it's about making opportunities for yourself. You need to *put* yourself in the right situation and right headspace. That's what gives you a chance at succeeding.

Suggested Listening:
Annie Lennox: *Diva*, Arista, 1992; *Medusa*, Arista, 1995
Frankie Goes To Hollywood: *Welcome to the Pleasuredome*, ZTT, 1984; *Liverpool*, ZTT, 1986
Paul McCartney: *Flowers in the Dirt*, Capitol, 1989
Grace Jones: *Slave to the Rhythm*, ZTT/Island, 1985
American Idol: *Greatest Moments*, RCA, 2002

Simon Climie

The Accidental Producer

*I*t's always nice to meet someone who enjoys their work. Based on our conversation, there's no question that Simon Climie is one of those people. "I love collaborating," he says. "It's a wonderful thing to go into a room with a talented artist and three hours later you come out with a song where there had been nothing. That has got to be the best day's work you ever do, and you can look back on it for years and remember what a great day that was."

Indeed, collaboration has been the common theme in Climie's career—first with the late Rob Fisher (with whom he co-wrote several hit singles and formed the cult 1980s pop band Climie Fisher), then with Eric Clapton, with whom he has co-produced seven albums as well as the 2005 live Cream reunion CD/DVD. Climie's other production credits include three albums with Michael McDonald, and his songs have been covered by the likes of Aretha Franklin, Smokey Robinson, Pat Benatar, Rod Stewart, Nick Lowe, Roger Daltrey, Jeff Beck, Carlos Santana, Vanessa Williams, and Amy Grant.

Climie's slick and thoroughly modern loop-based production style had its genesis in his early adoption of digital technology and his apprenticeship with ace producer Steve Lillywhite, for whom he did Fairlight programming. But on the day we meet, it is his equanimity that impresses just as much as his technical skills. Despite what has to be a killer jet lag (he's only just flown in from LA the night before), a constantly ringing telephone, and several shouting workmen on his roof, he remains remarkably focused and unflappable—two unquestionably important skills for a record producer to have.

Did you have aspirations to be a record producer from an early age?

I actually started as a songwriter and eventually landed a publishing deal with Chrysalis Music. I'd roll up each day and sit in their little eight-track demo studio, where I'd try and write a song. By the time I met Rob Fisher, we both had 16-track machines of our own. Neither of us were really interested in production, but after we formed a band and got signed, there was that question of, who's going to produce us? Then I met Steve Lillywhite; he'd bought a Fairlight, and I would help him with programming it, as well as doing arrangements. So we had the blessing of working with Steve for a number of tracks, and it was fantastic. These days, of course, everyone's got a bedroom studio, but when you compare it with going into a professional studio with someone like Steve who really knows what he's doing, it's like the difference between driving down the road in a car versus flying in a jet.

As much as we enjoyed working with him, we soon got the stage where we thought it would be nice to do our own production. Truth be told, it was a rather difficult decision to make because we'd gotten used to writing a song in three or four hours and then staying up late every night going to parties with our girlfriends, whereas it always seemed that the producers were

getting up really early and were then staying behind in the studios after we left; you could look at them the next morning and tell that they hadn't gone home. [*laughs*]

So, no, I wasn't one of those kids sitting at home with a tape recorder dreaming of making records. In fact, I think of myself as the accidental producer—it was something I just fell into, and the best training I got was having the opportunity to work in so many different genres with fantastic songwriters, trying to make good-sounding demos for next to nothing. That gave me the versatility to be able to interact with all sorts of different artists. Funnily enough, we didn't seem to have all these different categories of musical styles when I started out. Over the course of time, things started to grow into niches, and then the niche eventually became more important than the song.

How did you first hook up with Eric Clapton?

It was through songwriting. I bumped into him at a fundraiser somewhere and he was somewhat familiar with my work. We just got chatting, and at some point I told him, "I'm always happy to write with other people." One day he came around to my house with his guitar—at the time I had a couple of ADATs, and an early Pro Tools system—and within an hour or two we'd written something together. I just started playing something on keyboard and he joined in—he wasn't even aware that I was recording him. A few months later, he came by again, and I'd taken what he'd done and looped it, and I played it for him. He was amazed: "Is that me? What guitar was I playing?" Then he started playing along to the loop, and I recorded that as well. Afterwards I showed him how we could move things around, and he realized this was something new: I'd taken and looped an idea of his—which in the tape era may have been lost forever—and I'd recorded my response to it on top, and then he recorded *his* response. Out of that came one of the T.D.F. tracks, and that really was a lot of fun. [*Ed note: T.D.F. is an acronym for "Totally Dysfunctional Family," a techno/dance album collaboration between Climie and Clapton that started as a soundtrack for an Armani fashion show.*] After that, I would get things together for him to play to and he'd come around and add his bits or we'd just start on something of Eric's and build on it.

That looping style became a very integral part of Eric's sound, especially when we were making the *Pilgrim* album. I'd stay overnight and set up these loops and he'd come in the next morning to have a listen, and he loved playing to them. Live jams just go into the ether, you know—they're played and then they're gone. But what we were doing was more like a great photo shoot: we'd react to each other's work in order to create a lasting image. This approach evolved and became part of our recording/writing process. At the same time, I was introduced to a world of exceptional musicians, which made me realize that having the technology is nothing without wonderful performances.

Before you worked with Eric, he seemed to operate within a well-defined genres—first he was a blues guitarist, then he was making AOR-type records—but since you started collaborating with him, he seems a lot harder to categorize. Do you agree?

That's an interesting observation. Well, Eric's always listened to an incredible diversity of music. Within Cream, he had a framework where the limitations of the three-piece defined the sound, as it did with Jimi Hendrix. But Eric has also always evolved. People have only ever heard what's been released, but there's really no limit to what he can do; his ability is amazing. We've recorded him guesting on numerous projects and there really is no challenge he can't handle.

Similarly, when we were making *Me and Mr. Johnson*, the job was never about, "let's see if we can copy this record exactly," nor was it about, "Let's see if we can make a Robert Johnson song sound like a Britney Spears record because that's what's selling this week." Unfortunately, that's where most of the music business goes most of the time: they look at *Billboard* and they think, "Let's make it more like that." I find it really hard to do that, anyway. For me, the main goal was always to get the feeling of the song over. I've never been driven by the "this is my style of record" approach; it's always been about the voice, the song, and the feeling. I think that's a good formula.

How would you describe the producer/artist relationship?

There has to be a level of trust, for a start. Trust is like respect; you're not given it, you have to earn it. Part of that trust actually comes from simply making sure that everything is working before the artist comes into the room. When an orchestra comes into a studio, you know that every mic has been scratched, every preamp has been checked, every hum and buzz has been eliminated in advance; that's been done because you only have the musicians for three hours and they're really expensive, so you need to be able to start recording the minute they turn up. But try plugging a keyboard into a DI box in the same studio later that day, and it takes 20 minutes! That's guaranteed to get the artist really frustrated.

> **"Trust is like respect; you're not given it, you have to earn it."**

When it comes to Pro Tools and digital technology, it's a lot deeper than just checking cables and mics and preamps: you need to make sure your hard drives are working and that everything is locked to a stable clock. And whether it's a professional room or a home studio, the room needs to be set up in such a way that everything is not only working properly, but working to your best advantage. It's like flying a plane: you want to be able to reach for the control that makes the plane turn left or land without having to look for it. Unfortunately, many studio planners don't think like that, so you've got to go in ahead of time and create a homey environment where, if the artist gets an idea, you can just go ahead and record it without anything standing in the way. As Quincy Jones has said, capturing the magic is the most important thing a producer can do.

> *"There always seems to come a certain point where a singer just gets on fire and his voice gets this fantastic quality."*

Especially when you're recording a slow blues, the first take is often the keeper, so that's particularly important to an artist like Eric. We used to have a running joke in the studio about [engineer] Alan Douglas scrambling to get a guitar sound together, though Eric's got no time to waste; he just wants to record. In fact, he'd usually prefer that we *not* have a good guitar sound for him, because often a perfect guitar sound isn't what you want, anyway—sometimes you want a gritty, nasty little thing that just does the job, at least for certain parts. Similarly, there also always seems to come a certain point where a singer just gets on fire and his voice gets this fantastic quality—I've found that to be equally true of both Eric Clapton and Michael McDonald. You need to be completely ready to record at those moments.

Do you record a DI of Eric's guitar signal as a safety net, so you have the option of sculpting the sound later?

No, we don't, which I know is actually quite risky. We usually just use two or three close mics as well as a room mic, and we blend them together into a single mono track, so we do make an absolute commitment to a guitar sound. That was a technique I learned from Steve Lillywhite. The idea is to craft the sound into something that really works, and then stick with your decision. I know there are producers or engineers who are very concerned with isolation, but I don't subscribe to that view. A really good example of that was Eric's *Riding with the King* album, where there was a lot of leakage in the room, but the sound was right. We had to sacrifice some takes for the overall sound and feeling of the record, but that's fine, and I had to do a lot of editing on some tracks—"Key to the Highway" was a mixture of three versions and there wasn't a click track, so there were all these interleaved edits in order to keep the room sound—but what you got was real. If I'd gone down that clinical road of having a DI and perfect isolation without any bleed, the record wouldn't have been the same.

Eric may not understand all the technicalities of the recording studio, but he has an incredible ear; if there's a valve [tube] gone wrong in his amp, he'll know straight away. Like most amazing musicians, he's very sensitive to tonalities. So much of it is to do with touch, anyway; I can pick up a guitar and Eric can pick up the same guitar with exactly the same settings, and it's not going to sound the same.

So, yes, it's a risk that we don't have a DI and can't go to Amp Farm, but I think it's far better to take that risk, because we're building on every part. My approach is that every track is a building block, and we go from there. It's true that with Pro Tools the options are limitless, which means that it's possible to get yourself into a huge mess.

Nonetheless, you're a big proponent of digital recording.

Well, I know a lyric writer who comes up with four alternatives for every single line, and it drives me mad; beyond the fact that you've got five pages to read through, it's a lot of extra work figuring out which line is best. It's the same with recording: if you get something grooving and working, you need to make a commitment. I think your mind works at a much faster speed when you're recording something than when you're analyzing something.

But with analog, you almost had to be a prophet in that you had to know what things were going to sound like coming back off tape. I don't think people always did know it in advance; you'd play things back and then people would say, "Oh, I like that." Honestly, a bit of saturation and tape compression is very unlikely to make something worse; more than likely, it's going to work, and who would ever know what the original input signal sounded like anyway?

So is the goal to get every sound as close to the finished product as possible?

It varies. If we're recording a vocal or a guitar solo, I try to get it to sound as good as it possibly can, and to sit well with the backing track; to me, that defines the record. An artist might have to sing two or three passes before you feel you're getting towards something, anyway. At that point, you might be well advised to stop and invite them in to have a listen and make some decisions as well, so you're all tuned in. That also gives you a second chance to listen to the various takes and refine your thinking. Just as importantly, a singer needs periodic breaks. There's a kind of crispness to a voice when it's fresh, and sometimes if you've sung too many times it becomes over-compressed and it loses that edge—literally, the EQ of the voice changes dramatically. Having said that, it's different for every artist: some singers are just warming up on the eighth pass, while for others, it's over.

On the other hand, when it comes to drums, it's very difficult to record them exactly the way they'll sound in the final mix, and during backing track sessions the musicians just want to get going as quickly as possible, so you don't want to take forever getting the drum sounds. So instead, I'll work quite hard at shaping the drum sounds afterwards, often substituting samples with tools like Sound Replacer.

What yardstick do you use to decide when a record is done?

That's not a question I have to ask myself very often; it just seems to present itself. There's nearly always more than you need, because creative people will come in and want to try all sorts of things. The great players will give you what you want, and usually a bit extra too, and if you don't have what you need from them to make a record, you're in the wrong business.

Of course, you have to listen really hard and you have to make extensive notes. The question I continually ask myself is, "What is it going to take to make this feel right?" As the producer, you're under a lot of pressure because there are all these incredibly talented people looking to you for your opinion . . . and you'd better be right.

Interestingly, I've noticed that it's the last minute of a track that dictates how most people feel about it. There have been many situations where the first verse didn't feel right to me, and it took a lot of effort to convince people to go back and redo it if the rest of the track felt good to them; because everything was slamming by the end, they simply didn't realize there was a problem. Don't forget that a lot of records actually have long fades that we never hear—a lot of recordings are six minutes long, but we only ever get to hear the first three minutes. One of the jobs of the producer is to make sure that you get what you really need in those three minutes.

How do you deal with the inevitable differences of opinion that crop up in every project?

Well, I recently got a puppy, and I've learned that if you get to the point where you want to take the dog for a walk but he won't move so you end up dragging him, you've already lost the battle. The idea is to give him a little tug just to encourage him along; do any more than that, and it's very unlikely that you're going to get him to budge.

It's the same when it comes to dealing with artists. You need to be careful to avoid getting into a head-on collision with any artist, because the record is ultimately going to reflect their feelings and their will. The real problem with conflict is that it sets you back, and you may never recover from it. You've got to be mindful that you're continuing to move forward, or at least moving in a positive direction. Sometimes being a producer is more about performing a service than making a statement.

You've also got to understand that there are so many different reasons for an artist to have a block. It might just be that they're tired, or have come off a long tour, or whatever. Somehow you have to unlock the creativity in the artist; you've got to get in there and loosen things up so that people get in a creative frame of mind.

There are certain types of artists that need an enormous amount of guidance, and then there are other artists where you've really got to just step back and let them do their best and take it from there. There are very few people I know that are actually happy with something that's not good enough. Usually if I think a verse needs redoing, they're realizing it too.

That's all in a day's work for a producer: making sure you get to the right place without stopping or getting diverted. Unfortunately, though, you sometimes get stuck in the middle, with a record company or management trying to overtly influence your thinking. Sure, sometimes you absolutely have to work with them, because they may have a brilliant idea...but it's equally true that not everybody is a Clive Davis. For various reasons, everybody's got their own opinions, and it's good to try lots of things out, even if only to convince people that their idea didn't work. The problem is, you can't explore every idea, especially if you're on a limited budget, so you and the artist need to understand that some ideas simply *won't* work.

Is the goal to make a great record, or a hit record?

The goal for me is to make a great record, something you'll want to play over and over again. Some say that no one actually knows what a hit record is, but if you make a great album, there will inevitably be some hit singles on there. And it's not necessarily always the artist who wants a great record while the label wants a hit. [Reprise CEO] Tom Whalley, at Eric's label, is a very bright guy and he offers a lot of brilliant comments, but he's coming almost from where I'm coming from: he's said it's more important to make a quality record we're proud of than to just aim for a commercial radio record.

But with a really established artist like Eric, the label is pretty much assured that they'll turn a profit regardless; with a new, unproven artist there must be considerably more pressure to turn in a hit.

That's true, and in those kinds of situations you have to mediate between the two needs. I recently did a project with an artist that wanted to make a sparse, slow-to-mid-tempo album, but the record company wanted something more full-blown. Thankfully, I've got a pretty good track record, so I was able to phone up the label and say, "You know what? We need to cut at least seven or eight songs the artist's way so we at least fulfill their need creatively, and then it will all evolve naturally so we can deliver you the singles the way you want them." I think that's the only way to get through those situations, and in this particular case it worked out well.

I've got this thing about framing the vocals, and so I've found it's often best to leave things sparse. Take a song like "River of Tears." Eric's guitar sound speaks for itself, but a lot of it has to do with his composition process, coming up with all the *other* brilliant guitar parts. Another example would be Eric's solo on "She's Gone," which was one take, although it was done only after his long-suffering roadie had to spend hours driving clear across London to fetch a Pignose amp. [*laughs*]

It does seem that, with his guitar playing having long been at such a superlative level, Clapton has been focusing more on his songwriting and singing in recent years.

Well, whoever you are, you have to find something interesting in what you're doing—otherwise, why bother going to work? Maybe that's the reason he also often changes arrangements drastically when he plays songs live, and some of the live versions are staggeringly good. Our purpose in the studio is to record the song wherever it is at that particular point in time, but the feel of a song can change over time, and Eric is not afraid to adapt and change.

You've got especially strong arranging skills. How important is arrangement to the sound of a record?

It's hugely important. Arrangement is a factor that's really volatile, too, just like songwriting. For instance, you may have a great melody, but the words aren't as good, and the chords aren't going anywhere. So where do you start? You start by tweaking the arrangement a little just to get things to feel right. Then it's easier to come up with a more interesting chord progression, build from there, and then finally rewrite the words.

As the producer, you are ultimately the filter, and you need to understand that there are things that can completely ground a record. It might be something as simple as the tempo, which may be dragging, or it could be the bass part that is holding the record back. Or it could be the rhythm guitar part, in which case the best approach is to ask the player to come into the control room with you while you just have the drums, bass, and vocal play the song down. He'll be sitting there on the sofa, thinking, "Hmm, I've never really heard that," because he's been too busy playing this big, thunderous part which is pushing all the time and taking up an enormous amount of space sonically. So instead you might have him hold a single note through a distortion pedal, and see how that affects the track; you can really open up a record that way. Once you've simplified things, you can compare take five to the first take, and it will sound like a totally different band, even if you haven't touched a thing on the board or changed a single sound.

Often it's great to have the band play a slow blues as a warm-up song, because that's the kind of thing where everyone is cautious about what they play, and they all listen to each other closely, whereas if you have them play an up-tempo thing with a lot of chords in it, everyone is just too worried about their own part to listen to the whole. Usually the take you get after the musicians have played a slow blues is great, too, because everyone is locked together.

> *"In the control room, you need to make sure that all the equipment is locked ... and synchronized together. In the studio, you need to do the same thing with the musicians."*

It's a funny thing: in the control room, you need to make sure that all the equipment is locked to word clock and is synchronized together. In the studio, you need to do the same thing with the musicians.

Maybe ultimately that's the role of the producer.

Maybe. But it's mostly down to the material. A fantastic song recorded with a single stereo pair of mics is always going to beat, hands-down, a fully fleshed out 48-track recording of a piece of rubbish. The producer's job really is to bring the best out of the person in front of you, not to be a Svengali who tells everybody what to do.

Suggested Listening:

Eric Clapton: *Pilgrim*, Reprise, 1998; *Riding with the King*, Reprise, 2000; *Reptile*, Reprise, 2001; *Back Home*, Reprise, 2005

T.D.F.: *Retail Therapy*, Reprise, 1997

Michael McDonald: *Motown*, Motown, 2003; *Motown Two*, Motown, 2004; *Soul Speak*, Universal, 2008

Steve Parr

The Spiral Paradigm

Steve Parr may be one of the top surround sound and film music engineers in London, but his career began in his native South Wales, where, he recalls, "At the age of 11 or 12 I was buying old surplus Army microphones and connecting them up to speakers with bits of wire and a battery, fiddling with stuff and trying to make things work." At the same time, he was fiddling with the piano in his parent's living room, which led to work with local bands and an eventual move to London, where he joined jazz/punk band Burlesque before taking over the keyboard chair in the legendary pub band Trans-Am.

Well, at least some of the *pubs* they played were legendary. In the interest of full disclosure, I am compelled to admit that back in the glorious seventies I was the bassist in said band, touring endlessly up and down England's motorways in search of fame and fortune, which somehow managed to remain tantalizingly out of reach. It is perhaps no coincidence that Mr. Parr's career—and mine—took a distinctive turn for the better following the amicable break-up of said band.

But I digress.

Parr's childhood curiosity about technology stayed with him as he transitioned to the life of a session musician, when an interest in synchronization led to an unexpected opportunity. "I had bought one of those really early Fostex synchronizers that you had to sort of coax to work," he explains, "and one day I was doing a session where the engineer was trying to use one too but it broke down, so I ended up fixing it for him, even though I had just been hired as the keyboard player. The next day I got a call from the studio manager, who happened to be running one of the first recording courses in the country, and he offered me a job as a teacher! It was something about which I had virtually no knowledge whatsoever, but I was a starving musician and I needed the money, so I said, 'Yeah, sure, I'll do it.'"

With a laugh, Parr recalls surviving the gig by "basically just staying about an hour and a half ahead of the students." Eventually he landed his first engineering job, for an independent reggae label. In 1990, he made the momentous decision to open his own commercial studio, but even as he struggled to attract clients, opportunity beckoned. "It was when we weren't busy making records that people started bringing in films," he relates, "and I started to find that kind of work very appealing...plus there was a demand for engineers that could handle the technical aspects and time pressures of the job."

Nearly two decades later, Parr finds himself almost exclusively doing film work and surround sound mixing in his London studio Hear No Evil, taking on an eclectic array of independent and feature projects, including 2008's widely acclaimed HBO series *John Adams* and the 2004 live Steve Reich DVD *Reich at the Roxy*. He's also the guy responsible for the stunning surround sound mix of "Who Are You" that opens the *CSI* TV series, and even got to record the "Wheel's On Fire" theme song for Absolutely Fabulous with comedians Jennifer Saunders and Adrian Edmondson. In this wide-ranging interview, he reflects on his unique approach to recording

and mixing orchestral works, including the world premiere of his so-called "spiral paradigm," which he laughingly threatens to trademark as soon as he can find a lawyer who can understand it.

Why did you gravitate to film music work, as opposed to making records?

A lot of it is down to one's personality. I like things that present a challenge, and recording music for film is actually much more difficult than sitting around making a record. I used to find it so tedious making 23 comps of a vocal track and 17 comps of a percussion track, doing the same stuff with the same people over and over again. Recording music for film is, for me, intellectually much more stimulating. I like the fact that you've got to work really, really fast and under a lot of pressure, which means I don't have time to get bored. I used to hate it when I was working with a band on a song all day long and at eight o'clock at night they'd announce, "Oh, we're just going to go out and get something to eat" and then they'd come back three hours later and you'd play the track for them once —having sat around for three hours waiting for them to return—and they'd say, "Oh, fuck it, let's just go home." That sort of thing used to drive me crazy, and I just decided that I did not want to do that anymore.

My first exposure to surround sound back in 1987 was mixing in three-track—left, center, and right—which led to quite a revelation, because when I'd finished the three-track mix, I had to collapse it back into stereo in order for the client to take home a reference. To my surprise, I found that the center image was suddenly much more solid. Something was going on that I didn't quite understand, and eventually I learned that it's all to do with phase relationships, which I found utterly fascinating. When I started shopping around for a new console, I was very interested in the Euphonix, because it had a whole section on it devoted to 5.1 mixing. I'd never heard of 5.1 at that point, so I did some research and learned that there was a new medium coming out called DVD that would actually be able to store that signal.

Then I started thinking, well, here I am with this fantastic 5.1 system, able to throw sound effects all around; has nobody ever thought of doing music or advertising in this way? So I set up some appointments and met some of the dubbing mixers and explained to them that they could actually have their music mixed and delivered to them in 5.1, instead of them simply putting some delays and reverb on a stereo mix so that some of the sound appeared in the rear speakers. They were a little bit reluctant at first, thinking that I'd probably just screw it up, so it took some time to build up a trust, but it did take hold, and I ended up doing the first-ever surround sound commercial in the U.K., for Peugeot. I had to explain to the advertising company that we could do this. Nobody had any commercial rates for doing it at the time—even Dolby had never done it—so they had to work out a whole new rate card for the commercial. My premise was that, since every film projector today has to be able to accommodate a 5.1 soundtrack as well as stereo, there's absolutely no reason why you couldn't sneakily put on a 5.1 advert in the midst of everybody else's boring old stereo advert; after all, nobody's going to change the projector in the theater. Suddenly, your car advert is putting music all the way around the theater audience, as opposed to everyone else's advert, which is coming solely from the front speakers, so you sell more cars. It was amazing; the sound just came alive, and over a period of a few years it became the normal thing to do.

What's the main difference between a music-only session and a music for film session?

Primarily time, or, more accurately, lack of it. I once got hired to play keyboards on a small film session, only to find out that the composer somehow hadn't written the music yet, so he wanted me to help. I made what I thought was a reasonable request, asking, "Well, can I at least see the film to get some idea of what to play?" and he said, "We don't have time for that; the best I can do is show it to you at double speed." [*laughs*]

True story, and it illustrates how fast everything happens. It's a major problem if everyone isn't thoroughly prepared, because film orchestral recording sessions here in London are almost always done in blocks of just three hours. The way things will usually begin is that a composer will phone up, book the session, and give me the lineup—it may be 15 violins, six cellos, whatever—as well as the formats being used: most of them work in Logic, or in Digital Performer. I'll set up and test all my equipment—mics, headphones, etc.—hours beforehand, but no matter how much preparation I do, on the day of the session, the composer will inevitably turn up exhausted from having been up all night finishing up the final writing of the music. A little before the scheduled start time, the musicians will start drifting in, but even if the last of them arrives two or three minutes before 10 o'clock—and very often the composer himself does dash in at the last minute—it doesn't matter, because at exactly 10 o'clock, the conductor is in front of the orchestra and my recorder is running.

I take everything, needless to say. It's rare that the first run-through is perfect—the musicians are still getting used to their headphone balance and the score in front of them—but I'm ready, and if it *is* the perfect take, I've got it.

In a typical three-hour session we may record anywhere from 10 to 30 pieces of music, each anywhere between 15 seconds and four minutes in length. In all, we'll record a total of about 20 minutes' worth of music in a three-hour session. But the rules are very strict: the musicians get a 15-minute break after the first hour and a half, and if it's one minute to 1 o'clock and you've got a two-minute piece of music to record, you can't start it—we actually synchronize our clocks at the beginning of the session. If you do run into that situation, you have to ask the musicians if everybody is willing to do 15 minutes' overtime, and at that point anyone who says no can get up and leave.

Every second in a session like that is invaluable, and the musicians are expensive, so you can't afford to spend any time at all on anything technical, fixing things, or even repositioning microphones. You do it in any tiny little pocket of time you can find when something else is happening. Everything is absolutely full-on all the time; you even have to minimize the time between takes, because even if you only spend a minute or two setting up each new cue, that's nearly a third of your three-hour session gone right there.

And there's no time for full playbacks, either; you might listen back to the first cue or two, but once you've got everything sorted out, you rarely have time to listen back again until after the session is over and it's time to start mixing. All your time during the session is spent actually getting the music recorded, so it's my job to make sure that there is absolutely no chance of anything going wrong, because if something does go wrong, it's going to cost a lot of money.

To that end, I even have a complete backup recording system in place—a full-on multitrack RADAR system that I keep in Record the entire time, from the minute the conductor picks up his baton to the moment everyone leaves. I start it at the time of day the session is starting and I just let it run in the background in tandem with my other hard disk system so that if anything drops out or there's any kind of technical problem, I can actually look at the time in the file and trace it back, then fly the problem area back in. The main hard disk system is only put in Record when we're ready to put down a take, but the RADAR is running wild; it's got absolutely everything that's running through the board, all on separate tracks, so I'm duplicating the system. That's my fail-safe.

Since there's no time for experimentation during a session, presumably you have fixed mic selections and placements, all set up in advance.

Absolutely; there's no time to fiddle on a session like that. You can experiment on the simpler sessions, where there might be just a single instrumentalist coming in to record some cues and you can try to hone in on a specific sound. Or sometimes things are a little less set in stone and so the musicians are going to be trying stuff out for half an hour; while that's going on, you can try a few things out. You just have to be very practical, and you have to grab your opportunities when you can.

What are your usual mic choices for string instruments?

In many rooms, classical engineers utilize classic mic techniques like the Decca Tree, but my room is quite specific, so what I do is mic the sections individually and then I use an M-S [mid-side] pair as my surround mics, fed directly to the rear channels. Not only do I really like the sound of it, this technique keeps the imaging absolutely solid. I retain enough control over the various sections so that I can balance them, but really I let the room do most of the work. That way, if the conductor gets it right then pretty much I get it right.

I generally use AKG 414s and 3000s for the section miking, even though the 3000s are quite inexpensive. I actually have a philosophy about that, which goes something like this: because every mic manufacturer is hopefully trying to make the best microphone that they can, there's got to be a trickle-down effect on their cheaper, mass-market mics, because presumably they want to make those mics as good as they can, too. After all, the same diaphragm manufacturing techniques have got to be used, no matter what the mic. So you can pay two or three thousand dollars for a manufacturer's top-end mic, but I think you'll find that that same manufacturer's lower-end mics—which may sell for just a few hundred dollars—may well have only slightly lesser quality: logically, there's got to be only a few percent difference between the two. In fact, the lower-priced mic may not be worse at all—the differences may only be cosmetic.

> *"You should always spend as much money as you can possibly afford on one very good mic, because most of the time you're only going to be recording one person or instrument at a time."*

So are you saying that if you're on a limited budget, you're better off buying a lower-priced mic from an established manufacturer, as opposed to a more expensive model from a manufacturer with a lesser reputation?

Exactly. Of course, even having said that, you should also always spend as much money as you can possibly afford on one very good mic, because most of the time you're only going to be recording one person or one instrument at a time, whether it's a vocal or a guitar overdub. So you need that one great mic, but then supplement it with some lower-priced mics from a good manufacturer. The quality of the manufacturer is what's most important.

It's interesting, because while the difference in quality between a top-end mic and a not-so-top-end mic may be only 10 or 15 percent, the difference between a world-class musician and an average musician can be a hundred percent—you can actually have somebody who can't even play the part! So that is a far more crucial part of the equation than the microphone you're using. In the perfect world, you'd want the best of both, but if you've got to sacrifice one or the other, spend the money on the better musician.

Similarly, a good engineer will make a good, listenable record on even the worst equipment, because he's got good ears and knows what he's doing. But take an inexperienced engineer and put him in the best studio in the world, outfitted with the best equipment in the world, and the result will be a pile of crap if he doesn't know what he's doing.

There does seem to be a misconception among many novices that all you need is great equipment.

And it *is* a misconception. Look, manufacturers have to keep making new models, because they've got to stay in business, and they've got to keep people thinking that they need these new pieces of equipment. But of course we don't. We all love new toys; we'd all love to have this new stuff, but we really don't need it.

No, what you need is a huge amount of common sense, a reasonable amount of experience, a lot of practicality, some gear that will do the job, and great musicians. And, of course, good ears are absolutely vital. To be a good engineer, you have to have good musicality. If you don't have that, if you don't understand music instinctively and how things fit together, and how to balance things, then you should become a maintenance engineer. The whole thing comes down to musicality.

While it is true that you can be very musical without actually being a musician, it's certainly a help if you are one, especially in tricky situations where you're trying to explain your point of view or are trying to understand what the artist is trying to accomplish. Certainly it helps me in my chosen area, because my life would be a hell of a lot more difficult if I couldn't read a score.

There are many ways that I can use my experience to help both the sound of a film and the budget at the same time. For instance, I've learned that if you don't have enough string players for a particular part and they're playing loudly to try to compensate, the sound can be a little bit brittle. In that circumstance, the musicians are far better off taking the dynamics down and letting me balance the sound afterwards in the final mix, because the end result will be a much better sound. A composer may not understand that quite so well. Similarly, he may not understand that it's sometimes useful to use mutes on violins in order to make a small section sound bigger, because the mutes damp out some of the high frequencies which allow the listener to identify the number of instruments that are playing. There are lots of little things like that, which have nothing to do with twiddling knobs. Sometimes a quiet word in the composer's ear during a session can save a lot of time and money and also yield a much better sound; it really can make all the difference.

Do you sometimes find yourself imposing artificial constraints on what you're doing in order to make the most efficient use of your time?

Absolutely. I deal with people who write music to order all the time, so they're not like a band who can be a bit more self-indulgent. They're asked to write very specific things, and usually, within those constraints, they do a very good job. But if you took away those constraints, they wouldn't know where to begin, because freeing them up to write absolutely anything would actually hinder their creativity instead of enhancing it. Sometimes the best creativity occurs when you have a problem you're trying to solve and you're trying to work within certain parameters.

> ## "Sometimes the best creativity occurs when you have a problem you're trying to solve and you're trying to work within certain parameters."

A good example of that kind of approach was on some of the eighties Phil Collins records, where the producer removed the cymbals from his drum kit. Some of it may have been done because they were trying to accomplish something musically, but I get the impression that a lot of it was, let's work with some kind of restriction and see what results. And what happened? All of a sudden he had a whole identifiable little stamp. So I'm a great believer in setting up situations in which accidents can freely occur. Setting certain limitations can sometimes lead to my discovering a new type of sound, or a new way of working.

For example, not long ago I bought a few of the Universal Audio plug-ins. I've got some of the old original hardware and I've compared them, and they're really spot on. I was mixing an album recently and I decided to individually bus out all 40 tracks of it and leave all the faders on my console at 0, with no EQ, and instead do all signal processing and balancing with those plug-ins, just to see what would result. It was very interesting; I got a great sound, and I've gotten a lot of compliments from people about the vocal sound in particular. Actually, I didn't do that much to it—I just tried a different approach.

I made a similar kind of revelation recently concerning my digital-to-analog converters. On one big project, I was using up all 24 channels of my usual D/A converters and I needed a few more channels, so I connected up a couple of extra interfaces. I'd wired them in so I could easily switch between the different converters, and in doing so I could easily hear that they sounded quite different from one another. I wouldn't actually say that one was better than the other, but they were definitely different, and one was far more suitable for transient sounds and drums—the cheaper one, in fact. The more expensive converter, on the other hand, was far better for vocals and less transient instruments. So now I've gotten in the habit of using my converters almost like effects processors, deliberately putting drums and transient sounds through one set of converters, and the other sounds through the other set, effectively exploiting the difference in sonic quality.

Other than having to break out stems and mix in surround, do you find there's any real difference between mixing pure music versus mixing music for film?

Not really. But working in both genres has led to me to develop a pretty unique approach to mixing—something I call the "spiral paradigm." It goes something like this: When you first start mixing a piece of music, you're presented with a load of tracks, and your first job is to figure out what's going on musically. To that end, you're almost putting faders up at random, just trying to learn what's recorded on each track. At that point, you're probably not thinking consciously in terms of EQ adjustments or compression settings, but you start getting hooked into it, bit by bit, and you stop answering the phone and you really start to concentrate and hear things. And here's the key: the more you listen, the more you hear. So you keep going, and after an hour or so you're deep in that concentration zone, and you're hearing all sorts of stuff you didn't hear the first time around, because now you're focused; you're really concentrating. It's almost as if you've gone down a tunnel, and the last thing you want is someone bothering you at that point, or the phone ringing, or having to get engaged in some conversation, because it brings you out of that tunnel very quickly...and then you've got to take another hour or so to get back down there again. That's why you switch the phone off, and that's why you don't want an artist or an assistant asking you lots of questions.

It's only when you're down in that concentration tunnel that you're able to hear the minutiae of your recording: in effect, you're looking at the foliage down at the bottom of the forest, but you're not seeing the forest. At that point, you really can't do any balancing because you have no overall picture of the music. Instead, you're hearing every sound in its individuality; everything is all bare and crunchy and laid out before you. That's the time when you can hone in on the sibilance on a vocal or the EQ of a bass drum or whatever.

> *"It's only when you're down in that concentration tunnel that you're able to hear the minutiae of your recording: in effect, you're looking at the foliage down at the bottom of the forest, but you're not seeing the forest."*

I have found that the best thing to do when you're at that level of concentration is to fix what you need to fix and then quickly move on to something else—a different song altogether. So I actually work on four or five different songs at a time—getting down into that tunnel on each, fixing what needs to be fixed, and then moving on to the next one.

Then, when I get to the end of that process, I'll return my attention to the first song, make some notes, fix what I have to fix, move on to the second one, make notes and fixes, etcetera, until I've gone through all four or five songs. Then, and only then, will I get the artist and producer in to have a listen. I'll give them notepads and let them hear the song once and write down all their notes. We'll have a little conference afterwards to make sure we all concur, then move on to the next song and do it all over again. I've found that working this way really helps me keep my perspective…plus it keeps me from getting bored. That's the "spiral" I'm talking about: going around in a big circle, then in a smaller circle, and so on, gradually approaching the center when theoretically everything will have been ironed out and we'll have the "perfect" mix that satisfies everyone's artistic criteria.

Similarly, a film may contain 30 or 40 music cues, and I'll split the score up into four or five basic genres and work the same way. If I were to sit in a room with a director and composer and they see the whole process of what I'm doing, I'd get so many suggestions that I'd never finish. Plus they'd get bored, and that's really counterproductive. It's a good idea never to let them see too much of the process, so when I finish recording, I'll send everybody away for at least half a day and I'll put together the mixes in a fairly rough but reasonable state. Then I'll invite the director back and we'll play through the film from beginning to the end, with me pulling up the mixes as we go so that we can hear the music in context. While the director is looking at it and seeing how the music is working with his film, I'm thinking about what's wrong with my balances and making notes. Then I'll send the director home so the composer and I can sit down and start finalizing all the mixes. This is actually a much more efficient use of time—especially when we've got very limited time in the first place—than spending four hours on the first mix getting everything absolutely right before moving on to the next one.

Suggested Listening:
Rob Lane: *John Adams* (original television series soundtrack), Varese Sarabande, 2008
LTJ Bukem: *Planet Earth* (6.1 surround mixes), DTS, 2005
Studio Voodoo: *Club Voodoo* (6.1 surround mixes), DTS, 2004
Steve Reich: *Reich at the Roxy*, Sweetspot, 2006 (DVD)
Soundtracks recorded by Steve Parr can be found on the IMDb website http://www.imdb.com/name/nm0663348/

Andy Bradfield

Kinetic Energy

"Even as a little kid, I was fascinated by the recording process," Andy Bradfield tells us. "When I was nine or ten, I got a little microphone and tape recorder and I used to go around recording everything in sight."

Fortunately, Bradfield's parents encouraged the precocious child's interest, enrolling him in a formal course being taught at a local studio in his native Essex—appropriately enough named Diploma Studios—when he was just 14. Even after completing the 30-week program, Bradfield would bicycle the four miles to the studio every day after school just to soak up the atmosphere and continue the learning process.

Upon his graduation in 1986, Bradfield applied to most of the major studios in London, eventually landing an assistant engineer's job at Richard Branson's Townhouse studios. Through his company, Virgin, Branson owned a mobile as well as a second, residential studio in Oxford called The Manor; he eventually purchased London's famed Olympic Studios as well. "Being able to work in all these different facilities provided me with a fantastic grounding because I got to meet up-and-coming bands as well as established ones, as well as some great engineers and mixers," Bradfield recalls. "That was also the era when people were doing a lot of remixing. Clients would book a weekend and come in and sample the entire vocal on a computer, then construct a new backing track on synths and drum machines. In some ways, that was the precursor to the modern way of using a digital workstation, except that it was a hell of a lot harder!"

Rising quickly through the ranks to full engineer, Bradfield would go on to work with a broad range of artists, including Rolling Stones drummer Charlie Watts as well as Elton John, David Bowie, Tom Jones, Pet Shop Boys, and the Spice Girls, and garnered his first Grammy nomination for his work on Robbie Robertson's 1998 album *Contact from the Underworld of Redboy*. In recent years, Bradfield has gravitated more towards mixing and has opened his own studio in conjunction with his engineer/mixer wife Avril Mackintosh, putting together tracks for Rufus Wainwright, Josh Groban, Marc Almond, Alanis Morisette, and England's latest girl power group, the Sugababes, as well as recording soundtracks for big-name composers like Howard Shore and Danny Elfman.

On the rainy summer afternoon we meet, Bradfield throws himself into our interview with the same kinetic energy that undoubtedly drives him behind the mixing console. English reserve be damned; this is one Brit who's unafraid to display his enthusiasm.

Looking back, how much do you think formal training helped in your career?

That's a difficult thing to quantify. I suppose my training gave me the impetus to go forward, but I was so young that not much of the formal knowledge ended up being of great benefit; I learned a lot more when I started actually working as an assistant. Having said that, there are basics like microphone techniques or getting headphone balances or doing monitor mixes that don't change whether you're working in 24-track analog or Pro Tools. I also had to become adept at tape editing and dropping in, and I'm glad I learned those things even though they aren't skills you need today; if you just jump into digital recording, you miss out on all that.

Do you consider yourself a perfectionist?

No, I don't. When I started in this business, I was under the misguided impression that everything had to be perfect, but I quickly learned that it's far more important to have everything sound exciting. Whether it's a performance or a mix, the idea should be to

> *"When I started in this business, I was under the misguided impression that everything had to be perfect, but I quickly learned that it's far more important to have everything sound exciting."*

make it as exciting and as engaging as possible for the listener. That's why mixing in isolation, without the benefit of direct contact with people, can be difficult. I much prefer having the artist there with me while I'm mixing; however, these days, a lot of projects are done remotely, with the artist sending me a file that I have to mix on my own and then send back for comment.

That said, I have worked with some producers and artists who are perfectionists—to call them "detail merchants" would be an understatement—and it can be a bit trying. But, as they say, the devil is in the detail, though I try not to get too hung up on those things, because sometimes wrong can be good. Whether I like to admit it or not, sometimes I've just slung things together and it's glued together perfectly. I'm actually amazed at how often I'll think a mix is going to be really difficult, based on the number of tracks and the complexity of the

> *"Sometimes wrong can be good."*

arrangement, and it turns out to practically mix itself. I've talked with other mixers and that seems to be a very common experience, but I find it very weird. Other times, you think a mix is going to be easy and you get halfway through and you just think, "No, this isn't going to work." When that happens, all you can do is pull all the faders down and just start over again.

Similarly, most songwriters say that their best songs are either the ones that they wrote very quickly with very little effort, or the ones they slaved over for months; there seems to be relatively few great songs in the middle.

That's definitely true when it comes to mixing, too. But it's getting harder and harder to do a quick mix because of track counts, which are getting totally out of hand. No one seems to be bouncing anything down any more, which is a big issue for me because it takes such a long time just to wade through a song when it's got 128 tracks, let alone actually mix it. More and more, the arrangement itself seems to occur in the mixing stage now. Because you don't have to make decisions any more, people put them off until the last possible moment, which can sometimes make mixing a lot harder; certainly it gives the mixer a lot more responsibility as to how the final song shapes up. It's as if you're working with a slightly moving target these days, which can make things a bit tricky. Young people coming into the industry seem to know this instinctively, and they are embracing that way of working, but I also think they sometimes don't realize the huge responsibility they are passing along to others.

The goal today all too often seems to be to make a perfect record, not necessarily a great record.

I quite agree, and I have to say that I don't buy the perfection thing at all. If you go back and listen to the records that really excite you, they are rarely perfect. Even classical records fall into that category because they *have* to have to tuning issues in order to sound big and exciting. It's simply a question of how far you push the rules in order to get that excitement without actually sounding out of tune, which is where it suddenly becomes wrong. That said, you'd be hard-pushed to get a less-than-perfect record past some artists, because they strive for perfection regardless.

The real problem comes when you're called on to mix tracks that weren't well-recorded to begin with. Sometimes I wonder if their speakers were switched on at all! [*laughs*] In those cases, you have to just grit your teeth and get on with it. Personally, I view those kinds of projects as a challenge.

How do you go about getting the best performance from an artist?

Recording is a really big deal, even for established artists, because it's a very unique situation. That's why I think you need to do everything you can to take the load off them and make them feel comfortable. It's when an artist feels comfortable that they do their best work.

There are some producers, though, who have made great records through intimidation, by keeping artists on edge.

I don't think that works most of the time. I was involved in a project a few years ago with a co-producer and he was doing just what you describe, purposefully trying to intimidate the artist, and, frankly, I don't think he got the best out of that artist, so I've seen it backfire too. With all the pressures that are on artists today—pressure to perform and pressure to deliver—I think it's generally better to make them as comfortable as possible. That ties in with experience, because after awhile you know when an artist benefits more from one approach or the other; you know whether they're having an off day just because they're tired, or because they're not taking things seriously enough, which is when you do need to get tough with people a bit. I'm not really comfortable giving artists a hard time, but if they're not doing their work properly—if they're showing up late, or hung over—they're going to get a very frosty reception from me, because that's just unprofessional.

Do you think that record-making has gotten overly complicated?

A lot of people say to me, "Hasn't recording gotten really technical?" and my reply is, "Recording's *always* been a technical exercise." In some respects, it used to be even more technical, in terms of things like tape biasing, and technical issues have always gotten in the way, which is why one of the important jobs of the producer and engineer is to carry that load for the artist so they don't have to worry about those aspects. That's the one downside to the rise of the home studio: modern artists try to do too much. Yes, it's good to know about these things, but there's a saying in England: "You don't keep a dog and bark yourself." It's very true. If you're going to employ someone to do something, let them do it. It's fine to get involved, but you've got to let the people you've hired do the work they're trained to do.

Of course, you're not always going to see eye to eye with the artist you're producing, but that's part of the creative process. The danger, though, especially with young artists coming up, is that they think they have to do absolutely everything and be hands-on all the time. Much better to have someone around with experience, because they can take a lot of the pressure off.

At the end of the day, all of this stuff still comes down to the two things attached to the side of your head. Don't ignore them: they're very, very important . . . and they actually tell you everything you need to know. Whether you choose to listen to them or not, and whether you choose to act on the information they're giving you is entirely up to you, but, really, they're giving you everything you need. True, it's easy to get dissuaded and persuaded by what you see on a computer screen or by what somebody is telling you, but if something bugs you, you can't

ignore it. My usual rule is that if I play a track three times in a row and something consistently bugs me, then I'm going to have to do something about it. That's how I know that something isn't right—my ear starts complaining and my brain keeps bringing it up to me.

So you're saying that, ultimately, you have to rely on your own personal taste.

Exactly, although it's also dictated by the tastes of the artist and the record label. You just have to do the best you can with whatever is put in front of you. You have to have a good idea of what it is you want to achieve, but above all, it's supposed to be *fun*. All too often, that's the difficult part. [*laughs*]

I imagine it's not a lot of fun when you and the artist aren't seeing eye to eye on what it is you're trying to achieve.

No, it's not. The only way around that is to try it both ways—your way and their way—and then use the gentle art of persuasion to attempt to convince the artist that you're right. But if they steadfastly refuse to see things your way, you need to remember that at the end of the day it's their record, not yours. It can be very frustrating sometimes when you see clearly that someone is misguided, and it can eat up a lot of valuable time, too, but all you can do is try to be a diplomat and resolve things amicably. You can only do so much, after all. Eventually you sometimes have to say, "Well, if that's what you want to do, that's the way we'll do it." You're stuck between a rock and a hard place, because if you don't say that, they'll just go to someone else who will give them what they want.

Everyone seems to agree that people skills play such a large role in being a successful producer or engineer.

That's absolutely true, and students in particular should never underestimate the importance of people skills. I get the impression that recording schools focus mainly on technical and practical realities, and that's all well and good, but it can send the wrong message to people who attend those courses, because they finish their training and think, "Okay, now I'm an engineer." No, what they are is a *technician*. To actually properly call yourself an engineer, you need that other aspect too. Sadly, that art seems to be disappearing because we don't have the number of studios that were in existence 15 or 20 years ago, so there are fewer training grounds where people can learn those non-technical skills—the intangibles as well as the tangibles. People who started at the very bottom at places like Abbey Road or Olympic had a real advantage in that they were able to work on all kinds of sessions with all kinds of people. You learn a lot that way.

I remember working on a series of difficult sessions at one point when I was assisting at Townhouse—we were working really long hours, people weren't getting along, there was a lot of tension—and I was complaining about it in the canteen one afternoon to one of the more experienced engineers. He said, "Let me give you a piece of advice: the way to view those kinds of sessions is that they're teaching you what *not* to do." That really stuck with me, and from then on I started looking at things in a completely different way. It suddenly turned a negative into a positive—a difficult session became an interesting experience for me.

We've talked about how digital technology has impacted on the recording process, but do you feel that it has improved the *sound* of today's records?

Well, one thing that does seem to have changed is the idea of doing something over and over and over again until it's perfectly right; people today tend to think, "Oh, it's good enough; we'll fix it later." When I first started making records 20 years ago, the attitude was very much that you do it until it's done, or until you fall over, whichever comes first. [*laughs*] You would just work like a dog, and there's something to be said for the idea of "no pain, no gain." But there is also great truth to the law of diminishing returns, and when I look back at some of the things I did when I was under immense time pressure, it's not pretty.

> **"One big problem with digital recording is that people tend to rely on their eyes, not their ears."**

One big problem with digital recording is that people tend to rely on their eyes, not their ears. That's something I try to avoid, because it's all too easy to get fooled by what's on the screen. The good thing is that you can do amazing things today on much less expensive equipment than you needed 20 years ago, but the thing that hasn't changed is the experience you need to be able to pull it off successfully and overcome problems in the process.

Suggested Listening:
Charlie Watts Quintet: *Warm & Tender*, Continuum, 1993
Robbie Robertson: *Contact from the Underworld of Redboy*, Capitol, 1998
Rufus Wainwright: *Want One*, Dreamworks, 2003; *Want Two*, Geffen, 2004; *Release the Stars*, Geffen, 2007
Josh Groban: *Awake*, Reprise, 2006
Alanis Morisette: *Flavors of Entanglement*, Maverick, 2008

Part Five

Music City

Tony Brown

Able to Leap Tall Buildings at a Single Bound

Superheroes exist only on the pages of comic books, not in real life, right? Hmm. There are some people in Nashville who might disagree.

Almost singlehandedly, a soft-spoken producer named Tony Brown saved Music City from economic disaster some 20 years ago, changing the musical tastes of an entire nation in the process. The story of how he did so is the stuff of legend.

The son of an evangelist preacher, Brown was forbidden to even listen to secular music as a child. A self-taught pianist, he began touring with professional gospel groups as a mere teenager—a connection that led him to an association with Elvis Presley (and a seat in The King's backup band) in the last years of Presley's life. Following Elvis' passing, Brown started playing piano for Emmylou Harris, who gave him a crash course in all the music he had missed as a child and turned him into a country music fan.

Tiring of the road and seeking a "real" job, Brown hooked on with RCA—then the preeminent record label in Nashville—as an A&R man, but left after a couple of years, frustrated at the company's refusal to allow him to actually produce records. After doing a short tour with Roseanne Cash and Rodney Crowell in 1983, Brown briefly returned to the RCA fold before being lured away by MCA honcho Jimmy Bowen, who gave him free reign to find new artists. It was there that Brown blossomed, eschewing the standard formulas that made country music seem stale and old-fashioned in a time of changing, more sophisticated tastes and instead signing and producing pop crossover artists like the group Alabama, as well as a raft of so-called "young country" artists that included Nanci Griffith, Vince Gill, Steve Earle, Patty Loveless, and Lyle Lovett.

Their success throughout the 1990s wasn't just a shot in the arm for an ailing industry; it was more like a revolution. Within a few short years, Nashville became reborn as the new center of American music, attracting some of the best musicians and songwriters in the world. The resurgence also led to the construction of dozens of state-of-the-art recording studios, creating hundreds of new jobs and revitalizing the entire community. . . just the kind of thing you'd expect from a Superman.

But in his secret identity as a mild-mannered record producer, Brown has crafted more than a hundred number one hits—a string that continues to this very day with new artists like Trisha Yearwood as well as established legends like Reba McEntire and George Strait, for whom he has produced eight and fifteen albums, respectively. In keeping with his superhero persona, Brown made a miraculous recovery from a life-threatening brain injury in 2004, which led to a recent decision to start his own independent production company. . . situated, as he is quick to point out, in Chet Atkins' old office.

You spent a lot of time with Emmylou on the tour bus, listening to all the records you'd missed growing up.

When I was working with Elvis, he was just a celebrity to me—I wasn't aware of the history of what he had done musically. But when I got on the bus with Emmylou, it was like having a continuous history lesson because she was constantly playing music—old-time country or bluegrass, or songs by songwriters she'd discovered. She turned me onto country music, which I never had been into before.

The thing about country music is that it runs a pretty close parallel to the way I was raised in the church, because most country artists are pretty God-fearing. Of course, some of them are also as wild as any rock and roller ever thought about being, but for the most part it wasn't a hard transition for me. I couldn't have gone from playing gospel music to playing in a rock band, because it would have been too much of a culture shock.

How did you land the gig with Elvis?

Elvis had formed a group from three gospel music singers that he knew were out of work, and he called them Voice. They were literally his house band because he loved to sing gospel songs around the house. I was playing with the Oak Ridge Boys at the time, and the lead singer for Voice called me up one day and said they needed a piano player. I referred him to a guy from Sweden, who got the job. That fellow called me about a month later and thanked me for putting his name in there, and then he said, "You know, we're in a Mercedes limo right now, riding down Sunset Strip with Elvis, and he's firing a gun out the window. It's really cool." [*laughs*] I started thinking, god, I should have taken that job myself! Ultimately, the guy wasn't able to get his green card, so he got shipped back to Sweden and I ended up getting the job.

Eventually Elvis brought us on tour with him as an opening act. The very first show we did, I was waiting backstage, all excited about seeing him make his entrance. But when the door to the limo opened, Elvis literally fell out of the car. [*laughs*] He was very medicated in those days, and it was an awful show, needless to say. It kind of freaked me out.

Another time, Elvis had someone call us to say, "You guys need to come to Graceland tonight, just to hang out." But one of the guys in the group didn't want to go because he had a hot date and so we said, "We'll come tomorrow." We drove down the next day and as we pulled up in front of Graceland there were 15 Cadillac Sevilles lined up in the driveway. The guy who had called us said, "I told you—y'all should have come last night." [*laughs*]

I was with Voice for a year and a half, and then I actually started playing in Elvis' own band, after his piano player, Glen D. Hardin, left. We'd all arrive in a big bus before the show started—there was a 10-piece band and a 12-piece orchestra, maybe 25 backup singers, so it was a pretty big crowd of people. We'd creep up onstage in the dark and pick up our instruments so we were ready to play as soon as the lights went on. But one night in Baton Rouge, Felton Jarvis, who was Elvis' road manager and producer, came up to each of us and whispered, "As quietly as you can, walk back to the bus—Elvis has gone home." So we tiptoed off the stage and got back in the bus and drove off. As we were driving away, I saw the lights come on in the Coliseum and you could just hear these screams coming from the audience. Apparently on his way to the show, Elvis decided that he didn't feel like singing that night, so he just went home. Now *that's* a superstar! [*laughs*]

After your stint with Elvis, it was a while before you began producing records.

Yes. After Elvis passed away, I began playing with Emmylou, and then she stopped touring because she got pregnant. At that point, I started thinking, I need to get a real job, so I began working for RCA. This was just after they had received the first platinum album by a country

artist [for *Wanted! The Outlaws*, featuring Willie Nelson and Waylon Jennings], so all of a sudden a lot of attention was focused on Nashville. This new country music had crossover possibilities, so RCA decided to start a pop label called Free Flight. I was sent to LA to work out of their office there. I was just an A&R person; I wanted to produce but they wouldn't give me a chance to do that.

So even though your roots were in gospel and country music, your job was to look for pop acts.

Right. But the kind of pop acts I had grown to love were people like the Eagles and Linda Ronstadt—that kind of music was just starting to happen. Unfortunately, that was also when the Clash came on the scene, and the Ramones, all the things I just didn't get. So after about a year I returned to Nashville, and this time I was put in the country division. That's when I discovered the group Alabama.

But RCA still wouldn't let me produce records, so I quit and went out on the road with Roseanne Cash and Rodney Crowell—both at the time hot, new trendy, ahead-of-the-curve artists. Roseanne kept getting pregnant, though, and Rodney couldn't get himself a hit, so I decided that was God telling me I needed to get a real job again! [*laughs*] I returned to RCA for a year before Jimmy Bowen hired me away to join him at MCA, where I ended up staying for 24 years.

And that's when you were finally allowed to start producing records?

Well, actually while I was still at RCA I co-produced a Steve Wariner record. That's how Bowen heard about me, and the carrot he dangled in front of me was that he would not only make me a vice president but would give me several acts to co-produce with him, including Wariner and Jimmy Buffett. After awhile he told me, "I'll take care of the established acts like George Strait and Reba McEntire; you go find me something new." That's when I started going out and signing and producing people like Patty Loveless and Lyle Lovett and Steve Earle. That sort of established me as being on the cutting edge. At the time, I wasn't trying to be that, but that's the reputation I developed.

And eventually things came full circle and you ended up producing George and Reba too.

That's right. When Bowen left and went to Capitol, I inherited them. By then I had signed Vince Gill, and I also had produced Rodney Crowell's huge *Diamonds & Dirt* album, which had five number-one singles on it—a real thrill for me because he was my mentor. So all of a sudden things started happening for me.

Is your overall philosophy as a producer to let the artist do things the way they want to do it?

That was Bowen's philosophy, and I adopted it. He once told me, "You know, most country artists are puppets: the producer tells them what they're going to sing, how they're going to sing, where they're going to cut the record, all that kind of stuff. But it's their record, so you should let them have their way, because nine times out of ten, the artist is right." That's what he did with Reba McEntire and George Strait—he gave them co-production of their records and that's when Reba exploded, and so did George. Jimmy was one of the most positive things that ever happened to this town: the studios got better and the record budgets got bigger.

> **"Sometimes an artist gets a little confused; that's when, as producer, you've got to step in and actually produce."**

Sure, sometimes an artist gets a little confused; that's when, as producer, you've got to step in and actually produce, but for the most part, you need to trust them. That's what I've always done, and it's always worked for me.

What do you do, though, when it seems that the artist is taking a record in what you feel is completely the wrong direction?

When an artist gets so huge that they sell millions of copies of every album, they usually don't want to go in a different direction. It's not that they're settling, though that's what happened to Elvis in the last five or six years of his career, as he deteriorated health-wise. Jimmy Bowen taught me about time management: how to take advantage of the available time and get as many things accomplished as possible. I know all too well that when a record works, the artist is a genius, but when a record fails, it's the producer's fault. [*laughs*] It's like Kenny Rogers sang: "You've got to know when to hold 'em, know when to fold 'em, know when to walk away." I've walked away from a couple of projects, but I generally love it when an artist does something unexpected and tries to buck the trend. I'm glad when talented people attain success.

> **"When a record works, the artist is a genius, but when a record fails, it's the producer's fault."**

Do you take different approaches to making records with different artists?

I do. This town is full of great musicians and great studios and great engineers, so I always like to cast each artist with a specific engineer, and put them together with certain musicians, and I'll encourage them to use a certain studio too. Some people like a funky vibe, and other people like a shiny, glitzy kind of studio, for example. It's all part of the psychology of making a record—something that's almost as important as your musical knowledge and your savvy and taste.

How do you handle things when you see an artist spending inordinate amounts of time trying something out that you're convinced isn't going to work?

Well, most country artists don't do that. Everybody sort of knows what they need to do to get on radio, because radio is still king in country music—we need it in order to tell people that a record exists. We only have two TV channels—CMT and GAC—and they're not in every major city, so we don't have the luxury that a pop act has, where there are plenty of music channels. In country music, the drill is either you get on the radio or you're only going to sell 50,000 records at the most.

The boundaries of country radio have always been pretty narrow, although they're expanding a bit now, thanks to artists like Shania Twain, Keith Urban, and Rascal Flatts—sonically, it's bigger than it's ever been before. You couldn't have gotten some of the crunchy guitars that are on some of these records onto the radio 15 years ago. I remember that when I did Vince Gill's "High Lonesome Sound," there was a little bit of banjo on that record. You could barely hear it, but it was there. We were going to put it out as a single, but the promotion department said, "Hang on...the first thing you have to do is to take that banjo out." I said, "Why?" And they said, "Because they won't play it on radio." Later on the Dixie Chicks came along and there was banjo on all their records and then Keith Urban came along and he had this thing called a "ganjo" and now it seems like everybody's record today has a little banjo plucking in the background. [*laughs*] Same thing with Hammond organ. I used a little B-3 on the first album I did with George Strait. Next thing I knew, B-3 was on every record coming out.

Do you need to personally enjoy an artist's music in order to successfully produce them?

Not necessarily enjoy it, but certainly I need to understand it. I don't love bluegrass music as much as I love traditional country music, but I can at least understand it. I feel I could produce a bluegrass record because most bluegrass artists already know what they want—it's just a matter of being the person that helps them get their music on the disk.

With rock 'n' roll and pop music, it's more about attitude, so you have to almost consciously create what the next big thing is going to be. Mind you, country is slowly getting that way. I think that's because of artists like the Dixie Chicks, and Keith Urban and Rascal Flatts, and because of what Mutt Lange did with Shania [Twain], which I love. Things are really different now.

George Strait doesn't even think of himself as a country singer; he sees himself as a crooner in the Sinatra vein.

Well, the kind of music that George really loves is Western Swing—Bob Wills' stuff—which is actually derived from the kind of big band music Sinatra did. If you listen to a Bob Wills record, the ensemble does with fiddles and steel guitar the same kinds of things that a big band does with horns. George actually did a duet with Sinatra for the *Duets* album. It didn't make Sinatra's album, but at my urging, George did put it on his box set.

Does George like to sing live with the band, like Sinatra did?

He sure does. He's had the same band for years so they know every move he makes. Unless they write their own songs, a lot of artists today will come to sessions not even knowing the songs. They just record a guide vocal with the band and then work out what they're going to do afterwards. But George—who doesn't write—comes to the sessions knowing the songs we're going to cut that day inside out. So nine times out of ten his final vocal comes from the tracking session, and the band responds to that; he performs, and they perform back. We cut a lot of his songs in the first take, too.

You've produced well over a hundred number one hits. How many of them would you say were first takes?

Maybe ten of them. It's interesting, when I worked with Don Was, I noticed that he would run over just the intro with the band until they got it perfect, then he'd move on to another section—maybe focusing on where the band might stumble—and he'd rehearse that, then he'd rehearse the ending, all separately. He told me, "Never let great musicians play the whole song until they get all the rocks out of the road. Then I guarantee you they'll get it in the first or second take." And he was right.

These days I take that same approach when I work with George, and with Reba. Of course, there are other artists who like to work things out in the studio—people like Vince Gill, where the arrangement might change ten times as we're rehearsing. "I Still Believe in You" started out as an up-tempo song. But Vince said, "This just does not sound right—let's send someone over to Tower Records to get Bonnie Raitt's 'I Can't Make You Love Me'—I want it to sound like that." So we went out and got the record and played it for the band, and when we put the red light on they just nailed it, first take.

George's "Give It Away"—the song that won the ACM Single of the Year and CMA Song of the Year—was a first take too. But that's such an obvious George Strait tune, and it's so simple. George has never tried to push the envelope because he doesn't have to. I really respect him for that because I think when you look back on his body of work years from now you'll be able to play any of his cuts and instantly know it's him. I hate when an artist loses his identity. Take Babyface, for example. I loved his first record—he was almost like a country R&B artist—but then he got huge and started making his records more hip-hop, more like Outkast, and he lost the things that I liked about him.

What is it that makes you want to work with an unknown artist?

It's an intangible thing. With Patty Loveless, it was her voice. With Lyle Lovett, it was charisma. He's the same today as the way he was back then—the hair, the suit; he just has a presence that is undeniable. His first album is still amazing to me, even though it was basically just his demos; I simply replaced a few acoustic guitars that were a little noisy, and I added fiddle to one song. That was it.

Of course, you need a strong song too. People think that all I like are singer/songwriters. That's not true; I just happen to be attracted to those kind of people because they tend to be more focused, they have more of a vision, so it's more fun.

> *"I happen to be attracted to [singer/songwriters] because they tend to be more focused, they have more of a vision, so it's more fun."*

Are you a big fan of modern digital recording technology?

I am now, even though I fought it for so long. But I would never go back [to analog]. The technology just makes the recording process so much easier, at least in terms of replacing things. If you've got a guitar lick played with the perfect performance except for one note being slightly ahead of the beat, you can go right in and move it ever so slightly without having to do the whole thing over.

Of course, it can't take people who can't sing and turn them into singers. Some people think, "If you can't sing, Pro Tools can fix that and make you sing really good." That is not true. But what it does do is it allows you to use the best pass of a vocal, the one that's the best emotionally, even if it has one note that's slightly sharp or flat. In situations like that, I'll always give the artist the opportunity to go in and redo it, and they'll usually want to sing the whole thing again, but if they can't match it, you're able to take that one great performance and just fix that one little spot. I don't consider that cheating.

You had a serious accident a few years ago in which you nearly lost your life. How did that experience change your approach to making records?

I think that's the reason I decided to do what I want to do, as opposed to what I thought I had to do. It made me take a real look inside myself. I thought, now that God gave me a second chance, what is it that will really make me happy? I decided it was having the freedom to make records with anyone I want to work with. I realized that I had been in a rut because I had gotten used to the rigid structure of a record label—every Monday there was a staff meeting, that kind of thing. I was spending far too much time on administrative things and not enough time being creative.

The accident also showed me what great friends I've made in this town, and it definitely taught me not to ever take things for granted. When I go into the studio now I realize how fortunate I am, what a great job I have. Plus I'm working out of Chet Atkins' old office. It doesn't get any better than that!

Suggested Listening:

George Strait: *It Just Comes Natural*, MCA Nashville, 2006

Rodney Crowell: *Diamonds & Dirt*, Sony, 1988

Vince Gill: *I Still Believe in You*, MCA, 1992

Steve Earle: *Guitar Town*, MCA, 1986

Patty Loveless: *Honky Tonk Angel*, MCA, 1988

Lyle Lovett: *Lyle Lovett and His Large Band*, MCA/Curb, 1989

Kyle Lehning

The X Factor

A Hammond B-3 organ—the bane of every roadie's existence—weighs nearly four hundred and twenty pounds.

I know this because I have just helped veteran producer Kyle Lehning load one of these behemoths (along with its accompanying hundred-pound Leslie speaker) into the back of his pickup truck after a gig. It's not every day that an interviewer is pressed into schlepping duties, but it's a small price to pay for the privilege of spending a couple of relaxed hours in Lehning's gracious home in the Nashville suburbs, chewing the fat about the current state of the music business.

Kyle Lehning's love of the Hammond is a reflection of his love of jazz—an unusual quality in someone best known for his production of country records. And even though it was his proficiency on keyboards and trumpet that led to touring work with superstar Waylon Jennings, he remained determined to follow his main passion and forge a career in engineering and record production. After finding success in the studio with pop duo England Dan and John Ford Coley (their single, "I'd Really Love to See You Tonight," was a huge national hit in 1976), Lehning started to transition into country music as he began working with "England Dan" Seals as a solo artist, as well as mainstays Ronnie Milsap, Kenny Rogers, and Jimmy Buffett.

By the mid-'80s, Lehning was firmly established as one of Music City's top producers. It was at around that time that he helped broker a record deal for a then-unknown singer named Randy Travis, leading to one of the longest-running relationships the industry has ever known. Over nearly a quarter of a century, the duo has made more than a dozen albums together, records that have practically redefined country and gospel music from the ground up. In 1992, Lehning was recruited to head up Asylum Record's Nashville office, an experience he now describes as "liberating...but also somewhat scary." During his six-year tenure there, he signed and produced records for a number of up-and-coming new artists, including Bryan White and Neal McCoy.

Today, Lehning has resumed his career as an independent producer, continuing to nurture emerging talent while taking an active role in the various initiatives of the Grammy Producers and Engineers Wing. Thoughtful, articulate, and just plain fun to hang with (despite the fact that he won't trade in that goddamned Hammond for a less weighty keyboard!), we covered a lot of ground in our long, enjoyable conversation.

Why do you think you and Randy Travis have had such a long-standing professional relationship?

Well, I think he appreciates the role I've played in his career and the fact that we've been together through ups and downs—we've had hits and we've had misses. In the 23 years we've worked together, he's only made three albums that I didn't produce; other than that, I've worked on all his records.

One of the reasons I enjoy going into the studio with Randy is that he's really consistent. He's a terrific singer, with a great, iconic voice, and he's adventurous when it comes to material. We have a "benefit of the doubt" clause, where if I run into a song that I strongly feel he should try, we'll record it and see if it works. And the same with him—if he's got something that he's written or found and I'm not sure of it, we go in and give it a try anyway. That doesn't happen very often with other artists.

I'm guessing that, after 23 years, you probably see eye-to-eye more often than not.

A lot of times, yes. I like the fact that he will venture out there and try new things, and he's got a great sense of humor, which I think is a really important factor in having a long career. He's very competitive, but at the same time he's got a clear sense of himself in the world—you're not dealing with some massive ego here; you're dealing with someone who's basically the same guy he was 23 years ago. In many ways, he woke up the country market and sort of dusted it off. After his success, people realized that you could make true country music and still compete in the charts.

How has the role of the producer changed since you first started making records?

Well, for one thing, we're probably not going to see many more people who are just doing record production alone. Maybe "producer" will morph into another title, like musical director. That might be more apt, anyway.

When I first started in the business, I came in through engineering, and there weren't that many engineer/producers at the time—it certainly wasn't as prevalent as it is now. And now musicians are starting to get proficient in Pro Tools, so they're actually wearing all those hats at once. I suspect that's the way it's going to continue to go.

> **"The most difficult thing to establish is how to be honest in a non-threatening way."**

But do you think artists will ever be capable of producing themselves? Don't most people need a sounding board, an objective set of ears?

I doubt that it's ever a really great idea for artists to produce themselves, but that other person in the room can be an engineer that they have trust in. The most difficult thing to establish is how to be honest in a non-threatening way—a way that allows you to say what you really feel about a performance and be able to move through that. Sometimes people are afraid of losing their job, or offending the artist, but the more successful an artist gets, the more important it is for them to find somebody who will actually tell them what they really think.

And sometimes the more successful an artist gets, the more insecure they get.

That's right. It's a delicate balance, but that's the most valuable thing to an artist, particularly if you're working with them over a long period of time.

You once made the observation that record producers used to be more like the listening public than they are today.

I was thinking of specific people who loved music but had no technical concept of what was going on, so they just went completely with their gut. They'd sit in a studio and produce records and their input would basically be either "that's good," or "that's not good," and it would be up to the musicians and the technicians to interpret what "not good" was. Usually getting a thumbs down from one of those guys forced the musicians to come up with something more interesting, more surprising, and/or more energetic.

There's something about that innocence that is more like the attitude of the general public. I recently shared an experience with [veteran producer] Norbert Putnam that came a little late in my life because I wish I'd had the experience ten years ago. I had been invited to speak to an undergraduate class about record production, and Norbert happened to be in town, so I asked him to come join me. We talked about ourselves for about an hour and a half, and then Norbert turned it on the class, asking them, "What is it you're looking for when you go online?" This kid in the front row raised his hand and he said, "I just want to be surprised."

That comment woke up the teenager in me—that same teenager who was always looking forward to the next record that was going to come out. It was a real "wow" moment for me, because, frankly, I'd forgotten that part of the job was to surprise people. All of which returns to the problem of being so technically savvy that you forget that it's really all about keeping the listener interested enough to want to hear the next section of the song, that it's all about keeping them wondering what's going to happen next.

> *"It's really all about keeping the listener interested enough to want to hear the next section of the song."*

So are you saying that there's too much emphasis on technology today?

It's hard to know, because kids today are going to tackle Pro Tools one way or another. People complain about autotuning, but if Frank Sinatra had had it, even he might have considered using it on occasion. He certainly didn't complain about using a great microphone, or the great echo chambers they had at Capitol studios.

Surely there's a difference between wanting to accurately capture the actual quality of somebody's voice and fixing their pitch.

Maybe, but it's all technology. What I mean is that if there's an actual great performance that just has a slight irritant that keeps it from being exactly right, that might be a good case for using autotuning, perhaps just to bump one syllable up or down a little bit. I'm not suggesting that Sinatra would have ever needed to use it consistently, or that it should ever be used to compensate for someone who can't sing in tune at all, even though the bottom line is that the public wouldn't be aware of it anyway.

How close to perfect do you need to get things when you're making a record?

Well, I think I'm like a lot of other guys in that, if something doesn't consistently bother me, then it's okay. [*laughs*] If something haunts me, on the other hand, I won't be satisfied until I go in and fix it. In general, though, I try not to belabor things too much; I'm not one of those guys who has to put every high-hat on the grid—I've only ever done that on rare occasions.

Today's technology has just given us lots of options to consider, and I, for one, don't miss analog. Given a choice, I wouldn't go back. Pro Tools sounds good enough to me, and it still allows me to just capture a performance without messing with it. After all, doing nothing is one of the many options it offers.

Are you using digital plug-ins too?

Yes, for mixing. Part of that is because the industry now has an expectation that they can ask you to change something two weeks after you've turned a mix in, and get a remix delivered that same morning. In a lot of ways, the industry is like the public in that they don't care about details—they just want what they want when they want it. Digital technology has given us the ability to do that, so I've learned to be happy with using plug-ins, because it's the only way you can do an exact recall and satisfy that need. I was never able to do a recall on an SSL or a Neve that felt exactly right to me—it always felt like a variation on a theme, and somehow never quite as good; somehow it never came back *better*. [*laughs*]

Mind you, I still break out all my Pro Tools tracks to an analog console, and I still use analog outboard gear across the stereo bus because I'm not convinced yet about mixing in the box. But the console is just set at unity gain, so I'm really just using it as a big summing system.

Do you do a lot of signal processing on the way in?

Yes, I try to get everything to sound like it ought to, right at the get-go. Sometimes I'll even print effects if we've got something special going on. I'm not the least bit afraid to commit.

What kind of tricks have you come up with to elicit the best performance from an artist?

I'm not sure I'm actually that good at doing that, because, to me, all of that should get done before we go into the studio. It gets done by spending time with the artist beforehand, building some sense of respect and trust between us. Then it's a matter of knowing where we're headed, combined with the joy of adventure. There are producers who form an image in their mind beforehand of what they want to hear coming out of the speakers, and they beat whoever it is into fitting that image. I've always gone into the studio with a pretty good idea of what I've wanted, but I've also always had a pretty good expectation that the people I surround myself with are going to surpass that. That way, the worst case outcome was that it was going to sound the way I'd imagined it, and if that's the worst we do, it'll be okay. For me, it's a little like Christmas morning; I want to go in there with a sense of anticipation, expecting that it's going to turn into something better than I could come up with.

Do you see the producer's role, then, as simply facilitating the vision of the artist, as opposed to having a vision of their own?

Well, that would be the ideal scenario, even if it makes me the weakest link in the chain. Of course, if you're a team player, that's a win-win situation! [*laughs*] You never want to be the smartest guy in the room, anyway... which is something I can generally count on. [*laughs*]

But, yes, for me it's a lot more fun to work with someone who has a good sense of who they are, someone who knows what they want to do. I'm not one of those Svengali characters—I never have been, and it's never been an aspect of my personality. I've always been much more interested in collaboration and helping people accomplish their goal.

What is it about a new artist that makes you want to work with them?

I'll never forget something the late, great Arif Mardin [*interviewed in the first edition of* Behind the Glass] said to me: "The secret to making great records is, don't make records with people who can't sing." It's unfortunate that we often spend so much time trying to make somebody into something that they just aren't. So I've tried as often as possible to latch onto what I think is a compelling voice. Sometimes I've been right, sometimes I've been wrong, but that's what I look for. It can be like trying to catch lightning in a bottle, but I've tried to stick with that approach.

It's true that, with the very best artists, you pretty much get to just sit there and go along for the ride. Having said that, they still need to be certain that they're going to get honest feedback from their producer; that's something that's really invaluable. The equipment is seductive, and the power you think you have by being able to manipulate all this stuff is incredibly seductive, but it can just allow you to spin and spin and spin. You think you're getting somewhere, but all you're really doing is playing with the equipment; you're not actually accomplishing anything.

How do you handle personal tensions in the studio?

My approach is really simple. The way I keep the table clear is that I tell the artist very early on in the process that there will never be a tie: whatever we find ourselves disagreeing on, you win. But because there won't be a tie, I have the freedom to tell you exactly what I think. At the end of the day, it's your career, so it will be your responsibility to decide whether what I have to say is helpful or not.

Do you find you have to sometimes remind artists of that conversation?

No, I haven't, because every artist I've ever worked with has seemed to get it right away. They understand that for me to be able to give them my best work, I need for them to be able to listen to my input in the spirit in which it's given; they need to understand that I'm simply giving them my opinion, for whatever it's worth. If it rings true, fine, let's play with it. If it doesn't, no problem.

What were the main lessons you learned from your stint as a record company executive?

Well, I went straight from being a record producer to being president of the record label, and I was pretty much given carte blanche, with no indoctrination. My only training was basically, "Here you are; now go make some money for us." [*laughs*] Frankly, I didn't know what I was doing, but I went in there thinking that hit records were made because you spent a certain amount of money making sure that they got promoted and marketed, and if the public had an opportunity to be exposed to the record, they would respond.

All of that is absolutely true, except for the fact that "respond" doesn't mean that they will necessarily *buy* the record. They can hear it all you want them to hear it, but if it doesn't connect with them, they won't buy it. I learned the hard way all about that great concept of the turntable hit: a record that gets a ton of radio play but doesn't sell. In a way, they're like passive hits: if people hear it on the radio, they won't turn it off, but they also won't get out of their cars and go buy it. I had a number of those kind of hits; I think everybody does. Then there were other times when we were just kind of lukewarm about something—we'd say, "Well, let's just put it out and see what happens"—and we couldn't keep people from buying it.

So I guess I thought that as a record company executive, I'd have some degree of control over record sales, but I didn't. I found that experience to be liberating . . . but also somewhat scary. [*laughs*]

What was the X factor?

I don't know, and that's the beauty of it. I don't think it's something that can be quantified; it's just a question of whether the public responds to a record or not. There had to be something about every record that got through my system to the point where it got released, but beyond that I couldn't predict whether it would be a million-seller or a dud. Of course, I was always happy to take full credit when we *did* put out a hit. [*laughs*]

So, yeah, we're all geniuses . . . not. You just do the best you can. There were records that I really believed in and really worked hard to try to get the public to respond to, and they died a death. Sometimes no matter what you do, it just doesn't work.

Sure, we've all heard apocryphal stories about producers that predict in the control room that a record will be a hit, and it is. Somehow, though, you never seem to hear the other 10,000 stories about producers predicting that a record will be a hit, and it isn't.

That's right. Frankly, the odds are against *ever* being right when you make a prediction like that. I don't know what we can even say about the way things work now, because that golden age is gone. And if there's another golden age coming, I don't quite see it yet. We all feel that, goddamn it, there's got to be some way to make this all work in the age of the download, but somehow the solution just keeps slipping farther and farther away.

> *"We all feel that, goddamn it, there's got to be some way to make this all work in the age of the download, but somehow the solution just keeps slipping farther and farther away."*

Yet the idea that music should be free for everybody, like the air we breathe, is not a new thought. It's actually a very tainted idea, because the fact of the matter is that music is *not* free; anybody who's downloading music has actually invested money in being able to do so, making technology the new distribution system. Unfortunately, that new distribution system is ignoring part of its responsibility, because none of the dollars that are being invested in computers and broadband connections and iPods are being used to compensate the people creating the content.

Sadly, most of the general public doesn't view things that way, and the industry got so far behind trying to figure out what was going on that it wasn't able to clearly see what was happening until it was way too late. Unfortunately, the precedents are already set, and sitting around waiting for Congress to do something is frustrating. Of course, they've got their hands full with a few other things.

So if a well-meaning record company executive like yourself wasn't able to successfully promote music he really believed in, why does anyone need record companies at all?

That's a good question, and maybe the answer is that we *don't* need record companies. The role that record companies traditionally played through the years was that they served as the filters—they were the conduits that gave us access to what was supposed to be good music. In many cases, it worked, but in many cases, it didn't. In the '70s, when I first started making records, I was in competition with every other record, I knew who I was up against, and it was a very clear competition. Now, I don't have any clear idea of who the competition is—there's just this huge mass of information floating around out there, and Top Forty radio is really more like Top Forty Million radio. [*laughs*]

It's hard not to feel like a deer caught in the headlights when you start thinking about it that way. We don't even seem to know what it is we're shooting for anymore. But perhaps the bright side is that the change in distribution has made it harder to manufacture a hit; the cream rises to the top now by virtue of an artist's actual performance, whether live or online.

Yet every generation seems to breed another Britney Spears.

Well, there's always been a confectionery aspect to music entertainment, and I'll be the first to admit that I actually like some of it, same as I like chocolate cake; I find it to be satisfying for what it is. Some of those records are actually great pop records with terrific production values. And even if they're more to do with the talent of the producer than the talent of the artist, they still satisfy the listener, and they still can be great records.

What is the difference between a great record and a hit record?

These days, I'm not even sure what a hit record is; it's getting to be a more and more difficult concept to wrap my head around. Maybe that's why I wasn't a great record company executive. [*laughs*] A really great record company man wouldn't have any trouble with that question. To me, a great record is one that sells, and god bless them because that's what keeps people in business; the soul-satisfying art record that doesn't sell doesn't pay anybody's bills. Chet Atkins used to say, "The higher up the chart a record gets, the better it sounds." [*laughs*] Maybe that's the answer to your question.

The most beautiful time for me in any project is when the idea is to make a great record, with no preconceived notion about whether anybody else is going to like it. That's the point at which the perceived audience is very small: just me, the artist, and the record label. But that's a very ephemeral place, and it very quickly turns into, "We've got to get our money back; we're not doing this as an exercise in record production." Before then, there's a short period of time where there's absolutely nothing to lose and everything to gain; it's kind of magic, because there's no outside pressure to try to turn the record into something that's going to compete in any way. I like to keep that going as long as possible, because I think there's gold in that—it improves your chances of coming up with something that's uniquely attractive.

The question is, how do we get from that starting point to the point where large numbers of people get to enjoy the record? In particular, how is a new artist going to find that mass audience? My thinking is to do it slowly and consistently. These days, it takes a good year to get the first single through the system; everything has slowed down so dramatically that it's hard to get a feel for anything. What makes the problem worse is that a record label today will typically spend all their money on that first release, so if it doesn't sell well, you don't get a second chance; the idea of sticking with somebody has become a financial impossibility. Sadly, there's no more nurturing of artists these days.

What advice can you give to someone who wants to be the next Kyle Lehning?

You know, I went to the Southern Books Festival not long ago, and one of the authors had some advice for an attendee whose grandson had recently left medical school to become a writer. He told her, "I would advise you to tell your grandson to quit writing and return to medicine…if he can." I don't know if there's any better advice than that, if for no other reason that the odds of success in this goofy business of ours are so slim. So if you can think of any other way to make a living, and you can convince yourself that you can be happy doing it, you should go do it.

I certainly don't have any regrets about the life I've lived, though. I consider myself incredibly fortunate to have had the career I've had, and to get up in the morning still loving what I do and the people I work with. The level of ability that these musicians have, and the fact that I get to bring them together in a recording studio, play them a piece of music, and then just keep my mouth shut and let the pot stir is still exciting to me. It's just an incredibly privileged place to be.

Suggested Listening:

Randy Travis: *Storms of Life*, Warner Bros., 1986; *Always & Forever*, Warner Bros., 1987; *No Holdin' Back*, Warner Bros., 1989; *This Is Me*, Warner Bros., 1994; *Inspirational Journey*, Warner Bros., 2000; *Rise and Shine*, Warner Bros., 2002; *Around the Bend*, Warner Bros., 2008

England Dan & John Ford Coley: *Nights Are Forever*, Atlantic, 1976; *Dowdy Ferry Road*, Big Tree, 1977; *Some Things Don't Come Easy*, Big Tree, 1978

Dan Seals: *Stones*, Atlantic, 1977; *Harbinger*, Atlantic, 1980; *Rebel Heart*, Liberty, 1982

Ronnie Milsap: *Heart and Soul*, RCA, 1987

Bryan White: *Bryan White*, Asylum, 1994; *Between Now and Forever*, Asylum, 1996; *Right Place*, Asylum, 1997

Derailers: *Here Come the Derailers*, Lucky Dog, 2001; *Genuine*, Sony, 2003

Paul Worley

I Produce, Therefore I Am

I t isn't every day that you get to meet a record producer who's a philosopher. I'm not just talking about a record producer that *has* a philosophy—I mean an honest-to-goodness *philosopher*.

Like many of his Nashville peers, Paul Worley started in the music business as a guitar player and studio gopher (as in "go-fer"), but not before he had earned a Bachelor of Arts degree from Vanderbilt University studying the intricacies of existentialism and phenomenology. "Spending four years trying to figure out what 'to be' actually means was quite interesting," he says, "and one of the great Hindu philosophers had an outlook that really stuck with me. He argued that, given perfect knowledge of the facts, the best path to take in all situations is the one right in the middle. I've learned to adopt that approach when I'm in the studio making a record: I always try and listen to the voices around me, accepting that everyone's point of view has validity, and that's been beneficial to my music."

An accomplished session guitarist, Worley has played with everyone from Glen Campbell to Hank Williams, Jr., but from the mid-'80s onward he made a left turn into record production and was soon making hit albums for Martina McBride, Pam Tillis, Highway 101, Trace Adkins, John Anderson, and the Dixie Chicks (for which he received two Grammys). In 1987, Worley shifted gears and began playing for the "other team," eventually serving as an executive vice president at Sony Music Nashville (where he shook up the industry by signing the aforesaid Dixie Chicks) before becoming head of A&R for Warner Brothers Nashville in 2001. A couple of years ago, he made the decision to leave the front office and return to independent record production ("I felt that if I stayed, I was on a path to creative irrelevancy," he explains in this interview), but not before discovering, signing, and producing the debut and sophomore albums for Big & Rich, one of Music City's hottest new acts.

Today, Worley continues to craft hit records in the studios of Music City while also serving as one of the principals of Skyline Music Publishing, which has recently entered into a joint venture with veteran producer Russ Titelman [*interviewed on page 59 of this book*]. Though our conversation took some unexpected detours into the deeper aspects of life (hey, what do you expect from a philosopher?), it was nonetheless made highly enjoyable by Worley's infectious laugh and self-deprecating humor.

Did you always want to be a record producer?

Well, I always thought it would be a really cool thing to do. From reading the backs of album jackets, I had the sense that the producer was the person who put all of the elements together for the artist. But I honestly thought I was going to be an artist when I first started out. You just go and follow the music, wherever it leads.

I still primarily think of myself as a musician rather than a producer; to me, that encompasses all things musical, whether you're playing a guitar or an audio console. When I'm producing, I go into the same zone that I do when I'm playing; I'm always trying to get myself right in the middle of the sounds and the performance so I can feel the tensions in the rhythm—the push and pull—in order to make sure things are right. Not correct, but right.

Do you generally play on the records you produce?

Up until five years ago, I did. I used to be most comfortable sitting out in the studio with headphones on, playing rhythm guitar with the band while they were tracking, living in that little world between the kick, snare, and high-hat. That was where I could make most sure that the rhythm feel was right. But everything has an ebb and flow, and I've pulled away from that in recent years; for now, I'm enjoying the other aspects of recording, plus I always love finding new musicians and hearing what they play. After all, I've already heard everything *I've* ever played! [*laughs*] Plus my chops aren't as great as they used to be...though my ideas are just as good.

Are you very hands-on in the control room, or do you leave all the tweaking to your engineers?

I know just enough about engineering to be conversant in it, but I usually work with great

engineers, let them do their thing, and then adjust it to my own tastes. Setting attack and release times on compressors, for example, is a very subjective thing. A lot of engineers tend to do it mathematically so that the compressors react with the tempo of the song, but I quite often prefer to set them a little off-kilter so that they're letting some peaks through and not recovering exactly in time. It's just a matter of using your ears.

My attitude is that every piece of gear has a sound, so you might as well become knowledgeable about their sounds. The same way that you might choose a Strat over a Les Paul for a particular song, you might choose a [Universal Audio] 1176 over a TubeTech for a particular sound. That's what so great about recording: everything you do imparts a slightly different color.

That said, people love all kinds of sounds. I don't know of anybody out there who says, "Oh, I don't like that track because the snare drum sounds too radical." They either like the song or they don't like it; they're not going to sit there and break it down to its component instrumentation or tonal colorings.

You've developed a reputation for doing things a bit differently from the usual style of Nashville recording.

If I have, it's because I like to do the arranging at a rehearsal hall, not in the studio. I get the musicians set up in a circle in a nice, comfortable environment off-site and work out the arrangement with them over a period of a couple of days so that everybody understands what the song is, what the lyrics are about, and what the vibe is. That way, each musician gets a chance to figure out what *not* to play as well as what to play, and to work out when it's their turn to step up and carry the ball.

It's not an idea I invented—when I was an A&R guy, I had a chance to work with [producer] Peter Collins on a project, and that was his approach—though it's a pretty unusual way to do things here, because there typically is no rehearsal for Nashville sessions. Personally, I think that's a problem. I would much rather go rehearse beforehand than sit around in a studio all day figuring things out. That's the way we used to make records, after all.

And, by doing things that way, you end up with just four or five musicians covering all the bases, the way any good band would. You end up saying, "Okay, it's the second verse, so something new has got to happen here. Let's see, hmmm, we don't have a fiddle player... but we do have a bass player. So, hey, Mr. Bass Player, make something happen." Next thing you know, something *is* happening... and you don't need an extra musician to make it happen.

As an added bonus, the musicians know ahead of time what arsenal of sounds to prepare for those two or three days you're going spend capturing the music. So they bring specific guitars and amps and drums with them, and they've got them set up and ready to go; there's nobody sitting around waiting for the strings to be changed on their old '55 Strat because they know ahead of time to have the axe ready. That in turn allows the producer and engineer a little more time to actually think about how we're going to capture what's being played, and that allows for more variation in the texture of the sound, too.

So that may be why my records sometimes sound a little different than other records made here in Nashville. Frankly, I think more people need to do that, because otherwise we get so much sameness: everybody's playing the same crap on the same instruments through the same amps, miked with the same microphones, all playing the same licks they played yesterday because it's the Favorite Lick of the Week. There's only one way around that, and that's to allow the musicians to spend time with the music. They need to understand what the artist is trying to do and they need to get the lyrics under their skin so that when they think of a lick to play, the lick has as much to do with the lyric as it has to do with the melody. And then, of course, the great sound of nothing is always a possibility—a wonderful possibility.

Are you constantly in search of new sounds? Because that's also outside of the usual "Nashville formula," where each instrument always has to sound a certain recognizable way.

> **"I don't make my record; I make the artist's record."**

Well, first of all, there *is* nothing new. [*laughs*] But I'm always in search of something unique—something that has a character and flavor that's specific to that song from the incredible array of possibilities that exist out there, from all the previous recordings that have ever been made in the world. I've been doing record production for 30-odd years, and I've been a musician for 45 years, and all those sounds are inside my head. If I just give myself time to think about them, I can use that palette to help the artist express himself.

After all, I don't make *my* record; I make the artist's record. I like to work with true artists, as opposed to just singers, and mostly I do first albums and second albums—I don't do third albums, for some reason.

Why not?

I'm just usually not interested in doing more than one or two albums with a new artist. Once they're up and running and their sound has been set, then it's basically just repetition. I'd rather let somebody else do that, or perhaps somebody else needs to come in at that point and help the sound evolve. The only exception was Martina McBride; somehow, we made 13 or 14 albums together.

Why was she the sole exception to the rule?

Because she wouldn't let me go! [*laughs*] Even when I began telling her, "Martina, you need some new blood; you need someone with new thoughts and new ideas," she was just very steadfast and said, "No, Paul, I'm going to pull it out of you." And she did, too. For many years, she forced me to get beyond myself. It was a real gift to me, and we had a good, long run together. Eventually, though, it got to the point where it clearly made sense for her to move on.

"The music that really works—the music that really rings the bell and makes people go crazy—is the music that doesn't sound like everything else."

I guess it's that I love launching new artists—not only discovering them, but helping them discover themselves in the studio. And I love fighting for them when the forces that signed them want to shape them in a way that is not their essence. After all, the music that really works—the music that really rings the bell and makes people go crazy—is the music that doesn't sound like everything else. But when you turn an album like that in, it sometimes scares the shit out of the record company. They'll say, "I don't know anything that sounds like that." Well, that's a good thing, right? But they don't think so. They worry about the so-called "gate-keepers" and how they might react. I say, fuck the gatekeepers. And fuck the gates. Who needs a gate, anyway? [*laughs*]

That's particularly interesting, coming from someone who used to be an A&R person.

Yeah, well, you can't hold that job forever if you have that kind of attitude, obviously. [*laughs*] I ultimately had to make the decision to leave that end of the business because I felt that if I stayed, I was on a path to creative irrelevancy. Although it was a comfortable living and the material rewards were good, I'm just not ready to be irrelevant.

Do you feel that your experience working for a label influenced the way you make records today?

Everything is an influence. One of the best things about being an A&R person at a major label is that you get presented with a huge array of music from producers and artists all over the world, and so you get a much broader perspective. The danger of being an independent producer and staying that way for too long is that you can get very insular in your thinking and creativity because you've just got yourself and your team around you. If you don't work hard to open your ears and your mind to other music, you won't grow.

I don't think that having been an A&R person necessarily changed my approach to making records, but I probably understand the record company's point of view, right or wrong, a little better as a result of that experience, and I know better how to talk to them. I also know some of the danger signals to watch for. If, for example, you have those first few meetings with the label and you realize that they really don't get the artist—that is, they actually want the artist to be someone else—well, I know that I'm not that guy. In situations like that, I'll just quickly withdraw myself from the process. That's just too unhappy a life to live; it's just not worth it.

So I look for situations where I not only love the artist and have respect for their abilities, but where the record label also not only loves the artist but understands what they are all about, and will not try to make the artist sound like every other artist on their label. If all the relationships are lined up that way, then I'm happy to go to work.

But does every new artist have a clear sense of where they want to go?

Maybe they do. I try to work with artists that have a pretty good sense of themselves, but that doesn't necessarily mean that they know how to get there, and that's where I can help. But I'm not the artist, and I don't want to be the artist. I just want to help the artist recognize their potential. To that end, I'll sit down with them beforehand and ask them what their goals are. Is the idea to simply express yourself and then just get out on the road and accept the life that comes with that? I can get with that. Or perhaps the goal is to somehow hit mainstream radio and yet not sell out your individuality. I can get with that too. But those are different goals, and I want to know up front what the artist is trying to achieve.

You once said that the best advice you can give aspiring producers is to "Never stay in one place; always look for new studios, new engineers, new artists, new music."

Well, the other way of saying that is that there's no way of figuring it out, because there's no "it" *to* figure out. In other words, if you've had a hit, you can't just sit there and say, "Okay, now all I have to do is repeat that." That won't work, because the next time you do that, it won't be a hit. Why? Because it already *was* a hit. Whether you did it or somebody else did it doesn't matter. Copying a hit is not the same as making a hit.

> ## *"Copying a hit is not the same as making a hit."*

Instead, you have to keep moving. It just fits with Darwin's theory of evolution: we're supposed to evolve on all levels in order to live a happy and healthy life; staying still is dying. The wonderful thing about my being 58 years old is that I've come to realize that there's more I *don't* know than what I do know. That's what wakes me up every day. I don't wake up thinking about what I already know—what's the fun of that?

Suggested Listening:

Martina McBride: *The Time Has Come*, RCA, 1992; *The Way That I Am*, RCA, 1993; *Evolution*, RCA, 1997; *Emotion*, RCA, 1999; *Martina*, RCA, 2003

Pam Tillis: *Put Yourself in My Place*, Arista, 1991; *Homeward Looking Angel*, Arista, 1992; *Thunder and Roses*, Arista, 2001

Highway 101: *Highway 101*, Warner Bros., 1987; *Paint the Town*, Collectables, 1989; *Bing Bang Boom*, Collectables, 1991

The Dixie Chicks: *Wide Open Spaces*, Monument, 1998; *Fly*, Monument, 1999

Big & Rich: *Horse of a Different Color*, Warner Bros, 2004; *Comin' to Your City*, Warner Bros., 2005

Clarke Schleicher

On Prime Numbers and Multiple Miking

Veteran Nashville engineer Clarke Schleicher is fighting a bad cold on the day I meet with him, but like the professional that he is, he gamely carries on. Between sneezes and sniffles, he tells me how he got into the business: a childhood flirtation with trumpet and then tuba, which led to a switch to the decidedly hipper electric bass when he got to high school, followed by college-level clinics in jazz theory and steady gigs around his native Louisville, Kentucky. All signs pointed to Schleicher becoming a professional musician until his father laid down the law: young Clarke would be going to college whether he liked it or not.

Fortunately, he found a college he wanted to attend, and it happened to be nearby as well. Middle Tennessee State University, located just outside of Nashville, offered one of the few audio programs in the country back in the mid-seventies, with an innovative curriculum that allowed the enthusiastic Schleicher to study both music and recording. Following graduation, he landed his first internship, with the Nashville division of ATV Publishing, which housed an eight-track demo studio in the basement. "Nobody there knew a thing about operating it, so they let me loose and I learned all the gear and began recording song demos for some of the staff writers," he recalls. "I was scared to death at first, but I discovered that this was something I loved doing."

Additional internships around town followed, allowing Schleicher to gain additional experience and confidence, until one day he learned of a job opening at a suburban studio called the Bennett House, run by veteran producer Norbert Putnam, an ex-bass player from Muscle Shoals who had enjoyed huge success with Dan Fogelberg, Joan Baez, and Jimmy Buffett. "I called every day and bugged the hell out of the studio management," Schleicher recalls with a laugh, "until finally, at the end of the summer, they decided to hire me."

At Bennett House, Schleicher was exposed to not only the top artists of the era, but the top engineers and producers as well. After two decades of making hit records for many of country music's most recognizable artists—Martina McBride, Pam Tillis, and the Dixie Chicks among them—Schleicher joined forces with producer Paul Worley [*interviewed on page 234*], with whom he helped craft hits for contemporary artists like Big & Rich, Sara Evans, Mark Chesnutt, and Kevin Montgomery. Today he serves as chief engineer and head of studio operations for Warner Brothers' Nashville recording facility, located on the site of Mike Curb's former label Monument Records and, briefly (and intriguingly), Mary Tyler Moore Productions.

How do you feel that technology has impacted on the quality of today's recordings? Do you think that albums sound better today than they did when you were starting out?

Well, these days, of course, almost anyone can afford to have a Pro Tools rig in their bedroom. Overall, it seems a shame that there's no apprenticeship system anymore—something which was of such great benefit to me—but on the other hand, it also means that the people are able to do a lot more experimenting intuitively than I was ever able to do. There are times when I wish I'd had a Pro Tools rig up in my bedroom back in 1976—who knows what I would have done with it?—but it's a double-edged sword, because I'm not sure if that freedom compensates for not having mentors to learn from.

Back in the eighties, I was lucky enough to be able to work with some of the best engineers of the time: people like Bill Schnee, Bill Szymczyk, Neil Dorfsman, and Jack Joseph Puig. That's when I really learned to be an engineer. Before then, I just *thought* I knew how to be an engineer. Working with folks of that caliber gives you an opportunity you just don't get any other way. With those guys, the name of the game was change; everything was different, and nobody ever did anything the same way twice, or the same way as anyone else. I learned that there are so many different ways to skin the cat; just because this guy mics an instrument one way and another guy mics it a different way, that doesn't mean anybody's right, or wrong, or weird—just different.

Ear training was the most important thing I learned from Bill Schnee: recognizing what a good snare drum sounds like, what a good vocal sound is. Bill always knew where he was going, and that was a huge lesson to me. So many engineers come in and just fiddle and fumble around until they stumble onto greatness, but Bill was the first guy I saw who would come in and immediately start working towards a sound. He had a picture in his mind from the second he would start listening: he'd shove up all the faders, listen to the song for awhile, then shove them back down and start working towards a goal. By the time all the faders were back up again, you had an amazing record.

> **"If you know ultimately what things need to sound like coming through speakers, you're halfway there, because you'll probably eventually figure out how to get there."**

Having said that, there's no question that experimentation is key. You may not have a Jack Puig around to show you how to get a great drum sound, but if you study records and practice and play, you can still kind of get there, just in a more roundabout way. If you know ultimately what things need to sound like coming through speakers, you're halfway there, because you'll probably eventually figure out how to get there.

These days, I've found that a lot of singers even know what mic sounds good on them, especially the ones who have been singing demos for years . . . and a lot of country artists were demo singers for a long time. A lot of them now own not only their own mic but sometimes even an entire vocal chain that they know works well on their voice. Folks seem to have gotten a lot smarter now that a lot of them have become engineers too. Of course, a little bit of knowledge can be a very dangerous thing! [*laughs*]

One thing I can say for sure is that the sounds on records have changed, for better or worse. It's a bit frustrating in that, where I used to have to spend hours to make things sound big and open and tall and deep, I now have to work to make everything super-compressed and pumping and bright. I was never oriented that way, and as I work with younger producers, I find that I now have to change the way I work in order to accommodate what their ears want to hear.

What do you do if a producer is asking you to give them sounds that you subjectively feel are not good?

Well, I worked for years assisting an engineer by the name of Ed Seay. He was the king of the clean sound—he had the ability to make densely packed records with lots of country instruments and you could hear them all. I was always amazed at how he could take five acoustic guitars, three electric guitars, a B-3, a piano, all the drums, and 15 tracks of background vocals, mix them together and you'd hear everything. He accomplished that with three-dimensionality; he'd not only place instruments left and right, but front and back, plus he'd use the height dimension as well.

The problem these days is that we've lost depth; we've lost the three dimensions, and in my opinion it's due to what I think of as audio-inferior plug-ins and audio-inferior buses. So now you're having to deal with music that's primarily two-dimensional, and a lot of the newer producers want it that way on purpose. I've actually had to shy away from working on some projects because I just didn't want to go that route.

Mind you, back in 2003, I did put a Pro Tools rig in a bedroom in my house, and I spent a lot of time mixing custom projects in the box for private clients. As a result, I figured out a couple of ways of actually making it sound pretty good. That's when I realized that you could make the in-the-box concept sort of work. I could make the sound wide, but it was always so hard to get any kind of depth, and it was very time-consuming to figure out ways to get height. It took a long time to figure out tricks with delays and different kinds of reverbs and compression—and ways of *not* using compression—to come up with good-sounding mixes in the box.

What were some of those tricks?

The biggest thing that I learned was the importance of the clock. If you're using the internal clock in Pro Tools, the end result is going to suck. You must invest in a good external clock; the difference it makes is huge in terms of opening the depth of the mix.

The other aspects aren't as cut and dry because they depend upon the particular elements you're mixing together. They mostly have to do with delays and reverb—as well as panning—to give instruments their own individual spaces, as well as depth and height. The great thing about Pro Tools is that you can have as many reverbs and delays as you want: back in the old days you were generally restricted to just a few of them; either there was only so much outboard gear at the studio, or you had only so many available channels on the console for returns. But nowadays, by having so many reverbs and delays available, and by being able to freely pan them anywhere you want, you can use them in really creative ways: not necessarily to give an instrument a particular reverb, but to put the instrument in a particular acoustic space.

> **"Knowing how much to compress is important, but it's equally important to know when not to compress at all."**

Knowing how much to compress is important, but it's equally important to know when not to compress at all. I've found that there are a lot of people making home recordings that don't really understand the interaction between threshold, ratio, attack, and release. That's the kind of thing that can really make a difference in the sonics of a recording.

How do you know when *not* to compress something?

When the compressor starts making the sound so small that it no longer has any life. That's what happens to a lot of mixes; even when you turn it up very loud, the sound becomes very small, because there's so much compression being used. That's a huge mistake because it diminishes the dimensionality of a recording; you lose whatever depth is there because you have crushed the life out of it.

What so many people also don't realize is that compressors become musical only when they're in time with the music, which means that your attack and release times have to be in tempo with the part being played. These days, all too often, I hear compression that's fighting

the timing of the track instead of accentuating it. All too often, the vocal is being squashed down just at the point at which it was supposed to be exciting…and then it's popping up at times when it's not necessarily an important part of the song. The same with guitar licks and drum fills. All too often the compression doesn't flow with the song; it fights it.

Equalization, of course, is another huge aspect of recording. There are so many schools of thought there: some engineers don't equalize when they're tracking, only when they're mixing; others do just the opposite. I'm from the school of, do whatever you have to do to make it sound great right now. A lot of it is simply about ear training: unfortunately there are a lot of folks making home recordings who don't know what 3k sounds like; they don't know what 100 Hz sounds like; and they don't know what happens when you boost a frequency area too much or too broadly. It's easy to make something bright, but you have to realize that making it bright can also make it harsh, and by the time you or the mastering engineer compresses the hell out of it, you have this harsh little thing that simply isn't musical any more.

I think every aspiring engineer should get a copy of one of these charts that shows the exact frequencies of the piano notes, along with the frequency range of various acoustic instruments, and study it. That chart allows you to learn, for example, what the fundamental frequency is of a bass guitar playing in the key of G.

That recalls an interview I did with Tony Visconti [*published in the first volume of* Behind the Glass] where I asked him what his typical equalization was for bass, and he told me it depended on the key of the song. If the song was in A, for example, he'd be dialing up 110 and 220 Hz.

Exactly. Even some advanced engineers don't think in those kinds of terms, but of course Tony is a bass player. That's one of the things I really love about working with Paul Worley—we can communicate like that. We know what the frequencies of the different keys are and so when he says, "Turn up 466 Hz," I know exactly why he's saying that. Yes, you can sweep the frequencies and find the sweet spot, so memorizing a chart is not strictly necessary, but that basic knowledge is still a great thing to have: if nothing else, it will explain why boosting a particular frequency is working or not working.

Here's another potential application for that knowledge: an Aural Exciter basically just adds a third harmonic to the incoming signal. So if you're working with an electric guitar that sounds lifeless and dull, it can be very useful to know what the third harmonic of that guitar part is and turn just that frequency up. That will instantly give life to the guitar and bring out the part that the musician is playing.

The point is that the key of a song, and its tempo, shouldn't be just random numbers to an engineer; they have real meaning, and knowing those meanings can help you bring new life to the music you're recording and mixing.

Which brings me to the subject of delay times. One thing I've noticed about a lot of records being mixed in the box is that there hasn't been a lot of attention paid to delay times. That's because Pro Tools makes it easy to type the tempo in, click on the Long Delay, and tell it to do an eighth note for, say, 120 BPM. But one of the things I was taught a long, long time ago was that, regardless of tempo, prime number delays always work especially well. There was a delay unit popular in the seventies and eighties called a Prime Time, and that's exactly what it did; it gave you delay times of prime numbers: numbers that can only be divided by 1 or by themselves. The Prime Time would spit out delays of 31 ms, 37 ms, 41 ms, etc., and it was always interesting to me how those delays added an extra dimension to music.

Don't get me wrong: obviously, I use delay times that are in time with the tempo: eighth notes, sixteenth notes, triplets, etc. Those help underlay and reinforce the groove. But I also use prime number delay times, to create depth. So just because a delay time isn't an exact eighth note or sixteenth note, that doesn't mean it shouldn't be used. I always put a 29 or 31 ms delay on a vocal, for example: I just like the way it gives the vocal depth, regardless of what the tempo is. Similarly, I use 61 or 71 ms delays on guitars a lot.

Why do you think that is? Why, for example, would a 31 ms delay sound better than a 32 ms delay? Is it just mojo, or is there a physical explanation?

I don't know. All I know is that it sounds a lot better to me, and I can hear a big difference between a 31 ms delay and a 32 ms one. Those prime number delays just add a kind of dimensionality, and I use them all the time, especially when doing mixes in the box. A lot of times I'll actually stand above the speaker and adjust the amount of delay level to where I can feel the singer's head get bigger—it's like I can feel a real head singing to me, instead of a one-dimensional voice.

Despite the fact that you've come up with some great techniques for compensating for the limitations of mixing inside the box, do you still prefer breaking the tracks out to an analog console?

I do. It's not only better sonically, but I find it easier as well. That said, I have heard some pretty good mixes that have been done in the box, but perhaps because of my background as a bassist, my ears are always drawn to the lower frequencies, and I don't feel that the internal software in computers can reproduce those frequencies as well as the op-amps of analog consoles. Maybe it's just a sound that I've grown to like, and now I'm used to it, but I'm the type of guy who has a big-ass pair of JBLs at home; I just love bottom end. With some work, I can achieve all brightness and even a good degree of dimensionality when mixing in the box, but I can't get that primordial gut low-end sound from software yet.

Do you ever mix to analog tape to try to capture that sound?

I did it for a long time, but it's become cost-prohibitive, and the quality of tape has dropped off too. With all the inconsistency, you can't get a machine to align, you can't keep an alignment, and the tape sometimes sheds like crazy, so there's tons of worry as well as expense involved.

There's a perception that there's a formula way of recording in Nashville, with perhaps less experimentation going on in the studios here than in some other cities. Would you say that's justified?

Well, you have to bear in mind that there's two types of recording here: there's masters, and then there's demos. In a demo recording—which is the majority of the recording work being done in town—you have to record the basic tracks for five songs in three hours, so, no, there's not a lot of time for experimentation: you absolutely have to use what is tried and true. If I'm booked to do a song demo, then, sure, I'm going to set up a [Shure SM]57 on the snare and guitar amp, and [Sennheiser] 421s on the toms, and I know pretty much how to set the equalization curves for them beforehand—in fact, I can do them in my sleep.

But then we get to make records here, too, and that's a whole different world. For one thing, we generally only have to record the basic track for one or perhaps two songs every three hours, and then we'll spend hours and hours on overdubs and hours and hours on mixes. That's when I have fun and get to experiment a lot. One thing I really like to do is to put up all the mics, even if they're not actually on anything, even if they're just sitting in a corner; I fill up the board with mics. After all, that's what we're here for, aren't we? [*laughs*] It doesn't cost anything, so why not? Plus it's a good way to make sure the board is working correctly. So I'll put a different mic on anything in a heartbeat.

Are you saying that the microphones are just literally in random positions?

I'm saying that any extra microphone that isn't otherwise in use on an instrument will just get plugged in, wherever it happens to be; then we'll start moving them around to see how we can improve the overall sound. So it depends on what the setup is, what we're going for, and what instruments are out there. But if one or two of those "extra" mics start sounding good, I'll open up an extra track and record them. Years ago, I would record each mic to its own separate track, but [producer] Paul Worley, who I work with a lot, would say, "Man, can't we just get the backing track to be that way now instead of having to pull up four faders to get that sound?" and I saw his point. [*See the interview with Paul Worley, page 234.*]

> "The different tones and depth that can be achieved by just blending microphones instead of using equalizers is phenomenal."

Here in Nashville, we record a lot of traditional country instruments, of course, and each one is expected to sound a certain way; a steel guitar is supposed to sound like a steel guitar. But the subtleties of that instrument, the different tones and depth that can be achieved by just blending microphones instead of using equalizers is phenomenal. I'm not saying that I never equalize, but I find that I generally prefer using multiple mics. That's something I learned from [engineer] Neil Dorfsman. When he records electric guitar, he positions one microphone—usually a 57 or some other kind of dynamic—straight on to the speaker cone and then some kind of condenser off-angle, and then he blends the two mics together and records them onto a single track; that, in effect, is the equalizer. What was always kind of baffling to me was that the 57 would be the brighter-sounding of the two mics; because the condenser was off-axis, it would be the woofy one. Neil would start out with the condenser mic signal and then blend the 57 in to the point where it had just the right amount of high end. That seemed kind of backwards to me, but it worked, and he was able to get huge guitar sounds just by moving those two faders.

And with all the tones coming out of a piano, you can put a dozen mics on it and completely change the sound with every little move of a fader. I'll typically use at least three mics. I like to put [Telefunken] 251s on the hammers and a [Neumann U] 87 in the middle of the piano, set about a foot back from the hammers. I'll always have a room mic open too, and I'll record it on a separate track.

As a bass guy, do you favor using bass amps or DI?

Both. I usually put the bass amp in a hallway, the longer the better, because that really allows the fundamental tone to develop; then, by moving a couple of mics closer or further, I can get some really cool sounds. I generally start with two mics—one right in front of the cabinet and a second one all the way down the end of the hallway—and I almost always end up using a blend of the direct and amp sound in the mix. The direct gives a the bass definition in the 1k–2k range, whereas the amp gives that warm fuzziness down in the 50–100 Hz range. I'm always messing around with the controls on the amp and I usually find myself having to EQ the amp signal at the console so that it's really bright. The goal is to come up with the biggest bass we can get away with and still get the song played on the radio.

Believe it or not, I've noticed that even cartage can impact on a recording. That's because people roll up with so many cases, and there's no place to put them, so you end up stacking them in the hallway—which, as I said, I like to use for bass amp—or even in the studio itself, where they can interfere with the acoustics of the room. Sometimes musicians wonder why the big studio they recorded in sounds tiny—well, it wouldn't if they'd move some of the stuff out of there! [*laughs*]

I'm guessing that you've come up with some pretty novel ways to mic drums, too.

Yeah, I do a lot of weird-ass stuff. [*laughs*] For one thing, I insist on bottom tom mics, and I'll place as many mics in or around the bass drum as I can fit in there and mess around listening to them all. I may end up only using one of them, but I want the option of being able to pick and choose, being able to play with different mics and different positions.

I like to experiment with different mics on the snare, too. Right now, I'm loving using Royer ribbon mics on snare, about eight inches from the drum. I'll usually have an SM57 on the top skin, too, just for insurance, and a 452 on the bottom. A lot of times I'll just mix the Royer and the 57 together to get the snare sound I'm looking for.

As for overheads, I've found that when you're working with a really good drummer, he'll balance his kit for you, and in those cases I'll use just two mics for overheads. If you position them correctly, it should sound just like the kit does out in the studio, with the snare drum imaged directly in the middle. Of course, the sound of the room itself dictates where you place the mics. If the room is really bright, for example, all a drummer has to do is tap a cymbal and it engulfs the entire kit. In that case, you'll have to move the overhead mics further away, or choose different mics altogether.

Trina Shoemaker [*interviewed on page 256*] showed me a drum trick that was one of those light-bulb-over-a-head moments. Most engineers will point their room mics at the drum kit and move them back about ten feet. Trina turns her mics parallel with the kit, looking out, and that puts them in phase with the rest of the kit. When I saw that, I started kicking myself: why didn't I think of that? I go to great lengths to keep things phase coherent, after all; I have a phase checker nearby at all times and I'm constantly having my assistant check every mic, every cable, every piece of gear, so that if a mic is out of phase it's because I deliberately put it out of phase. Phase coherency can make a monumental difference in creating a cleaner, more defined recording. When everything in that speaker is pushing and pulling at the same time, that's when you get the best results. Once again, it boils down to timing: when the bass player is thumping the string at exactly the same time the drummer is stomping on the bass drum pedal and both of them are pushing the cone out, that sounds a whole lot better than if one sound is pushing the cone out at the same time another is sucking it in.

Will you actually be slipping and sliding tracks forward or back a sample or two to maintain phase coherency?

No, but I do want all my mics in phase. In fact, I want to look at the Pro Tools files and *not* see them together, because I positioned the mics in different places specifically in order to shape the sound the way I wanted it. I believe in moving mics to get the sound; I don't like it when people go in and realign the recordings, because that changes the feel as well as the sound . . . which in most cases is a bad thing to do. Having said that, I have seen tracks that were cut in such a hurry that they needed a lot of editing to make them sound better. But generally I'm able to create a master take right there on the floor without having to resort to those kinds of things. I may edit a verse or a chorus in, but I'm not into sliding stuff. It's much better to get the musicians to play it right in the first place.

What are your favorite vocal miking techniques?

Well, in country music the vocal is the most important element, so I will go to great lengths to find the appropriate mic, preamp, and compressor for the specific voice I'm recording. I always rent in as many microphones as the budget allows and I will always hold shootouts; I'll have the artist keep trying different combinations until he or she is ready to shoot *me*. [*laughs*]

Actually, the tracking date provides me with a good opportunity to do a lot of that experimentation; I'll have a ton of mics in the vocal booth and ask the artist to sing on a different one for every pass. That gives me the best opportunity to hear the mics capturing a real performance, because I've found that when the singer is out there consciously doing a shootout, that's not a real test. I've been bit so many times with, "Yeah, that sounds good" during the run-through and then once the artist *really* sings the song, it's "Oops, no, that really sounds bad." So I like to use the tracking dates and the scratch vocal to get the vocal sound together.

Presumably sometimes the scratch vocal is actually the keeper.

Yes, with certain artists. I've worked so much with Martina McBride and Sara Evans through the years, for example, that I already know the best vocal path for them, so we don't need to do that testing. Then there are artists like George Strait, who could probably sing their whole album during the tracking date and never have to go back and fix *any*thing. We're lucky in the country market, because there are a lot of singers who really know how to sing, and it's really cool to watch what that does to the band, because musicians find that so inspirational. It's funny also to walk around and look at the headphone boxes and see how they're set; you'll see that a lot of these musicians will have the vocal turned way up in their cans because it's inspiring them to play better. These singers are so good, it's fun to listen to them singing even scratch vocals because they're so great at it.

Do you ever find yourself using two mics on a singer: one close and one ambient?

I tried that for years, but it became a real accounting nightmare. Paul [Worley] does a lot of vocal comping, and because he's a guitar player, he's the best I've ever seen at it. A lot of producers comp the life out of the vocal, but Paul is able to harvest every little special moment and still make it sound like a complete performance. To that end, we've come up with a pretty special technique. We'll usually have the artist do a couple of warmup passes, then we'll start recording. They'll sing five or six complete passes—not all at once, though. They'll do three passes, take a break, answer a phone call, then come back and do a couple more, and all that will happen over the course of a day.

Afterwards, Paul will sit down at the console and start mapping out the vocal on a sheet, after which an assistant and I will put the vocal together as per his instructions. I'll spend a lot of time not just riding the fader, but riding the EQ settings, the compressor threshold, doing whatever I have to do to make the comped vocal sound consistent all the way through, like a complete performance.

Then, if the budget allows, we'll give the artist a copy of the comp and let them take it home and live with it for a week or so. They'll come back into the studio and sing it again and usually the result is a hundred times better, because they've figured out what they want to do. Again, we'll have them do five or six passes and then create a second comp from those takes. Usually by that time it's finished, but if there's a verse or a chorus that's still bothering someone, we just have them run out there and sing it again, and that tends to be when we get the best stuff because they're not thinking about it or worrying about it anymore since they think we're done. [*laughs*] It may be an expensive way to do things, but I've found that it often yields the very best vocals.

Suggested Listening:
Martina McBride: *The Time Has Come*, RCA, 1992; *Evolution*, RCA, 1997; *Emotion*, RCA, 1999; *Martina*, RCA, 2003
Big & Rich: *Comin' to Your City*, Warner Brothers, 2005; *Between Raising Hell and Amazing Grace*, Warner Brothers, 2007
Dixie Chicks: *Wide Open Spaces*, Monument, 1998; *Fly*, Monument, 1999
Pam Tillis: *Thunder and Roses*, Arista, 2001
Sara Evans: *Born to Fly*, RCA, 2000; *Restless*, RCA, 2003
Mark Chesnutt: *Savin' the Honky-Tonk*, Vivaton, 2004

Justin Niebank

Finding the Spine-Tingling Moments

Most of us would say that something not feeling right is a definite warning signal to reverse course, but that's not the way Justin Niebank sees things, at least not when it comes to the recording studio.

"Actually, one of the greatest lessons I've learned is that if it doesn't feel right, pursue it," he explains. "Whether it's technical, musical, or whatever, you need to go down that road and find out what it is that's bothering you. Sometimes it takes a lot of hard work, but you have to stick with it, because it's amazing what you *can* discover after you determine what the problem is."

That's typical outside-the-box thinking from this very atypical outside-the-box engineer. Born in Chicago, Niebank's first foray into the music business was as a session bassist. But he found himself becoming increasingly enamored with the recording process, to the point where he literally used all his savings to purchase gear—a move that paid off when he found himself starting to get hired more for his skills behind the glass. After a stint doing jingle work, Niebank hooked up with Alligator Records and began engineering for Chicago blues legends Son Seals, James Cotton, Albert Collins, Johnny Winter, and Lonnie Mack—work that led to an association with Muscle Shoals keyboardist Barry Beckett, then a successful producer in Nashville.

The only problem was that by that point Niebank had relocated to New York in pursuit of success in the rock world. "I was commuting from New York for awhile," he recalls. "That's where I had the opportunity to produce and engineer the first Blues Traveler album, but at a certain point I realized that it was really all about people and that I should just stick with the community here in Nashville. Once I made that decision, things started going really well for me."

Really well, indeed. Literally within months of setting down roots in Music City, Niebank was making records with the likes of Asleep at the Wheel, Hank Williams, Jr., and Marty Stuart, followed by engineering and production work with George Strait, Keith Urban, Trisha Yearwood, Patty Loveless, George Jones, Pam Tillis, Vince Gill, and Rascal Flatts. In recent years, he's become more of a mix specialist, blending tracks for country mainstays Dolly Parton, LeAnn Rimes, Faith Hill, Brad Paisley, and Trace Adkins, as well as rock legends Bon Jovi and Aussie songstress Olivia Newton-John. In reflection of Niebank's chameleon-like ability to shift genres effortlessly, he's also produced two albums for the Iguanas, a band whose diverse musical identity practically defies description.

Niebank took some time out to chat with us between busy sessions at his custom room in Nashville's beautiful Blackbird Studios. Passionate and intense, his thoughts burst forth with the speed of a runaway freight train, leaving no doubt of his fervor for the art of making records.

You didn't have a whole lot of training before you became a professional engineer.

That's true. I didn't assist for very long—maybe just a month or two—before I was promoted to engineer. In retrospect I wish I had assisted a lot longer because I would have learned a lot more.

I would have liked to have spent additional time standing behind the other engineers, because there were a lot of basics I missed, and I wished I'd picked them up earlier on. But the one basic skill I had, the one thing that got me work, was that, as a musician, I could follow what was going on musically and be way ahead of the curve. I guess the producers I was working with were thinking, "Well, it's all about the vibe; maybe his snare drum sound will get good one day too."

I actually started producing records back in 1989, but I always had a day job too; I guess I just wasn't comfortable putting all my eggs in one basket. Nowadays I'm doing a lot of mixing. I get calls to produce, too, but I tend to be really particular about what jobs I take.

When you're producing, do you always do the engineering as well?

Most of the time, but I'm also comfortable with other people doing the mixing because I really love getting other perspectives. Sometimes it's hard to communicate things that are second nature to me—that can be a challenge—but I do want other people's input. The problem is that some people are wary about giving me their opinions; they don't realize that I really want them to be active participants.

You know, making records is not rocket science. It's just about putting great music together and seeing what happens. I love the U2 approach of pushing all the faders up to see what it sounds like—then, if it's no good, push 'em all down again. You can't get too precious about things.

> *"Making records is not rocket science. It's just about putting great music together and seeing what happens."*

Nashville seems to be the last remaining town in the world where recording is still all about getting a bunch of musicians in a room, playing live together.

It's an amazing thing, and it's one of the reasons why I've committed to living here. There's just nothing cooler than walking in a room and getting that live performance. That's the way I made blues records back in Chicago, too—with everyone in a room, playing together, including the vocalist. When it's all happening, it's just the greatest feeling.

That's not to say that I think it's wrong to build up records part by part, because some people can do that really well. But for me, personally, I still love the excitement and the danger involved in live recording, where things can blow up any second. There's that thrill of punching in on analog with the whole room standing around you thinking, "Will he get it?" I miss that. Everything is so easy now that the entire element of danger has been taken out of things, but it was that very danger that used to permeate the whole session and make things better.

I've watched a steady change in musician's attitudes, too; they've become so used to playlisting multiple takes, they don't commit to getting that one great performance. In the old days, the musicians would gather around the console for every playback and they'd be so into it. Now there's a lot of complacency; they're all on their laptops, checking their email and watching YouTube. I'm missing that edge, that sense of people worrying, "Is this it? Oh my god, is this going to be *the* take?"

Trust me—a lot of musicians leave today's sessions wondering what actually happened in there. They'll be driving home, thinking, "Did I actually give a good performance?" They may hear the final record and be happy with the result, but I think some of them miss that danger element too.

I gather you have a bit of a love/hate relationship with digital recording.

Perhaps, but in the long run I have to say that I think it's pretty fantastic. It's daunting at times for me as a mixer; I recently worked on a song that had 175 tracks! It can be hard to figure something like that out unless the producer has a great vision. But sometimes I get songs with tons of tracks, and people really haven't made those choices; they're kind of hoping that I'm going to stir things together and it will magically appear, which can be pretty unrealistic. I'm not totally against that, but sometimes I long for records that have a simpler arrangement, where you can feel equally passionate about every part in it. So the deferring of final decisions in Pro Tools bothers me. The process of doing multiple takes and not making choices on the date works for some producers, and I'm fine with that, but I personally like the idea of putting musicians in a room, live, and getting a performance where people hear each other and react to each other musically. I still feel that's the pinnacle.

What are the common mistakes people are making in their home recordings?

People try too hard. It's not necessarily a matter of inexperience either, because I sometimes get files from top engineers that are way overcompressed. That's one of the problems with Pro Tools—people can do things, and so they *do* do things. What is so hard about doing nothing? Before you start worrying about how to set the compressor, think about the performance first.

Pick up any music magazine, and they make it seem as if it's all about the equipment you use. Well, it's *not* about the gear. It's about the performance at the end of the microphone. Make that your emphasis and you'll be amazed at the quality of the recordings you'll get. If it's a spine-tingling performance, believe me, people won't care if there's some distortion on there.

You're saying that gear in general is not the important thing, but what would you say is the single most important piece of equipment in a home studio?

The song. [*laughs*]

Well, assuming you have a great song to record.

Probably the most important thing is having a recording medium that gets things down fairly accurately. Even a [Shure SM] 57 through a decent mic pre will give you a good recording if there's a good performance at the end of the mic—in fact, it can be an amazing recording. Sure, I love using great microphones and great mic preamps, but it's mostly about mic placement. Just get together as good a recording chain as you can afford, but realize that where you place that microphone is far more important than anything else. That, and always hitting Record the minute the musicians are out there, because it's all about capturing great performances. Don't dick around with EQ and stuff while a musician is sitting there losing energy; record right away.

Do you find that the first take is usually the best take?

Well, it almost always has the most emotion. The more you do things over and over again, the more you lose perspective on what it is you're doing, so even if you're working at home by yourself, you need to come up with a system that allows you to consistently record that first run-through.

I guess that's the immutable studio Law of Diminishing Returns: at a certain point in the session, every succeeding take gets worse.

Absolutely, and if you're only just starting to record at that point, you're in deep trouble. I think every engineer in the world would agree with this. I guess that's where knowledge of equipment does come in handy, because you need to know how to set up all the gear in such a way that, if you have to, even without hearing any music, you can hit Record and get a decent sound. Of course, with the benefits of a few run-throughs you can tighten things up—maybe move a few mics around or adjust the EQ. But you need to know that if that first run-through is jaw-dropping, you can get a decent recording of it.

Let's talk a little about your approach to mixing.

You know, people come in and give me all these compliments on my mixes, but the truth of the matter is that I'm really not doing much of anything because I'm basing everything upon balance. It's not about listening to each individual sound and getting everything perfect; it's about pushing up *all* the faders and coming up with a balance. I don't get into tons and tons of fader moves, either, because I tend to trust the dynamics of the performance. There are a lot of very successful mixers out there who use compression to pretty much mix their records for them, but the ones who are great are still musical about it; they find a way to make balance part of the process. I just feel that balance is way more important than EQ or automation, but people seem to give up a little too soon. They're also afraid to work for a couple of hours and then pull all the faders down and trust and believe in themselves. You need to know the song well enough that you can do that fearlessly and put up another mix at any time. And if that one doesn't work as well, try another one.

I think that's one of the reasons producers like having me mix for them: they know that I'm comfortable with scrapping the whole thing at any time, and they also know that five minutes later I'll have another mix up that sounds pretty damn good. That's because I believe in balance first.

I'll spend the early part of a mix just moving faders—I won't do hardly any EQ at all. I'm mostly just listening to the song as a whole, learning all the parts and finding those moments where the musicians have special relationships with the music. I need to figure out where those spine-tingling moments are so I can pull them out and emphasize them in the final mix, and I need to understand how the music is working against what the singer is doing, and what the dynamics are within the song. In other words, I'm listening for all the spots that will mean something to people.

Especially with new artists, if I turn around and find that they're not welling up at those moments, I know I haven't done a good mix. Balance creates emotion, because you're listening to how everybody is working together, as opposed to just focusing on any one part. So if you get people choked up, you know you're getting a good mix.

So are you saying that you begin a mix by analyzing the music, as opposed to analyzing the sounds?

Yes. Another engineer might listen to the file at that point and think it's the worst-sounding stuff they've ever heard in their life, while I might be thinking, "I don't know—it feels pretty good to me!" [*laughs*]

"It *feels* pretty good to me," as opposed to "It *sounds* pretty good to me."

Exactly. That's what I'm most interested in at first. And if the kick drum's not that good, hey, it's not that big of a deal to fix it. I occasionally have situations where the sounds are atrocious, but maybe that's charming; I have to take that into consideration, too. Maybe when the artist and producer sat in the control room, that's exactly what they were going for. I can't assume that my sensibility is the right sensibility. That's where going back in time and listening to rough mixes can be especially useful—they can tell you what people were thinking.

But in Pro Tools it's certainly easy enough to replace sounds. I rarely do full replacement, though—it's usually more about supplementing; if I feel a sound needs a little more girth or the ambience was not appropriate, I'll supplement it slightly. That's the beauty of having done this for awhile—I can just add slight shades to emphasize the emotion and feel of a track. My attitude is, hey, if it feels good, it *is* good. Who cares if the bottom end is shy, or if it's a little bit muffled, or if there's a little distortion in places? If what's coming out of the speakers moves me, I consider it a good mix.

Yet there seems to be such an emphasis today on achieving technical perfection in every record. So much of what we hear today is perfectly in time, and perfectly in tune.

Actually, I'm finding that, to their credit, a lot of the people at record companies today are saying, "Let's have it be real; let's have it be organic." They really do want you to make records that way, but a lot of times what they get back does not represent a full commitment to that. So I can understand why they're sometimes a bit wary—I'd feel the same way. People talk a great game but they don't always deliver, so that puts the labels in a difficult situation.

The problem is that a lot of records now stop halfway in the process; people somehow seem resistant to the idea that emotion is what's required to make a record right. Instead, they work hard to make a record surgically perfect, but that doesn't make it a great record—it just makes it a perfect record.

What are your thoughts about mixing inside the box?

I still prefer breaking tracks out to a big console, because that way there's still some degree of performance involved in the mix. When you're just sitting there with a mouse, there's really no performance aspect. I still use some outboard gear, but I have to also be realistic about the fact that if the record company wants a remix, I have to be able to recall things exactly, and plug-ins make that a lot easier. There are some plug-ins that sound great to me, but the vast majority of the ones I use are things that mangle the sound, as opposed to the tools that are supposed to make the sound pristine and perfect. I use those things that distort and saturate, just to give the sound a human quality. That said, I would still always advise that you try balancing first before you reach for any plug-ins. And if the end result is a little lacking technically—say, there's not enough bottom end—you can always print the mix to half-inch analog tape, or tweak it in mastering.

Do you like having the artist in the room with you while you're mixing?

I *love* having them there! I can't understand why some engineers like working on their own, with neither the artist nor the record company there. My attitude is, "bring 'em on!" To me, there's nothing more exciting than working on a mix for two or three hours and then having someone else walk into the control room and tell me what they're hearing, because that helps *me* hear it differently. If they walk in and their reaction is, "eh," then I know I need to rethink things. And, again, I need to interpret what that "eh" means: it may not be that the mix sucks—there may be just one thing that pulls them out of it. You have to figure out what it is, and a lot of the time it may actually be something that you yourself have in the back of your mind as an "eh," but you haven't taken the time to pursue. So maybe the mix isn't working because you've been a bit lazy. I love it when I get feedback during a mixing session, because it kicks me into gear more.

On the other hand, it's got to be kind of disheartening if you've come up with a mix that's really moving you, and the artist says "eh."

Fortunately, that only happens very infrequently. But when it does, I'm actually kind of excited about it, because I'm the kind of person who always thinks there's got to be more that can be done to improve a mix, even if everyone else in the room is jumping up and down, loving it. I always feel there's something I'm missing, anyway, so I don't get negative when somebody says they don't like a mix; I kinda say, "Cool. Finally, a challenge!" Believe me, I second-guess things as much as anyone, but if you find those things that are the core of the song and the performance and stick with it, it's amazing how everything else falls into place.

At the end of the day, though, you have to be true to yourself. If you really believe a mix is great and somebody else says they don't like it—and there will come a point where that will happen—you've got to have the strength to say, "Well, that's the way I hear it, and that's the best I can do; I know that everything is properly balanced and that it will translate well to TV and radio and also sound good to people listening on earbuds or their laptop speakers." If you've honestly done all that and they still don't like it, you just have to accept that and move on.

I guess the problem is that taste is not only subjective but also continually evolves and changes.

Yes, but the one thing that will always cut through changing tastes is emotion. Records today may be technically more perfect than in the past, but what they don't have is some of that rawness that comes with emotionally going out on a

> *"The one thing that will always cut through changing tastes is emotion."*

limb. It's thrilling for me when I can work with artists that understand that and are willing to retain some of those rough edges. It can be hard to convince people of this, but sometimes those rough edges can actually be the most commercial part of the record! One little moment of something gritty or nasty can actually be the reason why people want to listen to a song over and over again, so you have to make it a strength, as opposed to trying to hide it as a weakness. After all, if you keep hiding things from the listener, there's nothing left to catch their ear.

When I was a kid listening to records, I was able to imagine the people in the studio, and I sometimes think it's those rough edges that allowed me to visualize them there. If everything is too cleaned up, it just doesn't sound real any more. Maybe that's one of the reasons why kids are more interested in video games now.

Despite limited budgets, do you still do a lot of experimentation?

Oh, yeah. I'm always amazed when engineers are able to describe their drum setup or guitar setup, because I change it with every session. Maybe it's down to boredom, but I want everybody's record to sound different from everybody else's. That's the exciting thing about trying different mics and different mic placements: I want to have the ability to put different sounds in front of people and tailor everything. With every artist, I want to run through a different vocal chain, I want to use different reverbs, different effects. It's the same reason that I don't template mixes: I want every artist's record to be *their* record—I don't want to use the same compressor on every bass. I just feel it's part of my job to always push myself, same as the artist themselves would do if they were in my position.

What kind of tricks have you come up with to put an artist in their comfort zone and give their best performance?

Everything is based on a great, believable playback. You can't try to talk somebody into something; you have to let the music and the sound do all the talking for you. If an artist can walk in and hear their voice placed correctly in the mix with an arrangement that inspires them so that they get that tingle up their spine, then my job is done. At that point, they trust you, and you know you can trust them, so it becomes a solid working relationship. But when you try to talk somebody into something they don't really feel, you see that look in their eyes that tells you they don't necessarily trust you. As somebody who came up as an artist myself, I know how that feels, having someone trying to talk you into something that you know is not right.

So I just try to simplify, simplify, simplify, and let the playback do the talking. When I walk into somebody else's session and what I hear coming back through the speakers doesn't sound like a record, I wonder how they can sit through it for eight hours a day. I believe that it should sound like a finished record at every moment in a session. Even if you're just working with a stripped-down three-piece rhythm section at that moment, it should sound like a record, and the vocal should be up there—you should be thinking about the vocal all the time. Taking that kind of approach can clear away any concerns, plus if you make it sound like a record at every moment, you won't be compelled to use tons and tons of plug-ins when you mix it—it will sound good when you simply balance it.

That may be a lesson you learn from being in a band. When I look back on all the relationships I had when I was in bands, I realize I wasn't necessarily a really good person then, because I would fight for things. Looking back now, I realize that I should have just let the music do the talking. If my idea was great, it would have been obvious. So you shouldn't ever fight for ideas, because there are going to be a million good ideas, and the best ideas come from being open. Even if an artist gives you what you think is the worst idea you've ever heard, it still might inspire you, or someone else in the room, to come up with the *best* idea you've ever heard. You have to believe that, and you have to make sure the artist knows that you're open to new ways of thinking.

> **"You shouldn't ever fight for ideas, because there are going to be a million good ideas, and the best ideas come from being open."**

But what if the artist is getting a tingle and you're not? What if you know in your heart of hearts that what they want is not the best thing for the record?

It all comes down to interpretation. I believe that a big part of a producer or engineer's job is interpreting what people say. Most people got into making records because they had that experience of hearing something over the radio that moved them. If you're feeling that something is not working but they see it as magic—if it's evoking that experience in them—you need to interpret what it is about that thing that makes them think it's magic. At the same time, you have to figure out what it is that's preventing *you* from feeling that magic.

But isn't it true that, with today's limited budgets, you often have limited time to figure those things out?

Well, you just find a way to make it work. That's where Pro Tools does come in handy: if you're running out of time, let the band do some recording at their house and send you the files. Just adapt to what's going on while keeping the standard of your quality up. Studios want to stay in business, so they're always willing to talk when budgets are limited. You just need to find a way to use your time more effectively—it's as simple as that. Some of the most successful records I've made were the ones with the $30,000 budgets, not the $200,000 budgets.

Don't forget, this is an art form, and art requires time and patience and pushing envelopes. Every great producer has had to go out on a limb and do projects where they weren't getting paid. If you believe that you're making a great record, sometimes that's what you have to do.

You should view every record you make as an investment in your future; that's really the bottom line.

Selected Listening:
Blues Traveler: *Blues Traveler*, A&M, 1990
Marty Stuart: *Country Music*, Columbia, 2003
Keith Urban: *Be Here*, Capitol, 2004
Patty Loveless: *On Your Way Home*, Epic, 2003; *Dreamin' My Dreams*, Epic, 2005
Vince Gill: *Next Big Thing*, MCA, 2003; *These Days*, MCA/Nashville, 2006
The Iguanas: *Plastic Silver 9-Volt Heart*, Yep Roc, 2003; *If You Should Ever Fall on Hard Times*, Yep Roc, 2008

Trina Shoemaker

Determined and Fearless

Maybe it's just a side effect of the Starbucks jet fuel she's gulping down as we conduct this interview, but a couple of things soon become abundantly clear about Trina Shoemaker: one, she is supremely confident in her abilities. And, two, she takes no shit from anybody.

Shoemaker grew up in Joliet, Illinois, a small town near Chicago, where her hobbies included buying every album she could get her hands on and disassembling her dad's hi-fi equipment. At the age of 19, she moved to Los Angeles, with the express goal of becoming a record producer. "Mind you, I didn't know exactly what a record producer was at the time," she is quick to add. "But I had spent my entire youth looking at pictures of control rooms on the insides of album jackets and I knew that I wanted to be there. I would see photographs of Lennon or Hendrix sitting by a console and there would be some guy smoking a cigarette sitting next to him, and I just thought, 'I want to be that person.'"

Despite applying to every major studio in LA, Shoemaker was only able to land a secretarial job, albeit one at Capitol Records. "Unfortunately," she recalls, "it was soon made clear to me that the record company and the recording facility were two separate entities. Eventually they told me to stop lurking around in the hallways outside the studios!" Frustrated and pissed off, Shoemaker's next move was a long ways away: 6,000 miles, to be precise, where she had to make ends meet by working in a London pub. Fortunately, it was a pub frequented by a manager/film producer who needed someone to run his office while he was away in the States for a few months. Shoemaker took the job, and quickly discovered that a Capitol artist of her acquaintance—English singer Hugh Harris—had set up a demo studio in the basement. Without any fanfare, Harris put her to work punching in his vocals. "I peppered him with questions," Shoemaker remembers, "and his answers were classic. I once asked him, 'What's amplitude?' and his reply was, 'Volume, love; it's all just volume.'"

Unfortunately, the gig ended all too soon, and Shoemaker returned to LA, broke but more determined than ever. While there, she briefly attended a small private recording school, where she learned how to line up tape machines and make cables. One day, out of the blue, she decided to relocate once more, this time to New Orleans ("Odd, considering I didn't know anybody there and had never even been down south," she reflects), a move that proved fateful in that it led to her meeting famed Canadian producer Daniel Lanois [*interviewed on page 14*]. Lanois and his staff at Kingsway Studios took Shoemaker under their wing, utilizing her considerable soldering and tape editing skills... as well as, she notes wryly, her ability to keep the kitchen area clean.

The rest of Trina Shoemaker's biography reads like a chapter out of *A Star Is Born*. One day in 1995, singer Sheryl Crow turned up to begin recording her eponymous follow-up to the immensely successful *Tuesday Night Music Club*. On just the second day of the sessions, Crow had

a falling-out with her producer...and discovered that the not-so-shy female engineer standing in the shadows had an uncanny ability to punch in vocals—a skill she'd honed years before at a basement studio in London. Two Grammys later—including the 1998 Best Engineered Album (for Crow's *The Globe Sessions*)—Shoemaker's career was firmly established. In the years since, she has worked with an eclectic group of artists, including Emmylou Harris, Blues Traveler, Queens of the Stone Age, Nanci Griffith, and Steven Curtis Chapman (whose 2004 *All Things New* netted Shoemaker her third Grammy). Following the birth of her son and the terrible destruction of Hurricane Katrina just months later, Shoemaker relocated to Nashville in 2005, where she continues to be active in the music scene while balancing the demands of being a new mother.

Why New Orleans?

I don't know, to be honest with you. I knew that I couldn't afford to live in LA any longer, so I had to move somewhere, and I'm not crazy about big cities, so New York was out too. It wasn't because of the music scene there; something just came into my head one night and said, "You're going to New Orleans."

I was so broke, I stayed in a transient hotel at first. I applied to every studio in town and eventually got a job at Ultrasonic—but as a maid, not as an engineer. But it was through that gig that I started making the rounds of the studios and ran into the [Daniel] Lanois crowd.

Dan taught me so much. He and Mark Howard and Malcolm Burn essentially provided my career to me. I worked like a dog, but they were the ones who showed me how to make records, and they didn't hold back. Mind you, they made me pay for that knowledge with blood, sweat, and tears! [*laughs*] Dan was rough, but he was a genius. He could be a real taskmaster, but then we would be listening to five takes of something and he'd turn to me and ask, "What's the edit?"

and he'd allow me to cut the tape. He'd entrust me with those kinds of decisions, so he really built me up...but then, if I'd done something to piss him off, he'd retaliate by doing something really heinous. [*laughs*] It was always this up and down thing, but what that taught me was that nobody can psych me out in a studio—you cannot frighten me in there. I simply won't panic, and I guess he taught me that too.

Why do you think he hired you?

Well, truth be told, I was very ballsy and very mouthy, and I think Dan kind of dug that. I wasn't afraid to speak my mind, and you need to be able to do that in the studio—but then, having made your point, you also need to be able to sit back and shut up.

And I had two skills that were invaluable in those days: I could fearlessly punch in—and I never missed a punch—and I could cut tape like a surgeon. Those two skills are no longer valid, but they're the reasons I got the job at Kingsway, and also the reasons why Sheryl Crow asked me to work with her. I could get good sounds, too, but that's easy, and that's not why Sheryl hired me. From her point of view, she could just keep singing and be confident that I wouldn't erase something good.

Do you really feel that getting good sounds is easier, or less important, than developing other studio skills?

Yes, I do. How hard is it to put a mic in front of an instrument and turn on a preamp? People have trouble getting good sounds because they mess with it. They get it in their head that they have to change it some way—they've got to roll something out, or add something in. Just put a microphone in front of a guitar amp, walk into the control room and turn the preamp up good and loud, shove it through a compressor if you want some extra gain—don't compress it, just use it to get some extra gain—and send it to the recorder. Done.

But surely the art is knowing *which* mic to put up, and where to put it.

Right. But, again, that's not something you have to spend your entire career figuring out. Ask somebody, or do a little experimenting. You'll find out that a [Shure SM] 57 and a Royer [ribbon mic] sounds great together on a guitar amp. Truthfully, any mic is going to sound great if you place it in front of a great amp getting signal from a great guitar being played by a great guitar player. It's not about *getting* the great sound; it's about capturing a great sound that's already there, which means simply recording without interfering with it.

Your assumption, however, is that you're working with a great amp, a great instrument, and a great guitar player, which isn't always the case.

Well, if you don't have that, you're never going to get a great sound; all you're going to get from a mediocre player is a mediocre sound. That's the real truth of recording, and it's something that a lot of people don't want to face. That's why I'm saying it's not hard to get great sounds as long as you have great players; what makes engineering hard is having to focus for 14 hours a day and persevere when things aren't sounding great because the performance isn't working, or having to deal with broken gear or problems with the signal flow, or trying to maintain the big picture even while having to do minutiae like vocal comps. Plus you need to have strong people skills: you need to have a really great attitude, the ability to be a diplomat, and the instinct to know what the most important thing is to do next. It's all about knowing how to spend those 14 hours—which is costing so much money—really well.

> **"You need to have a really great attitude, the ability to be a diplomat, and the instinct to know what the most important thing is to do next."**

And at the end of the day, great sounds aren't all that important. There's that old joke about how do you fix a terrible snare sound? The answer is, a hit single. [*laughs*] It's true. Listen to [the Rolling Stones] "Gimme Shelter"—really listen to it. It's the worst-sounding garbage I have ever heard, but it's also one of the best songs I've ever heard. So we forgive that appalling recording and we say it sounds fantastic... because it *is* fantastic. Or listen to [Creedence Clearwater Revival's] "Fortunate Son." Let's face it: it's a terrible recording, but it's still compelling. I'm sure the engineer didn't intentionally blow out John Fogerty's vocal—nobody said, "Hey, let's get some distortion on this vocal—won't that be fun?" It just happened, and I'm sure somebody got some shit for it, but because Fogerty's performance is so exceptional, it becomes quintessential—the hallmark of the best distorted vocal you've ever heard.

So my approach as an engineer is to hope that the music is great and then throw up some mics. I might go into the control room and add a little high end or midrange to something; I might, for fun, sculpt the sound a little bit because everything's going so well, I'm bored and looking for something to do. But if it's a terrible band and it's sounding terrible, I know that there's nothing I can do about it except hack away... and even then it's still going to sound bad.

You still have to be creative, of course. You have to go, "Wow, I wonder what would happen if I miked this piano like I would mic a snare drum?" You've got to get in there and be inventive and have fun because you might stumble upon new ways for things to sound. But, again, that's not my definition of getting a great sound. My definition is putting a microphone in front of an already great sound and then recording it.

Does that truly mean that you can never fix it in the mix?

Well, I certainly can't fix a terrible performance, and I can't turn a bad singer into a great singer. But I can take what's given to me and create a really good

> *"I can't fix a terrible performance, and I can't turn a bad singer into a great singer. But I can take what's given to me and create a really good blend of what's been recorded."*

blend of what's been recorded. I can take the vocal you give me and make it present and fat-sounding and I'll place it right in the middle of the mix and put a great effect on it... but if it was awful to start with, it will still be awful, at least to my ears.

Blending is its own art form, and I can create a great blend of great sounds or of awful sounds; an out-of-tune guitar can easily be blended beautifully with an out-of-tune piano. Getting a mix properly balanced is the key. The great mixers—the Lord-Alge brothers, the Jack Joseph Puigs, the Andy Wallaces—can get a great blend on anything.

Of course, you have to know what sounds good. If you don't know anything about recorded sound, you can really mess up someone's recording. Ultrasonic, where I first started working when I moved to New Orleans, didn't have a bunch of gear. They were like Stax Records in that everything in the studio was already set up and never broken down; the musicians just turned up and played. I'd watch David Farrell, the engineer there, go out into the room and move a microphone an inch. I'd ask him what he was doing, and he'd say, "This will give me a little more punch." He didn't do it with EQs; he'd just move the microphone around for a few minutes until he decided, "That's the best I can record that drum with that mic through this channel on this day; now we've got to roll tape."

But tastes change, and the records of today don't sound like the records of 20 or even 10 years ago. How do you adapt to changing tastes?

Well, you've got to put a subwoofer in your car to begin with. [*laughs*] Seriously, you do, because 40 Hz exists now; it didn't exist in the past in recorded music. I mean, it existed physically, but nobody could hear it because the speakers of the era couldn't reproduce it and in any event vinyl couldn't hold it because the needle would jump out of the groove. So today you have to factor that in. We have real low end in today's recordings, so you have to work with it.

It's not all about low end, though. Today's records tend to be surgically precise, and today's vocals tend to be autotuned.

Not the records I make! [*laughs*] Mind you, I haven't had any hit records for awhile. But I take pride in the fact that my records sound fantastic. They are artistic, they are creative, and I refuse to use autotuning. I rarely will even cut to a click. I don't make those kinds of records, and as a result I don't make hit records. But that's okay, because I'm very happy with the records I *do* make. So I guess I'm a rogue, and sometimes I get work because of it, and sometimes I'm passed over because of it.

How do you balance the aesthetic demands of the artist with the commercial demands of the label that is financing the sessions?

Well, if I'm contacted by a major label to produce one of their signed artists, then my understanding is that the artist and I have both agreed to play ball: we have to give them a single, and we have to allow them all kinds of comments on what we're doing. As long as we're all willing to play ball, then, fine, let's go into the studio.

Actually, I prefer to work with indie people, where the label basically says, "Do whatever you want because we're not giving you much money anyway and we're going to be happy with whatever you give us." But either way, if there's a major difference between the artist and the label, then ultimately we all have to sit down together and discuss what we're going to do. The deal is between the label and the artist, after all. I'm just a hired gun—an independent contractor who is brought in to make a record. There's no way for me to side with a label over an artist—I could never do that—but

> **"There's no way for me to side with a label over an artist—I could never do that—but there's also no way for me to ignore a label that is paying for the sessions and owns the masters."**

there's also no way for me to ignore a label that is paying for the sessions and owns the masters. The artist needs to realize that they have to come to an understanding with the label, because if they don't, the label will simply shelve your record so it never comes out, but they will still own your masters. In short, you're going to be fucked. They have that power, and they will do that to you in a heartbeat, so you have to ask yourself if you really want to get into a battle with them. The best way is to come to a peaceful resolution by talking things through.

Do you take the same approach if you and the artist aren't seeing eye to eye?

You know, it's weird, but that's never happened to me. I always seem to find a way to figure out what the artist needs, and why they need it, and we always seem to find a way to resolve differences of opinion without it ever getting ugly. Maybe the key is that I always try to meld the artist's needs into something that the label wants, too. In other words, if an artist refuses to use a click track, okay, fine, they don't have to. But then they need to understand that I'm going to have to edit the shit out of the drums so the label will feel like the song is in the pocket. Okay, you've just made hours of work for me, but I'll do that so that the track will feel really steady and you can still say that you didn't use a click.

The people who hire me really trust me, and they usually recognize my abilities as an editor, a crafter. I can look at a body of work and see what needs to be removed and what needs to amplified, what's missing and what could use a slight arrangement shift to be more powerful for the listener. So if I say, "Look, this is not working; it just doesn't feel good," they usually say, "Alright, let's try it another way." I've never locked horns with an artist, and if it looked like things were going to go that way, I'd rather just give them back their money and leave. Out of the hundreds of projects I've done, I've only ever left a project twice in my life, and those were both mixes. I left because I knew it wasn't working and there was no way the artist and I could see eye to eye. Both times, I simply asked them to pay me for the hours I put in and, in exchange, I dissolved any other agreement we had.

Why do you think there are so few female producers or engineers in the industry?

Well, it's a really, really, really hard thing to do for *any*body, whether you're a man or a woman. Most people aren't going to make any money at this for at least 10 years, and you aren't going to be able to have any serious personal relationships, because you have to be committed to spending 14 hours a day in the studio for months at a time. For a woman, you absolutely cannot try to start a family in your twenties, and possibly not for most of your thirties. You have to accept that you're going to be alone for 10 or 15 years, and you may miss out on ever being married or having children as a result of that. Your male counterparts are not going to have to deal with that. If I had decided to have a baby when I was 28 or 29, that would have knocked me out of the business. Not because the business would say, "No people with babies allowed," but because, even assuming I would have been willing to spend so much time apart from my child, I wouldn't have been able to afford quality childcare.

I don't think there's anything else holding women back, so maybe it just comes down to the fact that a lot of women decide to have a child, which precludes them from going after this career full force. I really struggle now between being in the studio and being with my kid. I just don't want to sit there for 14 hours a day—I want to go see my little boy. What happens is that all the mommy wiring comes out and you find yourself thinking, "You know what? I'm not interested in your guitar part—I'm interested in my baby, and I want to go see him, so hurry up!" [*laughs*]

There are women astronauts who will tell the same story: it's really rough to have a highly competitive, highly desirable professional career and be a mom. The women who don't have babies are doing fine—they're out there making records and they're having a good time.

What advice do you have for someone who wants to be the next Trina Shoemaker?

[*sighs*] I really don't know how to help some of today's kids who want to get into this industry, because when I started out I could roll in as a maid—and I'm a very good maid—but I also knew how to line up tape machines and fix gear. I was also willing to be treated like shit and be paid nothing. They say pride cometh before the fall, but back when I started doing this, you couldn't have any pride; you couldn't have any dignity. You had to be willing to do anything, short of sexual favors, to get a chance to record music.

These days, I don't know how you make yourself hireable, other than that you have to know Pro Tools, and the best way to do that is to buy it and set up your own little home rig . . . but that costs money. I didn't have to have any money in order to become an engineer—I just had to be prepared to be a maid first, and to work hard. Nowadays you need $30,000 to get into the game, either to buy a rig for yourself or to pay school tuition so you have access to a rig. But when I first moved to New Orleans, my rent was $200 a month and I didn't need a car or insurance, so I could afford to work for free and then bartend to make a few dollars. I needed to prove to myself that I could be an engineer and I wasn't about to let anyone, or anything, stop me. Maybe it was my own damaged sense of self-esteem that pushed me to put up with some really undignified shit! [*laughs*]

I'm not sure that most people are willing to go through that. I meet a lot of people these days who seem to have a sense of entitlement: "Hey, I went to school, I paid my dues; I deserve to do this." I sometimes feel like telling them, "I don't know if you deserve it or not, but I gave up *every*thing to get to do this, and I focused on it non-stop." All I thought about in those days was editing, punching, and sounds—I was a real weirdo! [*laughs*]

What's the craziest trick you've ever tried in a studio that actually made it to record?

Well, I didn't actually come up with this, but I played a big role in it making it work. On the Queens of the Stone Age album called *R*, there's a song called "Leg of Lamb," and in the bridge it sounds like there are distorted guitars. But it really is [singer/guitarist] Josh Homme and [producer] Chris Goss saying "dum, dum, you idiot" over and over again. I distorted it so severely that you'd never know that it was actually vocals and not guitars.

Also, on the song "Kashmir's Corn" on Victoria Williams' *Musings of a Creek Dipper* album, I recorded one of her vocals with her head stuck in the bell of a sousaphone because she liked the way it sounded in there. I just had her move over for a second and stuck a 57 in there, down where the bell starts getting thin, and away we went. It was like one of those old Edison recordings, where they sang into a megaphone. I don't know if these qualify so much as tricks as they are just weird moments... but they sure were fun to do.

Suggested Listening:

Sheryl Crow: *Sheryl Crow*, A&M, 1996; *The Globe Sessions*, A&M, 1998; *C'mon C'mon*, Interscope, 2002

Victoria Williams: *Musings of a Creek Dipper*, Atlantic, 1998

Queens of the Stone Age: *R*, Interscope, 2000

Steven Curtis Chapman: *All Things New*, EMI, 2004

Grayson Capps: *If You Knew My Mind*, Hyena, 2005

James Otto: *Sunset Man*, Warner/Reprise, 2008

Part Six

Young Guns

Rodney Jerkins

Getting That Darkchild Sound

By his late twenties, superstar producer/songwriter Rodney Jerkins had already accomplished more than most of us would dream of attaining in a lifetime. Almost overnight, Jerkins took the music business by storm and became one of the hottest and most in-demand names in the industry, with a Grammy and literally dozens of multiplatinum records to his credit. Darkchild, as he is known, has produced hits for a staggering array of R&B, rap, and pop artists—names like Destiny's Child, TLC, Whitney Houston, Mary J. Blige, Brandy, Monica (including co-writing Brandy and Monica's megahit "The Boy Is Mine"), Jennifer Lopez, Britney Spears, LeAnn Rimes, Vanessa Williams, Will Smith, Toni Braxton, Joe, Coko, Blackstreet, Tatyana Ali, Kirk Franklin, and Debra Cox. He even teamed up with eighties superstar Michael Jackson for his 2001 comeback album *Invincible*. An unlikely combination? You might think so, but Jerkins succeeded in giving Jackson at least a modicum of street credibility, producing a record that, despite meeting limited commercial success, broke new ground sonically.

Grounded in classical and gospel music, Jerkins' career began to take shape when, at the age of 14, he met his idol Teddy Riley, who encouraged and mentored the young boy. After years of woodshedding in a home studio, Jerkins produced his first album, a collection of gospel songs performed by his brother Freddie. The record sold like hotcakes in their local New Jersey area and gave Jerkins the confidence to make music his fulltime avocation. In 1995 he hooked up with Mary J. Blige, co-writing, arranging, and producing five tracks on her multiplatinum *Share My World* album.

You'd think that all this success would go to such a young man's head, but that's not the case with Jerkins. Soft-spoken—almost shy—and refreshingly down to earth, he took some time between sessions at New York's legendary Hit Factory (now, sadly, no longer in business) to talk with us about his unique approach to arranging, writing, and production.

Why don't we begin by talking about how you got into the business; it's an interesting story.

Well, when I was five years old, I started taking piano lessons, classical music. I played a little bit in the church as I got older, played drums too. Then I started doing little four-track demos for people around the area, doing little productions in my house. I think people heard something different, because here I was, ten years old, and my demos were sounding better than anybody else's! I recognized it myself. One day I decided to try to copy a record, and my copy was so close, it was almost exact. I had a drum machine—an Alesis HR16, I think—and I didn't just program the beat, I copied the *sound* of real drums. I got so close, I decided that I could do the same thing these guys were doing.

I grew to love Teddy Riley's productions. There was something he had that I loved, and he was so musical. So I started following his career, listening to everything he did; I tried to write in his style. One day, when I was 13 or 14 years old, I had the opportunity to meet him. I was waiting in the parking lot, and when he arrived he invited me and my whole family into the studio. I had a tape of a dozen songs with me and he listened to the whole thing and he loved it. I could tell it was a genuine love—it wasn't like, oh, I'm going to nod my head because there's a kid in the room. I could tell by the facial expressions of everybody else in the room that they were blown away.

Then Teddy began to seek me out to sign with his company. I asked my father what he thought. He said, "Son, I've been around this world for a long time and if someone wants you that bad, you got something." So I didn't do the contract with Teddy and I began to work on my own instead. He offered me a great deal, but I just felt that I could make it on my own. And that's what I did.

You had real self-confidence.

Yeah, that's what it's all about. That's one of the keys.

When you're starting a project, do you have a vision, goal, or sound that you are working towards? Or does it develop spontaneously?

It's all spontaneous. I just sit down at the keyboard and I like to come up with the chord progressions or melody patterns first—whatever strikes me. Then I build the drums and other elements over the top of that. Some people start with the drums—the groove—first, but I don't.

When you do the drums first, you have to work according to the drums. My focus is not drums. Sure, I want them to be tight and crisp, hit hard and smack it in the face, but my focus is the song, so I want the melody first. I focus on the melody, and then I work the groove underneath that.

Very often, you co-write with your artists.

All the time.

What will their contribution generally be? Lyrics?

Yes, mainly lyrics. I mostly handle the music tracks myself. I have a sound, but I'm always using elements that I haven't used before. Normally, when people ask me to do a record for them, I'll say, "Okay, order me an [Akai] MPC, a [Korg] Trinity, and a couple of [Roland JV-] 2080s or a [Roland XV-] 3080," and that's the norm for me. There are certain sounds I will immediately go to—Mercato Strings and Steelaway Guitar and Harp and SubBass2 out of the hip-hop or techno card—and that's what I work off. I'll have 16 sounds lined up; I might not use all 16, but I want them all lined up. I may have a bunch of synths I never touched before, but I'll sit down and go through every sound and see what new sounds I can use that I've never used before. I'm always going with the mindset of creating a new sound.

Do you normally tweak sounds, or do you just use presets and add effects?

I'll tweak them, but a lot of the presets are so good, it's amazing.

Do you have a variety of drum samples that you've collected over the years?

Yes. I use an [Akai] MPC3000 to trigger the samples, and I layer and layer until I get the sound the way I want it. I did a song on Brandy's album where I had this kick that sounded real good, but I wanted some sub on it, just a short sub to round it off. So I went to my disk with all these [Roland TR-] 808 sounds on it and I reloaded the same kick and truncated it to take off the front of the sample so I got the woof I wanted. Then I tracked both of them together. I was thinking, if I add just the woof and not the whole sample, it may not cancel out what the other kick is doing, because sometimes if you combine two kicks, they cancel each other out. But no,

> *"When you do the drums first, you have to work according to the drums. My focus is the song, so I want the melody first."*

I was wrong, totally wrong—it *completely* cancelled out the other one. Then I put the attack back, and they worked perfectly together. It was the same 808 kick, and that's what messed my mind up; I thought, "this is not a different kick—it's the same kick, I just took the front off of it." It was really weird, but it worked out like that.

One of the characteristics of all of your records is lots of low end. What do you use for your bass sounds?

I used to use the Moog; now I'm into this [Studio Electronics] Omega. I used to use a lot of sub-basses, mixing the bass with a subharmonic synthesizer; now, I'm into the growling old-school synth bass that you mix with the sub. I think my records have good low end, but the top end of them are real cool, too—punchy and clear.

But I'm trying to create *elements* again in music. I feel like music has changed, especially in R&B, which has gone back to being beat-driven. I'm sticking with what I do, and I believe melody rules. It's like, if you watch a movie, you don't want to see things stop and start—you want things to keep going. I want music to be like that.

I give total respect to Dr. Dre because he has element. If you listen to his tracks, his tracks don't move beat-wise, but you hear in and out things all the time; you hear something coming from somewhere, whether it's left side, right side, all the time. It's like, "Whoa, what was that? A helicopter? What was that in the background?" All the time. That's element, and a lot of hip-hip producers don't do that. I think that's why people like him so much—because he actually does do those kind of things.

But when you talk about "element," you're not talking just about sounds, you're talking about musical changes too.

Yeah, key changes, things like that. There was one song I did with Brandy where, in the middle of the song, from out of nowhere, there's a countdown: "4, 3, 2, 1," and I go into a two-step groove for 16 bars, and then I go back into the song. I didn't have to go there—it was a ballad and I could have gone to a normal bridge—but this tells people, "Yes, it's a slow song but let's do something different that no one's done before." Totally different sounds, the drums change, everything changes. But you need to do things to make the transition correct. You can't just go from one kick to another—you have to do something to make it feel like you went into another song and came back. That's why I did the countdown thing for her, so it goes into a dance part for 16 bars, and then we're back into the ballad.

> *"Sometimes, new technology will make you change what you have been doing that is making you sound incredible. You can try something new and it can screw you up."*

You use both hard disk recording and analog tape. Do you make the decision as to which to use on a project by project basis?

I usually do all of the vocals on Pro Tools, though with Michael's album everything was recorded to tape because it made him more comfortable; he's used to that. But it depends on how I want it to sound. I like having things warmer—give me that low end!—so I'll usually track on tape; I still have this thing in my mind of having the tracks come up on the mixing console.

What are your thoughts about Pro Tools?

Well, you have to be careful. Sometimes, new technology will make you change what you have been doing that is making you sound incredible. You can try something new and it can screw you up.

But one thing I like about working in Pro Tools is having all those tracks: I'll do my talking thing and I'll say, "Give me another track and pan it to the left, then put this one to the right." You can play around with it a little bit more in Pro Tools. You can do it on the board, too, but it's easier in Pro Tools for those little tricks. That's what I really use Pro Tools for—for the tricks. Some of the effects we created for Michael's album were incredible. We did a thing on his vocal that made it sound like a machine gun—things that just make you go, "Whoa!"

Do you have any favorite plug-ins?

Autotuning, I guess. [*laughs*] But not on Michael! On everybody else....

How do you make the decision between using a plug-in or analog outboard gear?

I think a lot of engineers stick with Pro Tools effects because they're lazy. They don't want to go down there [*gestures towards rack of outboard gear*] and touch the knobs. With Pro Tools, access is easy—you just move your hand and the effects are right there. So it makes you become a little lazy, and that's the thing I don't like about Pro Tools. I was arguing just the other night about this. I wanted to listen to a song, and the engineer

said, "Oh, it's going to take me a minute because there's too many tracks and I have to dump it down to two-track." It kind of upset me because that's that Pro Tools crap—if you want to pull up a file, you have to go through this, whereas if I want to listen to something here [*gestures towards multitrack tape machine*], I just push a button.

They say Pro Tools is faster. I disagree. Let's be honest about this—you have crashes, you have to wait for stuff to be backed up. If you want to go back and find something, you have to deal with the fact that things need to be restored, or maybe something happened to the file. It's a lot of time for little things, all the time. Pro Tools is good for certain things, but I think it forces you to be sloppy. One of my vocal producers, his name is LaShawn Daniels, he knows Pro Tools so well—and he's an incredible vocal producer, one of the best—but of course this makes him more sloppy. He's not sloppy when you listen back, but he'll let stuff slide because he knows that he can fix it. When he just had tape he had to keep going until he got that perfect take. Now, if the singer falls off a note, or a note is a little sharp, he'll say, "Next track, let's go," and he'll make a mental note to fix it later. But when you're using tape you just work off your brain to make sure it's right. So I think it makes you more lazy.

Are you saying that it's less creative than using tape?

It's creative in its own way; the things you can do are mind-boggling. But what I'm saying is that it will really make you lazy; it will really make you not go for something. It will make you quit quicker because you know you can go and fix it later. So it's a good thing and it's a bad thing.

What was it like collaborating with Michael Jackson?

Oh, it was incredible. He's a perfectionist. He made me step my game up to a different level. It's a whole different thing; you have to really be focused in order to please him. From the day we started, we were always mixing, constantly mixing, even while recording vocals. Even when something sounded perfect, we were mixing again to try to beat it. It was different, because I am so used to doing the track, then adding the vocal, then mixing the song, and then it's over. But we were constantly touching up and going back and doing it over and over until we got it straight.

Was it constantly getting better, or did you reach the point of diminishing returns?

That always happens: "Where's the first mix we did? That's the one—let's try to get that back." To me, the first initial thought is always the best thought because it's raw thinking; you're just putting something up spontaneously and you're going for feel. You aren't trying to perfect it—it's just your first impression of what it might sound like. The first day you do it is always, I think, the best day. A lot of the mixing that I'm doing now is actually from the first day. When I put it up, that's my mix. I'm taking pictures of it on the console and I'm saving things, recalling the first day, and I build off of that—especially with the tracks. With the tracks it's that raw feeling, it's that first, "Whoa—why did I have that triangle so loud?" But there was a reason for it; maybe it gave a different movement in the track. I'm learning more and more about recording and mixing. Before, I never looked at it like that; I would just put it down to tape and then come back another day and mix it. But now it seems my first impressions always sound so much better.

What advice would you give to the reader who wants to be the next Rodney Jerkins?

It's so hard for people not to sell out if you're offered the world. Number one, you've got to mean it. It's about confidence and having faith in your own self, believing that you can do it, that no matter what happens, you can make it if you put your mind to it. There are going to be a lot of times when you go through tribulations, but that's what life is about; life is all about obstacles and getting through those obstacles.

> **"You need to accept who you are."**

It's also important to know what your calling is. You need to know that this music thing is really you, that you have it in your bones so bad you can't sleep at night. A lot of people, they may be led to be a doctor, or something else, but they don't accept it because they want to be a rap artist or they want to be a singer, so they do it for a few years but they never make it. That happens all the time; I've seen it happen to so many people. It's a shame, because they could have been something else. They may swear up and down that they're a singer, but they might not even be able to sing in tune. You need to accept who you are.

Suggested Listening:
Monica (featuring Brandy): *The Boy Is Mine*, Arista, 1998
Destiny's Child: *Say My Name* [single], Columbia, 1999
Mary J. Blige: *Share My World*, MCA, 1997
Whitney Houston: *My Love Is Your Love*, Arista, 1998
Michael Jackson: *Invincible*, Epic, 2001

Toby Wright

Pleasant Metal

They say that opposites attract, and Toby Wright's successful career as producer of some of the fiercest thrash-rock bands around would seem to lend credence to that theory. Easy-going, even-tempered and—well, we have to say it, downright *pleasant*—Wright isn't the kind of guy who would strike you as the in-your-face production and engineering force behind the likes of Alice in Chains, Korn, and Slayer. Wright's equanimity may be ascribed to his varied career, having starting out in the unlikeliest of all roles—as a maintenance engineer, of all things!—at New York's famed Electric Lady before making the move to LA and joining the techno-boffins at Village Recorders before landing at Cherokee.

Eventually tiring of fixing gear, Wright made the improbable transition to assistant engineer, then engineer, and finally producer. During the course of his journey, he's crafted hits for an eclectic group of artists—not just the thrashers he's best known for, but also more nuanced bands like Primus, Fishbone, the Wallflowers, and Third Eye Blind. Wright shared some of his unique recording techniques with us at LA's Record Plant one sultry afternoon during a break in finishing up some mixes.

Your productions tend to feature a lot of dense instrumentation, lots of distorted guitars, and lots of vocals, yet the separation is excellent. How do you achieve that with such thick backing tracks?

Well, [Alice in Chains'] *Jar of Flies* was done in about ten days. It was completely written, arranged, produced, recorded, and mixed in that period of time, and there wasn't a lot of time to think. It was basically, capture those guitars and go. We really didn't even have time to sit down and make a plan. "Set up and let's jam," was our motto.

So you didn't spend a whole lot of time in the recording process focusing on sounds? Was more time spent in the mix process?

No. We just slammed it to tape and slammed the mixes just as fast. I have a motto that if it takes five minutes to record, it should take five minutes to mix. If it doesn't, you're way over-thinking it. It's probably a very simple song if it just took one pass to record; it should be treated the same way when you mix it because that's obviously the intent.

On the other hand, if you spend a lot of time on a song and get out the microscope and get into every little tiny nook and cranny, then you should probably do the same thing when you mix.

> **"If it takes five minutes to record, it should take five minutes to mix."**

That way, it brings out the shine. I've found that, for a lot of the songs that I record and mix, I can go through them pretty quickly. Because I've recorded them, I know how I want to hear it, I pretty much know my vision for the song or the entire album, and I just keep pecking away at that. And as far as getting separation, it's just a matter of getting the tones. I have a few odd, special pieces of gear that I use for certain instruments here and there.

Can you run down a few of them?

Sure. I use a UREI 546 for my guitars. It's an old four-band parametric [equalizer] that has a really crunchy sound. I have Trident A-range modules, ten of them, racked up—I'm probably the only person in the world that has such an array. I'm also a big 1176 fan. I have purple ones, I have a black face, and a silver pre-black face, and every single one of them sounds different.

Have you hot-rodded them at all?

No, I don't really believe in all that hyped-up electronic stuff. I was a maintenance engineer for a long time and I've seen mods go bad.

Are these all guitar toys, or do you use them on other instruments?

I use them on pretty much everything. I don't use a lot of EQ; when I'm recording, I use mostly mic placement, dating back to the old school. I listen to the source carefully and then if I like what the source sounds like, I like to get that to come out of the speakers as well, so it sounds really close, if not better, in the control room.

> *"I don't overcompensate when I record . . . I record exactly what I want to hear."*

The problem is, if you go for a monster guitar sound every time, it's going to get pretty crowded in that little song if you also have big monster drums and monster bass. If everything's monster tone, you're not necessarily going to have a monster-sounding record; you're going to have a compressed, small-sounding record.

Plus it's going to be very hard for the vocal to sit on top of that track.

It sure is. Sometimes band members will say, "Hey, solo up my so-and-so," and it kind of sounds shitty to them in solo, but when you drop it in the track, sometimes it complements everything around it, and that's pretty much what I'm looking for. It doesn't matter what it sounds like in solo to me—it can sound like the weirdest thing on earth; as long as it fits and complements the track and what's going on around it, it's there to stay.

Obviously, the signal is passing through lots of tubes. Are you an analog guy, are you a digital guy, or are you both?

I guess I would be a "digilog" guy. I capture things on analog initially but I'll dump it into Pro Tools to preserve the sound, because, as all of us analog freaks know, once you run the tape over the heads five times, your sound is gone. Remember that sound you once fought with the guitar player over a third of a dB at 3k? The point is moot because it's now gone! So I use Pro Tools to save the sound, and then I'll edit it, push it around, clean it up a bit, and then spit out the drums and the bass, and any low end type of stuff back onto fresh tape before I mix, but I'll keep the vocals and the guitars coming digital out of Pro Tools. It keeps the crispness so that the original sound you've recorded makes it to your mix. I did one project completely in Pro Tools and it sounded thin and silly; it didn't have any balls at all, and I was not very happy with it. I don't know any digital medium at this point in time that can replicate warm music. It just doesn't happen, to my ear.

How are you getting from your rack into Pro Tools? Are you using stock A/D converters?

Just stock converters. I did a test a long time ago: I bought a 16-bit system and put it up against some drums I had recorded on tape, and I could tell the difference, so I got rid of it. I did the same thing when 24-bit came out, and I couldn't tell the difference, so now I own a 24-bit

system. I can't tell the difference; it doesn't matter after that. There are a lot of tech people that will tell you I'm wrong, but my ears don't lie to me. What I hear is what I hear, and I think that at the end of the day, the consumer can't hear the difference.

They *can* hear the difference, however, between an all-digital recording and a mixed recording. I can hear it on the radio quite well. Compression grabs digital on the radio in a very strange way—it's got a weird top end, even coming over a radio speaker, it's just strange, it's pointed. It's just not right, not pleasing to my ear, anyway.

That's probably because the transients are different.

Yeah, it's a strange thing. But analog tape will warm things up, though it can still be really crisp and clean on the top end. I don't overcompensate when I record, though; I record exactly what I want to hear.

So the basic signal chain is good mic positioning, rack of tube vintage gear, then to tape, and then Pro Tools...

Yeah, everything goes to tape. Sometimes I'll use that tape compression, and sometimes I'll hit it a little lighter and I'll just capture it. Generation loss, to me, just doesn't matter. I work at 30 IPS, +5, non-Dolby. Traditional.

Do you use plug-ins much?

Yeah, but mostly for effects. I don't use a lot of compression, but if it calls for it and I can get what I want with a plug-in compressor, I'll definitely put it on there. I'm not afraid to use anything, but I don't use things that I don't need. I'm a minimalist, I guess.

How do you decide whether to use an analog processor while you're still in the analog domain versus using plug-in processing?

It depends on what I'm hearing. If I just need a simple delay, I'll probably take it from an outboard source. But if I'm after something that's a little bit more insane or off-the-wall than I can get with normal outboard gear, I'll twist it up with a plug-in, because plug-ins can be a lot more drastic.

From what I've experienced thus far, I can twist sounds and make them more unreal in the digital domain than I can in the analog world; it just adds some weirdness. A reverb is usually a little smoother in the analog world than it is in the digital world. But for effects—flanging and ring modulating and all that kind of stuff—you can get a little more drastic in the digital world.

After you've done your editing and plug-in work, do you go back out again from Pro Tools to tape?

When I mix, yes. I'll take a rough mix out of Pro Tools as a starting point, but then I'll dump drums and bass to tape. Sometimes I'll use 16-track, sometimes I'll use 24-track.

So you don't dump all the tracks to tape, just the ones that need warming up?

That's right. I'll put the drums and bass back where they belong, on analog, and sometimes vocals, depending on how they're cut, depending on the DSP power of my computer. If I have eight tracks of vocals and I'm autotuning all of them, I'm going to print them to tape so that I can have the DSP power to help me out if I need a ring modulator on a guitar, for instance. I then send the signal into an analog console.

Is the final mix to half-inch?

Half inch, 30 IPS, ATR 104/102, always, and again at +5; I don't hit it too hard. I back up on Pro Tools, but I never use the digital mixes. Every time, the analog wins. Never had any kind of digital device win. And I've been through pretty much all of them.

With this recording technique, is there any kind of problem with tape hiss buildup? Because it sounds like some tracks are third-generation by the time you get to the mix.

Well, digital, to my ear, doesn't count as a generation. If I go off of tape to digital and then go back to a piece of tape, it's the same exact sound, so it's not a generation loss.

I gather you're not slamming the tape very much, though.

Not really. Sometimes I do for an effect, for the compression. But I'm pretty conservative. If I record a drum kit, for instance, and I really want the kick drum to be compressed, I'll compress it outside and then I'll slam it to tape and get that extra boom going on. Then I'll reduce it when it comes into Pro Tools 'cause it's usually too hot. I'll make it so the meter doesn't move, ever. The song starts, the meter moves, the song ends. [*laughs*] That's the last time it moves.

That's something that some engineers talk about with some degree of despair, but I suppose those are the demands of modern recording today.

Back in the days when I was a maintenance engineer at Cherokee, Roy Thomas Baker was working on a Cars record—*Candy-O*, I believe it was—and he owned a 40-track Stevens machine, two-inch. We called it the cricket machine, because all you heard was [*makes cricket noise*] and that was the sound of his meters bouncing off their stops, and if he didn't hear that, it wasn't good enough. So he got me into that train of thought a long time ago, and I guess when you learn from those who are considered the best, you tend to follow in their footsteps.

I don't believe in having all the songs on an album sound the same. I like to take one song at a time, build it until it's completed, and then sit back and listen to it and say, "Okay, I like where that's going, I like the vision that that song creates, I like where that takes me." Then I'll move on to the next song. There are certain records out there that use the same sounds from top to bottom, and they sound like one long song. Boring. I don't care who you are or who the band is, it's boring.

I like the listener to stay interested. It's my own personal thing: I get bored easily and can't even make it through a 400-page book! [*laughs*]

Does that extend to things like mic selection and placement? Would you re-mic the same drum kit for different songs?

Absolutely. On one album, I moved the drums six times in 14 songs and even changed out mics here and there. Some things stayed the same, some things didn't. I also used a few different vocal mics, depending on the song, depending on what I was after. Same thing with guitar mics: I used tons of different equipment. The guitar player came with one guitar, one cabinet, and we probably rented about $50,000 worth of gear because you can't do a record with one guitar and one cabinet. Well, you can, but it's not going to have a lot of variation in it.

You're the first person I've interviewed who made the transition from maintenance engineer to successful producer.

I don't think there are many. It's taken a long time; it's been about 20 years. But when it comes to physics and the properties of sound, and how sound travels and what instruments do and how their sound resonates, it's all very, very useful information. I can look at a guitar and pretty much tell you where is going to be the best place to mic that guitar after hearing it strummed once; it's all physics. And if you've got a little electronics background, you can figure out how things work under their specifications and then you can learn to push them even harder if you need to, and what they do when they're pushed harder, so you don't blow stuff up. [*laughs*]

It's real easy to blow stuff up, you know. I've seen people literally smoke modules and catch consoles on fire just because they had no idea what they were doing. I would love to see more engineers come up through the maintenance department.

Most people who want to be engineers don't gravitate to the maintenance department; they'll start as a runner or assistant.

Yeah runner, then assistant, and then go to engineer, but then you have really no background on how a Pultec works: why does it sound so sweet and why does this digital EQ sounds like shit?

But do you really need to know how to fix gear in order to understand that?

No, I don't think so. I just chose that path. I needed to know how to operate gear better than an engineer did, because if I walked into a room and there was a problem, I had to be able to solve that problem.

Some engineers know just enough to be dangerous. I was doing a demo about ten years ago in a little project studio and I asked the guy who was aligning the two-track machine, "When's the last time the azimuth was checked on that machine?" and he said "Oh, the azimuth? The azimuth is *great* in this room." [*laughs*] I got in my car and left.

I'll never forget that as long as I live. Obviously he had no idea what he was talking about, yet he called himself a producer. Very interesting.

I would imagine that tech engineers quake when they hear you're coming in to do a session at their studio, because they know that they're going to have to deliver.

Yeah, some do. Some get awfully mad at me, because I can't work under circumstances when I have no reference. I'll pretty much work anywhere, but technically it's got to be pretty close to correct. I can work around certain things, but if the monitors sound like shit and that's your reference, how are you going to tell what you're actually doing? My traveling reference is [Yamaha] NS10s, so I bring my CDs with me in a little CD player and plug it in and I know, "Okay, if it sounds like that, that's right." I can tell when NS10 woofers are worn and when they've been beat up by the client before me. A lot of people can't hear that; they haven't trained themselves to hear like that.

When I was at Cherokee, one of my fortés was monitors. I used to go in and tune the rooms and hear exactly what 3k sounds like. You know when you're EQing something and you think, "Oh, that needs a little dip at 2.5k"? Well, how do you know it's 2.5k? I've trained my ears to tell me it's 2.5k.

There are a lot of people who don't even know what phase is. You walk into somebody's house and they say, "Man! I don't have any bottom end on my speakers, what's going on?" I'll be saying, "Whoa, shit, I'm getting dizzy now, I'm going to throw up, you're out of phase." They say, "How do you know that?" "Well, put your face right here, don't move...hear that?" "Yeah, it's coming from all over the place." Then I ask them, "Where's the kick drum? Where's the bass?" "Well, I don't know...." Then you switch polarity, get it in phase, and then all of a sudden it's smaller, and then there's the kick drum and the bass in the center. "Ahh!" But a lot of people—unfortunately, even some engineers—have no concept of the difference.

What's the craziest studio trick you've ever tried that made it on to record?

Recording guitar through a fan. [*laughs*] I was doing the Korn *Follow the Leader* record, and we were looking for some weird, wobbly sound; that whole record is pretty much based on experimentation. I was messing around out in the live room with a little Pignose amp and I laid it on its back and there was a fan in the room going at half speed, so I put it on top of that, and I put one mic right down in it so you hear the sound of the fan. That's one of the guitar sounds on the record; I don't exactly remember which song, but it is one of the focal point sounds on that song. That one surprised me; it just worked.

> *"Never think you know everything; the minute you do, you don't."*

I notice that on the Alice in Chains track "Shame in You" you managed to do what a lot of engineers have told me they'd love to have the guts to do but never actually did, and that's putting the kick drum on one side.

Yeah.

Was that planned or an accident?

Planned, for sure. You know, "The whole record sounds like this, so let's make this song sound different." How? Well, it sounded exactly the same as every other song, so we decided panning was the best way.

It works because the kick drum pattern is so sparse, it's almost like another floor tom.

Exactly, that had a lot to do with it. I couldn't do it on a speed metal song—it just wouldn't be right; you wouldn't be able to distinguish anything!

Any final advice for our readers?

Just learn as much as you can. Never think you know everything; the minute you do, you don't.

Selected Listening:
Alice in Chains: *Jar of Flies*, Columbia, 1994; *Alice in Chains*, Columbia, 1995; *MTV Unplugged*, Legacy, 1996
Korn: *Follow the Leader*, Epic, 1998
Slayer: *Divine Intervention*, American, 1994; *Soundtrack to the Apocalypse*, American, 2003
Primus: *Rhinoplasty*, Interscope, 1998
Soulfly: *Primitive*, Roadrunner, 2000

Michael Bradford

Chunky Styling

As Mel Brooks once observed, it's good to be the king. In the sometimes fickle world of the music business, the line of royalty shifts from time to time, but it's gratifying to know that true talents like Michael Bradford can not only attain the heights of commercial success, but deal with it with equal doses of equanimity and poise.

Bradford is a producer, engineer, musician, and songwriter extraordinaire who was an integral part of the success of Kid Rock's multiplatinum *The History of Rock*, as well as Uncle Kracker's hit "Follow Me" (from the *Double Wide* album). His empathy behind the board stems, no doubt, from his long apprenticeship as a multi-instrumentalist sideman, playing everything from bass (his main axe) to guitar to keyboards and drum programming. He's toured extensively with a broad range of artists, from reggae's Heptones to jazz guitarists Earl Klugh and Grant Green, to R&B artists like Anita Baker, filling in the gaps between tours honing his craft in the recording studios of his native Detroit. It was there that he began assisting for Bob Seger's engineer Gerard Smerek, jumping on the Pro Tools bandwagon long before it was fashionable and learning how to tame the demons of digital recording.

Inevitably for a man of such talent, it wasn't long before the friendly confines of Detroit became too limiting, and Bradford made his move to the City Of Angels, where he quickly developed a reputation as one of the town's top programmers. His skills landed him a gig with legendary arranger Paul Buckmaster [Elton John], with whom he has collaborated on several movie soundtracks. The friendly, outgoing Bradford also soon developed working relationships with Terence Trent D'arby, Run-DMC, Madonna, Meredith Brooks, Youngstown, and with New Radicals' founder Gregg Alexander, as well as releasing solo material under his pseudonym Chunky Style.

We met up with Bradford in his studio in beautiful downtown Burbank (bet you haven't heard *that* phrase for awhile!), where we had a most enjoyable chat about his approach towards crafting hit records—a refreshing mix of old-school values and new technology tools.

What's your typical signal chain when recording bass?

Well, bass is my first instrument; it's the most natural instrument for me, so I take a lot of care in recording it, though the signal chain varies. My touring bass amp, which I use a lot in the studio now, is called the Mo'Bass, by SWR. It provides a complete signal chain, including a tube preamp, an analog Moog-style filter for auto-wah effects, analog distortion, parametric EQ, and a subsonic generator. It can also operate in a dual mode so that one channel is clean, while the other channel has effects. This is very valuable when I want distortion, but still need a full low end. I also have an 8 × 10 cabinet that can be split as well. I often go direct, but if I use the cabinet, I tend to mic it with an [Electro-Voice] RE20 or a [Sennheiser] 421.

Another thing I've been using is the Line 6 Bass POD, and my usual chain then is just to go from the bass straight into that and then take either a digital or analog output and record it into Pro Tools. If I'm in a studio where there's a console and a more standard signal chain, I'll tend to run it through something like an Avalon DI. I don't really use a lot of external gear for processing things because I think basses sound pretty good the way they are, and the more boxes you run things through—well, I don't know that it really helps the sound as much as it's just more stuff to write down! [*laughs*]

I've had to make records in all kinds of conditions that were pretty primitive—*The History of Rock* was recorded on our tour bus; Uncle Kracker's record was also done on a bus. I've recorded stuff in some pretty unusual places, places where I didn't have the benefit of a large format console and 30 pieces of outboard gear, and they still sold millions of records. I've reached the conclusion that although it's good to have a lot of gear for options, I think sometimes engineers make the mistake of piling stuff on to make a more impressive looking pile, rather than to make a better sound. It's hard to improve on a P-Bass or a good Washburn bass, or any of the good basses that have active electronics in them. Put it through a nice preamp, or, if you want a chorus or distortion, or compression on top of whatever tone the bass happens to have, use the Bass POD and chances are you're going to get a fairly good sound.

> **"Sometimes engineers make the mistake of piling stuff on to make a more impressive looking pile, rather than to make a better sound."**

So you don't use the DI signal from the Bass POD—just the processed output?

I use the processed output. If I'm going to use the POD, it's because of the sound that it makes. I don't really want to use it as just a volume booster; if that were the case, I'd just use whatever preamp is available.

You don't take the DI signal as well, just to give yourself the option later?

I don't believe in options. I'm radical that way. I don't like options, because they just mean you take more time. I've been in this business for 20 years, and when I started out, you didn't have nearly as many tracks to work with as you have now, and you had to make decisions—you had to say, "this is what I want it to sound like," and you went from there. You didn't cut three tracks of bass—one clean, one processed, one DI—and then decide five years from now which you want to use. It just takes too long. If you can imagine a sound in your head, that's what you should be going for from the beginning. I think the reason a lot of records sound so generic now is that everybody has too many options, so they never made a decision to begin with. I'd rather make a decision up front.

Back to the old school.

Yeah, I guess so. I'll give you an example: I did some Pro Tools work on the New Radicals album, and Gregg [Alexander] recorded a lot of tracks, lots of slave reels and alternate takes. It took a long time to edit all that into something usable—Gregg knew what he wanted, but each thing was on a different reel, and it was a big assembly process. A lot of stuff was recorded because there was the option to do so, but he probably would have gotten to the same end point anyway without all those extra tracks. Fine, that's his method, and that's what he likes to do, but, for me, I'd rather just decide how I'm going to do it in the first place.

Obviously, your point of view is valid, because you're making hit records. But the flip side is that it gives you a lot less leeway in the mix.

Yes, it gives you less leeway in the mix, and I don't think that's a bad thing. It's like if you have a band and there's a bass guitar player, a drummer, a guitarist, and a pianist, that's your rhythm section. You don't say, "Well, let's get five different bass players and three different drummers." You say, "This is the rhythm section." I think that the recording should be treated the same way: this is the sound, this is what we're going for, now let's get that sound.

If you can't imagine a sound, then you're really just on a search-and-destroy mission—sort of an experimental, exploratory surgery kind of thing—and so you're just hoping you'll come up with something. Then you'll either have a good accident or a bad accident—but you're going to have an accident. If, on the other hand, you've rehearsed with the band, you've thought about how it's going to go, you've tried some ideas out, and you've made a decision, I think it's a lot easier, because then you're going for a particular target. The best records—the ones that you're going to want to listen to 20 years later—are the ones where people made decisions, where they were going for a certain sound,

and they weren't trying to be so all-things-to-all-people. Those kinds of records might be popular for a short time, but no one wants to listen to them later.

You said that *The History of Rock* was recorded on a tour bus, but it has a lot of really well-recorded live drums.

There are lot of live drums, but a lot of them were cut in a little studio in Detroit after the fact. We would use a drum machine to get beats going, and then we'd do overdubs in Pro Tools, stacking up guitars and things like that. Even though we went into a little studio and added live drums later, the drums you hear on the record were heavily edited—they were put back into the computer and shifted around. So there are tracks where the performance of the drums doesn't bear a lot of resemblance to the way they were originally played. There are certain songs where, for example, I took a fill that I liked and stuck it somewhere else, or a song could have used something at the end that it didn't have, and since I had all these drums I could move them around and drop them where I wanted them. Also, some of the live drums were cut in the arena during a soundcheck, where I would have the drummer just play individual drums, and I would later make samples out of them. That way, when you listen back, you're actually hearing the sound of live drums, but they're being played like samples. So it's a combination of sounds—some of them are the complete performance of a live drummer, while others are the sounds of a live drummer, but sampled and played back either through an [Akai] MPC or a sampler, and then some of them are the original performances, but heavily edited.

The History of Rock has such a broad range of sounds. In every instance, were you working towards a specific sonic goal? Was each track really conceived beforehand, or was this one of those grand experiments you were talking about earlier?

I can't say they were entirely conceived beforehand, but to a degree they were. A lot of the songs on *The History of Rock* are re-cuts of older songs that Kid Rock had put out on his indie records. On some of the songs, we used the original masters and then overdubbed onto them; on other songs, we just made completely new recordings because he wanted them to sound as good as they could sound today. If that meant cutting them over, re-cutting a vocal, re-cutting the whole song, or rearranging the song, then that's the way it was.

It was actually pretty easy to get the sounds because, even though it's a pretty diverse record stylistically, sonically the band is what it is. Also, because Kid Rock and I played a lot of the guitar on the record, we already sound the way we sound. Using different effects is one thing, but the basic approach to the way you play doesn't change.

There's one song on there called "My Oedipus Complex," where we had our guitar player [Kenny Olson] play most of the rock guitar parts, but I was thinking in my head of the old Led Zeppelin records where it was like 30 tracks of guitars, really stacked, all playing the same riff. So I already knew how I wanted it to sound—I thought this would be great if it sounded like a stack of guitars, so that's what I did.

So you literally overdubbed the guitar multiple times?

That's what we did—eight tracks of the same riff, to really stack them up. Again, if you already know what you want it to sound like, then how you go about getting the sound is almost elementary. If you know you want it to sound really thick, then you know the way to do it is to have the guitarist play it several times. You can't use delay for that, because then they're all going to be exactly the same, unless you start putting an LFO on your delay, and then you start getting a phase thing, which is not really the same as real live multitracking. On a lot of *The History of Rock* engineering-wise, I took cues from classics like "Whole Lot of Love," "Are You Experienced"—records that were very innovative. Over time, you learn those techniques, and I've learned how to apply similar techniques in Pro Tools. I'm not going to take a reel of tape and turn it upside down to get a backwards reverb, but I can get the same effect in Pro Tools, plus it's a lot quicker, and I can make it very precise. If I want that trail to be exactly two and a half seconds long, then that's how long it's going to be.

Do you rely heavily on plug-ins for processing?

Yeah. I don't believe in outboard gear for processing. [*laughs*] No, I should take that back: I love outboard processing, but I don't believe in documenting patch bays, I don't believe in writing settings down. Plus, to me, the plug-ins in Pro Tools are very musical sounding, now that we're at 24-bit, and they're very versatile, and I can automate them. It's always nice to have a big, shiny rack of effects, but I'm having a hard time saying that they really sound that much better.

Even things like analog compressors and equalizers?

Analog compressors and EQs do sound really nice, and they're really good on the input of a signal chain. If I had all the time in the world and three assistants, I might use them more, but I don't. If I'm at a studio that has all that stuff and I can use it, I probably will, but mostly on the input chain, directly into the tape machine. For instance, I might put a bass through a Fairchild or an LA-2A, and then I might put it through a Neve EQ, and then I'll go directly into the tape machine, as opposed to through the console. On the other hand, if I had to overdub that same bass six months from now, I'd have to know how that stuff was set—I'd have to document that.

Now some people are going to say, "That's all part of being an engineer." Well, it is, but if you're in a different studio, even if they've got the same gear—even if it's all the same model number but you didn't know that they did a special tweak back in the shop—all this stuff changes. These days, I like the consistency that I get from a digital audio workstation. I know that it's going to be the same way next time, and, to me, that's more valuable than some of the esoteric benefits of using classic outboard gear.

> "My favorite mic technique is, first, picking a studio with a decent-sounding room—you'll save a lot of time and money in the long run!"

Do you have any special drum miking techniques?

I use fewer mics than a lot of people do. I like to use a kick, a snare, a couple of overheads, and a couple of room mics, but I don't like to very closely mic every individual drum, I don't like to put a mic on top and bottom of the toms, and I don't use X-Y or other fancy patterns. I think that a lot of people over-mic drums just because they can. The best sounding drums are pretty much the sound of the drums in the room. My favorite mic technique is, first, picking a studio with a decent-sounding room—you'll save a lot of time and money in the long run! [*laughs*] I think the main reason that big production recording studios are never really going to go out of business is that they have great-sounding rooms. And sometimes you need a great-sounding room and there's no way around it. You need the special floors, the special mass in the rooms, the ceiling height, plus if you've got a great-sounding room, you don't need as many microphones or other things to get the sound. So I say, if you want great-sounding drums, get a good-sounding room and tune your drums and get all the squeaks and noises out of everything. *Then* you can worry about microphones, and you'll find that you don't need as many of them.

What drum mics do you use?

Lately I've been using a lot of CAD mics. They've got a set that's designed pretty much for drums—dynamic mics for the toms and kick, and some really nice condensers—similar to the AKG 414—that work really well as overhead mics. For room mics, I'm at the mercy of whatever the studio has, but if they have some Coles ribbon mics hanging around, I love using those. If they have an [Electro-Voice] RE20, I love using that for a floor tom mic. If they've got a [Sennheiser] 421, I don't mind using that as an alternative kick drum mic. If they've got a [Tele-funken] 251, that can be handy sometimes if you really need a lot of sizzle. But, generally speaking, I'll tend to use dynamic mics up close and ribbon mics for room mics.

Do you use the tried-and-true [Shure] 57 on the snare?

Well, it's a great sledge-hammer; it can take anything and you can't hurt it too much. But it's not my mic of choice—instead, I've been using the CAD TSM411. It's a small dynamic mic and it's really good for use up close—you can beat the hell out of them, and they don't die. 57s work great, too, though. There's a larger mic that CAD makes called the KBM412, and that's a nice kick drum mic.

What's your technique for recording guitar?

I use the guitar POD a lot, because the effects are so good. If I'm miking an amp, I'll tend to use a combination of a 57 up close and maybe a [Neumann] U 47 for the room—if there's a room. The real problem with recording guitars is the same problem with recording drums: if you don't have a good room to record them in, you may as well just go direct and add ambience in later. Because what's the point of getting the sound of a concrete wall room? I recently had to record something in Texas, where the place happened to be basically just a cinderblock room, and so I ended up having to do the ambience after the fact because there was almost no point in recording the room—the kick drum sounded like a basketball. So how you record depends on what you've got to work with, room-wise.

What are your microphones of choice for vocals?

I'm going to sound like a CAD advertisement, but they had this mic called the VX2; it's got two tubes and variable patterns, and it's one of the best-sounding mics I've ever used for vocals. Interestingly, if someone's got a thin voice, sometimes I've found that a thinner mic like a 414 can actually work for them. A lot of people would go the other way, with a heavier duty mic like a Neumann or something, but sometimes, with a reedy voice, something like a 414 captures the reediness—if you're trying to capture them as they sound. Now if you're trying to change them or make them fuller than they really are, that's a different proposition.

> *"If someone's got a thin voice, sometimes . . . a thinner mic . . . can actually work for them."*

Another vocal mic that I've used a lot is the [Shure] SM7. I learned about that years ago when I was an assistant engineer working with Gerard Smerek, who recorded Bob Seger and Anita Baker. It's a dynamic mic, so it's got the punch and the impact handling capability of the 57, but, to me, it's a far superior-sounding microphone; it's got lower noise, it's just better all around. It's just about my favorite vocal mic if you have a powerful voice. When we cut *The History of Rock*, I used the SM7 on Kid Rock's voice most of the time. I also used it on Uncle Kracker, on Anita Baker, on Bob Seger, on a lot of different singers—that shows you how versatile it is.

Since you believe in making decisions early on, I'm guessing that you may not spend as much time on a mix as some other people do.

Yeah, if I get a good recording, I find that I don't have to spend as much time mixing it. In fact, I really try hard to make it sound good even *before* we start recording by working on the arrangement of the song. Even if I'm going to be the producer who plays all the instruments—I do a lot of that, too, whether it's all MIDI or whether I'm playing all the guitars and basses—I'm going to work out an arrangement for the song. It's not going to be like all this stuff is playing all the way through, and then the mixer has to do the arrangement by muting things. I want the song to be arranged beforehand. Paul Buckmaster, who's the arranger for Elton John, is a very good friend of mine, and I've learned a lot about arranging from him. When you arrange songs beforehand and you record them that way, you find that a lot of the time that it takes to mix goes away. Between having a lot of good sounds in the first place and having arranged the song, suddenly a lot of that Mute stuff is gone—you don't have to worry about that anymore. Plus a lot of the balances become less crucial, because when everything sounds good, things can blend a lot more smoothly, as opposed to having to do radical EQing and filtering just to make things cut through. Some of my mixes can be pretty complicated, because a lot of the sounds are heavily processed, but that sort of straddles the line between production and mixing.

Because of all this planning, do you find you use fewer tracks than other people?

Well, because of the computer, I'll have a ton of tracks, but that's because of the arrangements. For example, if I want a guitar to jump from left to right in a 16th note pattern, I'll set up that same guitar on two tracks and then I'll just chop them into pieces and leave the faders up so the tracks will play left-right-left-right, as opposed to having a panner go left-right-left-right and use up all that DSP. So I'll use up more tracks in that regard just because I'm laying things out visually the way I want them to happen, but I'm not using a lot of tracks in terms of recording a lot of instruments per se—though I might have the same instrument spread out amongst several tracks so that things can happen to them differently on each track.

Do you tend to set up a handful of effects that multiple tracks will feed or do you prefer to assign discrete effects to each track?

For vocals and things like that, I will tend to bus them to a stereo bus and then put the effects on that bus—for instance, a compressor, a reverb, and then an Aural Exciter; that might be my vocal chain. I'll end up having all those things going through a bus so that I don't have to replicate the same chain on every channel. Plus, it saves DSP.

It's interesting that you would place the Aural Exciter *after* the reverb in that chain.

I like sizzle, and I like the reverb to have sizzle, too. If you put the Aural Exciter before the reverb, you get the brightness, but you don't get the reverb excited, and I want the reverb to be as sibilant and as brilliant and shiny as everything else, so I tend to put the Exciter at the end of the chain.

How long do you typically spend on a mix?

Usually a day, two days at the most. If I've started the song from the beginning and I'm not just mixing someone else's song, it's usually pretty much mixed even before I get to the mix stage, because I'm working towards a goal all the way along. But if it's someone else's song that I'm just getting to do a mix or a remix on, then it takes a couple of days because the first day I'm just getting a perspective; I make a CD and listen to it in the car, and then I sleep on it. Then the next day I go for the fine-tuning. It really depends on how good the recording was in the first place, and also if the original recording needs a lot of excitement to happen.

For example, I did a mix for a rock band for their single recently. Even though the album version was already produced and mixed, the label asked me to do a new mix of this one song for radio. But I found that the original recording was kind of bland, so I ended up doing a lot of extra things to it—processing, even adding a few new parts by overdubbing—so that it would sound more interesting on the radio. That took some time, because first I had to get used to what they had already recorded, and then I had to figure out what to add to it.

A lot of engineers tend to specialize, but you have been able to work successfully in a lot of different musical genres. Why do you think that is?

I think it's because I just treat it all like music. Maybe it's because I'm from Detroit and I came up during a time of what they used to call free-form radio, where a DJ would play Miles Davis, then he'd play Santana, and then he'd play Alice Cooper. Back in the "good old days" when we still used steam-powered amplifiers [*laughs*], you could listen to a radio station and hear a lot of different music without having to change the channel. So I grew up thinking, "Well, that's all music"—sort of like in England, where they call it all pop music, whether it's the New York Dolls or Metallica or the Spice Girls; they don't break it down into R&B, rock 'n' roll, all these various genres. Maybe that's because there aren't so many radio stations there and they don't have these programmers who program 50 stations at once, so they play a lot of stuff. Similarly, my upbringing is that it's all just music—I don't really think of it in terms of style.

But do you take different approaches technically to different kinds of music?

Well, sure. If I'm recording something jazzy, I'll take more of an ambient approach generally, because you don't want just the sound of the instrument, you want the sound of the instrument reacting to the room. If you're recording industrial music, you want something extremely direct and in your face, because that's the whole point of the music. If it's an R&B record of the Anita Baker type, then you want it to sound very musical and played; if it's going to be an R&B record of the hip-hop type, then you want it to sound very upfront, in your face, obviously very technical, obviously very drum machine, obviously very synth-based, as opposed to, "maybe that's a real bass."

What's really cool to me is what Dr. Dre's been doing, because he's been using a lot of classic R&B-type music on his hip-hop tracks, and I'm a big fan of that. Maybe the other reason why I'm so versatile is that I've played so many different kinds of music as a musician, so I know how it all is really supposed to sound.

That's probably also why you were such a good match with Kid Rock.

I agree; we're basically a mirror image of each other. I was the kid from the ghetto who liked rock 'n' roll, and he was the kid from out in the sticks who liked hip-hop. We were sort of looking over the fence at each other; I was saying, "I like what you guys do" and he was saying, "Well, I like what you guys do." Also, when you're from Detroit, there's no one to tell you you can't. In LA and New York, there are a lot of rules: "I need a left-handed red-haired guitar player." In Detroit, it's just, "Well, he plays guitar. And drums. And he happens to noodle on the piano too." In LA, it's hard to find a lot of really good versatile people because they're not allowed to be versatile; there seem to be a lot of "rules" out here.

Is that true in Nashville, too?

You know, Nashville is very open because they just like songs. I really love Nashville, because there, they never talk about bands, they never talk about singers—they never talk about anything but songs. I go down there from time to time to write songs with other people and to fool around with ideas, and you'll be in a restaurant and if someone walks in who's a singer, okay, he's a singer. But if someone walks in that wrote a hit song, or if he's the publisher—that's the guy that they respect, and that's really cool.

If you want to boil all of this down to one thing, it's all about the song. If you've got a good song, then you can do something; otherwise, we've got a lot of work to do. And so, if it takes a long time to make a record, chances are the song wasn't that good, the recording wasn't that good, there were a lot of problems. But if you start with a really good piece of music and you arrange it and work it out, then the rest of it's fairly easy. All you need is a song.

Suggested Listening:
Kid Rock: *History of Rock*, Lava, 2000
Uncle Kracker: *Double Wide*, Lava, 2000; *No Stranger to Shame*, Lava, 2002
The New Radicals: *Maybe You've Been Brainwashed Too*, MCA, 1998
Butthole Surfers: *Weird Revolution*, Hollywood, 2001
Deep Purple: *Bananas*, EMI/Sanctuary, 2003; *Rapture of the Deep*, Eagle, 2005

Rafa Sardina

Covering the Latin Market

The Latin influence on American popular music runs long and deep. From Ritchie Valens to Jose Feliciano, from Carlos Santana to Los Lobos, from Gloria Estefan to Jennifer Lopez, from Julio Iglesias to Ricky Martin, Latin artists have played a vital role throughout the years.

Today's standard-bearers—artists like international phenomenon Luis Miguel and Alejandro Sanz (who has dominated the Latin Grammys since their inception eight years ago)—continue to break new ground. They also have one thing in common: the passion and commitment of ace recording engineer Rafa Sardina.

Sardina has been at the heart of popular Latin music for more than a decade. Born in Spain, he started his career doing live sound for local rock bands, but after a move to Los Angeles, landed an internship at Hollywood's fabled Ocean Way, where he apprenticed under studio owner/veteran engineer Allen Sides. As he quickly rose through the ranks, Sardina gained valuable experience working with artists like Dr. Dre, Dru Hill, Macy Gray, and Rod Stewart. It was there that he also first met Miguel, beginning a longtime collaboration that has yielded eight platinum albums to date.

A longtime aficionado of analog recording, Sardina made the reluctant transition to digital recording only recently. ("It's not a matter of preference, it's a matter of accommodation," he says, adding, somewhat wistfully, "these are just different times.") We talked with the affable 11-time Grammy winner (including Sanz's *El Tren De Los Momentos*, named the 2008 Best Latin Pop Album) at LA's famed Record Plant, where he now spends most of his working days when not ensconced in his new state-of-the art Pro Tools–/SSL-equipped home studio, After Hours.

Is there a qualitative difference in the sound of the records you mix for Latin audiences versus the records you mix for American audiences?

Not any more. There are some subtle differences within the different styles of Latin music, but there's really no difference sonically between the standard Latin rock or pop sound and the U.S. sound.

In the past, there has been a difference; there was that trademark Latin sound back in the '80s and the '90s, where you used lots of reverb and made everything super-large, with the vocals really up front with lots of effects on them. I guess some people still have that nostalgia for the old sound, but these days there is no difference, at least with the projects I get involved in. I think the Latin market is really following the taste of American music for the most part; of course, there is some completely original Latin music too, but that's a completely different world. By the same token, there is so much modern music in the Latin world that emulates or is in the same league as American music.

PHOTO BY ED FREEMAN (WWW.RAFASARDINA.COM)

Does the Latin market listen to a lot of American music?

Yes, especially these days with globalization. When I was growing up in Spain, we listened to a lot of local music, and a lot of music from Europe, especially England—we were hugely influenced by the British sound. There was this whole underground movement of buying and trading vinyl, listening to music other than what you would hear on radio. But these days, everybody listens to the same thing all over the world; you travel anywhere and you'll hear pretty much the same top 40 hits. It's weird—you go to Spain and you think you're in LA! Other than the local bands, the rest of the playlist is pretty much the same people that chart here.

You used to be a big analog tape guy, but now you seem to be working almost exclusively in Pro Tools. What are your reasons for making that change?

The whole industry has been forced to make that transition—it's not just a matter of preference or choice anymore, it's been unavoidable. It's a matter of accommodation, mostly. Digital has so many advantages over analog, anyway, in terms of workflow and what you can actually do or not have to do to accomplish the final result. I was actually recording to tape up until a few years ago, but since then I haven't done a project that way, other than a few isolated string dates.

Another problem is that people are not willing to pay the extra expense. They're not willing to pay for tape, or for all the extra hours you spend every day rewinding and fast-forwarding. These are just different times.

Do you try to get a lot of analog in the signal chain?

I work with a lot of analog gear, old and new. I especially love a lot of the newer tube products. I think most of today's engineers have learned to achieve a similar result, or at least as close to what we have in our heads, without using tape. Many of the things that we used to do in analog, we don't do anymore. For example, we used to equalize the top end of some instruments quite a bit during the tracking process to compensate for some of the loss that you might have. The first few times I had to do entire projects digitally I freaked out a little because the difference was so huge, especially back then with the kind of converters we had. But over time you learn to compensate.

What do you think of plug-ins that attempt to emulate vintage analog gear?

Well, one of the problems is, how do you model extremes? I have a tendency to push gear to extremes. Very often, in the spirit of the moment, you're working on something and you just go for it. I sometimes wonder, how will it sound if I push it in ways it's not meant to be pushed, if the circuitry is completely overloaded? Those are the kinds of things that some plug-ins don't take into account, and I guess those are the elements that are pretty difficult to model anyway. It's easier to create algorithms for the more subtle approaches.

What are your favorite vocal mics and vocal chains?

To me, the vocal is the most important element of every album, and I'm a big microphone geek. In fact, most of the money I spent on my studio was on microphones, though I waited to get the mics I wanted, the really exceptional ones. I have a collection of [AKG] C12s and [Neumann] M 49s and U 47s—all the classic microphones—and those are the ones I favor for the most part. But I've also come to love some of the Audio-Technica mics, and so I always try them out when I'm listening to a new vocalist.

I've been using Mastering Lab preamps for vocals for a long time now, and I still love them. They have a little bump in the low end and in the high end too; I wouldn't say they're really hyped, but they have a tone to them that works for vocals.

In terms of compression, I tend to use the Summit Audio DCL100, though sometimes I experiment with other devices, like the EAR [Esoteric Audio Research] 660. It all depends on what you're trying to achieve, but I try not to compress vocals too much during the recording— I'd rather do it during the mix. If I'm thinking about doing something radical, I'll split the signal and record one side of it in a more conservative way and the other side with a more adventurous approach, using a different compressor or chain. Whatever you do, though, it always has to accommodate the track and the purpose of the song.

> *"The recording quality is no more important than the monitoring quality you achieve in the headphones, because that is what truly excites and inspires an artist."*

But I'm also a firm believer that the recording quality is no more important than the monitoring quality you achieve in the headphones, because that is what truly excites and inspires an artist. I've worked with some really tough artists that can be extremely difficult; they won't even sing unless they have the perfect mix in their headphones—if not the final mix, then really close to it. It may not be the perfect sound per se, but it has to be the perfect sound for *them* in the headphones.

That changes so much from artist to artist, too: some singers like to have their vocals 10 dB louder than the backing track in their headphones, and others want it buried—I've sometimes wondered how some of those artists were able to sing at all, with the music so loud and their vocal so low. Whatever it is, they're so used to recognizing their own voice one certain way that they can't work any other way.

When you find the best vocal chain for an artist, do you tend to stick with it for an entire album, or will you change mics depending on the feel of the song?

I'll sometimes do that, but not often. I did do a project recently where the main vocal mic was a Telefunken U 47, but I ended up using a [Shure] SM7 on some tracks, and the Audio-Technica 4060 on a couple of other tracks. Some of those choices were obvious; others were not. There were times when we felt that the sound we'd achieved on some songs just didn't click with other ones. That's when you get to experiment, and sometimes that's the way the magic really happens. You need to be completely excited about the sound you're hearing.

So you're saying it's not just a matter of being acceptable; it's a matter of coming up with a sound that gets you excited.

Yes, I really feel that way. I need to be excited about the process, and I need the artist to be just as excited. I've learned over the years that you can either work hard in the studio or you can be a little lazier, but being lazy never worked for me. Sometimes when I'm creating a rough mix, people in the room might say, "It's okay, it's good enough; you don't have to try so hard." But it's *not* okay. Even in a rough mix, I want to create something that inspires the artist, because that in turn will affect his overdubs. Very often it's the little things that make musicians try harder. And it starts in the engineer's seat. If you're excited about what you're doing, that will translate to the musicians in the studio.

> **"Very often it's the little things that make musicians try harder."**

People also sometimes say, why try harder if it's going to end up as an MP3? But that's such a wrong way of thinking, because it actually makes a huge difference to have an amazing product *before* it gets turned into an MP3. A great mix turned into an MP3 sounds so much better than a poor mix.

I've only been producing for the past four years or so, and I have to say that up until that point I had a completely different view of things as an engineer. Not slightly different: completely different, certainly in terms of priorities. As a producer, there are times when you say to yourself, "You know, it could be sounding better, but that's not important right now; right now I need to get a better musical performance, or I need to get the artist to sing with more passion." At times, that becomes more important than getting the perfect sound. After all, you can always fix the sound, but you can't ever change or improve the performance or the emotional content. There have been times when a singer is trying out different approaches and I think to myself that I wish I were giving him a better sound, but then I realize that to stop the workflow and do so would be counterproductive, or I realize that a singer is simply not going to nail a performance on a particular day even if I stop and fix the sound. The biggest fear is that you'll come back the next morning and listen to the previous day's work and think, "Wow, that's really uninspiring; I really don't like it."

So, as a producer, my job is to focus more on intensity and emotion than on technical perfection. You also have to be aware of session management, knowing how to prioritize things during a session with the artist, with the musicians, with the songwriting process. All of those elements play an important role, even when you're thinking in terms of whether or not you want to ask a singer to try a different microphone. His head might be on some lyric that he needs to finish, and so bothering him with other things might just cause him to freak out... and you know you're not going to get *anything* from him if he freaks out. It's such a fragile process, and so much of production has to do with psychology. As an engineer, you're not so involved in that, but as producer, you have to really stay on top of it because you bear the ultimate responsibility for the final product.

What kind of tricks have you come up with to elicit a great performance?

It's very important to get the artist in his or her comfort zone. Some artists need to feel relaxed about the whole situation, while others need to get really excited. To me, it boils down to how people react to stress. Some get scared, while others get falsely enthusiastic, and you have to be able to recognize that. One artist I work with gets very relaxed by having the band hang around while he's tracking his vocals; it's as if he feels that the sole responsibility isn't just on him. For most singers, though, it's the exact opposite: they really need to be in a more intimate environment. Many singers don't want anybody in the room besides the producer; sometimes they don't even want the engineer there, so the producer has to do the engineering himself. Still other artists are truly performers—they aren't involved in the songwriting, and then you have to treat the whole process quite differently. Songwriters tend to be more adamant about how they want things to finally sound because they know what they really meant when they wrote the song.

In order to find out how different artists react to stress, do you sometimes experiment by putting them under stress?

[*laughs*] No, I try not to do that . . . not on purpose, anyway! On most sessions, stress is going to happen no matter what; it's just part of the process. But I have learned that the more successful an artist is, the more intense he is in the studio, and maybe that's one of the reasons for their success. They really are totally into the entire process, even when it comes to what seems like unimportant details. To them, it doesn't matter—it's *all* important to them at that very moment. It may not be that way in five minutes' time, but it's very important to them right now, so you have to navigate those waters and try to understand what the artist is thinking. That applies to the producer, to the engineer, even to the musicians. Even the assistant engineer! They have to be in other people's heads, at least a little bit. If things are going badly, for whatever reason, everybody's got to try to understand the thinking behind it in order to figure out how they can help. Sometimes the best way to help is by doing nothing, to get quiet and wait. But at least you need to be there in the moment, connected with everybody. That's the most important thing: being connected continually, not detaching yourself from the session.

> *"Sometimes the best way to help is by doing nothing, to get quiet and wait."*

Suggested Listening:

Luis Miguel: *Romances*, WEA Latina, 1997; *Todos Los Romances*, WEA International, 1998; *Amarte Es Un Placer*, WEA International, 1999; *Mis Romances*, WEA International, 2001; *Mexico en la Piel*, WEA International, 2004; *Complices*, Warner, 2008

Alejandro Sanz: *No Es lo Mismo*, WEA International, 2003; *El Tren De Los Momentos*, Warner Music Latina, 2006

Darryl Swann

Capturing a Unique Voice

The key to getting a great interview, as with most aspects of life, is to be in the right place in the right time. On a visit to LA not long ago, I dropped in on a good friend at the Record Plant and happened to mention that I was scouting around for hot producers involved in hot projects. "Ah, you want to shoot over to Studio D," she told me. "Darryl Swann is in there putting the finishing touches on Macy Gray's new album, and I'm sure he'd love to talk with you."

Macy Gray, as in the indescribably baby-voiced singer, as in the Grammy-winning Best Female Pop Vocal Macy Gray? "That's the one," my friend assured me. I took a little less than a nanosecond to reply: "Cool; which way's Studio D?"

A short time later, I found myself engaged in fervent conversation with Swann, a young, eager and thoroughly dedicated engineer/producer whose success has clearly not gone to his head. Talking expansively about the gritty street sound he created with Gray for her breakthrough hit "I Try," Swann gives an insider's perspective on how to start a trend and not just follow one.

Tell me how you got started in this career.

I grew up in Cleveland, where I used to do sound for local bands—after the show was over and all the guys were chasing the girls, I'd be the one wondering why this speaker blew up. Eventually I moved out to California, playing guitar for a mid-'80s group called Haven—our big claim to fame was that we used to play the Troubadour and hang out with Poison and Warrant before they were signed! [*laughs*] Through a friend, I was offered a job as a runner/second engineer at Silverlake Recording; within two weeks, I was doing my first session, engineering for L.A. Reid and Babyface.

I ended up living at the studio! [*laughs*] I used to sleep under the mixing board because that's the only place the carpet was clean. I'd do 30- or 40-hour sessions and then sleep for three hours, wake up like a glazed doughnut with sweat all over me, and do it all over again. But I really got to cut my teeth; in between sessions I'd put up my own reels and start playing with drum machines, bringing in artists late at night, working that whole thing out. I also discovered that I had a knack for interacting with people, which is so important in producing, like being a psychologist. You have to know how to pull something out of a person, how to make a person active, how to make a person feel good.

Then I went to college at UCLA, graduated, got back into music, and started living out of another studio [Straight Arrow Recording] with a bunch of gospel producers. I was their guy for years and years; eventually I got put on a Chaka Khan session, and from then on I was a producer.

How did you meet Macy?

Interestingly, we actually grew up about a half an hour away from each other back in Ohio but we didn't know each other then. What happened was that in '93, '94, I had a group called Cultural Revolution—it was kind of a Soul II Soul type of group, and I was the jazzy beat guy—and

Macy sang on a couple of our demos. We actually landed a label deal, but she opted not to be in the group; she said, "I'm doing my own thing." Six months later she got a deal with Atlantic and recorded a rock 'n' roll project that never came out.

So I have my deal, she has her deal; my record never comes out, her record never comes out; we both lose our deals. So I'm back engineering—this is around '95 or so—and she's a secretary somewhere, and, out of the blue, she calls one day and says, "Let's write something." We go into my buddy's garage studio and write "I Try" with a couple of other guys; we put it together in one night. From that evening, from that one song, it set such a new precedent in her sound because everyone who had heard her previously had thought of her as being like a black Janis Joplin, kind of crunchy with big drums—straight rock 'n' roll. Now all of a sudden she's got this whole new Al Green kind of flavor, and her publisher is freaking out: "Oh my God, it's a new sound!" Because no one wanted to hear the old stuff; you know, you get dropped from a label and no one wants to hear from you anymore, so you have to reinvent yourself. That one demo that we did that night got put in two films and two soundtracks: *Love Jones* and *Picture Perfect*, with Jennifer Aniston.

The demo, not the master?

The demo. It's funny—that demo vocal is the one that's on the album [*On How Life Is*] that won the Grammy. Anyway, we kept writing, and 15 songs later, we have a solid package and she gets her deal with Epic. It's ironic that on that first record, about seven of those vocals are the scratch vocals that we did at night at Paramount Recording; we'd sneak in, it was like guerilla recording. I'd have my drum machine and my guitar, and we'd write songs. That's basically how we came up with the whole first album. A lot of those original beats and vocals are the ones that ended up on the record.

Did you record that album analog or digitally?

We did everything on two-inch [analog tape]. We would mock it up in the [Akai] MPC60, or the MPC3000; that's pretty much my canvas in terms of coming up with sounds and ideas—the machine is just incredible. A lot of people think that it's just a drum machine, but I create entire spirits and entire moods with it. Even if you have just a kick drum, a snare drum, and one space sound, the way you mix those things can create a mood for what you're trying to do. And from there it evokes a hook, evokes lyrics, evokes a whole expression. So we sketched everything out with the MPC, and fleshed the rhythms out, because pop music today is all rhythm-based and hook-based.

Do you do your editing in the MPC as well?

I do a lot of editing in there. Obviously, when we have multiple tracks, then I'll use Pro Tools. But for the smaller stuff, I'm lightning fast on this machine; I fly all the backgrounds in with this thing.

I also use it as a MIDI controller, to trigger other modules and things; it's such a versatile machine. A lot of guys use computer programs, which are cool, too, but not as mobile as having one of these.

Hey, your axe is whatever your axe is.

Exactly; use whatever you feel good on. I started on the MPC long ago, so it's what I know. There are so many people that are so wrapped up in the gear, but they're just all tools. Just because something new comes out doesn't mean you abandon what you've been using if it works, if it serves your purpose. It's all about utility; it's all about what gets the job done. I can make that thing swing just as hard as the next guy who has got the newest thing.

Do you print the MPC sounds, or do you run it virtually while you are mixing?

Usually I'll print the sounds to analog tape, to smash it down nice. Or I may use the MPC as a slave machine. If I have, let's say, tracks 1 through 8 burning with all the drum sounds and we need the tracks on tape, I'll comp those eight down to one tape track and then, come mix time, I'll run the sounds virtually.

Do you go to tape for sonic reasons, or is it purely convenience?

I'm going for the sound; you get that saturation. I view it as electrons hitting tape, kind of like a bug hitting your windshield on the highway. It kind of splats, and the harder it splats the more it spreads.

That's a good analogy, if you'll pardon the pun. So it doesn't sound like you're a big fan of digital recording.

No, I love it. Like I said, it's all about the tool needed for the job. I love tape for the tangible qualities of tape saturation, the loud compression, the splat. Also, tape is much more forgiving, in terms of clipping and distortion. Tape distortion is good distortion, whereas digital distortion is scary distortion. At the same time, digital provides a lot of convenience. For this new album, we've printed everything on the two-inch, and then we've transferred everything over to Pro Tools, and we're mixing off of Pro Tools, just for the convenience of it. You know, something as simple as waiting for two machines to lock up when you're trying to do something, that alone is enough to drive you crazy. As much as I love those washing machines, there are definitely so many pros [to digital recording].

Yet you're mixing through an analog console [SSL 9000J], so you're going through multiple conversion processes.

Yeah, well, actually what we're doing is we're working everything. We're working tape, analog to analog, and then if we have to do some editing we'll drop it into Pro Tools and we'll drop it back over.

What do you mix to?

Mostly half-inch [tape].

Presumably for you, like most engineers, distortion is a tool.

Absolutely. It's a usable, tangible object. So the number of conversions really don't bother me that much, because I feel that, with the stuff that we're doing, we're using dirty-ass beats that are already crunchy, we're playing with heavy transient drums and really phat basses, plus Macy's scratchy voice. It may sound really naïve, but with that kind of material, all the different conversions are almost unnoticeable at the end of the day to the human ear. As long as our chain is clean, then we let the gear do what it's going to do. If we had a ratty chain, a bad signal path, then obviously things would be different, but we're here at the Record Plant, and the techies are great.

Do you ever record through analog tube gear on your way to tape, or do you leave all that for the mix?

Analog tube gear, absolutely. I like running the bass through a Neve preamp and a [UREI] LA-2; I love that combination. I also like running drums through the [UREI] LA-4. Those are my favorite compressors; they have such a soft yet hard push, like a trampoline, almost. I can devote a whole month on how compressors work; it's just something where you may never fully learn what they do—you just know what you want to achieve out of them. How they all have their own slip of a knob, which can make your stuff sound really nice, or kill it. For example, the Distressors are really unique. They put a certain thing on everything; when you want that thing, it does that thing—it's really unique in how their 3:1 ratio differs from everyone else's 3:1.

> *"If it sounds good, it is good; taste your food before you salt it."*

I teach engineering, and I tell my students, "If it sounds good, it *is* good; taste your food before you salt it." I know so many guys that feel that they're not earning their money unless they're pushing switches and turning knobs. No, you've got to *listen* to your sound. If it needs work, then plug something in or change a mic or move it.

At what point do you say to yourself, okay, I've got the right mic, and it's positioned as best it can be, now the only thing I can do to improve the sound is patch in some outboard gear. Where is that defining point?

> *"I know so many guys that feel that they're not earning their money unless they're pushing switches and turning knobs. No, you've got to* listen *to your sound."*

That defining point is when you are standing next to a snare drum and you're listening to the speakers, and it sounds exactly the same. Or if it sounds exactly the same and you want to take it somewhere else, that's when you tie outboard gear in. Or if you've got some weird acoustics and you've been playing with it for a while and what's out there just doesn't sounds as good as the mic placement that you have.

So you're saying you can actually *improve* the sound that's out there.

Absolutely. Again, if you taste your food before you eat it, you might like it bland, or you might want a spicy taste. My whole approach to producing and engineering is objective-oriented. Know what you're going for first; have an idea what you're going for first. It's like if you walk into a kitchen and you don't know what you want to eat, you end up opening the fridge and the cupboards, just looking around. If you know what you want, you get a pot, you turn on the fire, you put the water in it, you have an objective. You have a chain of command, you know what you want to do. Same thing with recording: you have to know what you're going for. I always work on the drums first and make sure that they sound lovely out there, make sure that they feel good in the room. Then I figure out what mics I think will capture the spirit that we're looking for, then place them and move them around. Once I hear in the control room what I hear out there, I know that at least I have a unity point, kind of a nice zero point. Then I ask: Do we want to go further? Is it dirty enough? It is *too* dirty? That's when I start tweaking.

You said that Macy has a very particular drum sound. Can you describe which mics you use and roughly where you position them?

First, let me say that the drum kit that we've been using is a special kit called Kik Drums. They're really dynamic and they have a really unique design, in that the shells are ultra-thin and there are absolutely no holes in them, so you get this nice resonance. You have to start with a great-sounding kit.

The mic that I love starting with on the kick drum is a [Shure] D112 on the front side. I'll use a [Sennheiser] 421 or an [Electro-Voice] RE20 on the beater side to get the attack, and then I'll put a [Neumann] U 47 FET two or three feet out to capture the full spectrum. That way, I get a nice, wide thing, a lot of air. The 112 gives me my 100 Hz, and the RE20 or the 421 on the beater side gives me my 2k and click. I get a really nice balance that way.

With all those mics, obviously you have to do lots of phase checking.

Absolutely. On the snares I use a [Shure] SM57, as new as possible. Lately, I've been positioning the 57 kind of far away from the snare. A lot of times you'll see 57s right on the skin, but believe it or not, I find that the mic shuts down when it's that close; the diaphragm doesn't breathe, it's just getting too much. I usually ride it off to an angle, maybe about five to six inches away from the head. I'll also use a 57 on the bottom.

I love using the [Shure] SM81 on the high-hat because it's thin, and it's real directional, so you get minimal leakage. I've devised this little technique where I'll take a pop stopper and put a ski cap over it and then wedge it in between the 57 on top of the snare and the high-hat mic. That cuts off literally 95 percent of the crosstalk between the snare and the high-hat. It's essential; I don't do anything without it.

Wool or polyester ski cap?

Lycra. [*laughs*] And I'll use [Neumann] KM 84s on the bottoms of the toms, and 421s on the tops. I've also been using an old Shure mic called a Salt Shaker; it's great for that old Motown thing between the kick and the snare and tom right in front. You get that great old crunchy sound. Plus I've been using a lot of cool ribbons on the kit.

What mics do you use for overheads?

I have a couple of tube [Neumann] U 49s close left and right and I've got some 77s a little bit behind those, left and right, and then we have some [Neumann] U 67s up high, left and right. And then right back behind the drummer we have a 44, an M 49 and a U 67. That's something else that I've found: in getting a room sound, a lot of people think you have to go out to the front of the room. But if you stand behind the drummer and listen, you can really hear all that is going on; if you stand right off the drummer's floor tom and he plays that kit, you can hear that attack of that kick drum, you can hear the drummer's perspective. I find that is the absolute sweetest spot for a room sound. You walk around while he or she is playing, and you'll find it's usually right over the right shoulder. Move two inches one way you'll get some weird phasing, but when you find that one spot, boom! Throw a nice ribbon up there, or a nice tube, a [U] 47 or something.

Do all the drum mics get printed to separate tracks?

Sometimes we'll comp a few down, like the kick drum mics; I'll usually find the sound and merge those down to one, but if we're going for something special, like a real ambient kick, I'll print the ambient mic on its own track and I'll print the attack-y ones on another track. We'll often do the snare the same way, and the Salt Shaker will go on its own track. That's the mic I use the Distressor on; it just gives it that nuclear sound, really unique. We usually have two mics on the toms, so it's just left and right toms. And then the room, depending on what we're going for, I'll print stereo rooms and then I'll print one or two additional mono rooms for a unique sound. There's one song on the new album called "Love Fanatic," where basically the entire kit is a U 47 right behind the drummer's right shoulder. Just the tone of it is so crisp and so phat.

But, of course, you have to be in a good-sounding room.

You have to be in a good-sounding room. And the Record Plant has a *great*-sounding room.

Do you ever use a bass amp, or is it always DI?

I do both. We're using one of those re-issued Ampeg amps and I've got an RE20 right up on it.

Do you use the two signals for different parts of the frequency spectrum?

Usually the DI will have that real present thing, and the amp will have the fuzzy kind of warm, wide thing. So depending on what we're going for, I'll print those on separate tracks so I can have the option.

You said you generally record bass through a compressor on your way in, usually an LA-2.

Usually so, but real light.

Do you recompress the bass when you mix?

A little bit. If it's just breathing nicely, I'll let it go. But usually I'll put a little something on it to give it a pump.

How do you record electric guitars?

I like to use amps as much as possible; very little DI. I'll put a 57 up against the grill on one speaker, a [Shure SM] 58 on another one, a U 87 about five feet back, and then I actually sometimes try a ribbon also. Sometimes I'll even throw a 421 in the back, especially if it's a Fender Twin, to give it a nice midrange kind of thing. Once again, you've got to check for phase frequently.

And acoustic guitar?

I usually like to use a [Sennheiser] 451 with either an [AKG] 414 or a U 87. I also enjoy the Royer ribbon mics, and also B&Ks; those are really nice on acoustics.

How do you position them?

I'll usually use two mics—a B&K or 451 up on the neck and then a wide condenser around the sound hole, so I'll get the nice attack of and the air of the whole. It gives a nice balance, a nice, wide full-body guitar.

Any tricks for recording piano?

Yeah, we've been doing a lot of really creative stuff with that. In some cases, we've been going for a low-fi kind of sound, so what I'll do is throw a dynamic in the room and crank the hell out of it. That gives a really nice low-fi ambient kind of thing. If I want a widespread sound, I'll throw a 451 and an 87 in there in kind of a V-position; that gives a nice stereo spread. Sometimes we'll even throw some mics underneath. On the song called "Psychopath," we threw some little percussion toenails on the actual strings of the piano to get a tack piano sound. Sometimes I'll just throw one condenser in there to get a low-fi kind of thing. Usually in the past, I've liked that widespread stereo piano sound, but I've been kind of liking the mono piano sounds more lately, because it's got more of an upright saloon feel. A Scott Joplin kind of thing, as opposed to the big Liberace spread.

Everyone is struck by the sonic qualities of Macy's voice. As her recording engineer, can you describe it technically?

Well, it's a very unique instrument, that's for sure! Take a voice like Luther Vandross, which I signify as taking some baby powder, throwing it up in the air, and when it falls you can kind of see through it. Macy's voice is like taking some finely granulated sand and tossing it in the air; you can see through it, but there are things there. From the unique scratchiness of her tone, it's almost polyphonic; you can almost hear harmonics in her voice. It's like, if someone is talking and their voice cracks, you can hear three different notes, three different harmonics going on. Well, you have that *constantly* with her voice! So I've found that sometimes a dustier mic actually sounds better on her than a transparent mic; for some reason, a really transparent mic just doesn't give the voice that resistance. It just says come on in, as opposed to a raggedy mic like a beat-up 87, which kind of pushes against it and makes the voice do something.

> "Macy's voice is like taking some finely granulated sand and tossing it in the air; you can see through it, but there are things there."

So you're talking about using a mic that imposes its own sonic signature?

Exactly. It's almost like a Focusrite EQ, which doesn't put anything on a sound, whereas a Neve EQ lays something on it. I've found that a less dynamic mic, let's say a more beat-up 87—meaning it has a lot of personality because it's been dropped and it's been tweaked a lot of times that kind of mic will sound better on her voice because it will press against her frequencies better than a mic that's so transparent that it doesn't capture all of those intangible qualities. Now, you would think that a really high-end mic would actually be the better mic, but for some reason her voice comes off thinner with a mic like that. It almost needs an imprint of a mic on there.

So what do you usually use, and what has not worked?

I find that basic 87s sound great, while U 67s, U 47s, or [Sony] C12s don't because they're a little too thin. On that first record, all those demo vocals were done through a beat-up 87, dents and all, through a [dbx] 160x and a really cheap mic pre. But the best chain I've found is an 87 with personality, through the Neve, through a LA-2.

Do you EQ Macy's vocals?

No, I usually go real easy on the EQ or have no EQ whatsoever. For some reason, her voice loves an old Neve pre.

What are the specific frequency areas that make up her voice? Where are those resonant nodes that make it so unique sounding?

That's a good question. Well, there's always that top, that 10–12k; that's the little girl sound in her voice. The mids are always there, too, though sometimes we'll have to dip out some of the 300 Hz a little bit. That's kind of a dusty frequency for her. It's all in those low mids—from about 800 to about 2500 [Hz]—and those highs.

You usually roll off the 2k in a voice, but in hers we usually push it a little bit. Sometimes that graininess is lost, so we want to bring it out a little bit. So we'll bump it up. 10k is good, 800 to about 2500 [Hz], and 100 [Hz]. Those are her tasty frequencies.

Are there any specific things Macy needs in her headphones to give her best performance? Do you strap a limiter across them, or do you give her effects?

Nope. It's usually pretty dry and she usually likes the lead vocal kind of tucked. I've found, like most producing engineers, that the more you tuck the vocal, the more the singer wants to perform because they want to be able to hear themselves; when it's way out front, they hold back. But Macy can get away with anything, just because the tone of the voice always comes through. I've got to give her Sony headphones though; I found that it makes such a difference.

Are there any special treatments that you give her vocals in the mix?

We usually put a nice harmonizer on it, using an Eventide H3000.

With what kind of settings?

The basic Micro Pitch Shift preset; that's always nice. I usually will run it through a nice LA-2 or an Avalon Pre, and smash it pretty hard, so it gives that pump, that warmth. I'll also usually use a very long and invisible reverb like a [Lexicon] 480, a Long Hall with the highs rolled off, so it's like another baby powder in the air, kind of a see-through reverb—not there, but you feel a presence. Then I'll usually use an invisible kind of slapback delay.

Set to the tempo of the song?

Usually set to the tempo, usually eighth notes. I'll obviously ride that on a separate fader to embellish certain things.

Again with the highs rolled off?

Yeah, absolutely, so it's kind of tucked underneath. And that's it, pretty much straight ahead. As we all know after you've been doing this for a little while, you shouldn't hear your effects. That's the key with her: it's all about the voice, the production—that voice just has to be out front. I put a nice smash on it, so it's right in your face but it's not hurting you.

When you're doing a mix, in what order do you bring the faders up?

I always visualize mixing like building a house: you create a foundation, then you build the structure, then you add the extras, and then you put all the ornaments on it.

The problem is that a lot of times when you're mixing, after you've done all the music, then you have to first tackle the vocals. But by that time your ears are usually a little numbed out, so sometimes what I will do is get the lead vocal sound first. I'll just push that one fader up and get the sound while my ears are still pristine and I have all my energy and my enthusiasm. Once I have that perfect sound where I can listen to it on 10 and I'm not mad at it and it doesn't hurt me, I'll pull that fader down and work on the root instruments—drums, bass, rhythm guitars, and keyboards. Then I'll bring the lead vocal back in but put it way up front so I have enough headroom in between the track and the vocal, where I can lay all the other stuff. From there, I'll bring in the solo instruments, all of the noisier instruments, background vocals, and then, very last, I'll bring in the DJ scratches and all the low-level ancillary—sparkles and things like that. I have found that by doing the lead vocal first, you are subconsciously keeping the focus of the song about the vocal. Especially with an artist like Macy, it's all about the vocal, as opposed to an R&B project where it's more production-driven.

What advice can you give someone just starting out in this business?

It's all about your axe; your weapon of choice. And the most important thing I can say is to have an objective before you get started. If you have an objective, then everything else falls into place. You can walk into a studio and it can be very alarming to see all these knobs and buttons and everything. But if you know specifically what you're doing, you go from seeing this wide thing to seeing a very focused situation.

Suggested Listening:

Macy Gray: *On How Life Is*, Epic, 1999; *The Id*, Epic, 2001; *The World Is Yours* (from the *Rush Hour 2* soundtrack), Def Jam, 2001

OPM: *Forthemasses*, Suburban Noize, 2004

El Pus: *Hoodlum Rock, Vol. 1*, Virgin, 2005

Ryan Hewitt

Lessons in Humility

Having a world-famous recording engineer for a father may present you with certain advantages, but that didn't prevent Ryan Hewitt from having to work through some, shall we say, issues when he was in his early twenties.

"My temper used to be outrageous," he tells us, "and I was constantly spouting off opinions without knowing what I was talking about. When I look back on those days, all I can think is, 'My god, I must have been such a jerk!'" Fortunately, apprenticeships with two of the industry's most notorious taskmasters—Sony's Michael Brauer and legendary producer Phil Ramone [*interviewed in the first edition of* Behind the Glass]—soon disabused the young Hewitt of his worst tendencies.

The son of live engineer David Hewitt [*interviewed on page 68*], Ryan Hewitt's story actually begins a decade earlier, when as a 12-year-old, he was invited to spend a summer working on his dad's mobile facility, Remote Recording. "I haven't held down a normal job since then," he says with a laugh. A few years later, at his father's insistence, he was forced to take a temporary leave of absence from the industry and earn a college degree; he elected to attend Tufts University and study electrical engineering. A crash course in studio etiquette—courtesy of the afore-mentioned Brauer and Ramone—followed, with history eerily repeating itself when the recently relocated Hewitt found himself at Cello Studios in Los Angeles, working under the tutelage of veteran Jim Scott [*also interviewed in this book, on page 88*].

A few short months later, Hewitt was working with Scott on the Red Hot Chili Peppers' *By the Way*, and his assisting days were over. Since then, he has engineered numerous solo albums for the Peppers' John Frusciante (including all five of the prolific guitarist's 2004 releases), as well as work with indie heroes the Alkaline Trio, Blink-182, and Tift Merritt. Most recently, he engineered and co-produced the critically acclaimed Flogging Molly album *Float*.

We chatted with the youthful Hewitt in between sessions at his Venice Beach loft studio Lock Stock, where he demonstrated a thoughtfulness well beyond his chronological years.

How did your experience as a 12-year-old helping out on your dad's truck shape your career?

Being on the road and working with my father had a major impact on the way I conduct sessions today. For one thing, it got me used to working adult hours—12 or 14 hours a day, getting up at eight o'clock in the morning, and then working until the gig is wrapped at two in the morning. That's been my life ever since! The idea of being on a truck, setting up the microphones, recording a show, and then tearing everything down again has informed the way that I record these days, because I can get things set up really quickly and deal with the session in a very succinct and concentrated way. It's an experience that has taught me to do things in a very efficient manner and capture the moment without overthinking things. And it taught me to be

prepared for any kind of contingency. When you're out on the road, you can almost expect at least one microphone to break every night, so you've got to be able to get out there with a new one in pretty quick order. Coming from an anything-can-happen situation like that into a more refined atmosphere in the studio certainly gives you a perspective.

Yet you chose not to follow in your father's footsteps in that you're not a live engineer. Was that because he discouraged you, or because you simply feel more comfortable in a studio environment?

From the time I first started getting into music and listening to records, I often asked my dad, "Why don't you want to be in the studio? Why did you choose to go on the road instead of staying in the comfort of the Record Plant?" His response was always the same: "I don't want to hear the same guitar solo over and over again; I don't want to punch in the vocal over and over again. I just want to do the gig and leave." He was really only interested in capturing the moment, not the whole refining process.

When it came to starting my own career, I thought a lot about what he said, but I also thought about the impact my father's job had on me as a kid when I wasn't working for him—namely, he wasn't around a whole lot. He's since expressed regrets about that on a personal level, but it was his job and it was his way of supporting a family. I ultimately concluded that it's a very limiting career move to just do live recording, because you have to become married to your business, and certainly spending time away from your family out on the road is a lot worse than spending time away from them in the studio, where at least you get to come home every night and have a certain amount of control over your hours and locations. Working on a truck appealed to me in terms of the excitement and the variety of artists we got to work with—an opera one day and a heavy metal band the next—but you're not as intimate with the music.

For instance, I got to record Jimmy Buffett, but I never got to meet the man. That was just kind of weird to me. But in the studio I'm constantly interacting with the artist, discussing sounds and parts and likes and dislikes. It's a bit more long-lasting, too, whereas live recording is more of a fleeting moment; it's all about showing up, doing the gig, and then handing the tapes or hard drives off to someone else. I prefer being immersed in the music and getting my hands dirty throughout the entire process.

You earned an Electrical Engineering degree in college. With the benefit of 20/20 hindsight, how important do you think that training was in terms of your career today?

Learning how to learn is the most important thing about going to college, so I advise people to get their degree in any subject that interests them, even if it's not specifically music or the recording arts. The important thing is that you gain some kind of expertise, regardless of the area. I was in a situation where my father said, "You can do whatever the hell you want to do in life... but you're going to get a college degree first, and it's not going to be in recording." I could see his point, because getting an education in something else gave me a different kind of perspective, in my case about equipment and all the other technical things that go along with recording. I don't know how to design gear—I'm certainly no George Massenburg—but, thanks to my EE degree, I can appreciate signal flow and I understand what's actually happening inside the gear I use. Technical specs actually mean something to me: when I see something like slew rate, I can picture all the equations in my head, and I can remember all the experiments we did back in school. I really like breaking things down to their component level and understanding what's actually going on.

> *"Learning how to learn is the most important thing about going to college."*

In hindsight, I wish that I had taken a double major of EE and music. Even though I've been a drummer since I was a kid—and you can make all the drummer jokes you want—I don't consider myself as much of a musician as I'd want to be. I wish I had taken some theory and composition classes while I was in college because having strong musical skills seems to be becoming increasingly important. One day I hope to take a few months off to learn as much as I can about piano and guitar; knowing that language is so essential to what we do.

So, yes, I would say that having that EE degree was beneficial in that it has influenced me to take a slightly different approach to audio engineering than some other people.

What were the main lessons you learned from Michael Brauer?

Michael was my main mentor when I was at Sony; I worked as his assistant for about two years, and the education I received from him was invaluable. The lessons I learned from him were mostly about bedside manner: how to keep a client's interest, and how to steer things forward in a direction you want to go. If an artist started questioning decisions Michael had made, he had the ability to say, "Just listen to what I've done and think about it for a minute." He was able to talk artists and producers off a ledge; he just had a great way of communicating with people. It really blew my mind watching him handle potentially volatile situations with major personalities and egos, but with absolute care and precision and humility. It was incredible to watch, and it made a huge impact on me. So now I always think about how Michael would handle things before I open my mouth in the studio. I always consider the impact my words will have, and I try to never lose sight of what my goal is, and what the goal of the record is.

So the basic lesson is, "place brain in gear before speaking."

Exactly. I see people put their foot in their mouth all the time, and it's so totally counter-productive. It's sometimes amazing to me that people with that lack of self-censorship can actually hold down jobs in a studio environment. There are more than a few engineers out there who just don't know how to talk to people, even outside the studio; they seem to be completely antisocial. It's bizarre to me, because we're dealing with people's art here; we're dealing with creative people who are putting their personal feelings and expressions out there for all the world to see, and that's something that needs to be nurtured.

After you left Sony, you worked for Phil Ramone for awhile. What were the basic lessons you learned from him?

Mostly how not to piss him off! [*laughs*]

Seriously, the main thing I learned from Phil is that it's always about the music, first and foremost; we're here to serve the artist, and we need to be able to facilitate whatever it is they want. I also learned the importance of always keeping your options open—whether it's a matter of last-minute changes to the arrangement or reseating musicians in the studio or changing to a different mic—and always remaining calm. No matter what was going on in the session, Phil would always maintain an even keel and would keep things moving along.

And it was through Phil that I learned to keep my then-notorious temper from getting in the way of solving a problem. In one of the earliest sessions I did with him, a microphone went down in the middle of a string date and the first thing I did was get very frustrated and flustered—I started pulling patch cords and so headphones were popping all over the place; things were starting to go awry in a major way. At the end of the session, Phil took me aside and he said, "You know, when something like that happens, you really need to just take a deep breath, step back, and figure out what's going on. You can't let your emotions take over." That was a lesson I had to learn repeatedly before it really started to sink in, but now if something goes wrong in the studio, my attitude is, "Alright, well, let's just figure this thing out," or "Hey, let's just put another microphone up and figure it out later."

Another one of Phil's major rules was, always be in Record; whenever the artist is in front of the microphone, that red light should be on. To this day I take that approach in all my sessions. It's all about capturing moments, after all; even if a take isn't going well, the drummer might play a badass fill that you can fly in later on. There's always something going on when musicians are out in the room; someone might play something and inspire an entirely new song, so you need to make sure that everything they do is on tape or on disk.

Who were your main musical influences as you were growing up?

Well, my dad is a big jazz-head, so there were always a lot of those records playing in our house, as well as things like Steely Dan. I became a big fan of the work of [jazz engineer] Rudy Van Gelder, even though all my friends were into eighties metal; I just never had any interest in that genre. Eventually I started listening to a lot of vintage British rock—Led Zeppelin, The Beatles, that sort of thing—but I never got into what I perceived as the heavily processed "LA sound." Looking back, I can see that I was very judgmental and a bit naive at the time. That's actually why I ended up being assigned to work with Michael Brauer when I was at Sony; the executives there thought of me as a pain in the ass. [*laughs*] I see kids doing that today, and I think, "I used to be the same way!" It's kind of entertaining to see it from the flip side: now I'm the one who has the assistant who's kind of a loudmouth, and I have to put him in his place. [*laughs*]

Working for Brauer instantly humbled me. As I said, I was a real cocky bastard at the time and the bosses at Sony apparently gave him instructions to break me. [*laughs*] They wanted to have me around, but they certainly didn't like my attitude. But once I started being put into high-pressure situations with Michael, that shit immediately left. In fact, not long ago, I sent a thank-you note to some of the people at Sony who had given me a hard time, thanking them for putting up with me and teaching me so many invaluable lessons in humility. Being taught that I didn't know everything was super-important to my development as an engineer, and as a person, and I'm grateful to Michael and a lot of the Sony people for teaching me that.

I sometimes think that maturity arrives at the moment when you realize that what you don't know is actually a lot more than what you *do* know.

You're right. I didn't realize it at the time, but as a 21-year-old, I was working with a lot of people who'd already forgotten more than what I knew then. That's why my advice to young people just starting in this business is to have an open mind and be willing to defer to people with experience, people who actually know what's going on.

> *"As a 21-year-old, I was working with a lot of people who'd already forgotten more than what I knew then."*

Jim Scott is pretty hard on his assistants, too, isn't he?

Yeah, it's interesting how shit rolls downhill, isn't it? [*laughs*] Never uphill! But the great thing is that Jim comes from a live recording background also—he ran the Los Angeles Record Plant truck for years, and so it turned out we had a very similar mentality about how to run a session in terms of always being prepared for anything. He made sure we had spares of everything on hand, from extra mics and extra DI boxes to extra bottles of water. Jim is probably one of the most inspiring people to work for, because he's always stoked, he's always happy to be there, and, just like Michael Brauer, he has a great bedside manner. There's always a lot of work getting done in his sessions, and getting done well, but Jim still maintains this party atmosphere that I've never seen anyone else replicate. He's got the tapestries hanging on the walls, he's got the Christmas lights strung up everywhere, he's got the margarita blender going on, he's got road cases full of fun stuff and toys and crazy percussion instruments. He knows how to have a good time in the studio—that's for sure.

What kinds of non-standard recording techniques have you come up with as an outgrowth of all these great influences?

Probably one of the most fun and experimental projects I've done as an engineer was [Red Hot Chili Peppers guitarist] John Frusciante's *The Will to Death*, where he wanted to make a record on 16-track tape with minimal mics on the drums, '60s style. His concept was that we'd get in for a week, mix it in a day, and the record would be done. I'd never done anything like that before—every record I'd made to that point had 12, 16, 20 mics on a drum kit, multiple mics on every guitar amp, multiple takes, tons of editing, etcetera. I'd never been forced to be a minimalist; I'd never miked a drum kit with just two mics before. So I had to kind of reverse engineer, pun intended, in order to figure out how to do all that stuff. It took a lot of reading and a lot of experimenting, and I had to listen to a lot of my favorite old records with a different ear. I had to train myself to understand the characteristics of a single microphone picking up an entire drum kit.

> *"The thing about using so few mics [on a drum kit] is that if you move just one of them a couple of inches, or angle it slightly differently, the sound changes completely."*

So whenever I had a little free studio time somewhere, I'd experiment and I actually came up with some techniques for miking a drum kit with just three or four mics that actually sounds pretty good. The thing about using so few mics is that if you move just one of them a couple of inches, or angle it slightly differently, the sound changes completely. For example, I like putting a [Telefunken] 251 in cardioid over the drummer's right shoulder, facing forward, but the exact position depends on how he plays, and how you need the balance of the kit to be for that particular song. If that mic ends up facing the floor tom, I might put another mic over the drummer's left shoulder in order to get a little stereo spread, but you need to be aware that those mics are going to be out of phase with the kick drum mic. You also need to make sure that the snare is somewhat centered between those two mics, but there's no point in taking exact measurements, because so much depends on the angle of the mics. I see a lot of guys chasing their tails measuring things, but it's kind of pointless because even the frequency response will change depending on how the drummer is moving his shoulders. The important thing is to listen to what's coming out of the speakers; that's what should ultimately dictate mic positioning. Just because a tape measure tells you both mics are the same distance from the snare drum doesn't mean it's going to give you a good sound with the snare imaged exactly in the center.

I've also recently discovered the joys of off-axis miking with a bottom snare mic. I used to put the mic straight on to the bottom of the drum, thinking that if it was parallel to the snares it would give me more impact, but now I'm finding that angling it a little bit away from the kick drum and using the polar pattern to increase off-axis rejection yields better results; that's been a fun thing to play around with.

With all the experimental work you've done with John Frusciante, I'm guessing that you're not just sticking a [Shure SM] 57 up against the grille to record electric guitar.

Well, John actually likes sticking a 57 about six inches off the grille, but ever since I've been working with [producer] Jerry Finn, I've been opened up to a whole different world of guitar recording techniques. Again, it's totally situation-dependent. If I'm going for a simple sound, I prefer using a single mic like a [Sennheiser] 421 or a Royer, and I've also gotten into using the Heil PR30 lately. If I'm going for a brighter sound, I'll go for a [Neumann U] 87 or 67 or something like that, a few feet off the grille. It's just a matter of finding the right tool for the job.

Do you have a standard technique for recording bass?

I usually record bass DI as well as amp, placing a 421 or a [Neumann] FET 47 a couple of inches away from the speaker cabinet, off-center to the cone. The FET 47 is actually my favorite bass mic by far—I've gotten great sounds with it and never had to touch an equalizer knob. I don't always use the DI track, but it's always nice to have in case you need to re-amp it later on. You also tend to get a little more finger attack from the DI, so if you need that later on in the mix, it's a good thing to have; it's all part of keeping your options open.

The majority of time I do compress bass as it's being recorded because it has a tendency to be uneven, though it depends on the specific player and the instrument itself as to how much you need to do that.

Do you prefer the sound of digital, or of analog tape?

I love the sound of tape, and I would record that way all the time but for budgets and time constraints—it takes longer that way, and if the band is sub-par and you have to do a lot of edits, it's a pain in the ass.

I also prefer analog outboard gear to digital plug-ins, with the exception of digital EQ, which allows you to cut tight notches into signals without the resultant phase shift. I've gotten so used to doing that on computers, in fact, that when I tried cutting notches using a console's analog equalizer recently, I was amazed at how much phase smearing I was hearing. The effects in Pro

Tools—the reverbs and the modulation effects that you can then sync up with your time base—are really tremendous, but other than that, I don't think plug-ins are quite there yet; they certainly don't sound as good as my pile of analog gear for tone control. Doing broad, musical sculpting with an analog equalizer is just a gorgeous sound, and the phase shift is part of that sound, and it's quite appealing in that regard. But when you're using a tight Q, trying to chop 15 dB out of something, it's not so pleasant, whereas computers allow the precision to do that without unduly altering the sound. My philosophy is, play to the strengths in whatever you're doing, and that's something a computer is quite good at. You always want to use the gear that's going to do the most amount of good and the least amount of harm.

What's the craziest studio trick you ever tried that actually made it to record?

Well, probably one of my favorite sounds—although I can't say that it was entirely my idea—is on the song "C'mon Girl," on the Chili Peppers' *Stadium Arcadium*. I was in the studio with John and he was doing a guitar part. We came to the solo section, and it was supposed to be a keyboard solo, but he just kind of noodled around and made some really cool noises. When he came in, I said, "You've got to hear what you did on that solo section!" He liked it and wanted to do another couple of passes—it was basically just a lot of sparse noodling with volume swells. I got the idea to put some backwards reverb on it, all sorts of lengths—short, long, infinite—so we just basically filled up the entire tape with backwards reverbs, then we comped that down to our favorite bits.

As a final experiment when doing a rough mix, I put that comp track through a [Dytronics] Cyclosonic Panner with some weird settings. John loved it, so I needed to use it on the final mix, but the problem was that every time the signal hit the Cyclosonic, it did something totally different. In the end I literally did 50 different mixes and sent them to John to pick out his favorite sections, which I then had to painstakingly edit together, cutting the half-inch tape master. It was totally insane—it just leaps out of the speakers like an ice storm and sweeps around—but it was really fun to do.

Selected Listening:
Red Hot Chili Peppers: *By the Way*, WEA, 2002; *Stadium Aradium*, Warner Bros., 2006
John Frusciante: *Curtains*, Record Collection, 2004; *Inside of Emptiness*, Record Collection, 2004; *The Will to Death*, Record Collection, 2004
Blink-182: *Blink-182*, Geffen, 2003
Saybia: *Eyes on the Highway*, EMI, 2007
Flogging Molly: *Float*, Side One Dummy, 2008

Ann Mincieli

Insomniac, Workaholic

If you had to pick one word to describe Ann Mincieli, it would be *intense*. The New York–based engineer's passion for her craft comes through in almost every sentence she speaks; try to talk about the weather, or the attributes of the cheeseburgers we're chowing down on, or pretty much anything, and somehow the topic always seems to return to recording. This is one very focused lady.

Mincieli's career started in the early '90s, when she began interning at not one, but two major recording studios in the Big Apple. Putting in over a hundred hours a week didn't faze this self-described workaholic one bit—it probably helped that she's also (surprise, surprise) something of an insomniac. "Whenever I wasn't working at one place, I was filling in at the other," she says. "I became a studio rat, and I loved it. I was living on the couch, but it was fine, and back then they paid interns decently, so it was rewarding too."

Her enthusiasm and gift for both the technical and musical aspects of the job soon netted her a promotion to assistant engineer. Interestingly, she opted to stay at that level even when she was deemed ready to climb the next career rung and become a full engineer. It turned out to be a prescient decision because it not only gave her an extraordinary opportunity to work with major artists like Mariah Carey, Lauren Hill, Jon Bon Jovi, and Courtney Love—even Yoko Ono!—but to absorb the techniques of master engineers like Bruce Swedien and Geoff Emerick.

Then one afternoon Ann Mincieli's golden opportunity arrived, in the form of a precocious—and startlingly talented—19-year-old artist/producer by the name of Alicia Keys. A decade later, Mincieli is still working with Keys, and not just as an engineer (she recorded parts of the breakthrough *The Diary of Alicia Keys*, as well as nearly every note of Keys' recent release, *As I Am*), but also helping Keys design and run her new recording facility, Oven Studios. It helps that Keys, as Mincieli is quick to point out, is every much of an insomniac and workaholic. "We're the only two members of the team that can outdo each other at the end of the day," she laughs. "When everybody else is dead and can't get up, there we are, working away." Sounds like a collaboration that promises more great things to come.

As a teenager you had some formal training, at New York's Institute for Audio Research. How valuable would you say that was in shaping your career?

Well, everything you learn is valuable, at least in terms of being able to put it on your resume, but the problem is that by the time you learn a piece of gear, it's old, so you still have to get plenty of hands-on experience. It's like anything else—if you take things seriously, you can make your way, but if you don't take it seriously, it doesn't matter whether you have any schooling or not; it's just not going to happen for you.

How did you manage to land two jobs simultaneously back when you were interning? So many people can't even find one.

I was always big into networking; in fact, I still am. I started at Skyline Studios at the end of 1992, and I was soon working 50 hours a week there, but almost from the beginning everyone on staff knew that they would be closing soon; in fact, they closed in August of 1994. So I was still sending resumes out, and the manager of Right Track offered me a job. She later told me that she needed an experienced person, and she liked the fact that I was already getting that experience at Skyline.

And you obviously felt that 50 hours a week at one studio wasn't enough to keep you occupied.

Right. [*laughs*] The thing is, back then, the interns had a lot of responsibility. You'd get the input sheets the night before—you'd know who was coming in and what their setup needs were, and the general assistants would set all of that up. It's a shame that it doesn't happen that way anymore, but it was a great way to learn and to get your feet wet—how to patch things, how to lay out a whole room: it was called dressing and undressing a room. Then, when the assistant engineer came in, he or she would check your work.

So you were actually working at a sub–assistant engineer level.

Yeah. You were building up to an assistant engineer position, and back then they didn't move you up the ranks quickly, because the assistants had a pretty critical job, what with running tape and doing punch-ins. Plus there was the fact that artists would lock out a room for a year; the studios back then had two or three rooms that were often locked out for a long time, so you were able to hang out and get a lot of experience. But you really had to know your Ps and Qs before you moved up; you really had to know who, what, why, where, when, why, and how in the room. I don't think that occurs much these days.

You know, with Alicia, I now work in studios all over the world, and I notice that things are very inconsistent these days. Years ago, every studio followed the same basic procedures; you'd walk in and in just a few minutes you'd be able to start rolling tape. Track sheets were written out the same ways, and the technical specifications were spelled out the same ways in terms of tape alignments, etcetera. That was the case even in terms of the ink colors you'd use: you'd mark your titles in blue, and if it were a master or a safety, you'd mark it in red. There was a whole way of working that I believe is lost with the technology now. There's no more community, there's no more learning like that, where you're learning how to do the little things right, and learning it incrementally. So I'm glad I came up during that time.

You made a conscious decision not to jump from assisting to engineering at the earliest possible time; instead you elected to wait until you felt you were ready.

That's right. I saw the industry changing before my eyes. I saw a lot of people who got promoted to staff engineer and more often than not, they would fall by the wayside because there just wasn't a lot of work; business was starting to decline, and more and more artists were putting studios in their homes and hiring just one person to run it. I'd actually been promoted to staff engineer by then, at Quad Studios, and it was at the height of their popularity, but what they actually needed was engineers who were willing to assist. That's because most projects by that point were going to outside engineers who would come in and want to get to work immediately, so they needed assistants who were past the basics, people who could do more than just put a mic up, people who were experienced with the console and could sit with them and keep them moving, so they didn't feel like they were stalled or helpless. In return, I got a lot of work out of it, and the opportunity to meet a lot of big names: I was assisting for everybody from Lauren Hill to David Kahne to Bruce Swedien to Geoff Emerick, and I was learning and taking something from each of these people and developing my own style. Personally, I'll take a gig any day sitting side by side with a Bruce Swedien or a Geoff Emerick, just learning.

So yes, I chose to stay back and pick the right time to make the jump, and I did it with the right artist, too.

Did you and Alicia click the very first time you met?

Yes, I would say so. It would have been 1999; she was producing a lot for other artists, and at the same time she was finishing up her debut album, *Songs in A Minor*. I met her in the elevator at the studio one day, and she said to me, "Wow, you're a girl and you're an engineer"—I was actually assisting at the time—and she started asking me a million questions. I remember thinking to myself, "Why is she asking so many questions?" But she was just really intrigued. Truth be told, I was a little distant with her. First of all, I didn't know who she was, and as an assistant you're taught not to do too much talking anyway, at least not until you get to know the artist.

But we got along well, and a year later, she started to get very, very busy. All of sudden she and I and her songwriting partner Kerry Brothers, along with Tony Black—a great engineer who worked at Hit Factory—started working together as a team. We just clicked—we were all from New York so we all had the same mentality. After *Songs in A Minor* was done and became a huge success, she hired me. I've been climbing ever since, little by little, until this last album [*As I Am*], which I pretty much engineered from start to finish.

One thing about artists, they look to give engineers and up-and-coming people a shot. When you're as serious and passionate about what you do as they are about what they do, they recognize it; there's always a need for good employees like that.

> *"One thing about artists, they look to give engineers and up-and-coming people a shot. When you're as serious and passionate about what you do as they are, they recognize it."*

Tell me the genesis of Oven Studios.

That was originally the nickname of the basement studio Alicia used to record in, in Queens. We called it "The Oven" as a joke because it was always so hot down there. After *Diary* came out, Alicia bought her own place on Long Island, and she officially named it Oven Studios. I was put in charge of equipping it and setting it up; I had everything in Excel spreadsheets, from paper clips to pencils, and I was running around 18 hours a day helping put it together. It was a huge learning experience. I learned a lot about tuning rooms and acoustics, about where sound travels and how it travels, and why certain things have to be designed certain ways.

Working in an established studio, you tend to take a lot of things for granted. But go into a studio that's being built from scratch, and you come to appreciate the little things. Alicia used to work in a place that wasn't designed right; it had padded walls that would make her voice almost sound compressed, but it wasn't compressed—there was almost no reflection, no feeling of being in a nice big room. She sings really loudly—she really projects—so the room size is very important, even more so now that she's doing a lot of vocal training; her dynamic range is just incredible.

What's your general approach to recording Alicia's vocals?

Mostly, I play a lot with proximities and with polar patterns. The one thing about Alicia is to get the vibe of the song: Are we going for a bright vocal, or a dark vocal? Are we going for a grimy vocal, or are we going definition and prettiness, or are we going for fullness? On *As I Am*, I used about five different vocal mics. I used a little $1,500 Telefunken M16 when I wanted a lot of transparency, high-end definition and transients. I also have an ELAM 270 stereo mic, reissued by Telefunken—not many of them have been made—and I used that on two of the songs; I get this prettiness out of it, but I also get this fullness and grit. Basically, I choose her vocal mic depending on the range that she's singing in and the vibe that she's going for—low-fi or high-fi.

I also re-amp her voice a lot—I'll take a feed of the mic and run it through a guitar amp and record it back in. Most of the time, I use the same vocal chain on her: a Neve 1073 and a CL1V compressor, although when I want a little more lower mid on her voice, I'll substitute an 1176 blackface. I'll also sometimes use a different chain on backing vocals, just to give them a different sonic quality than the lead vocals.

Another trick I sometimes use for backing vocals is the old Roberta Flack thing of putting a microphone up high in the studio and placing it in omni mode. Or I'll have a second microphone just a foot or two in back of the main mic—the one you use for the initial track. Then you record a double-track off the more distant mic, so there's a slight delay between the two. The two vocals combined sound really cool. The trick is to adjust the two mic preamps so that the balance is equal.

Do you ever use really cheap microphones to record her vocals?

Totally—Shure SM57s and 58s, just for variety. Bono, who I've also worked with, has this habit of doing his vocals in the control room with the speakers turned up really loud, and I kind of borrowed his technique a little bit. Alicia likes to collaborate with many different producers and players, so she always wants to have a mic around to pick up and sing through. At one point in the making of *As I Am*, just to catch the vibe, Alicia decided to work on 17 different songs in one weekend with a whole bunch of people. When she told me this, I thought, well, she'll probably be doing this in the control room, because musicians don't want to listen to ideas while they're tracking, and so I knew I was going to get bleed, so I just gave her an inexpensive mic and she sang in the control room like Bono does. We ended up using parts of those little vocals on three of the final tracks. Sometimes you've just got to throw the rules out the window.

What's your general approach to recording piano?

I've experimented a lot with M-S (Mid-Side) recording, but I take it a step further. The idea is to start with a great stereo microphone—I have a 414 with two capsules—and you put one capsule facing down over middle C, and the other facing sideways, in figure-eight polar pattern, which I mult, so they are patched into three separate mic pres. At the desk, the mic facing middle C gets bussed to both sides, and the other two are bussed left/right. Then you can play with the balance and phase. One of the two sides has to be out of phase, and which one it is depends on the balance; you just have to kind of keep flipping the phase buttons.

I'm also big on having a single room mic, about eight feet away from the lid, but not high up—just about even with the highest point of the lid. That gives you a little touch of ambience. You'll know you've gotten the perfect blend of the sources if you fold the signal back to mono and there's no cancellation, so you need to check in mono frequently. But with those multiple sources, you can totally mess with the image—it's like a ghost image, almost—and you can control how near or far it is, as well as how wide you want the image to be.

There are certain questions I always ask Alicia when she starts playing piano on a track: What key are you playing in? What range are you playing in? Do you want a close sound or more of an ambient sound? I need to determine beforehand how she hears the sound in her head, and then I need to select not only the right mics but the right piano for her. Fortunately, I have that luxury, but having that great foundation is so key.

Let's be honest: microphones are really just EQs at the end of the day. Newbies will just throw five plug-ins on a channel and EQ the hell out of something. More experienced engineers know to either change the microphone, or its position. If I'm looking for a brighter sound on the piano, I'm not going to reach for the EQ or throw a plug-in on it; I'm going to move the mics down closer to the hammers. If you know about microphones, if you know about polar patterns, if you know the difference between dynamic mics and condensers and ribbons, if you know what tones you get out of certain mics and mic pres, that's half your battle.

> *"Microphones are really just EQs at the end of the day."*

What's your secret for getting that ultra-deep hip-hop low end?

It comes mostly from a Yamaha Subkick, which I use not on kick drum, but on bass, which gives me a lot more control. I mic the bass cabinet with a [AKG] C12 or a [Neumann] TLM 103, and then route the signal to the Subkick. Printing all three signals—mic, Subkick, and a DI—gives me control over all three elements, with the DI providing the attack, the amp mic providing the roundness, and the Subkick giving me that deep bottom.

Also, the main bass used on the album was a 1956 Hofner 5001 violin bass with flatwound strings, which we ran through a [Ampeg] B15.

Wow, that's hardly what most people would think of as a modern hip-hop instrument.

Well, it worked, and so we probably used that bass on 80 percent of the album. We also experimented with a lot of drum tuning techniques; we would tune the toms with the underneath skin a half-step below so you'd get that subtle ring and note shift downward. We'd change skins—calfskin on the snare, coated on top of the toms and half-coated or uncoated on the bottom. It was just one big experiment; there were no rules. We'd put a [Hammond] B-3 through a Leslie, mic it, and then send the signal through a guitar amp set to full distortion.

We'd re-amp the harpsichord; we'd even re-amp the horns. I love re-amping: it gives me control between having things clean and transparent, or grimy and dirty… and everything in between.

What was it like working with Yoko Ono?

I really liked working with her. The engineer she used at the time—Rob Stevens—had a production room at the studio I was assisting in, and so she practically lived there for awhile. Sure, she did a lot of yodeling and a lot of singing that was almost this unique language, but she also had these incredible archives of John Lennon material in her vault that she was constantly working on. There was just a certain mystery about her: she would wear her wedding band when she came in and often talked about John. I'm a huge Beatles fan—I've studied everything about them—so it was an incredible experience just being able to get a feel from her about who John was as a person. One day, I was asked to transfer a tape that came from her lawyer's office, and it was one of the last interviews John ever did, the day before he died. Another time, I had the original 16-tracks of "Just Like Starting Over" and "Watching the Wheels Turn" in my hands. On *Double Fantasy*, before they'd actually begin playing, they'd be rolling tape and there would be five minutes of joking in the studio, with the session musicians just talking and being free. That's something you don't get to experience every day.

Is opening your own studio your ultimate goal?

It's one of them; I actually have many goals, including producing records. But my main goal is to just keep learning; I love studying. I'm actually pretty technical; I can take an SSL apart and put it back together. Probably 80 percent of the time when something breaks in the studio I fix it myself. Sometimes, though, you can only wear so many hats at once.

There are very few women in this business. Why do you think that's the case?

Well, it goes way deeper than just engineering—it's almost in every aspect of the music business: producing, being an artist, working at a record label. Sadly, many of the women that do get hired give up way too quickly. There were a couple of female engineers at Quad who got pretty far, and then all of a sudden they just gave up. They were 75 percent of the way there, and then they just couldn't hack it any more. Maybe it was just all that negativity of them thinking about how they were not going to succeed in a male-dominated industry that made them give it up and go work in the Gap. I just never thought about things that way.

Honestly, I think that some women get a little too caught up in the fact that there aren't many women in the industry. I've met a lot of women that gave up on it because they thought about it too hard. Maybe if I'd thought about it that much I would have quit, too! I just did it blindly; I never

> **"If you're overly sensitive to the fact that you're a woman in a male-dominated industry, you're not seeing things objectively."**

thought about it. I felt, even if it took me a year or two longer because I was a woman, so what? I was always everybody's sister, friend, buddy, anyway. Yeah, I've been flirted on and it can be tough, but I've tried to surround myself with sessions that weren't going to give me grief, so I try to work only with people that I'm comfortable with. You're not going to find me on a Wu-Tang session, you know what I mean? [*laughs*]

You try and get on the sessions that complement who you want to be as an engineer; that's what I always did. If someone came to me and offered me a session I really didn't want to be on, I'd just turn it down. Of course, that's something you can really only do when you have some seniority, but I've found it's better sometimes to say no than to put yourself in a session that's not you.

It seems to me also that if you're overly sensitive to the fact that you're a woman in a male-dominated industry, you're not seeing things objectively; if a label isn't busy, or an artist isn't busy, you're thinking that you're not getting work because you're a woman, whereas it might just be that the labels just aren't hiring right now, or the timing isn't good, or any one of the hundreds of other reasons why work might be slow.

All I can say to women who aspire to this is, don't even think about it. Just work, just perform. And if you perform, success will follow. It's hard, but you've just got to just gut it out. If becoming an engineer or producer is your goal, you can't let anything stop you.

What advice can you offer to young people today—both male and female—who want to get into the recording industry?

Try to get into the few good studios that are remaining. Try to get with an old-school producer or engineer and really study. It's so hard nowadays, but I believe the community is coming back, little by little. I'm sometimes a little sad about the state of the industry. Nowadays, too many kids come out of a recording school and they'll know Pro Tools, and they may work with a producer or two for awhile, and then overnight they consider themselves engineers. But having those skills alone is like just being able to put shingles on a house. That's fine, but the question is, can you build a whole foundation?

Suggested Listening:
Alicia Keys: *The Diary of Alicia Keys*, J-Records, 2003; *As I Am*, RCA, 2007

Mark Ronson

Making Music for the Sake of Music

You'd have to be a firecracker to be hotter than Mark Ronson is these days. Co-producer of troubled torch singer Amy Winehouse's smash *Back to Black* album (which won him the 2007 Producer of the Year Grammy), Ronson also recently produced two tracks on pop diva's Christina Aguilera's number one *Back to Basics* and co-wrote her hit single "Hurt." In between he somehow found the time to make records with Lily Allen, Robbie Williams, and Rhymefest, as well as his own second solo album—a collection of modern arrangements of cover songs called *Version*—all released to critical acclaim.

Like many of today's generation of record producers, Ronson rose through the ranks as a club deejay, though his background is decidedly more musical than technical. Born in the UK, Ronson moved to New York with his mother when he was just eight and quickly began absorbing the sound and culture of hip-hop. He soon realized that many of the samples being used in those records came from the same 1960s soul and R&B tracks being played in his household (Ronson's stepfather is Foreigner guitarist Mick Jones). It's that marriage of hip-hop and Motown/Stax, along with a healthy dose of Brit pop, that gives Ronson his unique musical identity, making him the perfect complement for Winehouse and Aguilera—singers that blend classic sensibilities with current sounds.

A multi-instrumentalist who is proficient on guitar and drums, Ronson has worked with an wide range of artists, including Macy Gray, Jay-Z, and Mary J. Blige. He was even recently given the opportunity to remix a classic Bob Dylan track (the results of which reportedly elicited an enigmatic "cool" from the equally enigmatic icon).

It may seem as if every door in the music business is opening for him at once, yet the soft-spoken Ronson seems to be taking it all in stride, with a maturity that belies his relative youth. "It was only when I got to the point where I was just making music for the sake of music and got outside of that bubble of overthinking or second-guessing what I was doing that the records I was making started having any real impact," he observes.

Wise words indeed.

Do you feel as though success has come very suddenly for you?

Well, I've been playing music since I was a kid and I decided I was going to try to be a producer when I got my first drum machine, when I was about 19, so I've been working on records for about ten years. But it is kind of funny how everything has kind of condensed into the last year and a half. About two years ago I started seeing a lot of my contemporaries—people I'd come up with in the early days, people like Chad [Hugo] from the Neptunes, or Kanye [West], or Brian [Burton, aka Danger Mouse]—really shoot by, and I began thinking, "Well, maybe I'm just not that good at this." I had just turned 30 and I was starting to think that maybe it was time to try to do something else for a living.

You know, even though you'd always like to say you're making art for art's sake, if you work in this industry, it can be hard to keep your vision. But starting with the work I began doing with Lily [Allen] a few years ago, and then with Amy [Winehouse] more recently, I stopped thinking about the charts. We weren't making music for anything or anybody: we were just sitting in a little room in my studio making the music we wanted to make.

I hear that story a lot: it seems as if it's when a producer stops thinking about making a hit record and focuses instead on making a great record that success often follows.

I think I needed a little bit of that abandon, of just being able to think, "Fuck it, I'm just going to make the records I want to make." That's the mindset I had when I met Amy. Most of the time, when you first meet an artist, you'll play them some beats or some chords over a drumbeat. I used to do that, but I don't anymore, because I find it doesn't really work. So the first time I sat down with Amy, instead of playing her anything, I just asked her, "What do you want your record to sound like?" I was kind of aware of her first album, but that had been

> *"Even though you'd always like to say you're making art for art's sake, if you work in this industry, it can be hard to keep your vision."*

released three years prior, so I thought maybe she was ready to go in a different direction. She just said, "I don't know, but I've been listening to all this '60s stuff"—and she played me some stuff by the Shangri-Las and Earl and the Cadillacs. There were a bunch of things there that I knew, a bunch of things that we had in common. I'd be playing songs to her and she'd say, "Oh, yeah—I love that." That's what inspired us to go in that direction with her album. "What do you like to listen to?" is the simplest question to ask any musician.

Then it was just a matter of seeing how I could take her purest conception of the songs to where she wanted to go with them. When she played them to me on a nylon-string acoustic guitar, many of them sounded like classic jazz standards to me. My job was to take them into this era that we were both infatuated with.

It seems to be a really symbiotic relationship, given that you both seem to have exactly the same tastes in music and the same aesthetic sensibilities.

Yeah, Amy loves classic great songs and '60s soul music, as well as a lot of the same modern music that I like—things like hip-hop and contemporary soul music. I could probably describe her taste as a mix of the Shangri-Las and Gnarls [Barkley], and that's very much an aesthetic I come from, maybe not so much as a songwriter, but as a producer. For example, I discovered a lot of the old soul stuff because that's what a lot of my favorite hip-hop producers were sampling; I would go back and listen to an old rare Stax record because I'd heard that rhythm on a Wu-Tang record. That's the reason why Amy's record resonates with hip-hop heads. It's actually gone beyond that now, to all kinds of people who like all kinds of music, but in the beginning the hip-hop heads were the ones who got it because of that kind of sensibility: the drum breaks and sounding like a record that could have been made 40 years ago and sampled today, but mixed with these beautiful songs and her vocals and the performances of the musicians. I guess that's where it had its initial impact: with people going, "Wow, what the fuck is this??"

Unlike many producers who aim to be invisible, it seems that you've created a very distinctive identity for yourself. There's a common theme that runs through *Back to Black*, and *Version*, as well as a lot of the other tracks you've produced; it's pretty easy to tell that it's the same guy behind the scenes—tons of horns, tons of tambourine, that whole Stax/Motown pedigree.

Well, I was always a big fan of the classic producer/arranger. Again, those records from the '60s are the records I got into when I was sampling from hip-hop. I'd go and pick up a record from the Modern Jazz Quartet, or from Quincy Jones, because they'd have these kind of wonderful, lush sonic soundscapes. If I saw Quincy Jones doing "Fool on the Hill" or something like that, I'd already know that it was going to sound amazing—it's pairing a brilliant song with a fresh new arrangement it never had before.

> **"Most beat-diggers go into vinyl stores looking for a song no one has ever heard of so they can create samples that no one has used before. I was always trying to find a cover of a song that I loved, but a version I'd never heard before."**

I was always doing things backwards anyway. Most beat-diggers go into vinyl stores looking for a song no one has ever heard of so they can create samples that no one has used before. I was always trying to find a cover of a song that I loved, but a version I'd never heard before, like Ike and Tina Turner doing "Whole Lotta Love." Those versions aren't necessarily better than the originals, but I always got something out of hearing a different approach, particularly when it was a soulful or a classic R&B arrangement of a modern pop song. I never really thought I'd be making a record like that myself; it's just that those are the kinds of records I've been buying for the past ten years. It was only after *Version* was completed that I had a "Eureka!" moment, where I realized this was obviously the kind of record I'd make because this is the kind of music I've always loved.

You've said that your concept with *Version* was that it would be the songs themselves that would serve as the guest stars, rather than the artists performing them.

The idea came about when I was asked to do a track for an album of Radiohead covers called *Exit Music*. In thinking about which song I wanted to do, I picked "Just," because there's a breakdown that happens two minutes into it with just two guitar harmony parts. You know how, when you have a favorite song, there's often one part that just kills you? That section is only about seven seconds long, but I'd always focus on it; if I was in a car with someone listening to it, I'd just keep rewinding that one section to the point where it would really start annoying people! [*laughs*]

I think it was Morrissey who once said, "The best moments in pop are fleeting." That may be bad paraphrasing, but I agree totally. So I thought if I was going to do my version of the song, I could take that part that I love and make it a minute long and start the arrangement with it.

That's where it all started, I guess. I realized that by taking some of these songs and changing the guitar hook into a horn arrangement, I could really remake them into something special. Most of the songs on *Version* started as fairly heavy rock songs, and heavy guitars over light funk beats don't really work—they tend to overpower the beats—which is why I came up with the idea of changing them to horns. The idea was simply to take the parts I loved in the original arrangement—like a bass line playing in harmony with a guitar line—and have a trumpet do it instead, or a clav[inet], or whatever. It was just like being a little kid again at Christmastime—taking my favorite songs and going to town with them. It was like when you're learning to play guitar and you master a song you really love and so you play it over and over again. It's just a touch of love for a song that you have to express somehow beyond just listening to it.

You seem to have a near-obsession with horns in your records; they seem to be an integral part of your sound, not just icing on the cake.

Part of that came from my dad being such a huge fan of the '60s era of soul, where horns were everywhere. Part of it came from my love of big band arrangements, like Quincy's instrumental things. And a big part of it came from the Dap-Kings, who played all over Amy's record and on a number of tracks on *Version*. It was just me playing all the backing tracks, but the one thing I couldn't do was the horns so I had them come in, and Dave Guy, the trumpet player, and I worked out some arrangements. I just fell in love with the way their horns sounded. Other than a few retro artists, I guess nobody was really using them in pop music for awhile except for little hooks here and there. It was just something that I keyed into that I really liked, plus I was aware that nobody else was really doing it.

You're not a singer and you don't do a lot of songwriting, even in collaboration with the artists you work with, so in many ways your career seems to emulate that of an Alan Parsons, where the production itself is the main feature.

In terms of *Version*, that's certainly the case, although I would say that some of the defining moments on it also have to do with the vocal performances. Still, I guess the sonic is what holds it all together—that mix of having the producer/arranger as artist, like Quincy Jones was, combined with the more modern interpretation of that with groups like the Chemical Brothers, where you're almost given a free pass, where people say, "Well, he's a deejay, so he's allowed to make a production-driven record."

But it's different with Amy's record, I think. As much as the production has to do with the success of that record, it's the modern feel of her songs and her lyrics that keeps it from being pastiche. Her lyrics on "Wake Up Alone" are so classic in some ways, yet she's expressing that sentiment in a way that's never been phrased that way before. There's no generic "ooo-baby" stuff like you hear in some retro-soul artists—not that she's a retro-soul artist, though she harkens back to that time. Or take a song like "Rehab," which couldn't have been written in any era other than now. It was the modern feel of her songs, plus her personality being so modern, which is what enabled me to go as old-school as I wanted with the production, even though it's still got the hip-hop sonic. With anyone else it could have come across as retro-pastiche. I doubt that I could have made the same record with Joss Stone, for example—in fact, I know that I couldn't. It would have just been another retro record.

***Back to Black* has the feel of an album that was recorded late at night, with the bleakness of Amy's lyrics underscored by extremely laid-back drumming. Was that a conscious production decision as well?**

Well, "Love Is a Losing Game" is the true heart-breaking ballad of the record. We had done a recording of it with her singing, just accompanied by acoustic guitar, and I'd become so attached to it that I felt there was no way we could top that emotionally. But there was a part of me that still wanted to hear the sonic of reverbed drums in the background, so I sat down with Gabe [Roth] and Homer [Steinweiss, bandleader/bassist and drummer with the Dap-Kings, respectively] and asked them, "how can we put a beat behind a ballad like that and not remove any of the sentiment?" That was a real challenge: coming up with a beat that wouldn't detract from the song and still

> *"Coming from deejaying, you're always thinking about the beat, but sometimes I find I have to shut down that side of my brain and remind myself it's not really about that."*

become an integral part of it. With a song like "Rehab" or "You Know I'm No Good" it's a lot easier because you can just put something hard behind it that's going to drive the track. Coming from deejaying, you're always thinking about the beat, but sometimes I find I have to shut down that side of my brain and remind myself it's not really about that.

PHOTO BY SKYE PARROT

I wrote the music to the song "Back to Black" and it's not a conventional beat that you'd hear in a club, yet there's still something driving about it. Usually when I start writing I'll come up with a kick drum and tambourine pattern first—that will usually come even before the piano. But on a lot of the other tracks on Amy's album it was really important to preserve the sentiment of the song.

In the studio, was Amy very sure of what she wanted, or did you do a lot of experimentation?

The very first night she came in I said, "I can just sit here and play you some tracks, but there's really no point because I want us to create something from scratch." She was only supposed to be here for one night, just to kind of try things out and see how we worked together, so after I listened to her songs and we played some old records together, I said, "Go back to the hotel and come back tomorrow and I'll try to come up with something overnight." I was definitely feeling some pressure. I really wanted to come up with something great because I really wanted to work on this record with her. So, inspired by the records we'd listened to, I came up with the piano progression and the kick/tambourine thing that defined what became "Back to Black." I was a bit worried that she might not like the bridge, where the tempo changes and the chords go a little more Baroque, a little more Radiohead.

But she came in the next day and in her understated, off-the-cuff way, she let me know she liked it. I remember she had her head down and she was listening intently and she finally said, "Yeah, I love it. It's wicked." [*laughs*] I said, "Do you really mean that? Do you really like it??" She just said, "No, it's wicked." I still wouldn't have known I'd gotten the gig if I hadn't gotten a call from my manager later that afternoon who said, "Amy loved the stuff and wants to stay an extra week."

She ended up writing the lyrics and the melody to "Black to Black" in just two hours, just playing along with the backing track over and over. That was the only song that came about that way; the other stuff we did, she would come in and just sing me the song while strumming an acoustic guitar until we came up with something she liked.

Are you very hands-on in the studio? Do you do your own engineering?

It depends on the project. Amy's album was really the first one where I had a whole band playing everything. On the rest of my albums, I pretty much played everything except for the horns. I've found, though, that inexperience is what gives you the happy accidents that make for different sounds, something unique. I pretty much know how to run Pro Tools, but I don't know if that means I'm an engineer. With Amy, we had been using every plug-in and every trick in the modern world to make her stuff sound old, and then I had this idea: why not just get the Dap-Kings to play it? They know how to make it sound like the real deal. So I left a lot of the technical side of things to Gabe, because he really understands getting those sounds.

It's interesting that you mention Pro Tools and plug-ins, yet most of the sounds that you admire so much were achieved using analog tape.

Absolutely, which is why all of Amy's tracks were recorded to tape. We sometimes dumped some of them back to Pro Tools, just for the luxury of maybe beefing up a kick drum or snare drum to make it a little bit more hip-hop in the sonic.

Version, on the other hand, was pretty much all Pro Tools because I didn't have the option to go to tape. I didn't have a record deal when I made that record; I was just messing around with demos, playing around with arrangements. It was one of those projects where, whoever was around at the time to sing a vocal or play a bass part would come in to the studio at one in the morning. With Lilly [Allen], I was in the middle of doing her album and I just asked her one night, "Hey, do you want to sing on this song?" I didn't have the luxury of even planning it out, much less using a real studio: we just did it. Despite that, it has a warm sound because the basis of a lot of the sounds that I used—the drum samples and things that—came from old records. I've found that, even if you don't record to tape, you can do a lot to compensate for it, though it will never sound exactly the same.

Anyway, since that experience with Amy's record I have been working mostly with tape. People sometimes think it's just a gimmick, that it's kind of a time warp thing, but I really do believe that there's something that you get from the sound of the tape, and from the sound of real musicians in a room playing together at the same time, miked up properly so that you can hear the air. It may sound pretentious or cheesy, but the music does actually breathe because there's air and lots of leakage. Usually, on modern-day R&B and soul records, someone starts by laying down a beat and then the bass player comes in and then the keyboard player puts a line on top of that and it just keeps getting layered in Pro Tools. But when you have a bunch of amazing musicians all in tune with each other, all playing in a room at the same time, it will make anything better, or at least make it more alive.

Some of my favorite records have been made in the last five or ten years—records by Radio-head or Fiona Apple or LCD Soundsystem. Any of these records are brilliant, but the thing is that we always go back to the era when all those classic records were made. I guess it was that mix of talent and inspiration meeting the technology of the time, the original four-track.

How did you come to do a remix of Bob Dylan's "Most Likely You Go Your Way and I'll Go Mine"?

Dylan has always been a bit of a remote figure to me—his catalog was always so exhaustive and people were so fervent about him that I never knew where to start. I've learned that you have to find something for yourself to really love—you can't just think in terms of something being a project that is going to lead to great things. But about a year ago I saw both those old documentaries on Dylan—*No Direction Home* and *Don't Look Back*—and that made me fall completely head over heels in love with his music. After that I just went Dylan-crazy so when, a few months later, Mike Smith, the managing director of Columbia UK—the label that I signed to—asked me to try a remix, I was totally into it. But I knew it had to not be an obvious song, that I couldn't do "Like a Rolling Stone" or something that iconic. So I listened to his stuff for hours and hours on end and when I heard "Most Likely You Go Your Way," I thought, this is something I could really do something with, get the Dap-Kings in and come up with a cool arrangement, put some irreverent hip-hop sonics on it, trumpets, sirens, flash things around in the background, and it would make sense. So that's what I did. I got the original four-track and played the *a capella* [vocal] over and over again, just jamming over it until we found the groove that sat well and complemented the song.

Has Dylan heard it? Do you know what he thinks of it?

I've never been able to speak to him personally, although I know his management played it for him and he said "cool." I think that's about all you're going to get out of him on the subject.

Hopefully that one word represents the stamp of approval.

Well, as long as he doesn't snap the CD over his knee and say, "Get this the hell out of my face!" [*laughs*] You know, a lot of people were up in arms about people doing Dylan remixes, about the fact that we were taking something classic like that and changing it. I do see the logic in that and you're always going to upset people when you change something so sacrosanct. But at the same time Dylan never would have played it the same way twice anyway. I don't know if he ever imagined it the way I did it, but it's definitely in the spirit of Dylan to view a song as something that's constantly evolving.

It was amazing to hear that original four-track because of the early style of that recording. There was no pure *a capella*, for example, because there's all this bleed coming from the room and lots of drums on his vocal track. So it wasn't like getting a pure vocal that I could put any beat over, because you're hearing the snare drum and the rhythm it was establishing. All we could do was play louder over it—it's almost like that scene in *No Direction Home*, at the end, where the crowd is booing him because he's brought The Band to play behind him for the second part of the set and he just turns to them and says, "Play it fucking louder." It's just the coolest moment in the film.

And hearing the outtakes was priceless—there are a few outtakes at the top of the track where you hear [producer] Bob Johnson go, "Let's take another one" and you hear the band kind of groan, like, "What was wrong with that one?" and you hear Johnson say, "The kid's gotta get his lyrics right!" [*laughs*] That was pretty amazing.

Selected Listening:
Amy Winehouse: *Back to Black*, Republic, 2006
Christina Aguilera: *Back to Basics*, RCA, 2006
Mark Ronson: *Here Comes the Fuzz*, Elektra, 2003; *Version*, Columbia, 2007
Lily Allen: *Alright, Still*, Capitol, 2006
Robbie Williams: *Rudebox*, Chrysalis, 2006

Patrick Stump

Fall Out Boy Falls into Production

F or someone who never wanted to be a record producer, Patrick Stump has amassed a pretty impressive discography in his young career. Lead singer and guitarist with Fall Out Boy (he also co-writes the band's songs with lyricist/bassist Pete Wentz), Stump seems almost surprised at the degree of success he's achieved in the producer's chair in the last few years with artists like Cobra Starship, Gym Class Heroes, the Cab, and the Hush Sound. "At first I really didn't think production was something I wanted to do," he explains earnestly, "but I found that I loved it."

"I only fell into it because I'm a multi-instrumentalist," he continues, "and having some kind of control over every instrument was something that appealed to me." Little surprise, then, that his role models include Prince and Brian Eno, as well as Neal Avron and Kenneth "Babyface" Edmonds, the two veterans who produced FOB's two studio albums. Though he disavows any intention of becoming the band's eventual producer, Stump nonetheless recently took the reins for the group's larger-than-life cover of Michael Jackson's "Beat It" (a studio track on their otherwise *Live In Phoenix* CD), featuring a smoking guitar solo from John Mayer.

Stump is almost a throwback in this day and age of technology in that his focus is more on songwriting than sonics. Though he describes himself as a "GarageBand nerd," he trusts his engineers to do the engineering, leaving him free to hone in on the artist's musical intent. It's an approach that has proved successful for many legendary producers—most notably, Sir George Martin—and, while it's way too early to predict that Stump will follow in those lofty footsteps, he certainly seems to have the right instincts to succeed in a job that's as much about simpatico as it is technical ability.

Patrick talked with us one afternoon on his cell phone, chatting affably as he ran errands in his Chicago neighborhood. Shifting gears effortlessly—in both his thought processes and, apparently, his driving—he shared his views on the art and craft of making records in the twenty-first century, interestingly citing film references as often as audio ones. Does a future in Hollywood await Patrick Stump? Only time will tell.

What do you see as the main role of the producer?

It depends, because producing is all about assessing the situation. I think it's a total fallacy to have one style as a producer and expect artists to meld to that. I've only done a few records to this point, but each has been a completely different experience. Some of the records I've produced have a lot of me playing on them, or even writing a lot of stuff with the band, and then there are other projects where I'm really not a musical producer—I'm almost more emotionally guiding the band, trying to focus them in one direction, trying to help everybody get along. I've learned that so much of it is psychology. I don't play games with artists, but I have met a number of producers who take the attitude, "I'm going to have to have somebody else come in and rerecord the part . . . but I'll have to lie to them about it." I don't like doing things like that, so my challenge is, how do I get what I want out of a player and not have to resort to fibbing?

One difference I've found between young producers and older, wiser ones is that younger ones will often go out of their way to put their stamp on something, whether or not it actually needs it. That's something I've tried to stay away from, personally. Again, it comes down to the fact that you can't produce every record the same way. There are going to be situations where the songwriting needs help, and other times when the songwriting isn't the problem—maybe it's just that the song is in the wrong key. There are totally different circumstances every time. It seems to me that restraint is 90 percent of good producing. Knowing when not to let your idea be represented is probably the most important exercise: knowing when you *don't* need to be heard.

You don't engineer the records you produce, though.

No. I actually made a very conscious decision to stay out of engineering. I feel like that's a legitimate job; the good engineers I know have spent their whole lives developing that skill. I think it would be kind of arrogant for me to come in and say "I know how I want things to sound." I trust my engineer to be good enough to know whether what I'm saying makes sense or not. I want everybody involved to have plenty of artistic liberty, and to feel like they're contributing something.

Fall Out Boy has always used outside producers in the past, but you seem to be sliding into that seat. Do you see yourself as eventually becoming the band's fulltime producer?

It's weird because I'm a producer and I'm in a band, but I don't really see the need to be my band's producer. If you're going to be a songwriter, you really need to have some humility about your songs. If you can't take constructive criticism, you'll never write anything worth a damn. So unless something unforeseen happens, I think we will always have an outside producer. Just as it would be arrogant for me to try to take on engineering, I think it would be arrogant for me to try to be the main songwriter and producer of everything. I'd be the singer and guitar player, and I'd be writing the majority of the music, and to then have the final say too seems like a very dangerous putting-all-your-eggs-in-one-basket kind of scenario.

On the other hand, you've just given a perfect description of Prince, who is one of your heroes.

Absolutely. But there are very few situations in which that can work. With artists like Prince and Tom Waits, it's almost like their style of production is part of their writing, so it would be kind of incongruous to have a separate producer.

Other than Prince and Tom Waits, who are your role models?

He gets overlooked all too frequently, but I love Eno. The great thing about him is that stylistically he can work with any artist. Even on the same record, even within the same song, he can change styles. Just listen to [David Bowie's] *Low*, or any of the Berlin trilogy: within the space of a single song it can go country and then disco or whatever. There's really no arrogance about what is pleasing to the ear, so he's a huge influence on me.

I also love the way Chic records sound. And all the same stuff everybody likes: of course I love George Martin; of course I love Quincy Jones. They wouldn't be such big names if they hadn't done such valid work.

So are there moments in the studio when you find yourself wondering, "Hmm, I wonder what Nile Rodgers would do here?"

Totally. But I guess I wouldn't so much be asking *what* would so-and-so be doing here as *why* would they be doing it. Prince might have done something one way, whereas a Nick Lowe might have done it a completely different way, so I'd be interested in learning why they took the approach they did.

Do you spend a lot of time in preproduction with your artists, or do you prefer to just jump right into the studio so that things stay fresh?

I generally look for things to be spontaneous and feeling as good as possible, but it really depends on the project and the artist. Jack Nicholson has talked about how crap it is to win an Oscar for Best Actor, because it's actually a collaborative effort: you're only going to be the best actor when everyone else is being awesome too. That's one of the things about preproduction: if everyone's on their game, you really can skip it and just press Record. So preproduction for me doesn't necessarily mean hammering out the arrangement of a song. It's more about hammering out the artist so that they're in a mindframe to give me, and themselves, the music that they want to make. That's one of my biggest challenges: looking at what an artist is shooting for, and com-

> *"Preproduction doesn't necessarily mean hammering out the arrangement of a song. It's more about hammering out the artist so that they're in a mindframe to give me, and themselves, the music that they want to make."*

paring it to what they're actually giving me. Someone might come in and say, "Here's something that sounds like Elvis Costello," and I'll be thinking, no, it really doesn't sound anything like Elvis. Or, "This was inspired by my love for jazz," and I'll be sitting there thinking that it actually sounds like metal to me.

How do you deal with potential production problems before going into the studio?

I've recently read a couple of books on screenwriting that stress that story is the most important thing; in other words, you can write all the explosions and flashy dialog you want into a film, but the story is key. I think the same is true of producing records. You can have the best recording imaginable, made with the best equipment, and you can put in the most creative ideas you can think of, but unless there's a song, there's really no reason to press Record. That's my biggest criteria when I'm selecting an artist to produce: unless I believe they can give me a strong song, there's no point in me even working with them. I'd say that's my biggest problem beforehand.

It's true that there have been situations where I've written with an artist I'm producing, or even written *for* the artist, but in all cases it's to support their existing songwriting acumen. I wrote a lot with Cobra Starship, for example—I probably wrote half of it with [vocalist] Gabe [Saporta], but Gabe's a good enough songwriter that the two of us just kind of bounced off of each other; it helped the record that way.

One of my all-time favorite records is *Thriller*. It's just the perfect storm: you have Quincy Jones and Bruce Swedien handling the arrangements and technical end of things, and you have Michael Jackson and Rod Temperton doing the writing, and you've got Toto playing on it. There's no weak link

> *"If everyone's on the same page in terms of what kind of record you're making, that's when the great records happen."*

in there, anywhere, but it's totally the child of compromise. To give another movie reference, [director] Sidney Lumet always said that the biggest compliment you can give each other on a set is that you're all making the same movie. That's true of producing and songwriting too. If everyone's on the same page in terms of what kind of record you're making, that's when the great records happen. The most recent Justin Timberlake record was an example of that, in my opinion.

But often everyone is *not* on the same page in the heat of making a record; there are always creative tensions in every session. How do you deal with those kinds of disagreements?

It's really hard, because you want to make sure everyone's ideas are represented. No matter what you do, though, there's always going to be a certain degree of error in record production—something that's true in any creative field—so at some point, you just have to say "This is my opinion, and I think I'm right," though it's a matter of being very careful in pulling that card. But every band has different things to say, and every musician is at a different place in their life, so a lot of times I look for situations that I remember being in, arguments that I remember having with my band, and how they turned out. I'll find myself sometimes looking at a young artist complaining about something that I myself remember complaining about, but then looking back on it I realize, "Wow, I was way out of line!" [*laughs*]

As a producer I have to be cognizant of what are legitimate concerns versus concerns of the ego. Mind you, sometimes you want to help ego. I've worked with bands where there's one guitarist who never gets his due and he's asking for it. You have to make that call as to whether he really deserves that boost. You have to decide whether the work he's put on tape warrants that much more attention. Sometimes the answer is yes, and sometimes the answer is, of course not! [*laughs*]

> **"You learn a lot from watching other people deal with problems, even if they're doing the wrong thing."**

I guess I just make sure to listen to everything that people say in the studio, even when I'm visiting; in my free time, I'm constantly sitting in on other people's sessions, just watching. You learn a lot from watching other people deal with problems, even if they're doing the wrong thing. You take notes and you think to yourself, "I'm not going to do that." Hopefully, anyway!

What's the craziest thing you've ever tried in the studio that actually worked and made it to the record?

[*long pause*] Well, I'm one of those guys who thinks I can find a noise I like in anything: if you give me enough time and the right context, I can make the right percussion sound out of a garbage can, or whatever. A pair of scissors once served for me as a kind of high-hat; my keys worked once as a tambourine; I had a suitcase that worked really well as a bass drum. I'm really into that kind of thing.

Another time I wanted to use a stand-up bass but we didn't have one, so I ended up miking the strings of an electric bass, unplugged, and EQ'd it like crazy. It ended up really fitting the bill; I was quite surprised. It didn't quite sound like a stand-up but it kind of had its own thing. It was just one of those magical recordings; I tried it again some time later and it didn't happen. For some reason, that bass and that mic just worked perfectly.

Was it a hollow-body electric bass?

No, it was a solid-body Music Man. That was what was so amazing about it! It just worked. It was just one of those magic moments, and it sounded incredible. I think I cranked up the midrange and it came out great. But any time I've tried it since then it hasn't worked at all.

Similarly, in the Fall Out Boy song "Dance, Dance," if you really listen to it, there are a couple of moments where you can hear what sounds like pizzicato strings, but that's just a mic right by the fretboard of my Gibson SG guitar, unplugged. It just kind of came off that way.

Do you feel as if you could produce any kind of artist, regardless of genre?

I do, depending on the song and the artist. You know, musicians have common experiences, no matter what genre they work in: I've heard hip-hop artists say the same things as metal

artists. I think it's a shame when a producer is genre-specific, because it limits them. I like music, period, and so I think there's something valid to every genre of music. That's not to say there aren't both horrible and valid examples in every genre. Dance music, for example, is something I can't suffer personally, but there is some dance music that's unquestionably great.

So far, you've worked mostly with artists that are contemporaries, people who are about the same age as you. Do you think you could work just as successfully with older, veteran artists? How would you deal with the authority issue?

I was actually thinking about that the other day—about how strange the situation must have been for Nigel Godrich when he worked with Paul McCartney [on the 2005 album *Chaos and Creation in the Backyard*]. Not only was the artist so much older than Nigel, but, jeez, he was Paul McCartney! [*laughs*]

I guess that no matter who the artist is, you have to have some confidence in what you're saying; otherwise, there's really no point. At the same time, obviously you're going to afford him a great deal of respect. That said, you should afford *every* artist you ever work with a great amount of respect, no matter their age or achievements. The Beatles were the extreme example of what you could accomplish in a studio, because they had unlimited resources and great creativity, but even with unlimited resources, sometimes it's going to be that one room mic, sometimes it's going to be that demo. Sometimes that first recording is the best you can get it; sometimes mic placement really isn't that important when the feel is right. Ultimately, you can never lose sight of the fact that the music is the most important thing.

Selected Listening:

Fall Out Boy featuring John Mayer: *Beat It* (studio version, from *Live in Phoenix*), Island/Def Jam, 2008

The Cab: *Whisper War*, Fueled By Ramen, 2008

Cobra Starship: *Viva La Cobra*, Decaydance/Fueled By Ramen, 2007

Gym Class Heroes: *As Cruel As School Children*, Fueled By Ramen, 2006

The Hush Sound: *Like Vines*, Decaydance/Fueled By Ramen, 2006

London Producers Panel

A Good Sound Is a Good Sound, Period

Panelists: Hugh Padgham, Ivor Guest, Steve Parr, Andy Bradfield, Cameron Craig

There really does seem to be something to this global economy thing, as is evidenced by this panel of English producers. For all the dissimilarities with our Nashville group in terms of background, experience, personality, musical genre, location, even climate (in contrast to the sunny skies of Music City, it is pissing down with rain the entire time we're convened), the answers these London-based producers give to many of my questions are remarkably similar to those of their brethren 4,000 miles away.

Our cast of characters on this gloomy British afternoon are: veteran producer Hugh Padgham, whose long collaboration with multiplatinum artists like The Police, Peter Gabriel, Genesis, and Phil Collins is documented in these pages; film music recordist Steve Parr, whose credits include the HBO series *John Adams* and numerous definitive surround sound mixes; mixing engineer Andy Bradfield, who's worked with a wide range of artists in both the US and UK, including Alanis Morisette, Josh Groban, and Rufus Wainwright; film scorer and producer Ivor Guest (Grace Jones, Björk); and Aussie Cameron Craig, whose engineering credits include Suzanne Vega, Amy Winehouse, and *American Idol* wunderkind Clay Aiken.

Parr and Bradfield are old friends, and Guest and Craig were actually ensconced in the studio next door, working together on a new Grace Jones album, when we snatched them away for an hour of chat, so there was an easy familiarity between them. However, none of the panelists had met Hugh Padgham before, though they certainly knew of him by reputation. The end result was an interesting mix of relaxed and slightly uneasy conversation, punctuated by the occasional dose of dry British humor. And if some of our panelists sound a mite cranky from time to time, bear in mind that most of them had gotten thoroughly drenched on their way to our arranged meeting place (the control room of Steve Parr's London studio Hear No Evil). Precipitation notwithstanding, their diverse perspectives made for a lively and informative discussion.

Do you think there is a British sound, as distinct from an American sound? If so, how would you quantify it?

HP: I don't know if the records themselves sounded any different, but I always thought the sound of FM radio in America was miles better than ours, probably because of the compressors they used. Even in the cheapest rental car, radio there would sound good, whereas it never sounds any good here.

It is true that a lot of English studios would tend to have Studer tape decks and we recorded using the CCIR curve. Then there were the American consoles—MCI and Harrison, whereas the classic British studio would have a Neve, or a Helios. When I first started working in American studios, they were full of Pultec equalizers and all sorts of wonderful gear that we never had over here. We'd have UREI 1176s and maybe some LA-2s, bits of American stuff, but not a lot of

L to R, (standing) Andy Bradfield, Hugh Padgham, Howard Massey, Cameron Craig, Ivor Guest, and (seated) Steve Parr

it. Abbey Road had some good Altec compressors, but there weren't very many studios here that had good old '50s and '60s gates and equalizers.

CC: Perhaps it's just down to a difference in attitude. Thirty years ago it was down to what was available to the studios, either here or there—a lot of the stuff that they had probably wasn't available here, either because of cost, or because it wasn't sold here, and vice versa. That's changed a lot, and now pretty much wherever you go, you find the same access to equipment.

HP: SSL changed that because suddenly every studio in the world had an SSL console, whereas when I was coming up, you used to worry about going into another studio because you weren't sure you would be able to work the console. Places like Trident wouldn't even allow outside engineers in; there were secrets in studios and many of them had custom-made desks that only their staff knew how to operate.

IG: I think that the whole approach to recording is a lot less formal in England. My experience working in America is that the studio staff are more formally trained—often they've studied the recording arts in college, for example—whereas here it's always seemed to be a lot more experimental and undisciplined. The last time I worked in a recording studio in LA, there was a very odd atmosphere, partly because the engineer I was working with had been exposed to a very different musical culture than me. There were problems getting the right amounts of bottom end, for example, and I think that's because there was no West Indian way of listening to music in him. It was a different musical approach—not better or worse, just different.

AB: American studios do tend to be a bit more strict in terms of workflow. Here in the UK, engineers and producers seem to be a little more flexible in terms of the last-minute overdub— something that doesn't seem to happen as much over there. It's more, okay, now we're recording, now we're overdubbing, now we're mixing.

IG: I also think that there's a difference in the way programs like Pro Tools or Logic are used. I've been surprised at how basic the use of Pro Tools is in some studios in the States—it's really just treated as a recording machine with the one or two basic effects that come with it. But here it's used more like a musical instrument, with everyone using as many plug-ins as possible.

HP: It seems as though it took the Americans longer to incorporate Pro Tools into their studios than we did. I would say it was being used here at least three or four years before it was fully accepted in American studios.

IG: Also, in the UK there's a "make music in your bedroom" culture that I don't think exists in the States to the same extent. Perhaps it's prevalent in places like San Francisco, where people are more into electronic music, but I don't know if it's as universal all over the States.

SP: I wonder how much of it is down to American mastering engineers versus British ones.

Have you found that mastering engineers in the two countries take different approaches?

HP: Not really. They're all caught up in the loudness wars.

AB: To be fair, it's not their fault—they have to please their clients. If you have an A&R man saying, "I want this to be the loudest record anyone's ever heard," what are you going to do?

HP: I think it's the mastering engineers who are most responsible for many of today's records sounding like shit, to be honest, though they are forced into it. My biggest problem is when you encounter mastering engineers who have the same ego as recording engineers or producers and are trying to put their stamp on it. I just want the mastering engineer to take what I've given them and make it sound pretty good coming off a piece of plastic. If they start EQing and compressing it to death, they can really fuck things up. My question is a simple one: what's wrong with the volume control? A well-recorded piece of music that's decently mastered will sound loud on the radio. It's the badly recorded stuff that has to be hyped up to compete on the radio.

IG: Where did the culture of loud come from, anyway?

HP: I don't really know. All of a sudden everybody wanted their song to sound louder on the radio than everybody else's. It's that conundrum of watching television and the ads come on really loud; everyone wanted their records to stick out the same way. But the concept is complete bullshit.

AB: This has always gone on, though; even back in the days of vinyl, everybody wanted their records cut as loud as possible, although there was a finite limit because things would distort, or the needle would jump out of the groove. Some cutting engineers were better than others in getting their records to sound as loud as possible without distorting.

SP: Those were the days when compression and equalization actually had a lot of meaning.

HP: These days, records may not be distorted, but there's so little dynamic range, your eardrums are being pressed in from the beginning to the end of the song; there's no respite.

AB: At least when you're banging your head against a brick wall you've got the space between the bangs! [*laughs*]

CC: I've never understood why everybody's so keen to make every track louder, because they all go through the same sort of compression when they're played on the radio. Unfortunately you even need to overcompress when submitting a mix to the record company because most A&R men don't understand what mastering does.

HP: It's interesting that it all comes down to what the A&R man thinks. Perhaps we should send them all copies of this book!

At least up until the '70s, I think most people would agree that American records sounded sonically different from British ones. Do you think that's still the case?

CC: I think they're starting to get really similar, actually. You can still pick out American records, but it's more because they differ stylistically; it's more to do with content than sonics.

HP: Nobody talks about whether records sound any good nowadays anyway, and consequently I don't hear that many good-sounding records these days.

Might that be because everyone today is listening to music as MP3 files played over earbuds?

HP: No, because that doesn't stop the producer from making a good-sounding record in the first place. It's probably more to do with limited budgets.

> *"Nobody talks about whether records sound any good nowadays."*
> *— Hugh Padgham*

IG: Again, there's that culture here of people working in their own bedroom. I don't know anyone who has Massenburg EQs or that type of gear in their home studios; everyone has quite basic rigs. There's just that mindset of get it down, get it down.

AB: Another issue with modern recording is that untrained people run everything way too hot. When you run out of headroom in the analog world, you can actually get some quite interesting results. But when you run out of headroom in the digital world, you just get crap. [*laughs*] The big problem is the lack of VU metering. That's got a lot to do with why people whack everything up to the top, whereas in reality that's a bad thing to do, because when it comes time to mix the song, all the components are too loud and fighting one another. I find that when I get material from other people to mix, I often spend a lot of time just turning things down because everything's been recorded right on the edge.

HP: I personally would stick my neck out and say that there is a direct relationship between the advent of Pro Tools and records not sounding any good any more.

CC: Then there's all the cheap, lower quality recording gear that's being used in bedroom studios.

HP: You know, I like Pro Tools in the sense that everything is non-destructive and you never run out of tracks. But it's a permanent safety net, and in some respects it takes the whole buzz out of recording.

AB: But it also makes you try things that perhaps you otherwise would be reticent to do—you can actually try a lot of quite risky things on the fly, with that safety net always in place.

SP: One thing I find really interesting is when I'm in an airplane and I put on the music channels. You can put on a classic rock station and sit there in your chair and doze happily for thousands and thousands of miles in half-consciousness. But if you put on the Top Twenty station, where everything has been mastered to a high degree, you can't drop off to sleep because everything's just kind of hitting you right over the head; you can't relax and just doze—you're either listening to it or not listening to it. There's no in-between state of just drifting in and out.

HP: Let's face it: a lot of music today is quite irritating-sounding.

SP: Well, it's certainly not conducive to relaxing.

CC: Is that because of the sound of it, though, or the music itself?

IG: Most likely both. But you *should* be able to have both: good material with loads of experimentation and flexibility, and everything really well recorded.

CC: For me, that's what Pro Tools is actually giving us, rather than getting in the way. The trouble is that we're almost the last generation of people who have been trained properly.

AB: I wonder if this is just a settling-in period, though, because this is really quite young technology if you think about it. The fact that Pro Tools gives us, for example, a virtually unlimited track count, has only been with us for a couple of years. Perhaps as things move forward, people will learn how to use it in more creative ways.

CC: Mind you, people probably had this same conversation when 24-track machines first came out.

SP: It's true; when 24-track first came out, people felt they had to fill up all those extra tracks, and that definitely affected the sound of recordings.

AB: If you go back in time to when digital first came out, it sounded appalling. Then they began improving the filters and things started to sound a bit better. It's an evolutionary process, and I wonder if maybe the whole connection between Pro Tools and the sound of today's records is a similar thing. In some ways, it's like a Pandora's Box—once you take the lid off, you can't really go back. For example, look at autotuning: at first, people tended to slap it on because it was slightly better than the dubious singer they were recording. But now people are starting to realize that there are better ways to correct tuning and they're willing to get in there and craft it. Perhaps that applies to a lot of these things we're discussing.

IG: I wonder sometimes if there's really a new generation of engineers who actually know good sound from bad sound, because there are no studios left for them to apprentice in.

How much of what we call "good sound" do you think is subjective? People who grew up listening to recordings on vinyl may hear things quite differently than the current generation, which grew up listening to CDs.

HP: Well, I think a good sound is a good sound, period.

CC: I don't know many people who mix a record and say, "That sounds like shit—let's put it out."

HP: I don't know; I've heard some records recently that seem to have been done *exactly* like that. [*laughs*]

IG: The big problem today is that budgetary concerns limit things tremendously in terms of production value. Cameron and I just finished a record that was self-financed by the artist, and if there had been a major label involved, I don't think we would have been able to make as good-sounding a record. The labels simply don't allow you to make that kind of big, textured record that costs a bit of money and takes some time to craft. I think that's a very, very important point: the major labels don't let you be creative anymore.

HP: You've broached on a subject that I think is actually the bottom line: one of the main reasons that our business is in the disarray it's in is because of record companies and the A&R people they employ. They simply don't sign music that Joe Blow wants to listen to out there. Instead, they sign what they think is good, based on what somebody else has told them, or because it's on the front cover of the newspapers that week. It sounds like a very cynical thing to say, but unfortunately it's true. In many ways, they've completely destroyed the art of the music business.

> *"These days, the only way an artist can make the record they dreamed about making is if they pay for it themselves."*
> *— Ivor Guest*

IG: As producers, if you don't do exactly what the label wants you to do, and quickly and cheaply, you won't get hired again. These days, the only way an artist can make the record they dreamed about making is if they pay for it themselves. If you get a major label involved, you simply can't do it, and that's pretty depressing.

AB: Then there's the "demo-itis" factor. Labels will get a basic demo and realize that it's not quite good enough to put out, so they ask you to better it . . . but then they're still in love with the demo, so you're caught in this vicious circle.

IG: Well, that's one thing that Pro Tools is great for: you can import the demo itself and then build on it.

HP: I defy anybody in this room to be upbeat about making money from making records for major labels at the moment. These days, a really big international hit album will only sell three or four million copies, which is way less than they used to sell years ago.

IG: And the problem then is, where does the producer get any money from? If you're on points, that won't add up to very much. You have to have a new kind of deal to see any kind of real money.

HP: Five points of nothing, after all, is the same as 50 points of nothing. And of course the record labels go out of their way to see that you get nothing.

Do you prefer working with an artist that has a very strong vision, or one who is willing to be guided?

HP: It's better from my point of view if they have a strong vision. For me, there's nothing worse than a wishy-washy artist who doesn't know what they want. Mind you, artists usually know what they *don't* want...

AB: ...which is everything. [*laughs*]

HP: ...which is everything, right. [*laughs*] But I'd rather work with an artist with a strong vision and help them attain that vision.

IG: I completely agree. Because what do you do otherwise? You can make a record sound five million different ways if they don't give you an indication of where they want to go.

HP: Exactly. There are one or two producers who are perhaps more famous than the artist they're producing, but there aren't many of those, and I wouldn't want to be one of them either.

How do you deal with an artist who comes to you and says, "I want you to make me sound like so-and-so"?

HP: Those are usually the artists to stay clear of. That's definitely a warning flag to me.

SP: If you work solely with artists who want to be molded or turned into something they're not, it's really nothing more than throwing mud at a wall to see what sticks.

AB: And in any event, you can only go so far in making person X sound like person Y, because they *aren't* person Y. So if that's what they want, you can never actually achieve it anyway.

CC: You can only end up with something second rate by taking that approach.

AB: At the end of the day, whatever you're working on needs to stand on its own two feet. Whether it's a film score or a record, it needs to stand on its own merits.

IG: One of the most dangerous things in all endeavors is this thing about having no rules. It's actually easier to experiment and create new sounds when there are some solid parameters set beforehand. It's only when everyone knows what they're doing that you have a starting point. You can actually experiment more if you begin from that point than if everyone's just sitting around saying, "What do we do now?"

AB: That's why tracking sessions always go much better if you've put in some rehearsal time with the band. Going into the studio unrehearsed is absolutely the wrong thing to do, because it makes everything take four times as long. In those scenarios, everyone is standing around scratching their heads trying to figure out what to play rather than recording, which is what you're actually there to do. Even with a small band, if you spend a couple of days in pre-production rehearsing them, it pays absolute dividends once you get in the studio. If you then experiment from that point, you'll get much better results because you're working from a solid footing. Still, there are some artists that don't work like that—they prefer to write in the studio—and those are the records that take years to make. These days, there are, thankfully, fewer of those artists around because there aren't the budgets to support them.

CC: Yes, the days of the 50-minute jams which might turn into a song seem to be disappearing.

A lot of home recordists have trouble recognizing when a record is done. What's the yardstick you use to determine when a project is complete?

HP: You know, I find that a really strange question. How does a painter know when he's put the last stroke on a painting? I've never contemplated that question in my whole life. I've never sat around thinking, "What else can I put on this?" I suppose there have been times when I would wonder if the lead vocal could be sung better, and then I might think that the record was *not* ready to be finished. But other than that, it's not a question that's occurred to me. As a producer, you make the decision to mix a record when it sounds ready to mix.

IG: Everyone has finishing issues, but if you're a producer and you can't make a decision as to when a record is done, then you probably are in the wrong profession, because the whole point of being a producer is taking responsibility.

AB: At the end of the day, it's a taste thing, a matter of opinion. You have to ask yourself if you achieved what you'd hoped to achieve. There's usually a general agreement where everyone in the room says, "It's great; it's done." You can carry on past that point but experience tells you that things will just get worse, not better; it's the law of diminishing returns. Similarly, you sometimes know when you've done one overdub too many because you ask yourself, "Do we really need this part?"

SP: Basically, a project is complete when you run out of things to do.

CC: It's when the budget runs out and you're so fucking bored of listening to it anyway. [*laughs*]

Obviously, one of the keys to making a hit record is starting with a great song. But can a producer and engineer make a big difference when the song is not so great to start with? Can you make a great recording out of a mediocre song?

AB: Yes, you can make a great production statement from almost any piece of music.

HP: But at the end of the day, doing that is not very satisfying. I know of several hit records that sound very good even though I think the song is crap. But then beauty is in the eye of the beholder.

IG: There needs to be an idea, though. It doesn't have to necessarily be a musical one; it can be sonic. But somewhere there has to be content of an artistic nature, whether it's an idea of melody or just a persona. It can't just be well-recorded; something about the song has to be strong enough to engage the listener. Some of the records that I grew up loving as a kid were far from well-made. They may have sounded like shit, but because of the feeling in them, they became lasting works of art.

> **"Records that are purely well-recorded but don't have a great song at their core tend to be short-lived. People will say, 'That sounds amazing,' but then they will forget about it."**
> **— Cameron Craig**

CC: Records that are purely well-recorded but don't have a great song at their core tend to be short-lived. People will say, "That sounds amazing," but then they will forget about it.

HP: I agree. So the answer to your question is yes—a skilled producer or engineer can make a great recording of a mediocre song—but who cares? [*laughs*]

What about in the world of film? Not every composer will turn in a great score, but can you still make a compelling soundtrack out of it?

SP: Well, some of the art of writing a film score is actually writing music that people *won't* notice, so in some ways it's a backwards thing: if a composer turns in something fantastic, it may make for a great soundtrack album, but it can be a lousy score for the film because the audience is listening to the music instead of the dialogue. Writing music for film is artisan rather than artistic in many ways. It's when you manage to combine the two—the artistic and the artisan—that you not only create a great soundtrack on its own but one that works perfectly with the image. That's the peak of perfection for film music. Bernard Herrmann scores are the supreme example of that.

IG: In films, as in pop music, there has to be an idea, and, again, it doesn't have to be a melody—it can be a sound.

AB: And, again, if the film itself is not great in the first place, you can do the best job ever recording the score, but it's not going to mean a lot.

Do you tend to "pre-visualize" how you want the finished record to sound, and then work towards that goal?

AB: I always have an idea of where I want to go, but whether you actually end up there or someplace else is dictated by the project to a great degree. You can't always predict how things are going to shape up. Sometimes you start working on a song that you think is going to turn out great, and it actually doesn't end up as good as you thought, whereas one that you were worried out ends up far exceeding your expectations. That's part of the thrill of the process.

IG: And by having a goal in mind, you know whether you're doing what you set out to do or not. It's having a true understanding of that goal that lets you know when something is sounding right or not.

HP: I try to make the recording sound like the finished product the whole way through. For example, when I'm doing vocal overdubs, I'll make sure the backing track sounds pretty much the way I want the finished record to sound.

What's the "magic fairy dust" that a producer can sprinkle on a piece of music to add that sheen and really bring it to life?

IG: Personally, I try to find something good about the artist that isn't necessarily what everybody else likes about them. And there's a lot of talking that needs to be done before you start as well. You need to get the concept of the project right in terms of exactly what it is you want to accomplish. The personality of the artist is really important, and the questions of what kind of record they want to make, and why they want to make it that way, are paramount. You need to conceptualize the whole thing beforehand—that gives you a ground zero point that you can keep turning to. If you've got a strong idea of what you're doing when you get into the studio, it's hard to get lost and you can surge forward.

CC: A lot of times mixing a project isn't really mixing it—it's more like finalizing it. Often my final mixes don't sound very different than the rough ones I was doing when we were two-thirds of the way through the overdubs. It's more of an evolution, but there's a sonic concept in place throughout. You know how you want it to sound at the end almost from the word go.

AB: I think it's mostly about having an outsider's perspective. Most artists are far too close to their music to actually see what needs to be done, or to recognize when something isn't working, in terms of arrangement, or instrumentation, or whatever. As an outsider, a producer can sometimes see the obvious when the artist can't. That's part of the art of being a producer. As long as there's a trust between the artist and the producer, great things can happen.

Acknowledgments

There is no gift more valuable than the gift of time, and I am enormously grateful to everyone who gave of their time and expertise to make this second volume of *Behind the Glass* a reality.

First and foremost, heartfelt thanks to the 46 remarkable men and women who agreed to be interviewed for this book. The wisdom you have imparted in these pages is invaluable, and I feel privileged to have gotten to know you. Special thanks to my longtime friend Steve Parr, not only for his insightful interview, but for putting a roof over my head during my time in London, and for his help in putting together (and hosting) the panel held there.

I am deeply honored by the thoughtful—and thought-provoking—foreword contributed by George Massenburg, one of the most gifted and principled audio engineers ever to grace a recording studio. Thanks, George, for keeping a perspective, and for keeping us all on the straight and narrow.

In each of the cities I visited during the course of writing this book, it seems I had a guardian angel pointing the way and smoothing the path. In Los Angeles, that angel was my dear friend Rose Mann-Cherney, president of the Record Plant, who left no stone unturned in her tireless quest to connect me with the best of the best. In Nashville, the unflappable Caroline Davis (*Performing Songwriter*'s director of communications and special projects) took on that role, single-handedly assembling and organizing the star-studded panel held there while effortlessly juggling multiple schedules to make it all happen. In London, Peter Filleul, executive director of the APRS, burned up the phone lines and sent out dozens of emails in support of this project. Rose, Caroline, and Peter, you have my eternal gratitude. I hope you know that I couldn't have done it without ya!

Sincere thanks also to Lyn Levine and Bea Swedien for their warmth and kind hospitality, and to my very special Ideal Reader, Deborah Gremito, for her love, encouragement, and painstaking reading of every word in this book. In addition, I would like to express my gratitude to Lydia Hutchinson and all the staff at *Performing Songwriter* magazine, as well as to Rusty Cutchin and Mitch Gallagher, my editors at *Home Recording* and *EQ* magazines, where a number of these interviews first appeared in truncated form.

John Cerullo, Mike Edison, Bernadette Malavarca, Carol Flannery, and Aaron Lefkove of Hal Leonard Corporation and Backbeat Books have done a sterling job of bringing *Behind the Glass* to life once more, and I am most grateful for their professionalism and support. I'd also like to express my appreciation to everyone who's emailed me at BehindTG@aol.com with comments and suggestions—I've done my best to accommodate you all. Keep those emails coming, folks...where there are two volumes, there might eventually be three.

Special thanks as well to Maureen Droney of the NARAS Producers and Engineers Wing, as well as Phil Ramone, Randy Travis, Alicia Keys, Alan Winstanley, John Gallen, Jay Joyce, Joe D'Ambrosio, Gina Schulman, Ken Weinstein, Ivy Skoff, Allison Elbl, Susan Levy, Karen Wiessen, Claris Sayadian-Dodge, Mel Hoven, Heather Edwards, Nina Mistry, Dee Harrington, Chuck

Ainlay, Geoff Emerick, Hank Neuberger, Tim Sanders, Ash Soan, Erik Lawrence, David Weiss, Karen Brinton, David Goggin, Jay Tavernese, Saul Davis, Caitlin Owens, Dean Serletic, Marc Mann, Francesca Smith, Trish Wegg, Matthew Freeman, Seth Swirsky, Lorena Mann, Jay Tavernese, Melissa Cusick, Aaron Wilhelm, Lisa Marie, Frank McDonough, Giles Stanley, Rob Whalen, Siobhan Paine, Veryan, Ros Earls, Alys Gibson, Carrie Ridley, Sharon Rose-Parr, Scott Anderson, Miriam Ben-Yaacov, Minda Zetlin, and anyone else who helped me along the way but was inadvertently omitted from this list.